Cosmetic Sets of Late Iron Age and Roman Britain

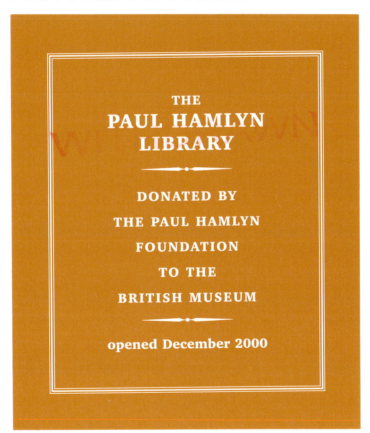

Ralph Jackson

British Museum Research Publication
Number 181

For Sylvia

Publishers
The British Museum
Great Russell Street
London WC1B 3DG

Series Editor Josephine Turquet
Assistant Production Editor: Katherine Candler

Distributors
The British Museum Press
46 Bloomsbury Street
London WC1B 3QQ

Cosmetic Sets of Late Iron Age and Roman Britain
Ralph Jackson

Front Cover: The finds from Hockwold and Itteringham (Cat. nos 261
and 286; see Pl. 8)

ISBN 978-086159-181-7
ISSN 1747-3640

Note: the British Museum Occasional Papers series is now entitled
British Museum Research Publications. The OP series runs from
1 to 150, and the RP series, keeping the same ISSN and ISBN preliminary
numbers, begins at number 151.

For a complete catalogue of the full range of OPs and RPs see the series
website: www.britishmuseum.org/research/research_publications.aspx

Order from www.britishmuseum.org/shop
For trade orders write to:
Oxbow Books,
10 Hythe Bridge Street, Oxford, OX1 2EW, UK
Tel: (+44) (0) 1865 241249
e-mail oxbow@oxbowbooks.com
website www.oxbowbooks.com
or
The David Brown Book Co
PO Box 511, Oakville
CT 06779, USA
Tel: (+1) 860 945 9329; Toll free 1 800 791 9354
e mail david.brown.bk.co@snet.net

Printed and bound in the UK by 4edge Limited, Hockley.

List of Plates, Figures, Maps and Tables

Acknowledgements

A catalogue of this kind, which comprises hundreds of objects recorded over several decades in many collections throughout Britain, has inevitably involved the assistance and cooperation of numerous individuals and institutions. To all I record my sincere thanks, beg the indulgence of any whose name I have failed to include below, and apologise for the long delay in bringing this book to fruition. I owe an especially deep debt of gratitude to Josephine Turquet, not only for her professional and flexible approach to editing but also for her unwavering support and seemingly inexhaustible supply of patience, tolerance and good humour; and I thank her willing assistant Kit Candler. I am also immensely grateful to Nina Crummy, who for long has shared with me her extensive knowledge of finds and, at short notice, read and enriched the text with new information, insights and bibliographical references.

As always, too, I have benefited enormously from the help, advice and unstinting support of my departmental and Museum colleagues, especially that of Catherine Johns, Val Rigby, Ian Stead, Tim Potter†, Richard Hobbs and J.D. Hill, and, more recently, Jonathan Williams, Jody Joy, Sally Worrell and Dan Pett, and from the unrivalled skills of our illustrators, Stephen Crummy (nos 286–7), Robert Pengelly (nos 22, 192, 261, 517), Karen Hughes (nos 77, 134, 139, 282, 349, 393, 474, 486, 509, 546–8, 566) and Meredydd Moores (nos 34, 50, 73, 213–14, 224, 260, 301, 318–19, 348, 362, 372, 479–80, 482, 518, 578–82 and Fig. 2), who provided a range of fine drawings to accompany my simple outlines. Judith Cash produced an early typescript, and I have been extremely fortunate over the years to be the recipient of Stephen Crummy's computer skills, here put to good effect in Maps 1–15, Fig. 25 and Tables 3–7; and, more recently, of the similar skills of Craig Williams who elegantly resolved the layout of Figs 4–24. To all these I offer my warm thanks, as also to Sandra Marshall† for Plate 5, to Saul Peckham for Plates 2, 7, 8 and 11, to Ian McIntyre for the splendid replica he made of the St Albans (King Harry Lane) cosmetic set (cat no. 436), to Louise Joyner for experimental work with minerals, to Keith Matthews and Michael Cowell for their detailed scientific analyses and to Susan La Niece and Duncan Hook for additional scientific input.

Beyond the British Museum I am particularly indebted to Bill Milligan, formerly of Norwich Castle Museum (NCM), who for many years not only kept me informed of the numerous Norfolk finds but also made arrangements for me to record them, as, more recently, have his colleagues John Davies, Alan West and Helen Geake (NCM), David Gurney, Andrew Rogerson and Steven Ashley (Norfolk Landscape Archaeology). Similarly, Jude Plouviez, Helen Geake, Faye Minter and Donna Wreathall (Suffolk County Council Archaeological Service) have unfailingly communicated information and images on the many Suffolk discoveries, while Angela Wardle (Museum of London Archaeology Service) and Jenny Hall (Museum of London) have kept me up to date with the increasing number of excavated examples from London. Their constant, kind, knowledgeable and generous help, of especial importance before the creation of the Portable Antiquities Scheme database, has enriched this catalogue beyond measure and I owe them all a very deep debt of gratitude. Through all of them, too, I relay my thanks to the host of un-named owners who made their finds available and supplied finding circumstances. I also record my special thanks to the late David Rogers, an assiduous and tenacious collector, who became fascinated by cosmetic grinders and liked to share with me his enthusiasm for each new purchase. His collection was acquired by the British Museum (Reg. nos P&E 1999,0802.1–96) following his death in 1999. Finally, I am most grateful to the numerous museum curators, conservators, illustrators, archaeologists, finders, owners, collectors and donors listed below, with whom I have had direct contact and who kindly supplied specific information and/ or illustrations and enabled the recording of objects.

R. Abdy, D. Abercromby, B. Ager, R. and L. Adkins, K. Ainsworth, P.H. Alebon, J.P. Allan, L. Allason-Jones, T. Austin, L. Babb, P. Barker†, D. Barrett, J.A. Bell, D.J. Benge, M. Biddle, B. Biktimir, J. Bircher, J, Bird, S. Bird, R. Boast, A.E. Bone, G.C. Boon†, M. De Bootman, H. Bowdler, G. Boyle, S.W. Bragg, K. Branigan, N. Brayne, R. Brewer, L. Brewster, D. Brinklow, A. Britten, P.M. Brown, R.A. Brown, H. Bullock, G. Burleigh, G. Carr, P. Carrington, C. Chippindale, P. Clarke, P. Clayton, S. Clews, S.R. Coleman, J. Collens, P. Collins, R. Collins, C. Conybeare, H. Cool, D. Coombs†, N. Crummy, M.J. Daniells, J. Darlington, A. Daubney, J.L. Dinn, B. Dix, A. Down†, S. Driscoll, T.B. Ellis, M. Erith, J. Errington, M.E. Farley, H.A. Feldman, K.M. Fellows, M. Feugère, A. Fitzpatrick, M. Foley, D. Ford, D. Fox, M. Francis, D. French, J. French, P. Frodsham, P. Garrard, R. Gilmour, C. Going, S. Greep, M. Griffith, N. Griffiths, M.A. Hall, J. Halliday, C. Hardie, C. Hart, A. Havercroft, R.A. Higham, A.P. Hobby, P.E. Holdsworth, V. Holgate, S. Holley, B.R. Hopkins, C. Howard-Davis, J. Hunt, A. Hurley, D. Hurst, J.D. Hurst, S. Hyde, L. Induni, J. Isaac, S. Jackson, C. Johnson, C.E.E. Jones, D. Kelly, R. Knox, E. Künzl, N.A.R. Lang, R.H. Leech, K. Liddell, G. Lloyd-Morgan, C. Longworth, M. Lyne, J.R. Magilton, H. Major, E. Man, J. Mann, F. Marsden, C. Martins, C. Mason, M. Matthews, P.C. McCulloch, C. McDonald, M. McElvaney, D. Miles, N. Mills, S.C. Minnitt, M. Moad, R. Moore, E.L. Morris, C. Mycock, D.S. Neal, S.P. Needham, J. Newman, R. Niblett, N. Nolan, J.M. Paddock, T. Padley, A.B. Page, R.M. Parker, J. Parsons, A. Phillips, R. Philpott, J. Pickin, C. Pinder, L. Pontin, F. Pryor, B. Read, P. Read, S. Read, N. Redhead, K. Reedie, T. Reynolds, C. Richardson, A.J. Roberts, D.J. Rogers†, P.G. Rose, G.E. Sandland, K. Sandwell, C. Saunders, J. Schuster, I.R. Scott, P.R. Sealey, F. Seeley, J. Sell, S. Sell, J. Shepherd, R.J. Silvester, B. Sitch, K.R. Smith, G. Speake, A.J.M. Spence, L. Staves, M. Stokes, M. Stone, J. Summerfield, K. Sussams, H. Swain, A. Taylor, T. Taylor, R. Thomas, D.J. Thompson, M. Thompson, F. Thuillier, S.J. Took, M. Tosdevin, R. Trett, A. Tyacke, M. Vickers, P. Ward, M.J. Watkins, K. Waugh, C.J. Webster, H.A. White, R.H. White, N. Wickenden, D. Williams, J. Williams, S. Williams, C.M. Wilson, C. Wingfield, M. Winter, P.J. Wise, P. Withers, W. and S. Wood, P.J. Woodward, D. Woollestone, B.R. Wooster, S. Wrathmell, S. Wright, R.J. Zeepvat.

Plate 1 Reginald Allender Smith, Keeper of the Department of British and Medieval Antiquities, 1928–1938

I. Introduction

In 1918 the Society of Antiquaries of London published a paper by Reginald Smith, then a 1st Class Assistant in the Department of British and Medieval Antiquities at the British Museum, entitled 'On a peculiar type of Roman bronze pendant' (Smith 1918). Smith illustrated 14 examples of these small bronzes (present catalogue nos 89, 111, 116, 121, 275, 279, 332, 427, 462–3, 469, 560, 565, 600) and noted three others (present cat. nos 184, 209, 550). With considerable ingenuity he interpreted them as pendant charms (for 'those who wished to wear something connected with the horse') derived from a rather murderous-looking piece of horse equipment, a form of serrated nose-band or cavesson, an idea repeated in his *British Museum Guide to Roman Britain* which was published four years later (Smith 1922, 48, fig. 52). Smith, who was made Keeper of the Department in 1928 (**Pl. 1**), maintained an interest in these small bronzes and progressively annotated brief details of new (or newly-published) finds on his interleaved copy of the *Guide* down to 1936. His 17 additions (present cat. nos 48–9, 64, 101, 103, 109–10, 112, 114–15, 117, 119, 124, 185, 292, 416–17), half of which were old finds from Colchester recognized and published by M.R. Hull (*Colchester Museum Report* 1930), included six which he termed 'solid' (two centre-looped, four end-looped – from Cirencester, Richborough and Brecon), indicating that he had now made a visual connection between the grooved and solid components – all of those included in his 1918 paper had been grooved components. While it may be supposed that there were some who Smith failed to convince on the question of derivation, the objects nevertheless came to be regarded as pendants or amulets, usually termed canoe-shaped, boat-shaped, keel-shaped or crescent-shaped. That identification persisted up to the 1980s, at which stage the number of published examples still stood at only a few dozen, and they continued to be regarded as a rather uncommon type.

In 1983 Robert Trett mustered some 44 examples in his review of the East Anglian finds, 'Roman bronze "grooved pendants" from East Anglia' (Trett 1983). Although he rejected Smith's fanciful derivation from serrated cavessons he still subscribed to the amulet theory. His use of the term 'grooved pendant', though cautiously objective, was hardly felicitous since it failed to take into account properly those of his examples that were not grooved. Furthermore, Trett, like most other commentators, was hampered by an assumption that the 'pendants' were complete as single piece objects, whether grooved or solid. Thus, Glenys Lloyd-Morgan, who, by 1981, had gathered details of several new examples following the discovery of one in excavations at Bedward Row, Chester (present cat. no. 91), took into consideration only the larger grooved component and regarded them provisionally as some type of amulet or pendant (Dr. G. Lloyd-Morgan *in litt.*).

Conclusive evidence had already emerged from the ground, however, to demonstrate that these small enigmatic bronzes were originally two-piece sets, comprising a greater, grooved, component and a lesser, solid, component. For, excavations at the King Harry Lane, St Albans site in 1965–8 had yielded a significant new find: one of the cremation burials (203 (SB40)) included an example of both the 'grooved pendant' and the solid rod-like 'pendant' (cat. no. 436). In the subsequent post-excavation analysis in the 1970s Val Rigby and Ian Stead formed the opinion that the two objects belonged together and that, taking into account their context and that of other finds, they had perhaps been used to mix or grind cosmetics. Shortly afterwards the author started research on two new examples from Stonea Grange, March, Cambs. (cat. nos 479, 482), and by 1984 had recorded 99 examples, including six complete sets. The most crucial set was that from Canterbury, excavated at the Cakebread Robey site in 1981 (cat. no. 73), in which the two components were found fused together in their operative position by their corrosion products, thus demonstrating unequivocally that the bronzes were two-piece sets. In addition, clues were found on many examples which pointed towards a specific function. In particular, a close examination of the groove of the greater component and the corresponding convex face of the lesser solid component revealed that in most cases where preservation was good traces of wear consistent with a to-and-fro or a rocking abrasive action could be discerned. As the sets were evidently a small apparatus for mixing or grinding, it seemed appropriate to name the two components 'mortar' and 'pestle', since those terms best-suited the perceived function. Furthermore, though conclusive proof was lacking, such evidence as there was indicated a use in the preparation of mineral-based cosmetics, and the terms cosmetic grinder and cosmetic set were coined. With evidence, too, for a virtually exclusive British distribution in the late Iron Age and Roman period it seemed timely to publish a provisional account of what amounted to a hitherto unknown type. That paper, published in the journal *Britannia* in 1985 (Jackson 1985) established the type and quite rapidly gave widespread currency to the new terminology, both within and without archaeological literature, as well as giving rise to a crop of other less appropriate terms – 'woad applicator', 'perfume grinder' etc.

Research on a particular artefact type almost invariably results in an upsurge of reported finds, but the increase in numbers of cosmetic grinders since 1985 has been truly remarkable: the raw statistics are 1918: 17; 1985: 99; 1996: 417; 2004 (this volume): 625. The hundreds of new examples have come both from museum collections and archaeological excavations and also from metal-detector activity. They testify to the increasingly good relationships between museum curators, collectors, archaeologists and metal detectorists. Although the numbers are continuing to rise, and there are still areas of uncertainty, it has seemed an appropriate moment at which to reassess the provisional conclusions reached in 1984, to discuss fully the huge amount of information gathered in the intervening years and to publish an illustrated catalogue of all those examples recorded by the author up to the 1st September 2004. The decision was taken not to incorporate examples from the database of the Portable Antiquities Scheme (http://www.findsdatabase.org.uk) even though already by 2004 some 61 examples had been recorded on it, but to treat those on the PAS database as complementary/ supplementary to this catalogue (albeit some pre-September 2004 examples are recorded in both places and selected post-2004 key finds on the database have been discussed here in the text). For an overview of the cosmetic sets recorded on the PAS database from 1997 to 2008 see Worrell 2008.

Plate 2 Complete cosmetic sets, end-looped, centre-looped and mixed, in the British Museum collections: top left Hockwold (260), top right St Albans (436), bottom left Itteringham (287), bottom right Itteringham (286)

2. Typology and Statistics

Cosmetic grinders are small two-piece sets made from copper alloy, comprising a greater component, the mortar, and a lesser component, the pestle (**Pl. 2**). Both components have in common two distinguishing features, a crescentic or elliptical shape and, with very few exceptions, a loop for suspension. In addition, and critically, the mortar has a channelled groove along its inner curve, while the pestle is a solid rod. For descriptive purposes both components may be divided into three zones, namely, for the mortar, *loop, bow* and *terminal(s)* and, for the pestle, *loop, rod* and *tip(s)*.

Smith's division into end-looped and centre-looped varieties (Smith 1918, 60) has stood the test of time, and virtually all cosmetic grinders can be classified according to that scheme.

As **Table 1** reveals, the present catalogue comprises rather more centre-looped than end-looped components (320:281), but of the surviving complete sets the end-looped variety is rather more common than the centre-looped type (9:6), while a not inconsiderable proportion are mixed sets (4), consisting of a centre-looped mortar and an end-looped pestle. With a sample size for the catalogued sets of only 19 it is not possible to draw firm conclusions from these ratios. That point is underlined by four important subsequent finds (not catalogued here), a centre-looped set from excavations in Colchester (**Fig. 1**) (Jackson 2006), a mixed set from Bures St Mary, near Sudbury (**Pl. 3**) (M. Mathews and J. Plouviez *in litt.*), and two probable sets, both centre-looped, found by detectorists at Battisford (Worrell 2008, 362–3) and Hempnall/ Topcroft, which result in a ratio of 9:9:5. It does at least seem likely that the catalogued complete sets are a broadly representative cross-section of the type, in view of the fact that the ratio of mortar terminal types in the sets corresponds quite closely to that of the sample as a whole (**Table 2**).

Table 1 Numerical breakdown of cosmetic sets and components

	2004	1985
mortars	418	77
pestles	207	22
end-looped components	281	60
centre-looped components	320	43
end-looped sets	9	4
centre-looped sets	6	2
mixed sets	4	-
end-looped mortars(including 9 in sets)	185	39
end-looped pestles(including 12 in sets)	96	17
centre-looped mortars(including 7 in sets)	209	36
centre-looped pestles(including 4 in sets)	111	5
anomalous mortars(idiosyncratic loop type)	10	2
indeterminate mortars(broken examples)	14	-
uncertain examples	4	-

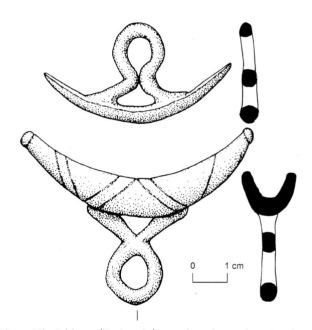

Figure 1 The Colchester (Garrison site) centre-looped cosmetic set. Drawing: Emma Spurgeon, © Colchester Archaeological Trust

Table 2 Data comparison between complete sets and whole sample

	Mortars with zoomorphic terminals		Mortars with knobbed terminals		Mortars with plain terminals		End-looped mortars and pestles with bird-headed loops	
	No.	%	No.	%	No.	%	No.	%
Sets (n = 19)	6	31	10	52	4	21	5 (n = 18)	27
Whole sample (excl. sets) (n = 343)	92	27	174	51	84	24	96 (n = 268)	36

At all events selection of the loop type appears to reflect both chronological and regional trends (see Sections 6 and 7).

The statistics also show that pestles have been much less frequently recorded than mortars (207:418), and the ratio of approximately 1:2 remains constant, also, between examples of both loop types (end-looped 96:185; centre-looped 111:209). This under-recovery or under-reporting is presumably due to the fact that the pestles are less robust, less distinctive and less decorative than their larger counterpart. However, recognition of the type has progressively redressed the balance in their favour, and the total number of centre-looped pestles, the erstwhile least-recognized component, has risen dramatically, from 5 in 1985 to 74 in 1996 and 111 in 2004.

The few exceptions to the loop typology (**Table 1**, 'anomalous mortars' 59, 91, 102, 134, 139, 389, 390, 403, 440, 576) conform to the type as a whole, namely that while all are united in overall form no two are identical and each new discovery brings with it the possibility of novel, idiosyncratic features. Nevertheless, some examples are very similar in appearance implying a common manufacturing source, while others, which share particular motifs or distinctive features are indicative of craft or workshop traditions (**Tables 7–8**).

Complete sets (Pls 2–3, Figs 1, 3–5)

Not surprisingly several of the complete sets show a distinct uniformity between the two components, either in their overall shape, especially the form of the loop, or in their décor. Thus, sets 22, 73, 74, 100/101, 154, 287, 436, 517 and those from Colchester (Garrison site) and Battisford, have matching loops, while, in sets 22, 73, 74, 100/101, 154, 287, 514 and 517, the overall shape and proportions of the pestle matches that of the mortar. It seems evident in all these cases that the two pieces were made together by the same craftsman, as also, probably, sets 92 and 501, although they lack any precise matching feature. Noticeable in all these cases, too, is the very exact fit of the pestle in the mortar, whether the 'chunky' form of sets 22 and 517 or the deep, slender, knife-like form of set 73.

Rather different are sets 192, 319, 437 and 438/439, all of which are from secure archaeological contexts but which appear, at first sight, to comprise non-matching components. In the case of set 192 both pestle and mortar are end-looped, but there is a very great contrast between the large, elaborate mortar and the much smaller, completely plain, pestle. However, it should not necessarily be assumed that they were made separately, for the form of the working end of the pestle is closely adapted to the profile of the groove in the mortar. Set 319, on the other hand, like set 438/439 appears to provide stronger evidence for non-contemporaneity of manufacture: not only is there no stylistic similarity between pestle and mortar, but the loop position is also at variance – an end-looped pestle with a centre-looped mortar. It may be that such 'mixed' sets simply reflect the ubiquity of the type, in that a broken or lost component could quite readily be replaced without recourse to fresh manufacture, albeit one might have to settle for a non-matching loop type. Alternatively, and in the light of the find from Bures St Mary, rather more convincingly, it is conceivable that the combination of a centre-looped mortar and end-looped pestle was an intentional and original choice. For, while the two components may have hung in a slightly less satisfactory manner when not in use there could have been

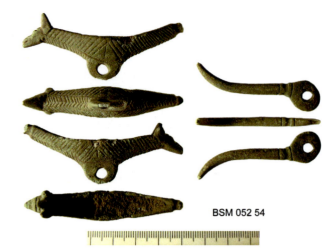

BSM 052 54

Plate 3 The mixed cosmetic set from a cremation burial group at Bures St Mary, Suffolk. Photo © Suffolk County Council, courtesy of Jude Plouviez

functional advantages when the set was operated. Certainly the very close correspondence between the sets from St Albans (438/439), London (319) and Bures St Mary, which combine a virtually identical centre-looped zoomorphic mortar with an end-looped pestle (**Pl. 3, Fig. 3**) (also near-identical in the latter two cases), hints at a common supplier of those mixed sets, while the stylistic similarity of the disc-like loops of another mixed set from St Albans (437) also implies contemporaneous manufacture. The mixed set from Itteringham (286), which combines a large ostentatious centre-looped zoomorphic mortar with a small plain end-looped pestle, recalls the similar contrast between the components of the end-looped Fishtoft set (192). As in that set the rod and tip of the pestle conform closely to the profile of the groove in the mortar and separate non-contemporaneous manufacture of the two components need not be assumed. The question must remain open, but for the present it may be observed that all of the recorded mixed sets come from contexts dated within the period late 1st to late 2nd century AD (**Fig. 25**).

Mortars (Figs 6–11 and 14–22)

Of the two components of cosmetic sets the mortar displays much greater variety in size, shape and degree of elaboration. At one extreme are tiny, absolutely plain examples (e.g.13, 124, 365, 512), at the other large and richly decorated pieces (e.g. 50, 261, 301). Within these extremes there is a wide spectrum, the form being constrained only by the need to provide a groove and, evidently, to keep to a 'pocket-sized' length. **Tables 3 and 5** graphically illustrate the length and weight values of complete mortars where those measurements could be determined. The whole-sample length range (n = 335) is 29–123.5 mm, but the great majority of mortars are between 45–85 mm long. Indeed, excepting only two examples (nos 50, 406) measuring 98 mm, the end-looped mortars (n = 143) are restricted to the range 42–88 mm. However, there is a wider spread of values for the centre-looped variety (n = 180), with the majority lying within the range 47–85 mm, but with both smaller examples (down to 29 mm – no. 282) and, especially, larger examples (five over 100 mm and one at 123.5 mm – no. 301).

Much more extreme than the length range (max. ratio 4:1) is that for weight, with a whole-sample range (n = 170) of

Table 3 Length values for complete mortars

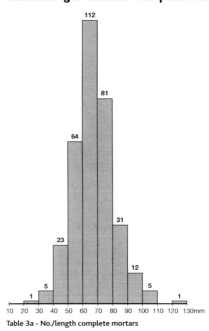

Table 3a - No./length complete mortars

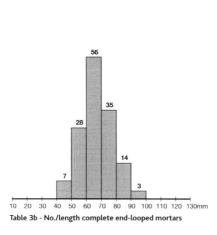

Table 3b - No./length complete end-looped mortars

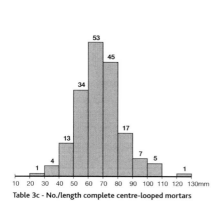

Table 3c - No./length complete centre-looped mortars

Table 4 Length values for complete pestles

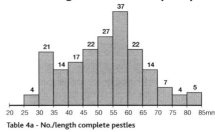

Table 4a - No./length complete pestles

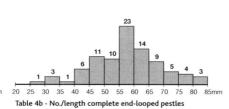

Table 4b - No./length complete end-looped pestles

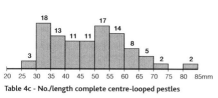

Table 4c - No./length complete centre-looped pestles

Table 5 Weight values for complete mortars

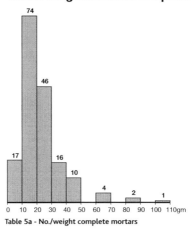

Table 5a - No./weight complete mortars

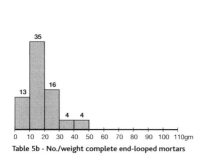

Table 5b - No./weight complete end-looped mortars

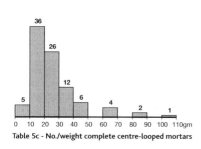

Table 5c - No./weight complete centre-looped mortars

Table 6 Weight values for complete pestles

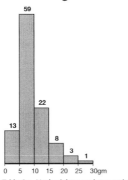

Table 6a - No./weight complete pestles

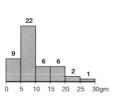

Table 6b - No./weight complete end-looped pestles

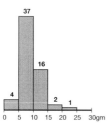

Table 6c - No./weight complete centre-looped pestles

5.0–103.2 g (max. ratio 20:1). As with the length measurement end-looped mortars display the more uniform weight, with all the measured examples (n = 72) lying within the range 5.0–49.5 g and all except eight weighing between 5.0 and 28.7 g. The weighed centre-looped mortars (n = 92) lie within the range 7.4–49 g, except for seven examples which weigh from 62.4 to 103.2 g.

The provision of a groove necessarily required the provision of a bow with walls. Variation in the size and degree of curvature of the bow, from virtually straight examples to very strongly curved pieces, affected the overall form, while differences in the wall height could provide greater or lesser scope for potentially decorative fields. The groove itself is similarly variable in length, breadth, depth and curvature. Its cross-section is generally U-shaped or rounded V-shaped, and its capacity varies from deeply-channelled to excessively shallow examples. Like the bow walls mortar terminals afforded great potential for elaboration. A few were adapted to function, but their prominent position made them a prime site for ornamental treatment in the round, and considerable effort was lavished on the decoration of some examples. The terminals can be categorized as zoomorphic/ornithomorphic, knobbed, spouted or plain.

The final defining feature, the suspension loop, was no less varied than the other parts of mortars. Beyond the functional requirement of a closed ring many different forms were possible, according the loop greater or lesser prominence. A few are tiny unadorned perforations through the end or base of the bow, while, exceptionally, one is a finely-modelled stylized boar's head, but most are projecting loops of ring-like, collar-like or plate-like form. Many of the end-looped variety take the shape of a more or less stylized bird's head, while the centre-looped mortars lent themselves to the provision of a projecting loop plate or a strutted openwork decor symmetrically arranged around the loop. An unusual variant has the loop set in a different plane. This feature, present on a small number of both mortars (50, 73a, 237) and pestles (207, 473), was perhaps a concession to function, though a regional explanation is possible since the majority of examples are from northern Kent. Other idiosyncratic mortars have multiple loops or have a slot or central aperture in place of a loop. The eye of the loop is generally circular, though there are distinctive D-shaped and heart-shaped varieties, and, where the loop was adapted to the profile of a bird's head, the eye is sometimes elliptical or tear-shaped.

Pestles (Figs 12–13 and 23–24))

Functional requirements limited the potential for decorative embellishment of the pestle component. The pestle had to be worked in the groove of the mortar, so its rod tends to be completely plain (though, exceptionally, see 12, 74b, 586, 603) and, as the surviving complete sets demonstrate, the shape of its tip or base generally corresponds closely to that of the groove. Thus, the rod may be broad or slender, and its cross-

section D-shaped, lentoid or knife-like. Despite those constraints there was still considerable scope for variety in the size and form of pestles and in the elaboration of their loop.

Like the mortars, pestles vary in shape, from strongly-curved ellipses to virtually straight examples, and in size, from a diminutive piece just 25 mm long (444) to an outsize example measuring 82 mm (74b). **Tables 4 and 6** provide a graphic illustration of the length and weight values of those pestles whose measurements could be determined. The whole-sample length range (n = 194) is broad, with extremes of 25 mm (444) and 82 mm (74b) but the great majority of values fall between 30–70 mm and peak at 55–60 mm. The centre-looped pestles tend to be rather shorter than the end-looped type, with the majority of examples falling below the 60 mm peak within the range 27–70 mm, with just two outliers at the upper end (586, 74b). The majority of end-looped pestles lie within the range 40–75 mm, with a virtually equal spread either side of the 55–60 mm peak and extremes of 25 mm (444) and 81 mm (151, 381). Weight values for pestles (n = 106) are concentrated within the range 4–14 g with a strong peak at 5.9–9.9 g and extremes of 2.1 g (137) and 25.1 g (127). Values for end-looped pestles (n = 46) fall mainly in the range 3.7–17.6 g, with a peak at 4–10 g., while most centre-looped pestles (n = 60) weigh between 4.3 and 15.5 g, with a peak at 6–14 g.

The majority of suspension loops on pestles are simple circular or sub-circular rings, sometimes of collar-like or plate-like form. The loop of the end-looped variety may be set on, above or below the axis of the rod. Occasionally it is coiled or ornamented with neck mouldings, but, like the end-looped mortars, the commonest elaboration involves the working of the loop into the form of a stylized bird's head. In common, too, with their mortar counterpart, a few end-looped pestles have their loop set in a different plane. Centre-looped pestles also tend to mirror the configuration of their mortar counterpart, and common variants include a ring-like loop with heart-shaped or D-shaped eye, and strutted or projecting loop plates. Rarer are loops with knobbed finials or sitting birds (Type N), while two examples with enamel inlay (Type O) match the decor of a distinctive group of centre-looped mortars (Types H and J).

A type of object with similarities to centre-looped cosmetic pestles is represented by two catalogued examples (513 and 593). Initially rejected, the type was re-considered on the strength of the wear pattern displayed by no. 593, which resembles that often encountered on cosmetic pestles. However, none has yet been found in a dated context and there is no obvious 'matching' mortar type, and, although the type has not been recognized as a product of any other era, the particular distribution of the examples recorded on the PAS database (Worrell 2008, fig. 3), which differs from that of cosmetic sets, suggests it is probably not a form of cosmetic pestle. Currently, therefore, identification as some form of fastening toggle, of as yet un-established date, seems preferable (Read 2010, 7, 10, no. 24).

Table 7 Distinctive sub-types

mortars

Type A (Fig. 6) — Bovid-headed mortar with end-loop positioned beneath the terminal.
Cat. nos 88, 163, 236, 318 (archetype), 325, 380, 394, 422, 495, 558

Type B (Fig. 6) — End-looped mortar with thick, sharply-carinated walls, incuse ring-and-dot and herringbone ornament and end-loop positioned beneath the terminal.
Cat. nos 483, 597

Type C (Fig. 15) — Centre-looped mortar with one bovid and one small knobbed terminal and incised hatching on the bow.
Cat. nos 319a, 357, 438

Type D (Fig. 21) — Centre-looped mortar with knobbed or plain terminals and large strut-encircled loop.
Cat. nos 429, 430, 541, 582 (with variants 90, 542, 581)

Type E (Fig. 16) — As Type D, but with stylized bovid terminals and more sinuous struts.
Cat. nos 36, 213, 496, 510 (with variants 65, 109, 358)

Type F (Fig. 15) — Centre-looped mortar with two bovid terminals and relief-moulded bow.
Cat. nos 53, 158, 174, 555

Type G (Fig. 16) — Centre-looped mortar with two different enigmatic zoomorphic terminals, a slender bow and a large ring-like loop.
Cat. nos 110, 241, 356, 523

Type H (Fig. 18) — Light centre-looped mortar with thin-walled enamel-inlaid bow, tiny simple knobbed terminals and a heart-shaped or D-shaped loop.
Cat. nos 37, 46, 74a, 83, 99, 106, 111, 112, 133, 138, 176, 208, 256, 258, 293, 311, 315, 360, 428, 469, 472, 487 580

Type I (Fig. 18) — As Type H, but without the enamel decoration.
Cat. nos 27, 58, 478

Type J (Fig. 17) — As Type H, but with highly-stylized and simplified bovid head terminals.
Cat. nos 92a, 129, 147, 215, 278, 281, 289, 302, 322, 361, 452, 455, 578 (with variants 16, 188, 501a)

Type K (Fig. 17) — As Type J, but without the enamel decoration.
Cat. nos 193, 309, 405, 559, 579.

Type L (Fig. 19) — Centre-looped mortar with knobbed terminals, angled bands of incuse hatching on the thin-walled bow and thin D-shaped plate-like loop.
Cat. nos 114, 191, 320, 349, 466, 476 (with variants 30, 113)

Type M (Fig. 22) — Triple mortar with central triangular aperture.
Cat. nos 134, 139

pestles

Type N (Fig. 24) — Centre-looped pestle surmounted by a swimming water-bird.
Cat. nos 297, 366, 543, 592

Type O (Fig. 23) — Large centre-looped pestle with inlaid enamel decoration and heart-shaped loop, the counterpart to mortar Types H and J.
Cat. nos 74b, 586 (with variant 232)

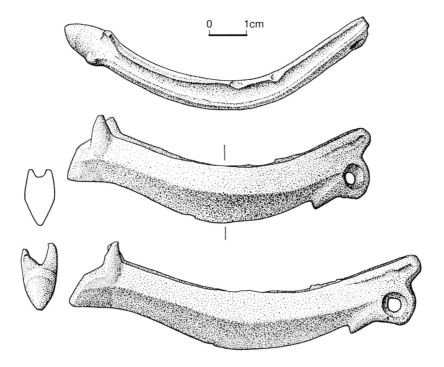

Figure 2 Skipton Street, London: lead model for the manufafcture of Type A end-looped cosmetic mortars. Scale 1:1

3. Manufacture and Function

Manufacture

With few exceptions cosmetic grinders appear to have been made by the casting process. One of the merits of casting is that it enables repeat production of identical objects, and at first sight this would seem to conflict with the evidence for cosmetic grinders, which shows the type to have been diverse rather than uniform. Indeed, the infinite variety may be regarded as one of the defining features of cosmetic grinders, and it is still true to say that no two examples are identical and many are unique (Jackson 1985, 169). However, as shown above, the increase in sample size has revealed a growing number of distinctive sub-types (**Table 7**). What emerges is that choice of variety lay partly in the overall design, controlled by casting, but even more so in the style and mode of decoration, the great majority of which was applied after casting. In this way virtually identical cast components could easily be adapted to individual taste resulting in a myriad of different forms.

In 1985 little technological evidence was available, but since then the data have expanded considerably. One find of particular significance was made at Skipton Street, London, in 1988, on a site excavated by the Department of Greater London Archaeology (**Fig. 2**). An object that initially appeared to be a cosmetic grinder in its own right was soon recognized as a lead-alloy model or archetype (318) for the production of end-looped mortars (Jackson 1993, 167–9). X-ray fluorescence (XRF) analysis has shown its composition to be almost pure lead, the malleability of which has resulted in a few scrapes and dents and a slight distortion of the bow. However, it is otherwise in extremely good condition, and the light patina preserves details of the original surface treatment. The vestigial groove retains its manufacturing score-marks, while working facets and file marks are clearly visible, too, on the rudimentarily formed stylized bovid-head terminal. It is evident that working of the piece had been completed and, with its overall form determined, it was ready for the casting process. The product, to be made via piece-moulds or, perhaps, by a 'lost-lead' process, could then be finished to a greater or lesser degree by cold-working (For the use of lead models as an intermediate stage in the process of casting see Branigan and Bayley 1989, 47 and Ager 2006, 248).

The archetype is related to a distinctive series of end-looped mortars, sub-type A (**Table 7, Fig. 6**). These have a characteristically long bow with steep carinated walls and a stylized bovid-head terminal, but their most idiosyncratic feature is their loop, which is not at the end of the bow, as is normal, but is set beneath and a little back from the end. As anticipated, while they all display an overall uniformity they vary in the type and degree of post-casting finish and decor. Of the nine catalogued examples six come from East Anglia. Eight are metal detector finds lacking an archaeological context, but they may be dated, broadly, by the Skipton Street archetype,

which was associated with pottery of the 3rd century AD, and by an excavated example from London (325) with a context date of AD 100–140.

Further evidence for repeat castings made either by use of an archetype or mould, or by direct moulding of an existing mortar or pestle, may be seen in the occasional occurrence of virtually identical components. These are listed in **Table 8**.

Table 8 Virtually identical components

End-looped mortars

Cat. nos	483, 597	**Fig. 6**

Centre-looped mortars

Cat. nos	319a, 357, 438	**Fig. 15**
Cat. nos	53, 158	**Fig. 15**
Cat. nos	36, 213, 510	**Fig. 16**
Cat. nos	129, 278, 578	**Fig. 17**
Cat. nos	112, 360	**Fig. 18**
Cat. nos	399, 584	**Fig. 20**
Cat. nos	429, 582	**Fig. 21**

Anomalous mortars

Cat. nos	134, 139	**Fig. 22**

Centre-looped pestles

Cat. nos	74b, 586	**Fig. 23**

The extent and degree of cold-working varied widely, from un-worked castings to carefully filed pieces, and from those only rudimentarily finished to immaculate and finely polished examples. Two centre-looped pestles appear to be unused castings: 190 was evidently unfinished as it retains extensive unsightly flashing, while 447 may have been a finished casting destined for re-melting since it has both un-cleaned flashing and a blemish. End-looped pestle 97 may also have been an unused casting with an untrimmed spur-like sprue. Other examples appear to have been used with little or no surface finishing after casting: 582, a centre-looped mortar, was poorly-cast with several flaws and an unfinished loop-and-strut assembly. Yet a marked basal wear facet in the groove shows it to have been used in that condition. Likewise, 605, an end-looped pestle, had been very heavily used despite the fact that its crude loop was never finished.

Rudimentarily worked castings are quite numerous (102, 196, 239, 271, 299, 338, 349, 372, 503, 517, 552, 590–1), as are examples with casting flaws or blemishes, mainly blow holes (67, 200, 229, 239, 292, 298, 310, 329, 425, 524, 552, 581–2, 591). Imperforate apertures sometimes appear to reveal a lack of finish (eg. 582), but they can also be a deliberate feature of a carefully worked decor (eg. 213). The overall design and decorative motifs are in some instances quite crude, ungainly, irregular, or carelessly done (34, 50, 67, 113, 349, 388, 393, 438, 474, 482, 581). On other examples cold-worked finishing marks can still be discerned, most frequently the facets and striations left by fine files (42, 200, 217, 310, 318, 329, 338, 397, 579, 581, 591).

Sometimes, however, the surface was given an extremely

fine finish which can be properly appreciated on a few examples where it has not been obscured or destroyed by corrosion. The finish was independent of elaboration, and simply-designed pieces like mortars 44 and 181 were very finely crafted and smoothly polished, while more ambitious designs could be quite cursorily finished. Nevertheless, the more ornate mortars offered greater scope for a thorough and careful finish, most notably 301 from Lakenheath, the largest and most elaborate example of all. An unblemished casting, it was subsequently extensively worked by sensitive modelling of the zoomorphic terminals, precise shaping of the bow and loop plate, and a carefully applied punched and incise decoration of the surface.

Prolonged, intense or careless usage occasionally took its toll, and several examples have undergone repair. The suspension loop of 392 wore through in antiquity but was restored by hammering together the broken ends, file-roughening one face and soldering on a repair patch, while apparent breakage of the loop of 389 was probably considered irremediable and the fractured end simply filed or hammered smooth. Likewise, one end of the rod of centre-looped pestle 470 appears to have broken close to the loop and then been smoothed off. Two further examples of repairs are on grinders blemished at manufacture: 425, a centre-looped pestle, has a cast-on tip at one end of the rod, presumably a repair effected after a failed casting; 229, a centre-looped mortar, was also flawed at manufacture by a partial fissure at one end of the bow. Re-working of the other end of the bow may well have followed breakage caused by a similar flaw, but wear in the groove shows that it was well-used anyway.

In just a few cases it is either evident or probable that manufacture was not by casting. No. 275, a simple, plain end-looped mortar from Hunsbury, was fashioned from a rod of copper by hammering out a thin-walled bow and turning down the end of the rod to form a butted loop. A more ornate and finely-finished end-looped mortar from Brettenham (51) also appears to have been worked up from a rod, and it, too, has a turned-over loop with its tip butted against the underside of the bow. Similarly, the idiosyncratic end-looped mortar from Felthorpe (186), with its coiled loop of rather irregular gauge metal, was more likely worked from a rod than cast. Working, as opposed to casting, more readily enabled economy in the use of metal, and all three of the foregoing examples are at the lower end of the weight range, with that from Hunsbury being the lightest mortar so far recorded. Three other examples, end-looped pestles from Brecon (49) and Norfolk (388), and an end-looped mortar from Stonea (482) have a turned-over loop with free end, which was more probably hand-worked than cast.

Function

The key to a fuller understanding of cosmetic grinders is a study of their function, and the basis for that has been a detailed and comprehensive examination of the objects themselves. It was, indeed, a misunderstanding of their function that impeded progress for some 60 years after the appearance of Reginald Smith's pioneering paper. Certainly there is much of interest in their varied decoration (section 6), but, by concentrating on their shape and decor attention was diverted from their primary function as small grinding kits. However, it has now been established beyond doubt that they

were used to prepare a substance or substances by crushing or grinding a small quantity in the groove of the mortar.

The main proof of this is in the traces of wear that survive on many examples of both components. The principal wear site on mortars is the inner surface of the groove, both on its walls and, especially, on its base. There is great variety in the degree of wear displayed. Some examples appear to have been used hardly at all, while at the other extreme there are mortars which have been substantially altered or damaged by prolonged, intense or heavy usage. On those examples that retain their original surface and are not obscured by corrosion the most commonly observed evidence is a distinctive wear-polish, which usually stands out in marked contrast to the finish of adjacent surface areas. Frequently, too, differential wear has resulted in the development of a basal facet running along the main axis of the groove. Sometimes the facet deepened the groove (eg. 124, 228, 314, 392, 467) or developed to one side of the axis producing a marked 'ledge' (eg. 129, 354, 403, 484). Occasionally, however, the line of wear can be seen to have deviated from the central axis, and the oblique facet which resulted sometimes developed into a deep 'rut' which encroached upon one end of each wall at diagonally opposing ends, occasionally causing severe attrition of the rim and wall (eg. 13, 60, 120, 199, 233, 288, 507, esp. 145, 424, 533, 559).

Corresponding to the wear patterns observed in the groove of mortars there is a distinct zoning of the wear traces discerned on pestles. The wear is invariably found on the convex underside of the rod. On end-looped examples wear-polish or wear-facets are located at the tip of the rod and usually extend back no further than the mid-point of the curve. Just as the shape of mortars could be altered by heavy wear so, too, the form of end-looped pestles could be substantially modified. This is seen most graphically on pestles 96, 219, 220, 382, 383, 605, where the rod has been shortened by heavy wear at the tip (**Pl. 4**). On other end-looped examples the wear was sometimes more evenly distributed, and this applies particularly to those of knife-like form with a wedge-shaped or shield-shaped cross-section (eg. 73b, 152, 192b, 285, 300, 514b, 516, 520, 564). They were evidently close-fitting in their mortar groove so that friction and wear were not restricted to the base but extended onto the sides as well (see eg. 192b).

Centre-looped pestles display less and different evidence for wear. The principal site is at the centre of the rod's convex face, but wear-polish and light wear-facets sometimes extend also along the full length of the rod to both its tips, and occasionally those sites take precedence (eg. 296). As on some end-looped pestles the shape of the rod of the centre-looped type was evidently sometimes closely adapted to the form of the groove in the mortar resulting in a more even distribution of wear. However, there was also a difference in the precise mode of use which would have affected the site and degree of wear. For the suspension loop on both types also served as a grip for opposed finger and thumb. This would have dictated use of the opposite end of the rod of end-looped pestles and likewise would have encouraged use of the central zone of the rod of centre-looped pestles, whether for a to-and-fro grinding action or a rocked crushing action.

That crushing and grinding were the primary functions seems indisputable when the wear patterns are examined as a whole. Anything less strenuous is unlikely to have caused such

Plate 4 Wear facets on the tip of three end-looped pestles (l. To r. 96, 383, 382)

marked abrasion. But what was the substance being ground, and what was it used for? It has to be admitted that neither question can yet be answered conclusively. For, no substance has been detected in direct association with any of the complete kits or individual components, nor, as yet, has any reference to the kits been found in the contemporary literature. This is hardly surprising. The type is unequivocally British (see section 6) so no native record can be expected before the introduction of writing at the time of the Roman conquest. Nor is there particular reason to expect a reference to the kits in Roman literature, since the type was clearly alien to that society. The most likely context for mention in Roman or Greek texts would be as an observation of, perhaps, a quaint British

tradition or custom in the writings of geographers, historians or social commentators. Martial, for example, draws attention to various regional commodities such as British baskets and German hair-dye. (*Epigrams* xiv, xxvii and xcix). However, the activity was probably so mundane or commonplace as not to merit attention. Furthermore, it was probably the kits rather than the product that differed from those in use in other parts of the Roman world.

It seems improbable, then, that a description will ever be found in any of the existing texts, but there is perhaps the merest chance that a British source, like the Vindolanda writing tablets, may one day supply a reference in a list, inventory or letter – always assuming that the word or phrase could be recognized. Greater, perhaps, is the chance of finding and identifying the physical remains of the substance or substances in association with a set, and potentially the most fruitful contexts are graves, for they generally combine controlled deposition with optimal preservation. In fact already in 1985 two grave finds had provided direct associations with toilet implements, if not the substance to be ground (Jackson 1985, 171), and this connection was strengthened by the discovery of the London set (319) in 1992 (Jackson 1993, 166–7). The former finds were from Chichester, St Pancras Roman cemetery (92) and from St Albans, King Harry Lane cemetery (436), both from cremation burials. That from Chichester was found with a ligula amongst other things (see section 6), while that from St Albans was associated with a set of toilet implements and a brooch. A subsequent grave find from the St Stephens Roman cemetery, St Albans, another cremation burial, yielded the unburnt remains of a bronze-studded wooden casket containing a cosmetic set (437) and a glass flask. No trace of mineral substances or pigments was recorded by the excavator, and scientific analysis of a residue in the base of the flask unfortunately proved negative (see cat. 437).

In the case of the London find the cosmetic set was fused together with a nail-cleaner and tweezers in an indisputably direct association (**Fig. 3**), thus giving firm support to the

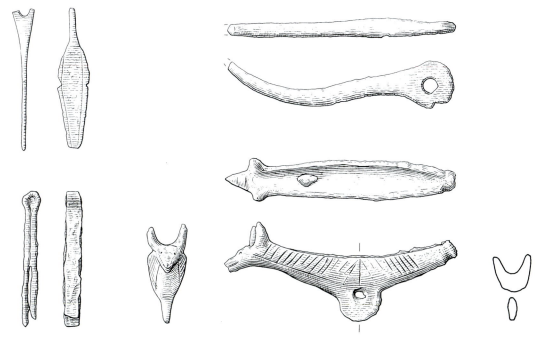

Figure 3 Blossom's Inn, London: the mixed cosmetic set (319) and the associated nail-cleaner and tweezers. Scale 1:1

supposition that cosmetic grinders were, indeed, employed in some aspect of body care or beautification. It was also virtually certain that all four implements had been suspended on the same cord or thong. For, unlike the normal Iron Age and Roman 'pocket sets' of toilet implements, usually comprising tweezers, nail-cleaner and ear-scoop, which were used individually and were therefore often conveniently secured on a closed metal ring, the two-piece nature of cosmetic sets required them to be detachable. Good fortune preserved the London cosmetic set intact and in its original juxtaposition with the nail-cleaner and tweezers, even though their securing cord or thong had long since perished. Similarly, the juxtaposition – loop-to-loop – of the two components of the Colchester (Garrison) set (**Pl. 10**) suggest that they were tied together when placed in the grave. But the use of a cord which might come untied, break or rot made cosmetic sets especially vulnerable to loss or separation, and this is reflected in the relative scarcity of surviving complete sets.

The loop on many mortars and pestles shows signs of wear on an arc of its inner surface. On some examples the wear was so extreme that the eye became elongated or wore away completely at that point (eg. 101, 178, 220, 314, 377, 392, 411, 462, 601). Such a wear pattern is consistent with free-running suspension of the components on a cord, which was fastened, perhaps, on a garment at waist level or on a belt or sash, similar to Anglo-Saxon girdle hangers. A few examples show little or no sign of wear in the loop yet had evidently been used since their grinding surfaces are worn (eg. 141, 474, 605). They were presumably either suspended in a manner that prevented free-running on the cord or were not suspended at all. Alternatives to direct suspension include storage in a box or, perhaps, in a pouch together with the substance to be ground.

As previously observed (Jackson 1985, 171; 1992, 165–6) the substance was one (or more) evidently required to be prepared in small quantities only, either because it was costly or because only a small amount was needed. It was then to be used immediately or decanted since the mortars were not designed to stand upright. Some, indeed, were equipped with a small lip or spout or an open end to facilitate control of the decanting process (17, 44, 51, 64, 308, 404, 423, 492, 576). The commodity seems unlikely to have been medicaments in view of the ubiquity of the type, and pepper may be discounted, too, since its import, from India, began only in the Roman period. Salt is possible, though such kits for its preparation are unparalleled in the ancient world. Were salt indeed the commodity there would in any case be little likelihood of ever establishing it's former presence, even in the 'secure' conditions of a grave find. There seems little to commend the theory of a connection to the use of woad (Carr 2005; Cuddeford 2008), the preparation and application of which hardly corresponds to the very particular design of cosmetic sets. Such indirect and circumstantial evidence as there is points rather towards the substance having been mineral ingredients for use in cosmetics, and there is a reasonable chance that these might occasionally survive as an identifiable deposit in an undisturbed context. For what kind of substances might be expected we can turn to the classical world, where the evidence for cosmetics is much fuller.

Roman perfumes and cosmetics were numerous, varied, often costly and frequently the subject of sarcastic or caustic comment by contemporary writers. A stock satirical portrait depicted the inevitably vain attempts by women and men alike to restore their youthful looks or mask the effects of age by over-lavish use of plasters, unguents, perfumes, pastilles, wigs and make-up. The reality was doubtless less extreme, but in Rome by the early empire it is evident that there was a general and widespread use of cosmetics by those women who could afford to do so. There was an extensive literature on cosmetics which frequently featured in works by Greek and Roman medical writers – Theophrastus, Dioscorides, Archigenes of Apamea, and Trajan's physician, Crito, amongst others. Galen considered cosmetic adornment one of the 'perverted arts' (5.821 K. Singer 1997, 60). From a passage in one of the *carmina* of the Roman love poet Propertius, written probably in the mid-20s BC, it may be construed that the people of Britain, too, were acquainted with cosmetics at that time:

'Do you even imitate the Britons, now, stained with woad, you crazy girl, and play games, with foreign glitter on your face? Everything's proper form is as Nature made it: Belgian colour looks foul on Roman cheeks.' (Propertius *The Elegies* II. 18B, 1–4. ('Painted Lady'). Trans. A.S. Kline).

That cosmetics were also extensively traded is attested both by the ancient writers, who comment, usually disapprovingly, on the unguent markets, notably the *seplasia* at Capua, and by the excavated remains of ointment pots, unguent phials and other cosmetic containers and impedimenta.

In addition to liquid perfumes, oil-based unguents, cerates and ointments Roman women used various cosmetic and dusting powders (*diapasmata* and *parapasta*), many of which were made from mineral substances. Despite its toxicity psimythion (powdered lead white – basic lead carbonate) was the favoured face-whitener, while minium (red lead – lead oxide), vermilion and cinnabar (mercury sulphide) were dusted onto the face as rouge. Galena (lead sulphide) and stibnite (antimony sulphide) were powdered for use as black eye-paints, as had long been the case in Egypt, where the copper ore malachite was also employed for its green colour (Forbes 1955, 17–21, 38–43). For all the foregoing manufactured mineral colours alternative, cheaper or more readily available natural materials could, of course, be substituted – white and red chalk, red ochre, haematite and powdered charcoal or soot, for example, just as they sometimes were for painter's pigments (Bierbrier 1997. Middleton and Humphrey 2001).

Preparation of the powders and eye-paints was no complicated business. The mineral ingredient was ground on a flat stone palette and the resulting powder was made into a paste by the addition of water, gum-water or spittle. The paste could then be applied, whether as eye-shadow or mascara, with the finger tip or the olivary terminal of a scoop probe (*cyathiscomele*), spatula probe (*spathomele*) or *ligula*, the Roman equivalent of the Egyptian kohl-stick. The same roles could have been performed using the mortar and pestle of the British cosmetic grinders, and it seems probable that the British kits were an insular version of the cosmetic implements used elsewhere in the Roman world. After Roman contact with Britain and the conquest of AD 43 it is apparent that both modes of preparation continued alongside each other, for there was no rapid decline in the use of cosmetic grinders after the introduction of the Roman range of cosmetic paraphernalia – stone palettes, bronze rods, glass phials etc.

The British cosmetic sets were differentiated by their suspension loop, and it may be envisaged that this portability extended also to the container for the cosmetic raw materials. In Egypt the mineral ingredients of eye-paints were carried in small pouches of leather or linen or in shells, reeds or leaf wrappings, all of which have occasionally been found in graves, while lumps of white lead have been found in pottery containers in Athenian tombs (Forbes 1955, 18, 39–40). The substances ground in the British cosmetic grinders are likely to have been mineral ingredients of this kind, perhaps in the form of lumps or pellets, which were probably contained in cloth or leather pouches and suspended on the same cord or thong as the kits. In time it is to be hoped that remains of the mineral ingredients, and even, perhaps, their container, will be found with a cosmetic set in a secure archaeological context. Something similar appears to have been found in Enclosure 1 at Stanway, where a tiny cloth bag containing what may have been mineral powder or paste, perhaps some kind of cosmetic, was part of the burnt pyre goods of an adult ?female cremation burial (AF18) of the second half of the 1st century BC (Crummy *et al.* 2007, 167–70).

In the absence of direct evidence for the identity of the substance to be ground an alternative intrinsic source was investigated – the contact surfaces of the pestles and mortars. For, although the instability of the mortars precluded the survival of any of the ground product in their groove, it was thought possible that the repeated grinding process might have caused the surfaces to absorb some of the material being prepared. It was hoped that scientific analysis might reveal traces of particular and identifiable materials. However, since it was considered that the substances ground were likely to have comprised, or to have included, the widely available and colourful compounds of lead, copper or antimony, which might be difficult to distinguish from the alloy constituents of the grinders themselves, the analyses of the contact surfaces were compared with analyses of other parts of the implements in the hope that enhanced values for particular constituents might be identified. In the event, however, no conclusive or consistent result was obtained (see section 4).

In order to test function and efficiency a brass replica was made of the end-looped cosmetic set from the King Harry Lane Cemetery, St Albans (436). Experiment showed that the tendency of right-handed users is to hold the rod by its loop between the thumb and index finger of the right hand, while the mortar is held in the left hand in one of two ways. Either it is gripped centrally by the bow walls, with the thumb opposing the four fingers, or it is gripped with the loop between thumb and index finger and the distal end supported by the little finger. A simple reversal of components accommodates the kit to left hand users (**Pl. 5**). In these operative positions a range of commodities was tested. Peppercorns and other plant seeds of rounded or spherical form proved resistant to crushing or grinding, as they were difficult to control and tended to shoot out of the mortar, but salt crystals were easily reduced to fine granules. Similarly, charcoal and chalks could be quickly powdered, but so, too, could a range of tougher substances, and the kit proved remarkably efficient in quickly powdering even a hard mineral like ilmenite sand (iron titanium oxide).

Other minerals tested included galena, malachite, azurite, haematite, realgar and graphite, which yielded respectively

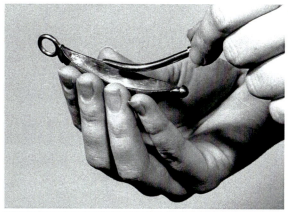
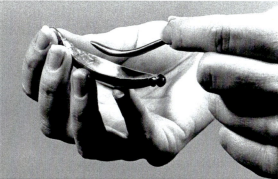
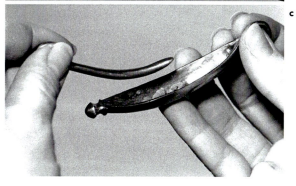

Plate 5 A replica of the end-looped cosmetic set from St Albans (436) showing two alternative ways of holding it when in use (a, b), and with samples of Egyptian Blue in the mortar (c)

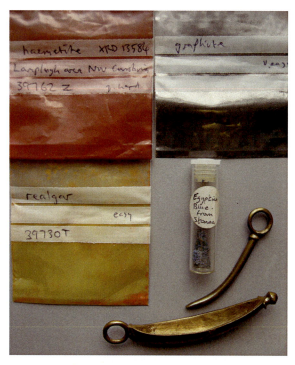

Plate 6 Some of the mineral powders prepared with the replica cosmetic set

powders of grey, green, blue, red, yellow and sparkly grey colour (**Pl. 6**). Best results were achieved by using a very small quantity and by first crushing the larger pieces by pressing them with the tip of the rod before grinding the product along the groove to convert it to a fine powder. All of these minerals would have been available locally in Britain or by means of trade. Haematite was especially widespread in Britain and was a very common pigment in Romano-British wall-paintings (see eg. L. Biek in Davey and Ling 1982, 220–2). As a cosmetic its powder makes a very effective rouge or eye-shadow, which adheres well to the skin whether applied dry or by licking the tip of the finger before dipping it in the powder. Its range of shades could be further widened by the addition of varied amounts of powdered white lead or chalk, while a sparkle could be added by dusting on a little powdered graphite. A reddish powder found in two glass *unguentaria* from the *colonia* of Celsa in north-east Spain (Hispania Tarraconensis) is suggestive of that sort of use, for analysis demonstrated that its constituents were haematite, gypsum, calcite and an organic binding substance (Perez-Arantegui 1996; Eckardt and Crummy 2008, 27).

In view of the suggestion that the Roman artificial pigment *caeruleum*, a calcium-copper silicate, known today as Egyptian Blue, may have had a cosmetic application as blue eye-shadow (Riha 1986, 97–8) as well as its more widely accepted usage as a pigment for painted plaster, a sample was tested in the replica kit. The *c.* 5–10 mm diameter sub-spherical balls in which Egyptian Blue was widely traded could not be accommodated in the groove of any cosmetic grinder, but the balls are quite friable and are readily broken into smaller pieces. These fragments were easily reduced in the mortar, though, as with some of the raw minerals occasional tiny quartzite grain inclusions had to be flicked out of the mortar with the tip of the pestle before the product could be reduced to a uniformly fine powder.

While some of the mineral powders proved to have good adhesion when simply rubbed on dry or combined with spittle, others, including Egyptian Blue, were less stable and probably required the addition of an oil or gum-water base. The tests also revealed, strikingly, how small a quantity of the minerals is required. For example, a tiny lump of haematite of 1–2 mm diameter yielded more than sufficient powder to shadow both eyelids and brush on to the cheeks. Appropriately enough, the kit was found to function most effectively when preparing a single lump of that order of size, and even the smallest mortars and shallowest grooves would have been capable of use in this way.

The experiments with the replica kit thus confirmed that the design of cosmetic grinders is very precisely adapted to crushing and grinding small quantities of mineral substances and that a broad palette of colours in considerable quantity could be carried in a small pouch or pouches containing tiny lumps of various minerals.

Who used these kits and their product? That it was no restricted group is evident from the sheer number of finds (over 600 catalogued examples) and their distribution (section 6), and we can infer that cosmetic grinders were in everyday and widespread use in Roman Britain. On the question of gender it might be anticipated that an unequivocal answer would be provided by the evidence from grave finds. However, as a summary of the available evidence shows (**Table 9**) the answer is neither as full nor as clear-cut as might be wished. Only five sets from graves provide evidence of gender, and of those only one is certain. Four of the burial associations of complete sets are female or probably female and one is possibly male, while a probable pestle accompanied the female inhumation at Saintes, and there is another female association in the early 6th century AD Anglo-Saxon grave at Horton Kirby. The possible male association is the cosmetic set from King Harry Lane, St Albans (436), which was found with a cremation burial in grave no. 203 (Stead and Rigby 1989, 103; Stirland 1989, 243). In contrast, the set from the St Stephen's cemetery, St Albans (437) was found with a probable female cremation burial. Niblett has drawn attention to the apparent gender bias in the sexed cremation burials in the King Harry Lane cemetery (out of use by the Flavian period) – 16% male/ 5% female – comparing them to the (as yet unpublished) results for the St Stephens cemetery (Claudian to early Antonine), where female burials outnumbered those of males – 28% male/ 35% female for the 1st to early 2nd century AD. Her suggestion that the dearth of males in the late 1st and early 2nd century may have been a result of local youths being recruited into the Roman army is tempered by the acknowledgement that cremated remains are difficult to sex (Niblett 2000, 103–4 and fig. 10.8). Likewise, in discussing another equivocal determination from the King Harry Lane cemetery – a possible male burial with an imported mirror – Eckardt and Crummy, while aware of the difficulty of sexing cremated remains at the site, raise the interesting possibility that the find reflects 'fundamental changes in the impact of Roman imports on the expression of élite and gender identities' (Eckardt and Crummy 2008, 31–2 and 89). The King Harry Lane and St Stephen's cosmetic sets could also be interpreted as possibly reflecting changes in the expression of identities, though as an essentially British type rather than an imported commodity. Whether or not that was the case the wider evidence indicates a predominantly female association with cosmetic grinders but male use cannot be entirely ruled out.

Table 9 Grave finds, sex of associated human remains

22	Beckford, set with female inhumation, Late Iron Age
436	St Albans, set with possible male cremation, AD 40–60
437	St Albans, set with probable female cremation, 1st–2nd cent. AD
---	Bures St Mary, set with adult cremation, probably female (mirror and casket included in grave goods), 1st–2nd cent. AD
---	Colchester (Garrison), set with inhumation, adult, sex unknown, late 1st–late 2nd cent. AD
92	Chichester, set with probable female cremation, 2nd–3rd cent. AD
501	Thérouanne, set with cremation, unexamined, late 2nd/ early 3rd cent. AD
273	Horton Kirby, mortar in female grave, early 6th cent. AD
444	Saintes, probable pestle with female inhumation, AD 40–50

4. Scientific Analyses

K.J. Matthews and M.R. Cowell

Introduction

Fifty-three cosmetic mortars and pestles were analysed in 1995 in order to determine their elemental composition (British Museum Department of Scientific Research, project 6610). The sample comprised: 2 complete sets (260, 436), 14 end-looped mortars (163, 181, 184, 212, 292, 318, 389, 441, 482, 492, 504, 508, 600, 601), 17 centre-looped mortars (147, 224, 261, 278, 301, 309, 348, 362, 399, 479, 496, 518, 578, 579, 580, 581, 582), 1 multiple-looped mortar (403), 5 end-looped pestles (96, 151, 152, 268, 604) and 12 centre-looped pestles (179, 180, 230, 310, 324, 372, 480, 493, 503, 528, 566, 591).

The aims were to establish whether or not the composition varied with style or form, or between the various geographical find areas. In the case of the complete sets, both components were analysed to determine whether or not the same alloy was used. Only 15 of the objects were considered sufficiently robust for a drilled sample of the alloy to be obtained from the interior of the body metal for quantitative analysis and to provide an indication of the validity of the surface analyses.

The interior surface of the mortars was analysed, in the hope of detecting the material that had been ground in them. The coloured enamel inlays on three centre-looped mortars were also investigated.

Experimental procedure

The mortars were examined using a low-power binocular microscope (x25–50 magnification) to see if any trace of the material ground up in the mortar was still extant.

The metal analyses were performed using energy dispersive X-ray fluorescence spectrometry (XRF), with a molybdenum target X-ray tube operating at a voltage of 45 kV (Cowell, 1998). The spectra obtained were calibrated by reference to those of standards of known composition.

The surface XRF analyses were carried out on the least corroded area of the objects – the surfaces were not abraded prior to analysis. In the case of the mortars, at least two analyses were performed: one on the outside, and the other on the inside i.e. the grinding surface. Multiple surface analyses were carried out on two of the mortars (184 and 224) in order to look for variations in the surface composition, both inside and outside. It must be emphasized that this analytical technique is a surface method and in most cases has only been used here to obtain a semi-quantitative elemental composition. Since minimal preparation was carried out to remove possible surface enrichment, patina etc., it may not accurately represent the composition of the body of the object (**Tables 10 and 12**).

Where the objects were relatively thick castings, and also not heavily corroded, a drilled sample of the body metal was collected, using a low power, slow speed drill with a 0.8 mm diameter bit. These drillings were also analysed by XRF (**Table 11**); the accuracy should be better than that obtained for the surface analyses.

The precision (i.e. reproducibility) of the technique is about $\pm$ 1–2% relative for the major elements (copper, tin and lead), 5% relative for iron and zinc, and about 25% or more relative for the trace elements (arsenic, nickel and silver). Although the accuracies are similar to these levels for the drilled samples the accuracies of the surface analyses are not clearly definable and may be less good than fully quantitative analysis of drilled material because of alteration due to corrosion.

Discussion of results

The surface analysis results are presented in **Table 10** as weight percentage ranges (major amounts 10–100%, minor amounts 1–10% and trace or not detected): the provisos outlined above relating to corrosion and other surface effects must be considered when using these results. The analytical results for the drilled samples are given in **Table 11a** as weight percentages and presented as a scatter plot in **Table 11b**. **Table 12** gives the results of multiple analyses at different points on the surfaces of the mortars from Faversham and Grimsby, illustrating the variability of results obtained by XRF analysis on the corroded surface within one object.

The analytical results confirm that nearly all of the objects are of copper alloys of the types common to Roman metalwork of other classes (Craddock 1978; Bayley and Butcher 2004; Hook and Craddock 1996), bronzes (defined here as alloys of at least 5% tin and copper), brasses (alloys of at least 5% zinc and copper) and gunmetals or mixed alloys (alloys of copper, tin and zinc). In many cases lead has also been added to the alloy and here the alloy is defined as 'leaded' if more than *c.* 5% lead is present. The only non-copper alloy object is an example of lead from Skipton Street, London (318), which is regarded as an archetype or model for the production of a mould for copper-alloy casting.

Comparison of the results of analysis on the corroded surfaces of the objects (**Table 10**) and of the samples drilled from uncorroded metal reveals the expected differences attributable to corrosion, in particular the loss of zinc from the surface and inconsistencies in the estimation of the lead content. Note also the variations in the lead to copper ratio detected across the surfaces of 184 and 224, and significant variation in levels of tin at different points on the surface (**Table 12**).

Table 10 Analysis by XRF of the uncleaned corroded metal surfaces of mortars and pestles

Key: ** more than 10%; * more than 1%, less than 10%; tr. less than 1%; n.d. not detected.

Cat.no., provenance, position of analysis	BMRL no.	Alloy type	Cu	Sn	Pb	Zn	Fe	Ni	As	Sb	Ag
Complete sets											
260a, Hockwold, Norfolk: mortar, outside	50475Z	leaded bronze	**	**	**	tr.	*	n.d.	n.d.	n.d.	tr.
260a, Hockwold, Norfolk: mortar, inside			**	**	**	tr.	tr.	tr.	tr.	n.d.	tr.
260b, Hockwold, Norfolk: pestle, top of loop	50476X	leaded bronze	**	**	**	tr.	*	n.d.	tr.	n.d.	tr.
260b, Hockwold, Norfolk: pestle, side below loop			**	**	**	tr.	*	tr.	tr.	n.d.	tr.
436a, St Albans, Hertfordshire: mortar, outside	50473S	brass	**	tr.	tr.	*	tr.	n.d.	n.d.	n.d.	n.d.
436a, St Albans, Hertfordshire: mortar, inside			**	tr.	n.d.	*	tr.	tr.	tr.	tr.	n.d.
436b, St Albans, Hertfordshire: pestle	50474Q	brass	**	tr.	tr.	**	tr.	n.d.	tr.	n.d.	tr.
End-looped mortars											
163, East Anglia: outside	50480U	leaded gunmetal	**	**	**	*	*	n.d.	n.d.	n.d.	tr.
163, East Anglia: inside			**	*	**	tr.	*	n.d.	n.d.	n.d.	tr.
163, East Anglia: inside, contents			**	*	*	*	*	n.d.	n.d.	n.d.	n.d.
181, Essex: outside	50445P	leaded copper	**	tr.	**	n.d.	*	tr.	n.d.	*	tr.
181, Essex: inside			**	tr.	**	n.d.	tr.	n.d.	n.d.	*	tr.
184, Faversham, Kent: outside	50449S	bronze	**	*	*	n.d.	tr.	tr.	n.d.	tr.	tr.
184, Faversham, Kent: inside			**	**	**	tr.	*	tr.	n.d.	n.d.	tr.
212, Great Sturton, Lincs.: outside	50478T	bronze	**	**	*	tr.	*	tr.	tr.	tr.	tr.
212, Great Sturton, Lincs.: inside			**	**	tr.	n.d.	tr.	tr.	tr.	n.d.	tr.
292, Keston, Kent: outside	50443T	bronze	**	**	*	n.d.	tr.	tr.	n.d.	tr.	tr.
292, Keston, Kent: inside			**	**	tr.	n.d.	tr.	n.d.	n.d.	tr.	n.d.
318, Skipton Street, London: outside	50452R	lead	tr.	tr.	**	n.d.	**	n.d.	n.d.	n.d.	n.d.
318, Skipton Street, London: inside			tr.	tr.	**	n.d.	*	n.d.	tr.	n.d.	n.d.
389, Norfolk: outside	50447W	leaded bronze	**	**	**	tr.	*	n.d.	n.d.	n.d.	n.d.
389, Norfolk: inside			**	**	**	n.d.	*	n.d.	n.d.	n.d.	tr.
441, St Albans, Hertfordshire: outside	50444R	bronze	**	**	*	n.d.	*	tr.	n.d.	tr.	tr.
441, St Albans, Hertfordshire: inside			**	**	*	n.d.	*	tr.	n.d.	n.d.	tr.
482, Stonea, Cambridgeshire: outside	50446Y	bronze	**	**	*	n.d.	tr.	tr.	tr.	tr.	tr.
482, Stonea, Cambridgeshire: inside			**	**	*	n.d.	*	tr.	tr.	tr.	tr.
492, Suffolk/Norfolk: outside	52063W	leaded bronze	**	**	**	n.d.	*	tr.	n.d.	tr.	tr.
492, Suffolk/Norfolk: inside			**	**	**	n.d.	*	tr.	tr.	n.d.	tr.
504, Thetford, Norfolk: outside	52056U	bronze	**	**	*	tr.	**	tr.	n.d.	tr.	tr.
504, Thetford, Norfolk: inside			**	**	*	tr.	**	tr.	tr.	n.d.	tr.
508, Tilbury, Essex: outside	50479R	leaded bronze	**	**	**	n.d.	*	tr.	tr.	n.d.	tr.
508, Tilbury, Essex: inside			**	**	**	n.d.	tr.	tr.	tr.	n.d.	n.d.
600, unknown provenance: outside	50448U	bronze	**	*	*	n.d.	tr.	tr.	n.d.	tr.	tr.
600, unknown provenance: inside			**	*	*	n.d.	tr.	tr.	n.d.	tr.	tr.
601, unknown provenance: outside	52060R	leaded gunmetal	**	**	**	*	*	n.d.	n.d.	tr.	tr.
601, unknown provenance: inside			**	**	**	*	*	tr.	tr.	n.d.	tr.
Centre-looped mortars											
147, Ditchingham, Norfolk: outside	52064U	leaded bronze	**	**	**	tr.	*	tr.	n.d.	n.d.	tr.
147, Ditchingham, Norfolk: inside (grey area)			**	**	**	tr.	*	n.d.	n.d.	n.d.	tr.
147, Ditchingham, Norfolk: inside (brown area)			**	**	**	tr.	*	n.d.	n.d.	n.d.	tr.
224, Grimsby, Humberside: outside	50456U	leaded bronze	**	**	**	tr.	tr.	tr.	tr.	tr.	tr.
224, Grimsby, Humberside: inside			*	n.d.	**	n.d.	tr	tr.	n.d.	tr.	n.d.
261, Hockwold, Norfolk: outside	50453P	leaded bronze	**	**	**	tr.	*	n.d.	n.d.	tr.	tr.
261, Hockwold, Norfolk: inside towards small end			**	**	**	tr.	tr.	n.d.	n.d.	tr.	tr.
278, Icklingham, Suffolk: outside	50459Z	leaded bronze	**	**	**	tr.	tr.	tr.	tr.	tr.	tr.
278, Icklingham, Suffolk: inside			**	**	**	tr.	tr.	tr.	n.d.	n.d.	n.d.
278, Icklingham, Suffolk: red enamel			*	*	**	n.d.	*	tr.	n.d.	tr.	n.d.
278, Icklingham, Suffolk: blue enamel			**	**	**	tr.	*	n.d.	n.d.	*	n.d.
301, Lakenheath, Suffolk: outside	50451T	leaded gunmetal	**	**	**	*	tr.	n.d.	tr.	tr.	tr.
301, Lakenheath, Suffolk: inside			**	**	**	*	*	n.d.	n.d.	n.d.	tr.
309, Lincolnshire: outside	50458Q	leaded gunmetal	**	**	**	*	*	n.d.	n.d.	tr.	tr.
309, Lincolnshire: inside			**	**	**	*	*	tr.	n.d.	tr.	tr.
348, Minster in Sheppey, Kent: outside	50454Y	leaded gunmetal	**	**	**	*	**	n.d.	tr.	tr.	tr.
348, Minster in Sheppey, Kent: inside			**	**	**	tr.	**	n.d.	n.d.	tr.	tr.
362, Norfolk: outside	50463W	leaded bronze	**	**	**	tr.	tr.	tr.	tr.	n.d.	*
362, Norfolk: inside			**	**	**	n.d.	tr.	n.d.	n.d.	n.d.	tr.

Table 10 cont. Analysis by XRF of the uncleaned corroded metal surfaces of mortars and pestles

Key: ** more than 10%; * more than 1%, less than 10%; tr. less than 1%; n.d. not detected

Cat.no., provenance, position of analysis	BMRL no.	Alloy type	Cu	Sn	Pb	Zn	Fe	Ni	As	Sb	Ag
Centre-looped mortars cont.											
399, Oakley, Suffolk: outside	50450V	leaded bronze	**	**	**	tr.	**	n.d.	tr.	tr.	tr.
399, Oakley, Suffolk: inside (dark brown area)			*	**	**	n.d.	**	n.d.	n.d.	tr.	tr.
399, Oakley, Suffolk: inside (beneath soil)			**	**	**	n.d.	**	n.d.	n.d.	n.d.	tr.
399, Oakley, Suffolk: soil from inside			**	tr.	**	n.d.	**	n.d.	n.d.	n.d.	n.d.
479, Stonea, Cambridgeshire: outside	50455W	leaded bronze	*	**	**	tr.	**	n.d.	tr.	tr.	tr.
479, Stonea, Cambridgeshire: inside, (silvery-looking area)			**	**	**	n.d.	**	n.d.	n.d.	tr.	*
479, Stonea, Cambridgeshire: inside, (brown area)			**	**	**	n.d.	**	tr.	tr.	tr.	tr.
496, Syderstone, Norfolk: outside	52835R	leaded bronze	**	**	**	tr.	*	n.d.	n.d.	n.d.	tr.
496, Syderstone, Norfolk: inside (at end)			**	tr.	**	n.d.	*	n.d.	n.d.	n.d.	tr.
496, Syderstone, Norfolk: inside (middle)			**	**	**	n.d.	*	n.d.	tr.	n.d.	n.d.
518, Warlingham, Surrey: outside (near loop)	50462Y	bronze	**	**	*	tr.	*	n.d.	n.d.	n.d.	tr.
518, Warlingham, Surrey: outside (side)			**	**	*	tr.	*	n.d.	tr.	n.d.	tr.
518, Warlingham, Surrey: inside			**	**	*	tr.	*	tr.	tr.	n.d.	tr.
578, unknown provenance: outside	50460R	leaded bronze	**	**	**	*	tr.	tr.	tr.	tr.	tr.
578, unknown provenance: inside			**	**	**	tr.	*	tr.	n.d.	n.d.	tr.
578, unknown provenance: red/orange enamel			**	**	**	tr.	*	tr.	n.d.	tr.	tr.
578, unknown provenance: blue enamel			**	**	**	tr.	*	n.d.	*	*	n.d.
579, unknown provenance: outside	50457S	leaded gunmetal	**	**	**	*	*	tr.	tr.	tr.	tr.
579, unknown provenance: inside			**	**	**	*	**	n.d.	tr.	tr.	tr.
580, unknown provenance: outside	50461P	leaded gunmetal	**	**	**	*	tr.	n.d.	n.d.	tr.	n.d.
580, unknown provenance: inside			**	**	**	*	*	tr.	n.d.	tr.	tr.
580, unknown provenance: cell with trace of enamel			**	**	**	tr.	*	n.d.	n.d.	tr.	n.d.
581, unknown provenance: outside	50465S	leaded bronze	*	**	**	tr.	*	n.d.	n.d.	n.d.	tr.
581, unknown provenance: inside			**	**	**	*	**	n.d.	tr.	n.d.	tr.
582, unknown provenance: outside	50464U	leaded gunmetal	**	**	**	*	tr.	tr.	tr.	n.d.	tr.
582, unknown provenance: inside			**	*	**	*	*	n.d.	tr.	n.d.	tr.
Multi-looped mortar											
403, Otford, Kent: outside	52058Q	bronze	**	**	tr.	n.d.	*	tr.	tr.	n.d.	tr.
403, Otford, Kent: inside			**	**	tr.	tr.	*	tr.	*	n.d.	tr.
End-looped pestles											
96, Chichester, Sussex	52065S	leaded gunmetal	**	**	*	*	*	tr.	tr.	n.d.	tr.
151, Dorset: loop	52057S	leaded gunmetal	**	**	**	*	*	tr.	tr.	n.d.	tr.
151, Dorset: dark area			**	**	*	*	*	n.d.	n.d.	n.d.	tr.
151, Dorset: white area			**	**	**	*	*	tr.	n.d.	n.d.	tr.
152, Dorset: loop	52061P	brass	**	*	*	*	*	n.d.	tr.	tr.	tr.
152, Dorset: grinding face			**	*	*	*	*	n.d.	tr.	n.d.	tr.
268, Hod Hill, Dorset: end of loop	50477V	leaded gunmetal	**	**	*	*	tr.	tr.	tr.	n.d.	tr.
268, Hod Hill, Dorset: worn area			**	**	*	*	tr.	tr.	tr.	n.d.	tr.
604, unknown provenance: grinding face	52055W	leaded bronze	**	**	**	tr.	*	n.d.	tr.	tr.	tr.
Centre-looped pestles											
179, Essex	50466Q	leaded bronze	**	**	**	tr.	*	tr.	n.d.	n.d.	n.d.
180, Essex ? (heavily corroded)	50471W	leaded bronze	**	**	**	tr.	*	tr.	n.d.	n.d.	tr.
230, Haddiscoe, Norfolk: grinding face	52059Z	leaded bronze	**	**	**	tr.	**	tr.	n.d.	n.d.	tr.
310, Lincolnshire	50470Y	leaded bronze	**	**	**	tr.	*	n.d.	n.d.	n.d.	n.d.
324, London	50468X	leaded bronze	**	**	**	tr.	**	n.d.	tr.	n.d.	n.d.
372, Norfolk	50472U	leaded bronze	**	**	**	n.d.	**	tr.	n.d.	n.d.	tr.
480, Stonea, Cambridgeshire	50469V	leaded bronze	**	**	**	n.d.	*	tr.	n.d.	n.d.	n.d.
493, Suffolk/Norfolk : grinding face	52062Y	?	*	**	**	tr.	*	tr.	n.d.	n.d.	tr.
503, Thetford, Norfolk: between loops	52054Y	leaded bronze	**	**	**	n.d.	*	tr.	n.d.	n.d.	tr.
503, Thetford, Norfolk: grinding face			**	**	**	tr.	*	tr.	n.d.	tr.	tr.
528, Wenhaston, Suffolk,	50481S	leaded bronze	**	**	**	n.d.	tr.	tr.	n.d.	n.d.	n.d.
566, Wymondham, Norfolk: loop	50482Q	leaded bronze	**	**	**	tr.	**	n.d.	tr.	n.d.	tr.
566, Wymondham, Norfolk: grinding face			**	**	*	n.d.	**	n.d.	tr.	n.d.	tr.
591, unknown provenance	50467Z	bronze	**	*	tr.	*	**	n.d.	n.d.	n.d.	n.d.

Table 11a Analysis by XRF of uncorroded metal drillings from mortars and pestles

The precisions of the technique are +/- 1-2% relative for the major elements: copper, tin and lead; 5% relative for iron and zinc, and about 25% or more relative for the trace elements: arsenic, nickel, silver and antimony.

Key: < less than the quoted detection limit

Cat.no., provenance	BMRL no.	Alloy type	Cu	Sn	Pb	Zn	Fe	Ni	As	Sb	Ag
End-looped mortars											
181, Essex	50445P	leaded copper	92.9	0.3	6.1	< 0.1	< 0.04	0.2	< 0.1	0.5	1.2
292, Keston	50443T	bronze	89.7	9.5	0.4	0.2	0.2	0.1	< 0.12	< 0.1	< 0.04
389, Norfolk	50447W	leaded bronze	68.3	10.2	20.4	0.8	0.2	0.1	< 0.2	< 0.08	< 0.05
492, Suffolk/Norfolk	52063W	bronze	91.5	5.2	3.1	< 0.2	< 0.04	0.1	< 0.1	< 0.1	< 0.1
504, Thetford	52056U	bronze	81.7	11.6	2.8	1.1	2.2	0.2	< 0.2	0.3	0.1
Centre-looped mortars											
348, Minster in Sheppey	50454Y	leaded gunmetal	78.6	8.1	8.9	3.6	0.3	0.1	0.2	< 0.1	0.2
479, Stonea	50455W	leaded bronze	75.0	7.4	16.7	0.5	0.3	< 0.05	< 0.16	< 0.1	0.1
578, unknown provenance	50460R	leaded bronze	84.4	6.3	8.1	1.0	< 0.1	0.1	< 0.2	< 0.1	0.1
581, unknown provenance	50465S	leaded gunmetal	76.0	6.2	14.6	2.7	0.4	< 0.1	< 0.2	< 0.1	0.2
582, unknown provenance	50464U	leaded gunmetal	84.6	2.9	6.2	5.7	0.2	< 0.1	0.2	0.3	< 0.03
Multi-looped mortar											
403, Otford	52058Q	bronze	86.1	12.7	< 0.1	< 0.2	< 0.1	0.4	0.8	< 0.2	< 0.1
End-looped pestles											
152, Dorset	52061P	brass	85.4	1.3	0.1	12.6	0.3	0.1	0.1	0.1	< 0.03
Centre-looped pestles											
179, Essex	50466Q	leaded bronze	77.7	6.5	15.0	0.6	0.2	< 0.1	< 0.2	< 0.1	0.1
310, Lincolnshire	50470Y	leaded gunmetal	78.2	8.2	10.6	2.7	0.1	0.1	< 0.1	< 0.1	< 0.04
372, Norfolk	50472U	leaded bronze	86.1	5.6	8.0	< 0.2	< 0.04	0.1	< 0.1	< 0.1	0.2

Table 11b Scatter plot of drilled samples illustrating the range of alloys used in the manufacture of cosmetic grinders

Lead is shown as low (0-2%: clear symbols), medium (2-10%: grey symbols) and high (>10%: black symbols)

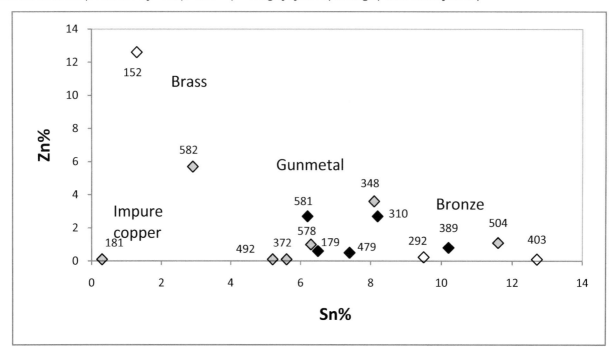

Table 12 Analysis by XRF of the corroded metal surface at several points on two mortars

Key: ** more than 10%; * more than 1%, less than 10%; tr. less than 1%; n.d. not detected

Cat. no., provenance	Cu	Sn	Pb	Zn	Fe	Ni	As	Sb	Ag
184, Faversham									
outside:									
knob (top side)	**	**	**	tr.	tr.	n.d.	tr.	tr.	tr.
side a	**	**	*	n.d.	tr.	tr.	tr.	n.d.	tr.
broken edge	**	*	*	n.d.	tr.	tr.	n.d.	tr.	tr.
side b	**	**	**	tr.	*	tr.	tr.	tr.	tr.
inside:									
near knob	**	tr.	**	n.d.	*	tr.	tr.	n.d.	tr.
quarter way along from knob	*	tr.	**	n.d.	*	n.d.	n.d.	n.d.	n.d.
halfway along from knob	**	*	**	n.d.	*	n.d.	n.d.	n.d.	tr.
threequarters along from knob	*	*	**	n.d.	*	n.d.	n.d.	n.d.	n.d.
adjacent to broken end	**	*	**	n.d.	*	n.d.	tr.	n.d.	tr.
224, Grimsby									
outside:									
end of animal's horn	**	**	**	tr.	tr.	tr.	n.d.	tr.	tr.
bird's head	**	*	**	n.d.	tr.	n.d.	n.d.	tr.	tr.
middle of side	**	**	**	n.d.	tr.	n.d.	tr.	tr.	tr.
behind numbered area	**	**	**	n.d.	tr.	n.d.	n.d.	tr.	tr.
inside:									
animal's head end	**	**	**	tr.	tr.	tr.	n.d.	tr.	tr.
bird's head end	**	*	**	tr.	*	tr.	n.d.	tr.	tr.
middle	*	tr.	**	n.d.	tr.	tr.	n.d.	tr.	tr.

The following examples were found to have features worthy of further discussion:

Centre-looped mortar from Stonea (479)
A shiny, silvery-looking area was noticed on the inside of this mortar. XRF analysis confirmed that this spot was indeed richer in silver than the rest of the mortar, though the significance of this is unclear.

Centre-looped mortars with enamel
Icklingham (278), Unknown provenance (578), Unknown provenance (580)

These three mortars had traces of enamel decoration on their sides, contained within very small triangular cells, although in all three examples only a small number of the cells still retained the enamel. The enamels were only of two colours, red or blue (**Pl. 9**). Both colours contained antimony, although the blue enamels were richer in this element, containing several percent. Antimony was used as an opacifier in enamels of this period (Tite *et al.* 2008, 67).

Centre-looped mortar from Oakley (399)
This mortar was presented for analysis in the state in which it had recently been excavated, i.e. there had been no cleaning or conservation of the metal, and, more importantly, the grinding area was still full of the soil that had accumulated during burial. It was hoped that some of the material that had been ground in it during its period of use might still remain beneath the soil. Unfortunately, the analytical results for both the newly revealed grinding surface, and also the soil, failed to reveal the presence of any substances other than those attributable to either the soil itself or to the body metal of the grinder. The mortar may of course have been cleaned before burial, or possibly the contents were organic and were not detectable by the methods used.

End-looped mortar from Faversham (184) and centre-looped mortar from Grimsby (224)
Surface analyses of these two items at several points on each showed that there were significantly higher levels of lead on the interior surfaces in comparison with the exteriors (see **Table 12**). In the case of that from Faversham (184), a maximum of a tenfold increase in lead concentration was observed and illite, a naturally occurring micaceous clay component, was also present. In the case of the Grimsby example (224), a two- to three-fold increase in lead could be detected by XRF.

Tiny amounts of the surface material were removed from both objects, inside and outside, for X-ray diffraction (XRD) analysis in order to determine the chemical form of the lead. It was shown that the lead compound is cerussite, a white lead carbonate. White lead compounds are recorded as being used in cosmetics in historic times, and the black lead sulphide, galena was used as an eye cosmetic. Cerrusite is a naturally occurring mineral and is also one of the corrosion products formed on lead and lead- containing alloys so it is not possible to be certain what form the lead material was originally, whether as a white compound of lead, the black sulphide galena, or the metal itself.

Summary of analytical results

The alloys from which the cosmetic grinders were made are, as expected copper-based alloys of the types used for metalwork across the Roman world. One end-looped mortar (181) was the only example which could be described as copper, with trace levels of other elements probably included as unintended contaminants from the ore. The majority of the cosmetic grinders are made of bronze with tin present at levels of 5% or more and relatively low levels of other elements except for lead. The ternary alloy of copper, tin and zinc, often with lead (described as 'gunmetal' for brevity), accounts for a number of examples. Interestingly there were only two which might be best described as brass: an end-loop pestle from Dorset (152)

with 12.6% zinc, and a set of mortar with pestle from St Albans (436) which had a few percent zinc and nothing else above trace level in the copper.

Lead carbonate was found at relatively high concentrations within two of the mortars (184 and 224) and a silver-rich area was detected in another (479). These were the only materials which were found on the grinding surfaces using these analytical techniques. Whether they can be considered to be evidence of what these mortars once contained, or simply contamination from burial and corrosion may need to await results of future analyses of similar artefacts.

(For the results of metal analyses by others see Cat. nos 22, 80, 154–5, 187, 275).

Plate 7 The bull terminal on Hockwold mortar 261

5. Decoration and Meaning

Within the constraints of their functional requirements cosmetic grinders, like other minor bronzes, afforded scope for artistic expression (**Pl. 7**). This might take the form of an aesthetically pleasing design, décor or finish but other aspirations might also come into play. It is, for example, more or less evident in some cases that the overall form and the choice of decorative motif had symbolic meaning. The difficulty, of course, is in gauging the extent to which this symbolism was 'read', since it often fell within the traditional decorative repertoire of both late Iron Age and Romano-British culture.

Most basic is the crescent shape shared by the great majority of cosmetic grinders (**Figs 4–24**) and seen most clearly in simple, unadorned pestles and mortars especially of centre-looped type (e.g. 159, 205, 299, 462, 536). The crescent moon was a common, virtually universal, motif with, in the Classical world, a specific apotropaic connotation and that symbolism may have been consciously registered in the overall shape of cosmetic sets. However, the crescent was invested with greater power when combined with phallic imagery, and a wide variety of crescentic/ phallic pendant amulets is known in the Roman world (e.g. Bishop 1988, 149–56; Johns 1982; Oldenstein 1976). Favoured in military contexts (see, e.g., Nicolay 2008, 226–36), a measure of their wider popularity is the proportionally large number of examples amongst the figural bronzes from the Roman town of Augusta Raurica (Kaufmann-Heinimann 1998). They served both to bring good fortune to the wearer and to protect him or her from the dark forces of the Evil Eye. This combination of motifs was not restricted to pendants alone but was a device to be found in many different Roman contexts, whether domestic or public. Two examples will suffice to illustrate how the crescent/ phallus permeated daily life. One is the phallic bronze head of a linch pin from Chelsham, Surrey (Bird 1997) the perceived amuletic power of which doubtless comforted travellers in the carriage or wagon of which it formed a part. The other, a rare survival, is an object in the hoard of ironwork from Blackburn Mill, Berwickshire, a wooden-handled iron sickle in which the crescentic iron blade was balanced by a curved wooden handle in the form of a phallus (Piggott 1953, 46–48, fig. 12, B.34). In addition to the apotropaic power of its combined crescent and phallus the sickle had a further clear link to fertility since its function was to reap the harvest of the sown seed.

In 1985 the present writer was wary of accepting a phallic amuletic interpretation of cosmetic mortars and pestles (Jackson 1985, 170). Since then, however, the number of more overtly phallic examples has increased and it is now considered likely that many of the kits combined a specific practical function with an amuletic role, often with a phallic or fertility connection. Some examples go beyond the 'natural' phallic shape of end-looped mortars with a knobbed terminal. Thus,

mortars 533, 191, 476 and an un-catalogued example from Sutton, Suffolk (Martin *et al.* 2008, fig. 144B) have knobs quite realistically modelled in the form of a glans, while 407, 298 and 363 add to that a simplified depiction of testicles (**Figs 19–21**). Furthermore, the knobbed terminals are closely matched on unequivocal phallic amulets of the *mano fica* type (see, eg., Bishop 1988, figs 48–49; Johns 1982, fig. 57), especially in the highly-stylized form in which they were sometimes made (Johns 1982, fig. 56; Lloyd-Morgan in Cool *et al.* 1995, 1537–9, figs 716–17, no. 6322, from a context dated *c.* AD 100–160 in the York fortress). There is even the possibility of a direct physical connotation, for the pestles, notably the end-looped type, are essentially phallic, while the groove of the mortar could be construed as vulvate. The placing of the pestle in the groove might then be perceived as symbolising sexual union and fertility. Although phallic amulets were common and widespread in the Roman Empire the use of phallic imagery is rarely found in pre-Roman Iron Age contexts in Britain. It would appear, therefore, that after the Roman conquest British cosmetic sets were sometimes adapted to Roman tastes or custom and that alongside their primarily practical use their amuletic role was enhanced through the protective power of the male organ.

If the amuletic use of phallic imagery was truly alien to pre-Roman Britain other powerful symbolism was not, and the heads of bulls and water-birds, either individually or in combination, are frequently found on the more elaborate cosmetic sets (**Figs 6–7, 14–17**). Many of the zoomorphic mortar terminals feature sensitive modelling, acute stylisation, exuberance and ambiguity and they can often be closely paralleled by other metalwork examples from the 'Celtic zoo' of the 1st century BC/ 1st century AD – bulls, cattle, rams, sheep, horses, stags, hinds, boars, dogs, hares, geese, swans, water-birds, crested and un-crested ducks, predatory birds, griffons and monsters. End-looped mortars had only one free terminal available for plastic decoration in the round, although the loop itself was often elaborated into a stylized bird's head (**Figs 6–7**). The centre-looped mortars, however, provided two terminals, and full advantage was often taken of the decorative potential (**Figs 14–17**). Furthermore, two terminals enabled a juxtaposition of imagery, a symmetrical confrontation or pairing of animal heads and motifs, and the various schemes selected frequently appear to transcend the purely decorative: they hint at meaning, albeit that the meaning is now hidden and the imagery itself obscured by what has been characterized as the 'abstracting ambiguity of Celtic art' (Megaw and Megaw 1989, 224). We cannot, therefore, hope to access the meanings of most of this imagery, but it is at least possible to suggest, for example, that the occasional twinning of a bull's head with that of a cow (4, 53, 158, 185, 211, 244) implies another link to fertility.

The fauna represented on cosmetic sets is dominated by bovids (77 occurrences on 57 mortars) and birds (26 occurrences on 23 mortars and pestles) as well as enigmatic or fabulous beasts (14 occurrences on 11 mortars) and many ambiguous bovid and highly-devolved bird heads (respectively 24 on 18 mortars and 76 on 75 mortars and pestles). Most numerous is the single bull's head, often juxtaposed with a knobbed terminal (e.g. 50, 192, 214, 292, 348, 373, 393, 479, 577 and Types A and C – **Table 7**; **Figs 6 and 15**). Where horns are depicted they vary quite widely in size and form, and in one instance, the splendid zoomorphic mortar from Hockwold (261), which combines bull and bird heads, knobs are depicted on the bull's horn-tips (**Pl. 7**). That arrangement is found more widely on Late Iron Age metalwork in Britain and Gaul, as on bronze mounts from Ham Hill (Toynbee 1964, 21, pl. Ia; Megaw and Megaw 1989, 223, fig. 372), Lexden (Toynbee 1964, 40, pl. IIIa) and Manching (Megaw and Megaw 1989, 144, fig. 224), on the mounts of an iron bowl from Lydney (Wheeler and Wheeler 1932, fig. 11, no. 9) and on iron fire-dogs from e.g. Baldock (James and Rigby 1997, 79, fig. 90) and Lord's Bridge, Barton (Megaw and Megaw 1989, 160, fig. 244). The sharp horns of powerful bulls present an obvious risk and the depiction of knobs may simply reflect stock-management practice – padded caps – as in more recent times (Jackson 1985, 170). Alternatively they may have been added to fire-dogs and mounts to avoid damage from sharp metalwork. However, in view of the ubiquity of terminal knobs on cosmetic mortars it seems more probable that the Hockwold knobbed horns were a part of the decorative apotropaic symbolism of cosmetic sets, a fusion of the symbols of virility and fertility. The power of the bull-imagery, enhanced by the crescent shape of the mortar, finds a counterpart in the Romano-Egyptian world where the sacred Apis bull was marked on its flank with a crescent moon (Pliny *Natural History* 8, 184 Kaufmann-Heinimann 1998, 226 GFV47, Abb. 174). It also connects to a particular form of Roman phallic amulet which juxtaposes a bull's head with one or more phalli (Bishop 1988, Types 8c, 10c. Menzel 1986, no. 411) and, in the case of an example from Hod Hill, the bull has knobbed horns (Brailsford 1962, fig. 3, A39).

Almost as frequent is the combination of a pair of bovid heads (Types E, F, J, K and 4, 34, 72, 109, 185, 194, 211, 244 – **Table 7**; **Figs 15–17**). There is considerable variety in the size, elaboration and degree of stylisation of the heads, from the minor masterpieces from Hockwold, Itteringham and Lakenheath (261, 286a, 301 – **Pls 7–8**; **Fig. 14**) to the simple devolved form found on the Type J enamelled mortars (**Fig. 17**; **Pl. 9**). Furthermore, the relative realism of the Lakenheath bull's head, thoroughly Roman in its essentially accurate and sensitively-modelled portrayal, is in complete contrast to the equally fine but highly-stylized bull with knobbed horns, lentoid eyes and flared muzzle on the Hockwold mortar, a true creature of the Celtic world, its style recalling *inter alia* the insular art of the even more highly-stylized bull's head with knobbed horns on the bronze spout from Kirmington (May 1971) and the handle-escutcheons on the Aylesford bucket (Megaw and Megaw 1989, fig. 316). The most stylized bovid mortar terminals consist simply of muzzle and horns, but ears, eyes, mouth and nostrils are often depicted, too. The portrayal was almost invariably restricted to the beast's head, but a fragmentary terminal from Wetheringsett (532) appears to show the mane and many incorporate the distinctive dewlap, which was readily contrived along the keel adjacent to the terminal (4, 34, 36, 109, 163, 213, 244, 301, 348, 350, 393, 496). In some instances the dewlap was enhanced by hatched decoration, a stylized representation of the animal's coat (34, 109, 244, 301), but a fragmentary example from Hacheston (227) has a much more realistic modelling of the rippled dewlap and shaggy curly coat on the neck and brow. Realism is also suggested by the ring at the end of the muzzle of the large idiosyncratic bovid terminal from Cossington (136), which gives the appearance of the bull's nose-ring. It is possible, too, that the Type A end-looped mortars were intended as a stylized representation of the whole animal, with the end-loop as the tail and the incised decoration on the bow of some of those examples may also have been intended to represent the coat (**Table 7**; **Fig. 6**, nos 163, 318, 236, 495, 558, 380, 325, 88, 422, 394, 595).

Mortar terminals in the form of a bird's head are restricted to a small number of centre-looped mortars (**Fig. 14**). The paired examples on two Type E variants (65, 358) from Caistor St Edmund and Norfolk, unprovenanced, and the bird's head juxtaposed with the knobbed bull's head on the Hockwold mortar (261) are sufficiently realistically rendered to be identified as water-birds, probably swans or shovellers. But other paired examples (39, 183, 228, 359, 524) and a second bull's head/bird's head combination (350, from Morton, Lincs.) are too heavily stylized for confident identification, though it is likely that they, too, were intended as water-birds. Stylistically close to the bull's head of the mortar from Morton is a fine uncatalogued example found during a geophysical survey at

Plate 8 Iron Age and Roman traditions: the bull on the Hockwold mortar (261) is confronted by his counterpart on one of the Itteringham mortars (286a). Above, pestles from Norfolk (366) and Itteringham (286b)

Litcham, Norfolk, with an imperforate centre-loop and a pair of large horned bull's heads (Andrew Rogerson and Michael de Bootman *in litt.*). A unicum is the centre-looped mortar from Chediston (87), the whole of which is modelled in the form of a sitting or swimming bird, probably a duck. Swimming water-birds are also featured on four centre-looped pestles (Type N – **Fig. 24**), one of which, an unprovenanced example from Norfolk (366), compares quite closely to the little ducks on the handles of the bronze cups in the hoard of bronze vessels found at Crownthorpe (Wickleword), Norfolk (Henig 1995, 35–7, fig. 17). However, the great majority of bird's heads occur as the loop on end-looped mortars and pestles. The curved form of the loop lent itself particularly well to the portrayal of a bird's neck, head and bill, and the motif is found on other contemporary looped metalwork, as on a bronze mirror handle from Ballymoney and the link of a bronze bridle-bit from Ireland (Megaw and Megaw 1989, figs 374, 376).

Like the bovid mortar terminals, the bird-headed loops display a broad spectrum of stylisation (Figs 6–8 and 12). Most realistic are the water birds – probably swans – on the end-looped mortars from Magiovinium (334) and Shelford (451) and the end-looped mortar/ brooch from Thelnetham (500), which develop the loop into a sinuous neck with prominent crown and long dished bill and incorporate carefully rendered eyes. In similar style are the loops on two idiosyncratic double-looped mortars from France, one a recent find from excavations at Actiparc 'la Corette', Arras, Pas-de-Calais (F. Thuillier *in litt.*; Jacques and Prilaux 2003, 67, no. 94; Guillaumet and Eugène 2009, 242–3, fig. 2), the other an old (un-contexted) find, only recently recognized, from the early excavations at Bibracte/ Mont Beuvray, Saône-et-Loire (Guillaumet and Eugène 2009, 241–2, fig. 1). Intriguingly the Arras example is reported to have an Augusto-Tiberian context date.

A more highly-stylized modelling of the loop on mortars from Mundham, 'Stonea' and Thetford (352, 485, 504) omits the eyes and highlights the distinctive crown and dished bill. There is a distinctive variant on the loop of a mortar from Tilbury (508), perhaps intended to show the tucked-back head of a sleeping water-bird (a suggestion I owe to Nina Crummy). The identification as water-birds of the numerous other devolved examples depends exclusively on the combination of the dished bill and the bird's eye – formed by the aperture of the loop. The example paired with the bovid head on the Fishtoft mortar (192) is surmounted by a knob, perhaps intended to represent the bird's crest or included as part of the apotropaic symbolism, or both. Like the Hockwold mortar the Fishtoft, Morton and Thelnetham examples twin a bull head with a bird head, a combination seen on other classes of metalwork, including a highly-ornamented pair of bronze dividers from Shouldham, Norfolk (Worrell 2005, 463–4), which also shares with some cosmetic sets the use of triangular enamel inlay and dot-and-ring punching. All distil and express the powerful Celtic symbolism of both bulls and water and, as such, they appear to parallel the continuity into the Roman period of bull-horned war gods, and goddesses associated with water. Perhaps, too, they combined things material with those spiritual, reflecting 'continuing Celtic preoccupations with the herd animals, which symbolized wealth, and with birds and boars, dwellers both in this world and the Celtic otherworld'

(Megaw and Megaw 1989, 192, 224).

The image of a boar, not as a terminal but skilfully adapted to the form of the loop, is found on an idiosyncratic end-looped mortar from Morton (351 – **Fig. 6**)) and, perhaps, in highly-stylized form, on a centre-looped mortar from Shouldham/ Fincham (460 – **Fig. 19**)). The Morton example, which comprises the head and elongated neck of the creature, is modelled in Celtic style but incorporates a ball-moulding, a common Roman gap-filling device for the provision of zoomorphic loops (e.g. Menzel 1966, 111, Taf. 82, no. 271), and it is another illustration of the fusion of Celtic and Roman traditions. Similarly novel is the centre-looped mortar from Hindringham (255 – **Fig. 14**), its form entirely given over to the depiction of a stylized fish. One terminal is modelled as the head, complete with eyes, mouth, gills and scales, the other terminal as the tail fin, while the curved bow comprises the body, with even the centre loop adapted to the form of the ventral fin. The rudder-like form of the tail fin, entirely Roman in style, is rather that of a dolphin than a fish and the Hindringham imagery may be compared, for example, to bronze lamps in the form of fish (Menzel 1986, 103–4, Taf 112–13, nos 239, 241) as well as to depictions of dolphins on a series of casket drop-handles (Menzel 1986, 186–8, Taf. 154–5, nos 515–9) and to the handle of a type of folding spoon (Crummy 1983, 69–70, fig. 73, no. 2020), all of which capitalized on the crescentic or sinuous form of fish and dolphins.

Singletons, too, are the Lakenheath (301) and Itteringham (286) mortar terminals depicting respectively a stag and a ram, in both cases twinned with a bull (Fig. 14). The modelling of the Lakenheath stag's head, like its bovid counterpart, is very accomplished, combining naturalism and stylisation to great effect, and its appearance would have been still more striking when its antlers were intact. It stands comparison with the larger, more naturalistic rendering of a bronze stag statuette found near Brighton and a bronze stag protome from Brampton, Norfolk (Henig 1995, 37–8, fig. 18, 97–8, fig. 62). Similarly, though of a slightly lower order of craftsmanship, the treatment of the Itteringham ram's head captures well the essence of the animal. More problematic is the identification of the very large broken zoomorphic terminal from Richborough (415): despite its resemblance to a horse head it was probably intended as a bovid. Ambiguous, too, is one of the terminals on an idiosyncratic centre-looped mortar from Wenhaston (522). From its pairing with a bull's head a second bovid head would have been anticipated, but the appearance is more of a human head than that of a cow or bull and its obscure imagery is mirrored by an assortment of other zoomorphic mortar terminals modelled in the form of ambiguous, equivocal, or fabulous beasts. Some, like the Wenhaston example, are difficult to characterize because of corrosion, more because of extreme stylisation (e.g. Type G, and 3, 245, 342, 460, 465 – **Fig. 16**) but a few appear intentionally fantastic or obscure, like the centre-looped mortar from Grimsby (224), which combines corvid-like and goat-like heads, and an unprovenanced end-looped mortar (596) which conflates bird-like and bovid-like imagery in a single carefully-modelled loop.

Particularly striking is another end-looped mortar, said to be from Yorkshire (573 – **Fig. 7**), its loop and terminal in the form of intricately-modelled devolved duck heads, their trumpet-like form and bossed tips recalling the terminals of dragonesque brooches (See, for example, Hunter 2008a, 139–41 and Hunter 2008b). This connection between cosmetic sets and dragonesque brooches, two specifically (near-exclusively) British types of artefact for adornment, with their heyday in the mid-1st to mid-2nd century AD, seems both appropriate and meaningful. The significance of the linkage is underlined by two further stylistically-related end-looped mortars (574, said to be from Yorkshire and 6, from Ashby Folville – **Fig. 7**), whose elaborate S-shaped bird-head loops, based on a tendril-and-volute or keeled roundel motif, also reference the form of dragonesques. The same motif recurs in miniature within an incised circle on the bow of the brooch/mortar from Thelnetham (500 – **Fig. 6**). This small ornate brooch, of exceptional form, is seemingly made in conscious imitation of an end-looped cosmetic mortar: its solid end, which accommodates the lugs for a hinged pin, takes the form of a bovid head, while the catch-plate (at the top, as worn) is designed to form a part of the re-curved neck of a sensitively modelled water bird and the convex bow, which gives prominence to the incised roundel at its centre, has a hollow back in the form of a broad U-sectioned groove. The brooch type is idiosyncratic and hard to parallel, but it has some features in common with another hinged zoomorphic brooch, from Finlaggan, Islay (Hunter 2009). The Finlaggan brooch is more accomplished and in more overtly Celtic style but it has in common with the Thelnetham brooch two opposed animal heads confronting a circular medallion on the prominent summit of the bow. In the twinning of a larger and smaller head and in the ambiguity of identity of the animals, the art of the Finlaggan brooch also resonates with cosmetic sets, and the date assigned (later 1st century BC to 1stcentury AD) would conform to derivations in the same stylistic pool.

Irrespective of whether the groove at the back of its bow was ever used for the preparation of cosmetics, the Thelnetham brooch, as a clear visual reference to cosmetic mortars, would have associated its wearer with the tradition and use of cosmetics and cosmetic sets. Given that the distribution and dating identify cosmetic sets as British and of pre-Roman origin, that association may not just have been with personal appearance and the use of cosmetics but with additional issues of identity and status, an assertion of Britishness (or, at least, an indication of allegiance to British ways) at a time of increased 'Romanisation', perhaps. In similar vein, is a gold, crescent-shaped pendant from Maker with Rame, Cornwall (PAS ref. CORN-955DE8), which closely resembles the commonest form of centre-looped pestle. It, too, is likely to have been made in imitation of cosmetic sets, sharing the ornamental and amuletic roles and perhaps serving as an indicator of identity, too.

The emblematic and functionally equivocal nature of the Thelnetham brooch is paralleled by another distinctive and exclusively British brooch type, the so-called chatelaine brooches which attach five or six toilet implements to the cross-bar of an enamelled umbonate or rectangular plate. The implements usually comprise one or more tweezers, ear scoop and nail cleaner together with, less often, file, ligula and spatula. The distribution of chatelaine brooches (Eckardt 2008, 121–3) is heavily biased towards southern Britain in contrast to the northern focus of dragonesques, and a different derivation

is probable (Bayley and Butcher 2004, 172–3), but the (admittedly sparse) dating evidence indicates a broad contemporaneity with dragonesques and cosmetic sets. Like the Thelnetham brooch, the chatelaines had the possibility to function as cosmetic or toilet implements, but it is considered probable that display – an explicit statement that the wearer was someone who took care of his or her personal appearance – took precedence over functionality (Eckardt and Crummy 2008, 173).

The design of the enamelled decoration on chatelaine brooches depends heavily on triangular cells, often interlocked, and triangular cells are also the motif of choice for those cosmetic sets with enamelled decoration – Types H, J and O (**Table 7; Pl. 9; Figs 17, 18 and 23**) – which invariably comprised the same arrangement on both walls. Indeed, there are at present only two mortars (188, 501a) with enamelled decoration not based on triangular cells. Plump equilateral triangles, of the type seen on chatelaine brooches, are encountered almost exclusively on the Type H knobbed mortars and Type O pestles (**Figs 18, 23**), while the enamel cells of Type J zoomorphic mortars are almost invariably of slender elongated isosceles triangle shape (**Fig. 17**). Similarly, while the apex of the cells on Type H mortars are directed towards the rim those on Type J are directed towards the keel. However a significant number of Type H mortars have slender isosceles or small equilateral cells orientated towards the keel and a further variant comprises panels of contiguous triangles. All three Type O pestles belong with Type H mortars, but as is clear from the three surviving complete sets (**Fig. 5**) an enamelled mortar did not necessarily have an enamelled pestle: while the Canterbury set (74) comprised a Type H mortar and a Type O pestle, both the Chichester (92) and Thérouanne (501) sets have plain pestles, as also does another Type H probable set from Battisford, Suffolk (Worrell 2008, 362–3).

The survival rate of the enamel inlays is variable, the most vulnerable to loss being the larger equilateral triangles of the Type H mortars and Type O pestles, but both type H and J suffer also from degradation of the enamel which sometimes prevents identification of the original colour. Nevertheless, the relatively large number of enamelled mortars has preserved a sufficiently large sample of coloured decors to enable comparison between the types. Type H mortars with equilateral triangles have an arc of between three and six cells and in all instances in which the enamel colour is identifiable the same single colour has been used for all the cells – red (472), black (293) and ?green (106, 112, 133). A single colour is also used for the Type H mortars with slender isosceles triangles, again between three and six in number – blue (428) and orange (256, 311) – and for the Type H mortars and one Type O pestle with panels of contiguous triangles – red (469, 232) and ?yellow (487). Type J, on the other hand, rarely employs a single colour and tends towards multiple cells (**Pl. 9**). In just two cases a single colour is used – green (361) and red (302) but as the number of cells increases additional colours are employed – red/ blue (188, 278, 289, 501), turquoise/ blue ('Suffolk' – PAS SF-665921), green/ red/ blue (129, 281, 578 and Burgate, Suffolk (Ipswich Museum IPSMG: R.2007-4)) and black/ green/ blue (452). Apart from the completely atypical mortar from Baldock (16) – three equilateral cells, red flanked

Plate 9 Type J enamelled mortars (278, 578)

by green – the cell numbers range from 6 to 26: 6 (92, 147, 322, 361); 7 (302); 9 (289, 455); 12 (215); 19 (452); 29 ((129); 25 ((281, 578); 26 (278). In all cases there is a near-symmetrical contrasting arrangement with a central colour flanked by one or more other colours in various combinations and permutations (**Pl. 9**). The enamelling technique is champlevé, the cells having been cast-in or cut and filled with a powdered coloured frit that was fused by heating. Analysis of the traces of blue and red enamel in mortars 278, 578, and 580 revealed the presence of antimony, which has been interpreted as an opacifier (p. 19).

The curved line of repeating slender triangular cells on Type J mortars was hardly ambitious in design terms but was clearly adapted to the limited available space on mortar walls. Furthermore, it appears to have been a standard, visually pleasing, border that was commonly employed at the base or rim of enamelled vessels, whether the miniature stoppered flask from Catterick, North Yorkshire (Allason-Jones 2002), the alabastron from Bartlow Hills, Essex, the vase from Ambleteuse, Pas-de-Calais, or the 'stylized vegetal' series of handled pans including those from Braughing, Hertfordshire, Linlithgow, West Lothian and Maltbæk Mose, Denmark (Henry 1933, figs 25–6, 45. Künzl 2008, 24–5) or, indeed, the miniature stands of uncertain, possibly ritual, function, like those from the Roman temple at Farley Heath, Surrey (Bird 2007, 49, nos 82–3, figs 22–3). Both on the vessels and stands as well as cosmetic mortars this 'toothed' design could be enhanced by interspersing different enamel colours, most commonly red, blue and green. Likewise, the plump equilateral triangles of the Type H mortars recur not just on chatelaine brooches but on other British enamelled products, including some examples of the series of hollow bronze cockerels, like that from Slyne with Hest, Lancs., which intersperses triangular cells of red, blue and green enamel on its chest (Worrell 2006, 436–7, fig. 4).

The Baldock mortar (16) looks like a local copy of Type J and the mortar from Thérouanne (501) is also a variant – it differs in form and size as well as in the unique shape and configuration of its enamel inlay. The Fincham mortar (188), on the other hand, conforms to Type J in size and style as also in

the arrangement of the enamel inlay (about 24–26 cells, red flanked by blue) and it differs only in the unique shape of the cells, which are of an ornate floral form, perhaps a highly-stylized lotus bud. Significantly, a version of that motif is also found within the decorative repertoire of the fired clay moulds for the production of enamelled vessels dumped in a pit in the fort at Castleford, West Yorkshire, around AD 90–100. Specifically it can be seen in the field of the lower register of Pattern 1 – the coloured enamel background for the reserved metal row of tri-lobed leaves – in Type A moulds (Bayley and Budd 1998, 204–11, figs 70, 71, 74, pl. 21). Those moulds were for the manufacture of the cylindrical part of enamelled flasks of flattened barrel shape, of the type best illustrated by the well-preserved example found at Pinquente, Istria (north-east Italy), but very likely manufactured in Britain (Henry 1933, 143, pl. 1. Künzl 2008, 24, left).

British enamelled metalwork, whether composite vessels, brooches or other ornamental bronzes, was popular from the 1st to 3rd century AD, with the heyday of production of vessels in the later 1st and 2nd century AD, and that chronology is broadly compatible with the current, albeit rather limited, contextual dating for the enamelled cosmetic mortars – 2nd to early 3rd century AD (16, 92a, 322, 501a). Künzl (2008, 25) believes that the enamelled vessels, some tricked out with Mediterranean-style motifs, others incorporating late La Tène style non-figural decoration, found a ready market overseas. Thus, it may be due to the popularity of British enamelwork that the sole complete cosmetic set found outside Britain, at Thérouanne, Pas-de-Calais, has an enamelled mortar. Certainly, as part of the flowering of British enamelled bronzes, Type H and J mortars and Type O pestles can be seen as a further assertion of insular British style and taste.

Other decorative inlays are restricted to a small number of examples. The bovid head terminal of mortar 479 from Stonea and the bird head loop of mortar 508 from Tilbury have deep round eye sockets, which were probably once set with glass 'eyeballs', like those in the eyes of certain zoomorphic clasp-knife handles (e.g. Jackson and Potter 1996, 352–3, fig. 113, no. 103). The four (now empty) deep circular cells, arranged in an arc on both walls of the mortar with phallic terminals from Sutton, Suffolk (Martin *et al.* 2008, fig. 144B), on the other hand, were more likely set with coloured enamel or with a metal inlay of contrasting colour to the body metal. The latter technique was certainly employed on a centre-looped mortar from Mileham, Norfolk (345), though in a rather unexpected position: at the base of the groove is an axial line of three small circular cells, one of which retains its silver-coloured metal inlay. The silver/ gold colour contrast would have been enhanced by the wear-polish of the grinding process. White metal is also encountered in the one instance of overlay, an end-looped mortar from Newport, Gwent (354) that appears to have been tinned.

Mortar bows are also quite frequently decorated with incuse designs, most commonly running chevrons, zig-zagging or zonal hatching (as on Types A, C and L as well as nos 34, 50, 119, 194, 260a, 261, 330, 362, 364, 440, 479 and 482 – **Table 7, Figs 6 and 19**), while ring-and-dot punching, a feature of Types B and F, is included in the elaborate decor of no. 301 (**Table 7, Figs 6, 14, 15**). The ring-and-dot motif is often characterized as 'late Roman' and is certainly present on some well-dated 4th century AD material, notably military belt fittings and Crossbow brooches as well as toilet implements (Crummy and Eckardt 2008, 54–5 and figs 21 and 66), but it was a simple motif probably not exclusively late and the question must remain open whether the Lakenheath mortar was residual in its 4th century context or whether the date should be applied to the mortar itself – and perhaps to Type B, too. An end-looped mortar from North Creake, Norfolk (393) combines both motifs in its design – incuse zig-zagging with ring-and-dot punching – and the combination of dot-punching and finely applied linear incision is also seen on nos 192, 218 and 577. Simple dot-punched designs are used to emphasize overall form, especially rim and carination, or to add detail to particular features, as on nos 4, 17, 185, 286a and 496. The ring-and-dot motif is found again as part of the raised design on some examples of Type F. A small crescent-shaped punch was used to enhance the rim of mortar 65 and an S-shaped punch employed very comprehensively over the entire surface of the idiosyncratic mortar 581.

Moulded bow decoration is a feature of Type F mortars (**Table 7, Fig. 15**) and there are individualized designs on

mortars 39, 261, 460 and 507. The free end of the loop of mortar 51, from Brettenham, has a moulded quatrefoil motif and other mortars with non-zoomorphic decoration focused on the loop include a coiled example from Felthorpe (186) and a large openwork trumpet scroll on a mortar from Wormegay (561). Alongside so much rich and varied decoration there were numerous other mortars which depended for their pleasing appearance on a fine surface finish and simple design, including those with a finely profiled and faceted bow (nos 265, 290, 454, 458, 467, 548 and 551). Most exceptional are the Type M triple mortars from Congham and Cranworth (134 and 139 – **Table 7, Fig. 22**) and another of unknown provenance (Murawski 2003, 88, 114–0308). There is no obvious functional advantage to the provision of three connected mortars of effectively identical size or to the three loops on a mortar from St Albans (440). The 'added value', if not simply from the pleasing symmetrical asymmetry, in the tradition of the Celtic triskele motif, may have come from the magical and religious potency of the number three, so powerfully expressed in the Celtic world through triple-horned animals and triads of deities (Green 1989, 169–205).

The wide diversity in form and almost infinite variety of decoration of cosmetic sets is perhaps to be accounted for by their personal nature – kits associated with self-presentation – and by the possibility that they were used by a broad social group. Significantly, as Nina Crummy has observed (*in litt.*), a similar diversity and inventiveness is exhibited by two other related types of *personalia*, British brooches and nail-cleaners. Of course, any attempt at a retrospective gauging of the relative value of cosmetic sets would be invidious, but purely in terms of size, quantity of metal and expenditure of time in manufacture they appear to represent a fairly wide spectrum, from small and rudimentary ('inexpensive') to large and elaborate ('higher status') examples. However, as this examination of the decoration has indicated, the choice of form and decor appears to have gone well beyond purely 'monetary', functional and aesthetic considerations into areas of identity and well-being – characterising, protecting and empowering the individual – and emphasizes the insular and late Iron Age origins and traditions that inspired the makers of cosmetic sets and those who used them.

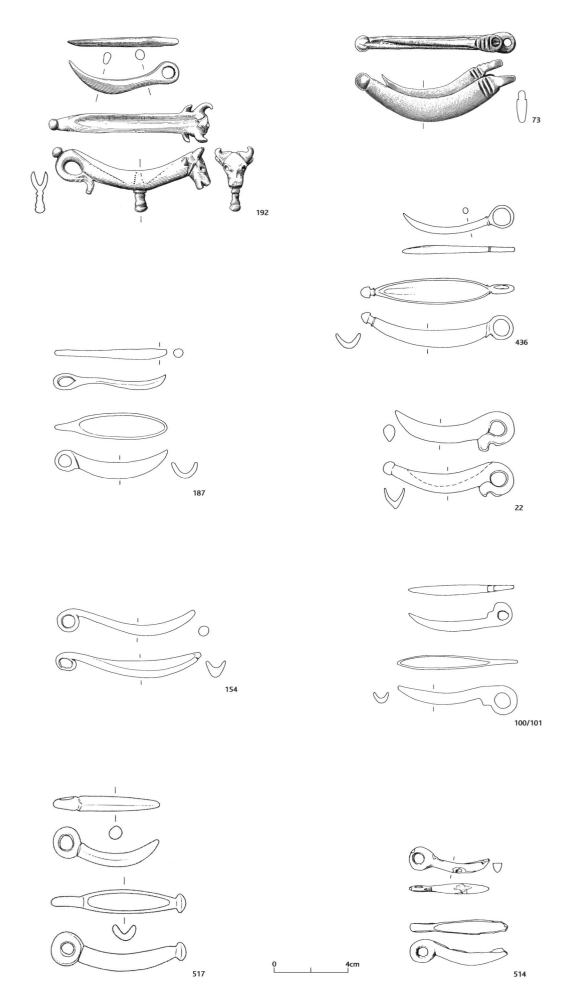

Figure 4 Typology: complete sets, end-looped. Scale 1:2

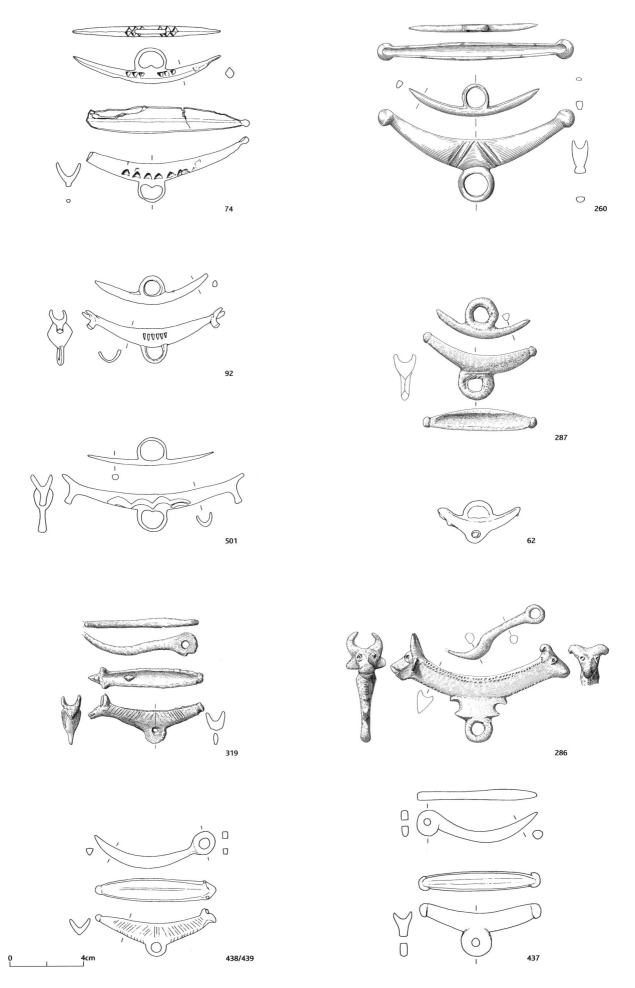

Figure 5 Typology: complete sets, centre-looped and mixed. Scale 1:2

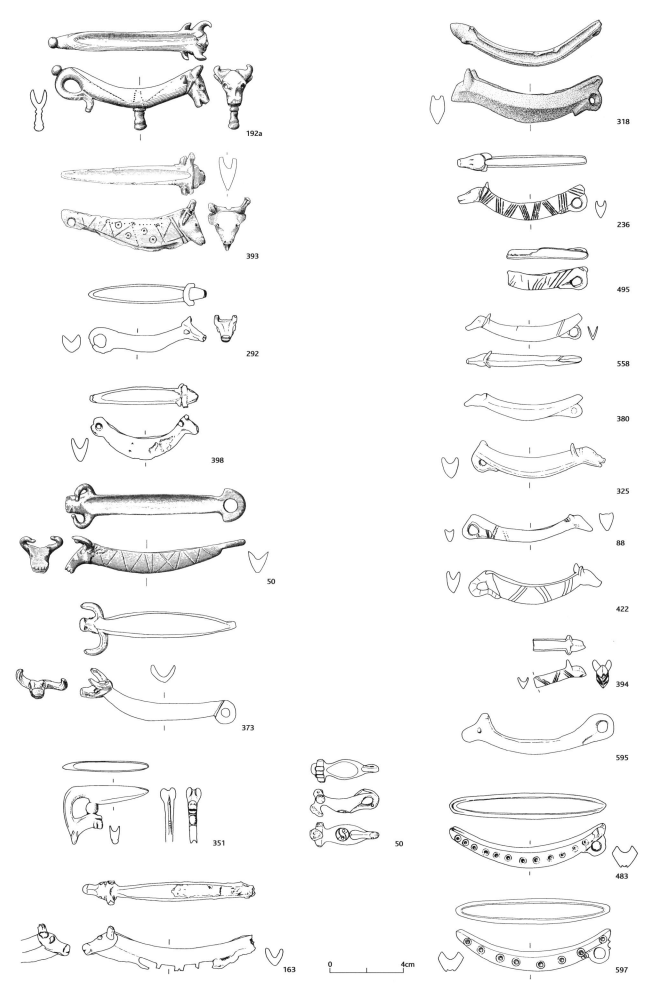

Figure 6 Typology: end-looped mortars with zoomorphic terminals. Scale 1:2

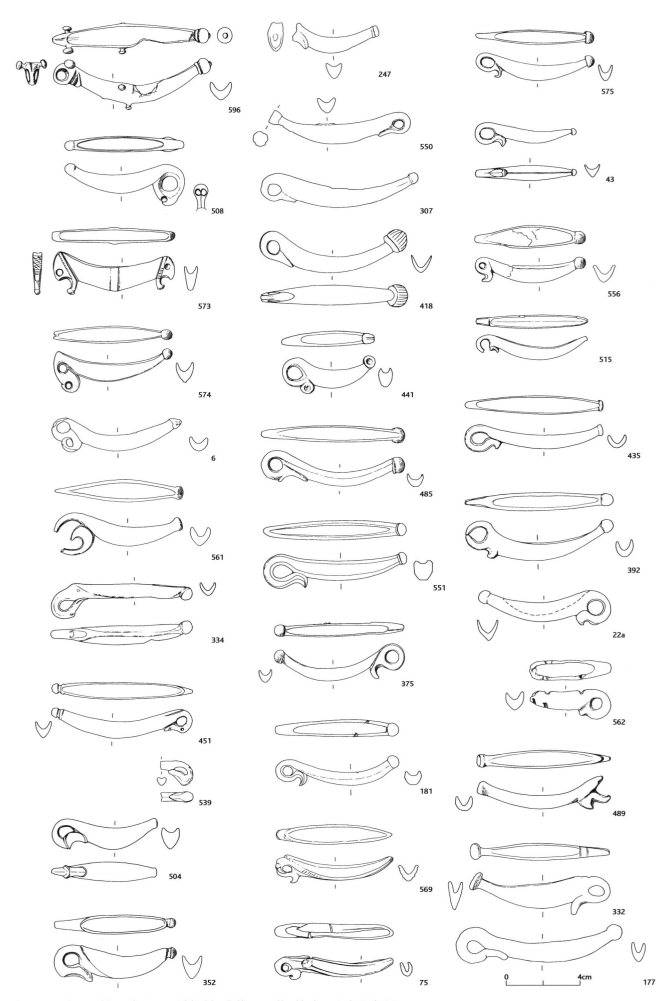

Figure 7 Typology: end-looped mortars with bird-headed loops and knobbed terminals. Scale 1:2

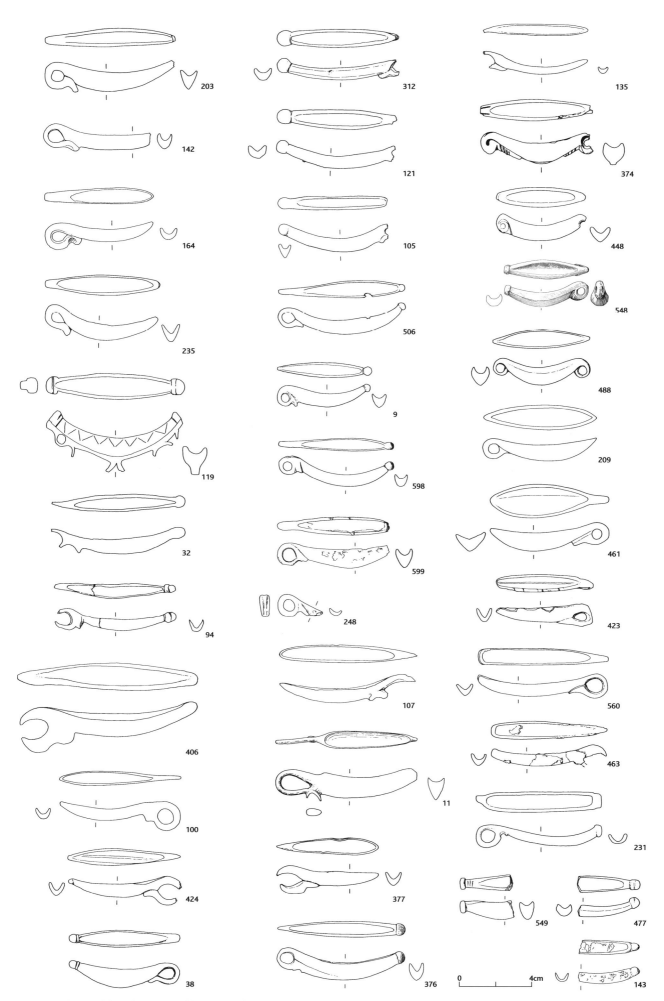

Figure 8 Typology: end-looped mortars with bird-headed loops and knobbed or plain terminals. Scale 1:2

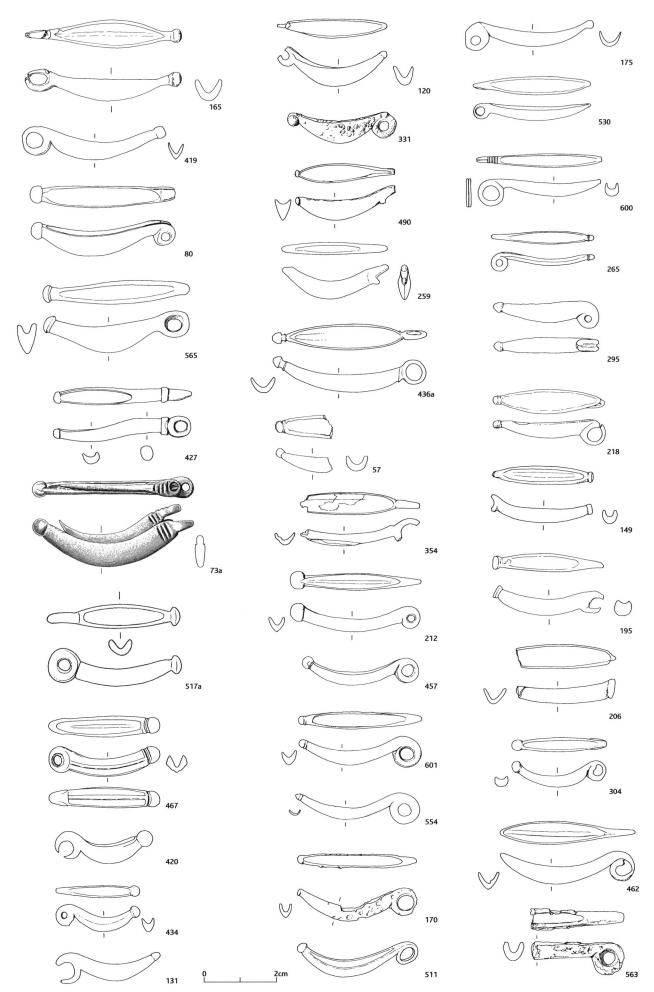

Figure 9 Typology: end-looped mortars with knobbed terminals. Scale 1:2

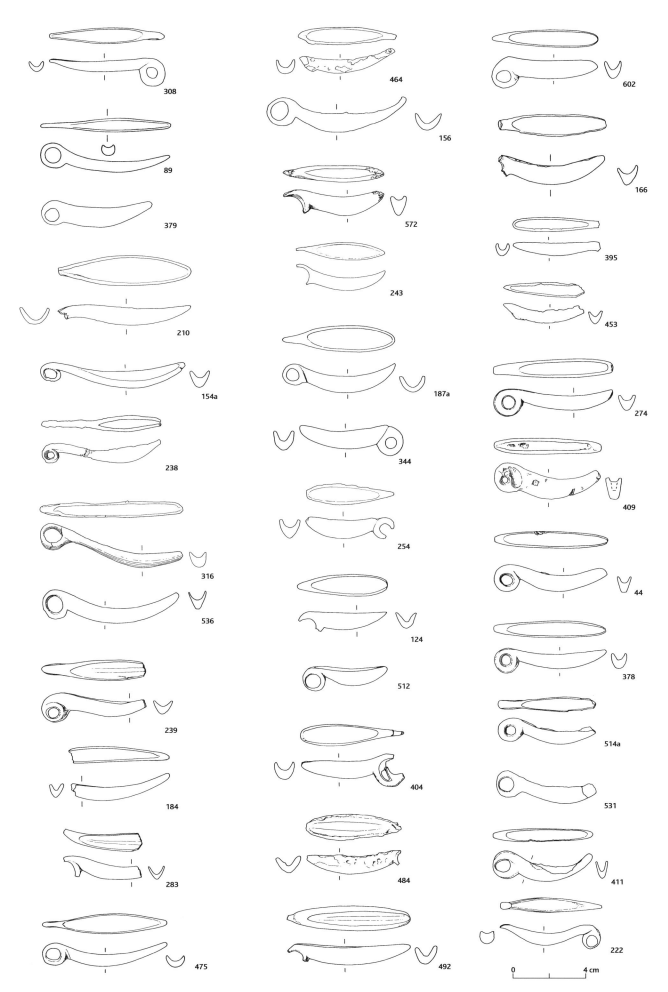

Figure 10 Typology: end-looped mortars with plain or spouted terminals. Scale 1:2

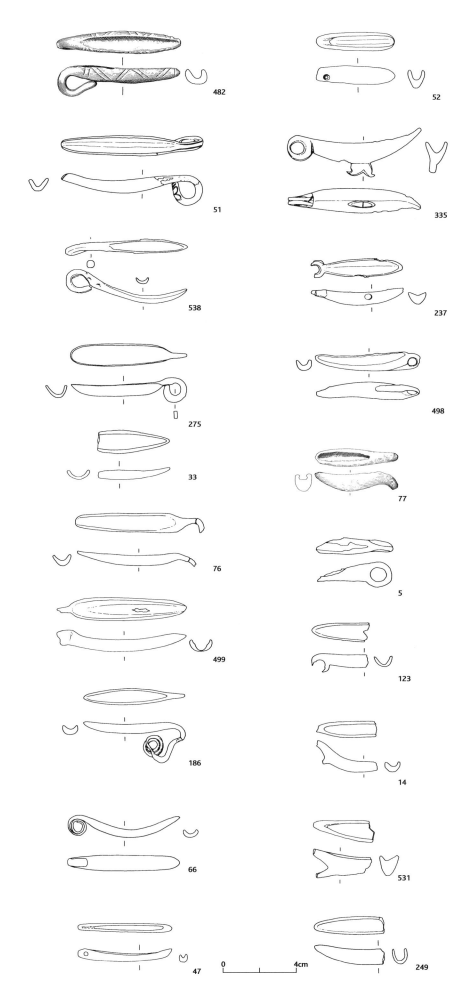

Figure 11 Typology: end-looped mortars with plain or spouted terminals. Scale 1:2

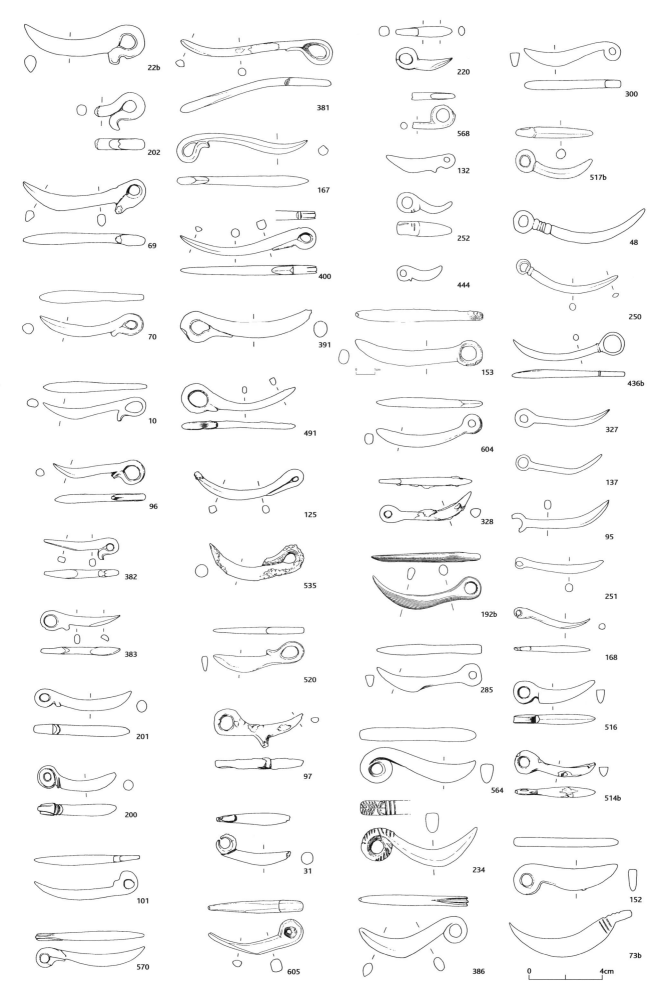

Figure 12 Typology: end-looped pestles. Scale 1:2

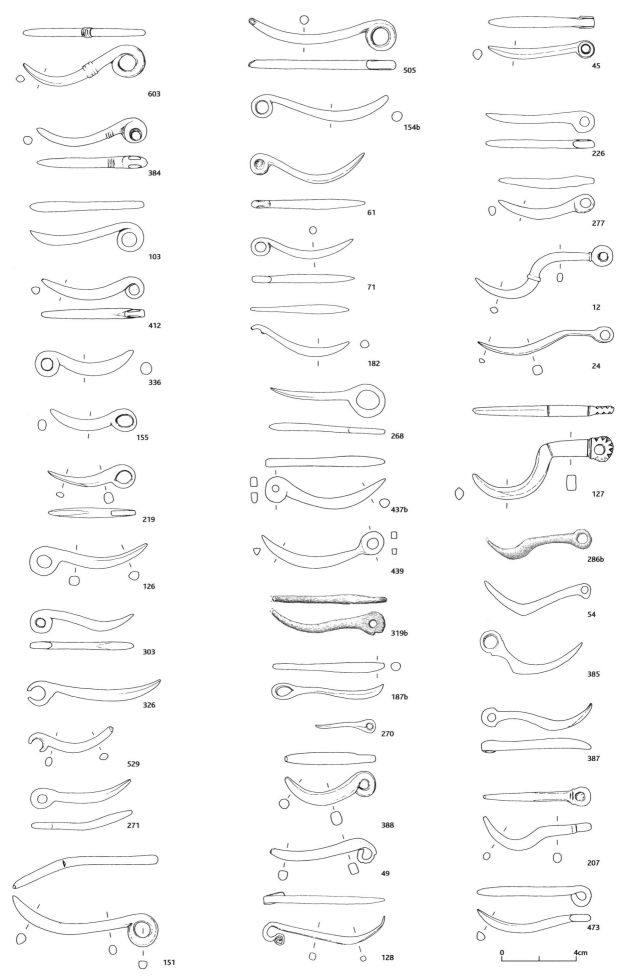

Figure 13 Typology: end-looped pestles. Scale 1:2

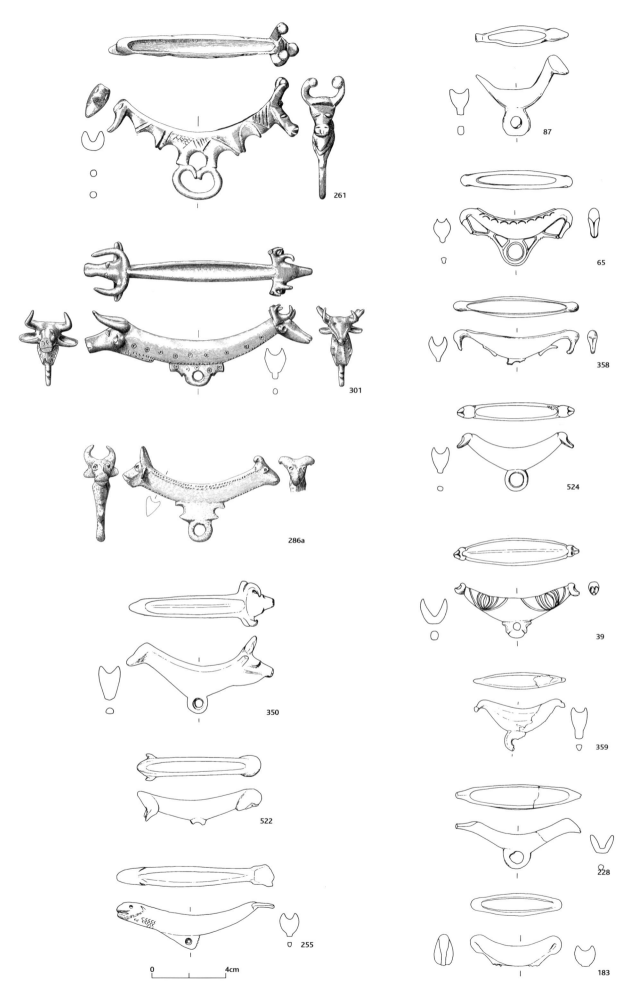

Figure 14 Typology: centre-looped mortars with zoomorphic terminals. Scale 1:2

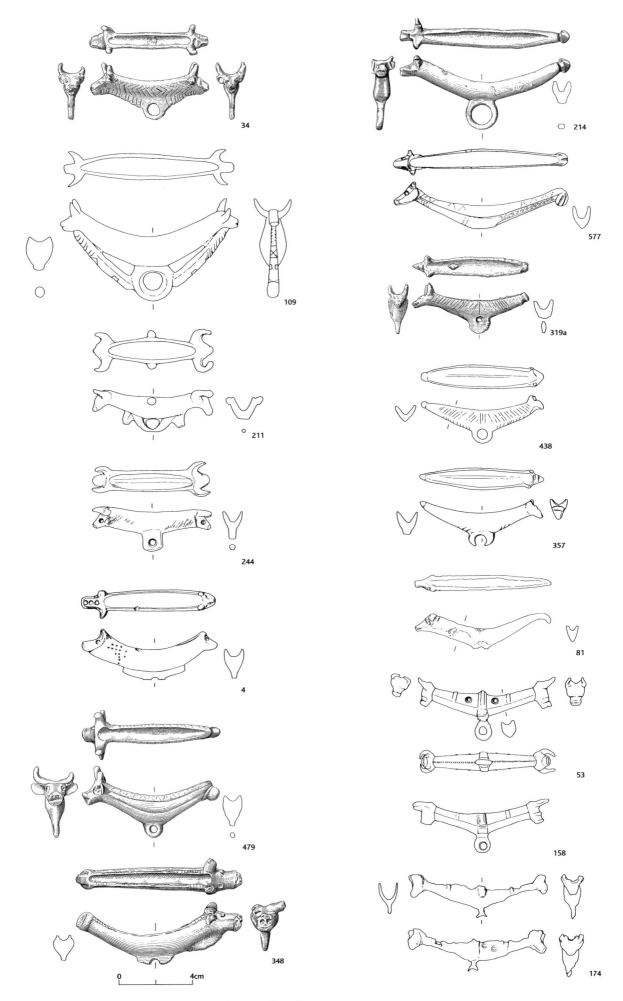

Figure 15 Typology: centre-looped mortars with zoomorphic terminals. Scale 1:2

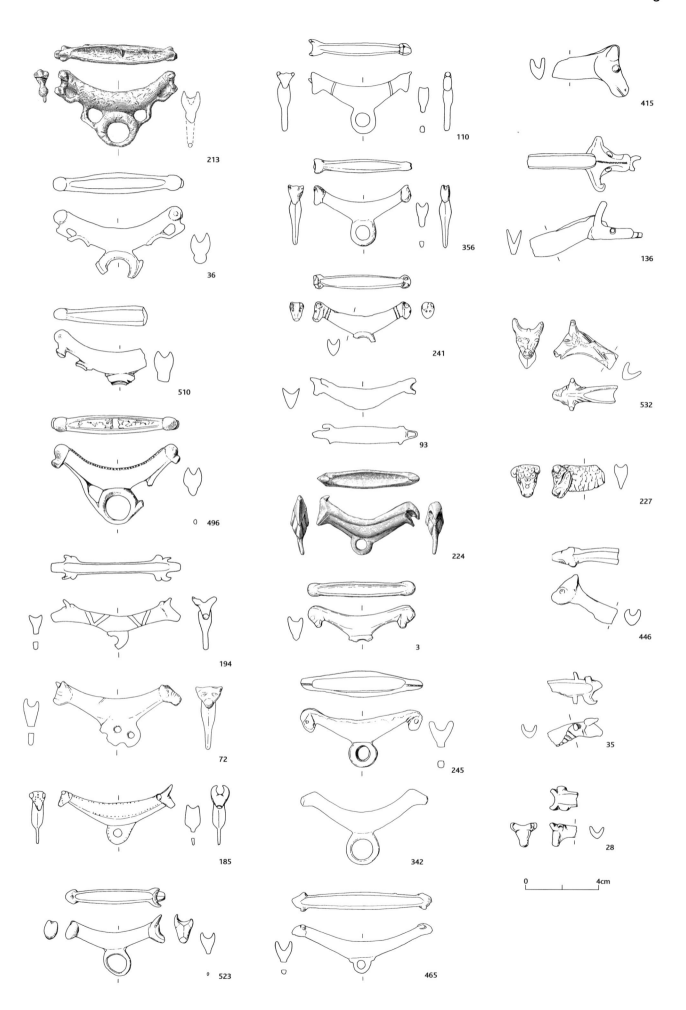

Figure 16 Typology: centre-looped mortars with zoomorphic terminals. Scale 1:2

Figure 17 Typology: centre-looped mortars, enamelled, with zoomorphic terminals. Scale 1:2

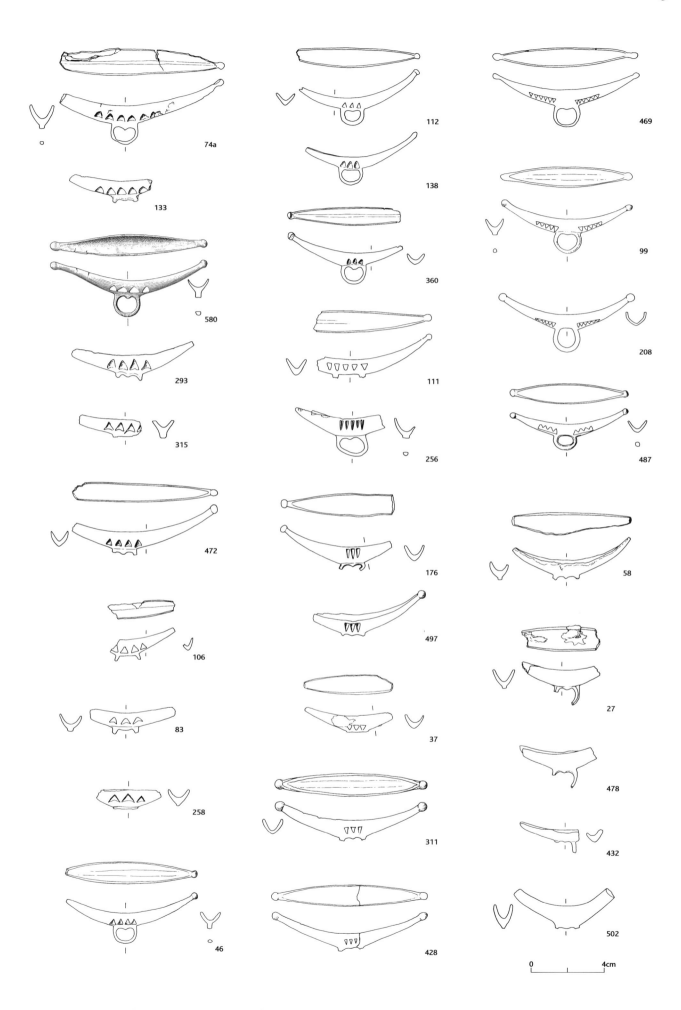

Figure 18 Typology: centre-looped mortars, enamelled, with knobbed terminals. Scale 1:2

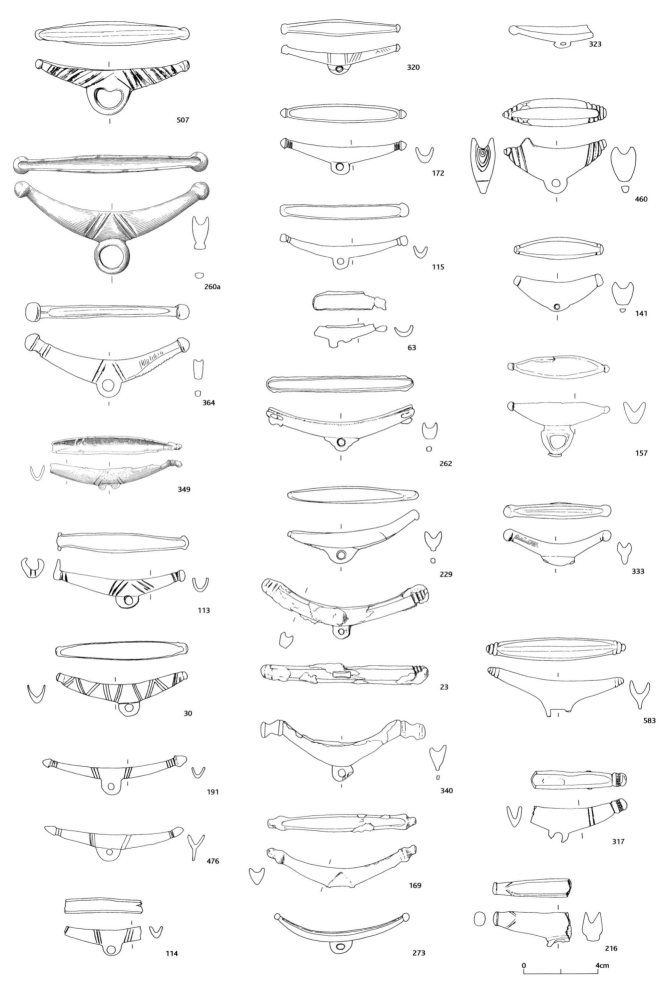

Figure 19 Typology: centre-looped mortars with knobbed terminals. Scale 1:2

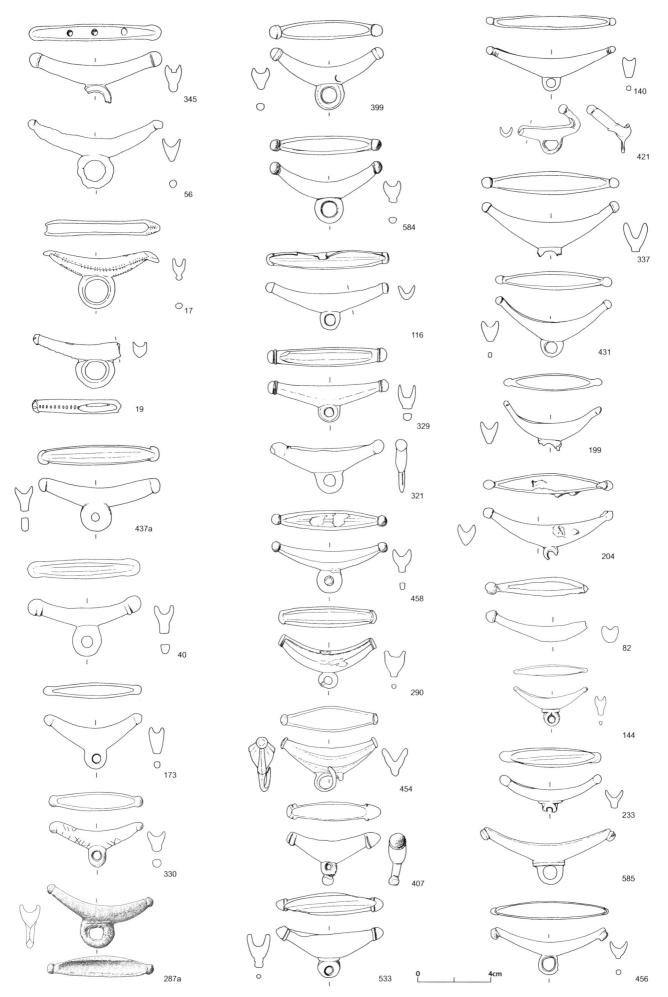

Figure 20 Typology: centre-looped mortars with knobbed terminals. Scale 1:2

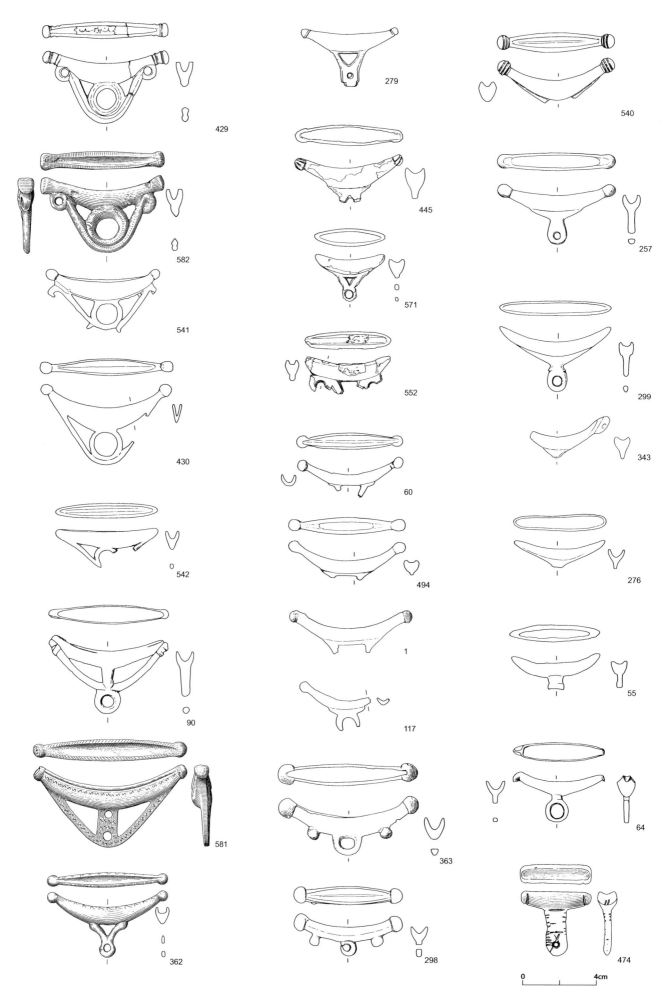

Figure 21 Typology: centre-looped mortars with strutted loops and/ or extended loop plates. Scale 1:2

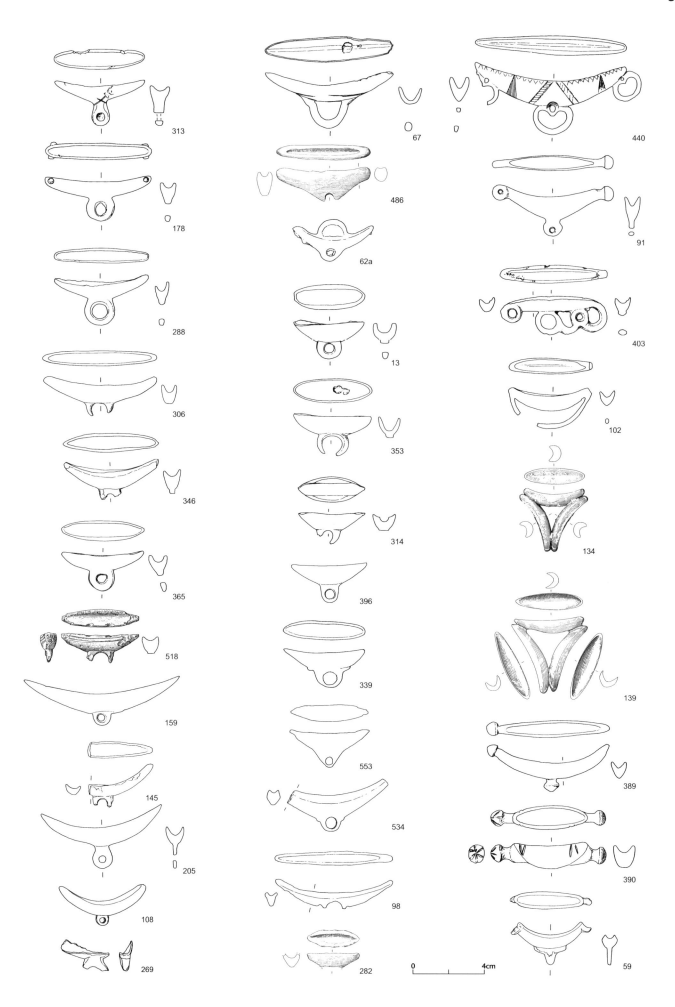

Figure 22 Typology: centre-looped mortars with plain terminals; multi-looped and anomalous mortars. Scale 1:2

Figure 23 Typology: centre-looped pestles. Scale 1:2

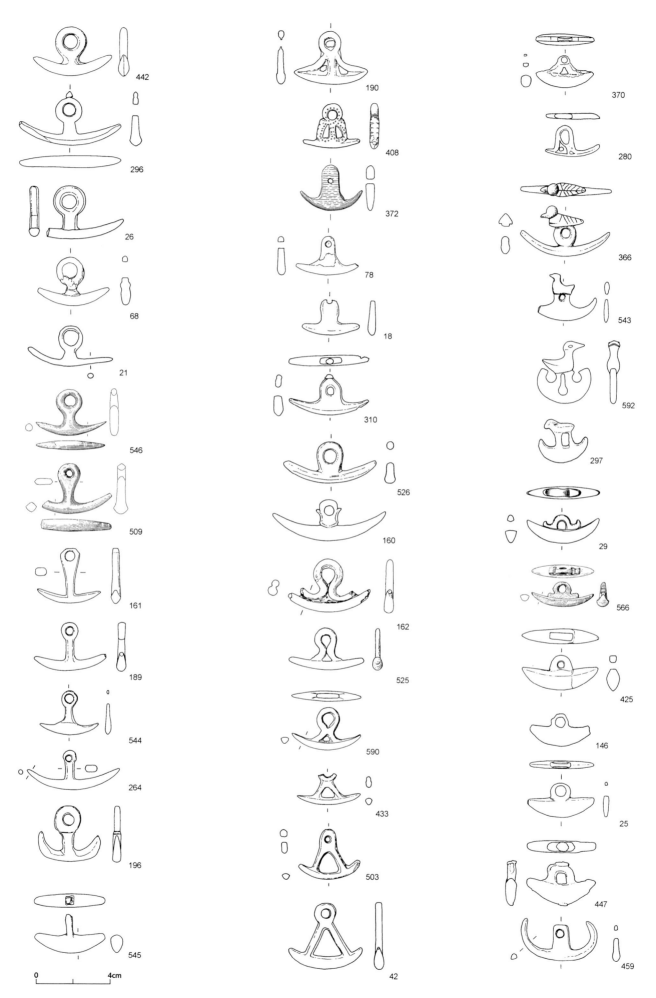

Figure 24 Typology: centre-looped pestles. Scale 1:2

Plate 10 The Colchester (Garrison site) cosmetic set *in situ* beneath the skull of inhumation JNF 439. Photo © Colchester Archaeological Trust

6. Context and Distribution

Cosmetic grinders are replete with intrinsic information of interest and importance, whether concerning their manufacture, function, usage, appearance or 'visual messages'; information that can be accessed to some degree from each and every example. However, a broader understanding of their role in the material culture and society of Late Iron Age and Roman Britain can only be achieved through an examination of the additional information derived from provenance, context and association. The quantity and quality of that information varies according to the manner of discovery and subsequent care of each find.

The present catalogued sample combines two datasets: 1) cosmetic grinders found as a result of systematic fieldwork, principally on archaeological excavations, and 2) those found casually, the majority with the use of a metal detector. The excavation dataset numbers 104 finds, the casual finds dataset 502. The evidence of the excavated sample comprises a precise findspot within an archaeological site, together, usually, with a secure context and, often, with associated finds and context date (**Pl. 10, Fig. 3**). The evidence of the casual finds varies but naturally is usually much sparser: of the 502 catalogued examples 136 have no recorded provenance or are of imprecise or uncertain provenance, while of the remaining 366 provenanced examples less than a third have an assessable potential broad site context. Thus, for an examination of contextual information ('social distribution') the sample comprises the 104 excavated examples (**Tables 13, 14, 16, 17**) together with some considerably less secure indications from about 100 casually found examples (**Tables 13, 15, 18, 19**). For the simpler assessment of geographical distribution the sample is larger – 366 casual finds supplementing the 104 from excavations to give a total of 470 plottable findspots (**Maps 1–15**).

Building on the initial publication of 99 examples (Jackson 1985) the data for the present catalogue were gathered over the period 1985–2004. In 1992 the author conducted a comprehensive survey of museums, county archaeologists, finds specialists and excavation units in Britain, circulating them with copies of the published drawings from the 1985 paper and asking for details of additional examples in their collections or records. This elicited a gratifyingly full and widespread response and the author made visits to record the many newly-reported finds as they were recognized in existing collections. It also ensured a subsequent steady stream of notifications as new finds were made on excavations or were identified among objects found by members of the public and submitted to museums for identification. At the same time, a growing number of collectors and metal-detectorists brought or sent their examples to the author at the British Museum, often via colleagues in other museums and archaeological

units. In parallel, enquiries continued to be made of overseas colleagues, but the 'nil return' of the 1980s continued until 1999 when the discovery of a complete set in a burial at Thérouanne, Pas-de-Calais (cat. no. 501) was reported (Jackson and Thuillier 1999). More recently, notification has been received of mortars from Arras (Pas-de-Calais) and Bibracte (Saône-et-Loire) and a third possible mortar from Corent (Puy-de-Dôme) (Guillaumet and Eugène 2009, 241–3). Once all existing cosmetic grinders had been recorded the new British finds settled into a pattern of rapidly increasing numbers found and reported by detectorists (who could now put a name to a hitherto unidentified type), with the occasional, and also increasing, number found on excavations – most impressively from London (cat. nos 318–28a) and from Heybridge (246–52).

Increasingly, too, cosmetic grinders were reported by collectors, who acquired examples found by detectorists and brought them for recording, a process through which the vulnerability of provenance information soon became apparent. In a troublingly not infrequent number of instances a cosmetic grinder, for which the author had already recorded a provenance, was brought in by a collector to whom it had been sold by a dealer, with reduced (e.g. county only) or no provenance information (see, for example, cat. nos 129, 140, 257, 260, 458, 566), or, even more disturbingly, with a 'new', completely bogus, provenance substituted (see for example cat. nos 29, 183, 211, 340, 426, 555). This was extremely damaging for it cast serious doubt on the given provenance of other cosmetic grinders acquired by the collector from the dealer at the same time (as cat. nos 46, 481, 485) and, furthermore, raised the spectre of other 'undetected' examples that had been through the finder/ dealer/ collector process. Thus, the unscrupulous or ignorant actions of a very small number of individuals jeopardised the painstaking work of those many detectorists and collectors who correctly reported their finds and supplied accurate finding details. For, the potential for loss or falsification of provenance of those objects that changed hands and ownership, often more than once, means that there will always be an inherent uncertainty in the given provenance of many of the non-excavated cosmetic grinders.

This negative aspect, however, was far outweighed by the tremendously important recording system, above all in Norfolk and Suffolk, which consolidated the dialogue with detectorists pioneered by Tony Gregory in the 1970s and 80s. In fact, it was information from the Norfolk and Suffolk SMR's (amongst others) that allowed the correction of lost and spurious provenances. Just as the importance of those recording systems was demonstrated for the 80s and 90s so the still greater benefits of recording through the PAS scheme, since its introduction in 1997, are underlined.

Context (Tables 13–20)

In the hierarchy of contextual information the complete sets from excavations are of greatest importance because they provide secure information directly relevant to the principal function of the type (**Table 13**). Individual components, even when they are from an excavated context, furnish a different, less clear-cut level of information (**Tables 14–15**). They may be present as detritus or as objects fulfilling a secondary role as, for example, amulets, votive gifts at temples, or exotica in Anglo-Saxon 'bag collections', but without their companion piece they were not capable of fulfilling their primary function as grinders. Of the 21 complete sets (**Figs 4–5**) 16 are from archaeological excavations and 12 are securely dated. In terms of their broad context (**Tables 16, 17, 20**) 10 are 'urban', 3 'rural' and 2 'military', while 1 is from an Iron Age settlement. Within those categories seven are from burials (4 accompanying cremations, 2 with inhumations, 1 uncertain) and one from a temple site. Of the five sets casually found that from Bures St Mary (**Pl. 3**) proved to be from a disturbed cremation while the two sets from Itteringham were part of a hoard (**Pl. 11**, **Tables 18–20**).

Most recent of the burial finds is the cosmetic set from inhumation JNF 439, excavated at the Garrison site, Colchester late in 2004 (Jackson 2006). The grave was part of a dense concentration of intercutting burials in a Roman cemetery comprising several hundred inhumations and cremations. On the strength of its stratigraphic relationship with adjacent features the burial was assigned a provisional date of late 1st–late 2nd century AD. Bone preservation on the site was poor and in the case of JNF 439 just the back half of the skull (of an adult of indeterminate sex) had survived. Sealed beneath its left side was a complete and intact centre-looped cosmetic set (**Pl. 10**). The distinctive loop assembly on both components, together with the knobbed terminals and incised zigzag motif of the mortar (**Fig. 1**), is suggestive of regional manufacture because the provenanced parallels are from Colchester, Norfolk and Suffolk (nos 113–14, 119, 362, 433, 525, 590).

As only the second recorded set discovered with an inhumation burial, and thus preserving evidence of its chosen placement in the grave, the Garrison find is of considerable interest. Although the potential significance of the position of grave goods in inhumation burials is a complex issue, and it is important to avoid simplistic conclusions or incautious generalizations, in Romano-British burials, as has been shown (e.g. Philpott 1991), personal ornaments, above all items of jewellery, are often encountered in positions that might be anticipated – rings on fingers or toes, bracelets on wrists and brooches (as garment-fasteners) on the chest. Pins found in close contact with the skull are usually assumed to be hair-pins, while examples found at the chest are sometimes interpreted as garment-fasteners. Combs are occasionally found on the breast or shoulder but were often placed by the head, in some instances with the indication that they were worn at burial. It is possible to suggest, therefore, not only that the position of the Garrison cosmetic set was carefully selected but also that, as with other personalia, that position was related to the set's former function: it is a significant additional piece of evidence in support of the view that cosmetic sets were used for the preparation of powdered colorants, principally, or exclusively, for the face.

Sadly, no trace was found in the Garrison grave of a container or of any lumps of mineral or cosmetic powders. In fact, the cosmetic set was the sole (surviving) grave good. Likewise, the only other set to date discovered in direct association with an inhumation, a Late Iron Age burial at Beckford, was also the only object found with the burial. An end-looped mortar (22a) was found close to the upper chest – thus, also, in close proximity to the face – of an adult female skeleton, which had been inhumed in a partially in-filled boundary ditch without a visible grave cut. The companion pestle (22b) was found in a disturbed layer immediately above. Selected as singleton grave goods, in this way, the importance of cosmetic sets is evident, and the position of the examples from Colchester and Beckford appears instructive.

The sets found with cremation burials – two from St Albans (436, 437), one from Chichester (92) and one from Thérouanne (501), together with that from Bures St Mary (**Pl. 3**) – lack any useful positional evidence but provide, instead, clues from the associated grave goods. At the St Albans King Harry Lane Late Iron Age and Roman cemetery, grave no. 203 (AD 40–60) was a cremation in a locally-made pottery flagon (*lagena*) (Stead and Rigby 1989, 96, 104, 324, 326, fig. 126; Eckardt and Crummy 2008, 78, 173–4). Included in the flagon were an iron toilet set, which had undergone cremation (and consequently preserved intact only the nail-cleaner component), and an end-looped cosmetic set (436), which had not been burnt, while another un-burnt object, a hinged Keyhole Rosette brooch, was placed just outside the flagon. Nearby, at the St Stephens Roman cemetery, grave no. 251 (late 1st/ early 2nd century AD), an urned cremation in a pit, was furnished with a mixed cosmetic set (437) and a glass flask, both apparently contained in a wooden casket fitted with copper-alloy rings and lion-headed studs (Unpublished). The Chichester centre-looped cosmetic set (92) was from the St Pancras Roman cemetery, in a box burial (Burial Group 228: late 2nd/ early 3rd century AD) which also contained ceramic and glass vessels, an iron bracket (probably from the box), a collection of personal ornaments, trinkets and amulets (two brooches, a copper-alloy pin, a ring, five beads, a perforated coin and a perforated dog/boar tooth), one copper-alloy and eight bone needles, a bone toggle and a bone ligula (Down and Rule 1971, 86–7, 113–15, figs 5.17–18 and 5.26). At Thérouanne (Pas-de-Calais, France), in a Roman road-side cemetery outside the civitas capital *Tarvenna*, a centre-looped set (501) was discovered in grave ST. 17 (late 2nd/ early 3rd century AD), an urned cremation in a pit (Jackson and Thuillier 1999). The other grave goods comprised ceramics (two flagons and a patera) and glass-ware (a cylindrical bottle and the stamped base of a flask). The mixed set from Bures St Mary was part of a disturbed cremation burial (1st/ 2nd century AD), apparently in a grey-ware lidded pot, with metal and bone fittings from a wooden casket, a glass flask, a brooch, a rectangular speculum mirror and a composite spherical vessel or container (M. Matthews and J. Plouviez, *in litt.*).

To these associations from burials may be added those from two notable finds of sets in non-sepulchral contexts. One was from a closely-dated context (*c.* AD 100–120) in a timber and clay building excavated at Blossoms Inn, London, a site near the Cheapside Roman baths. More importantly, it had a particularly intimate and indisputable association, a cosmetic

set (319) found with a tweezers and nail-cleaner (**Fig. 2**) fused together in a lump of iron-pan concretion: no doubt all were originally strung together on the same cord (Jackson 1993). The other was a ploughed-out hoard of the mid-2nd century AD found at Itteringham, Norfolk (**Pl. 11**), in which two cosmetic sets (286–7) were associated with 62 silver *denarii* and 42 bronze coins, the earliest a *denarius* of Vitellius (AD 69), the latest two *denarii* of the deified Faustina I produced by Antoninus Pius after her death in AD 141 (Leins 2002). In addition, there were two silver finger-rings – a snake ring and a gem-set ring – of types found in the Snettisham Roman jeweller's hoard (buried shortly after AD 154), a plain silver ring and a small copper-alloy key (for a rotary lock, probably on a casket or strong-box) as well as sherds from three pottery vessels, at least one of which (also probably dating to the 2nd century) was a container for all or part of the hoard.

Pooling the information from all this material associated with sets in secure, dated contexts certain trends may be observed even if the suggested function of the sets cannot yet be confirmed. Virtually all of the non-ceramic associated items may be interpreted as objects related to personal adornment and body care: jewellery, trinkets and amulets, from King Harry Lane, Chichester, Itteringham and Bures St Mary; toilet sets, *ligula*, mirror and (?unguent) flasks, from King Harry Lane, St Stephens, London, Chichester, Thérouanne and Bures St Mary; and wooden caskets with metal fittings to contain these personal possessions from Chichester, St Stephens and Bures St Mary. Crummy and Eckardt have demonstrated that after the Roman conquest there was a surge in manufacture and use of toilet sets in Britain. Furthermore, the nail-cleaners in those sets were an insular survival, mutating from an élite Iron Age object to an everyday and distinctively Romano-British grooming implement, though still, apparently, reflecting differences in social meaning (Crummy and Eckardt 2003, 61. Eckardt and Crummy 2008, 12, 118). So, the direct association of tweezers and nail-cleaner with the Blossom's Inn cosmetic set (319), as also the iron nail-cleaner with the King Harry Lane cosmetic set (436), serves to underline the connection of cosmetic sets to body-care implements expressing identity.

The Itteringham hoard, on the other hand, hints at relative value: the cosmetic sets (286–7) accompanied jewellery and coins of silver and bronze – objects and cash of everyday use, perhaps; however, the accompanying key may have been that to the real treasure concealed elsewhere – a strong-box, perhaps, containing gold coins and jewellery and silver plate. Another association with a key, a centre-looped mortar in a late 1st century AD context from excavations at Borough High Street, Southwark (no. 323) fused, loop-to-loop, by corrosion products to an iron slide key, suggests that the stringing together and suspension of keys and cosmetic sets might have been common practice, the one controlling security and personal belongings the other integral to personal appearance and identity.

Interestingly, cosmetic sets (as yet) appear not to have been included among the grave goods in élite burials of the Late Iron Age/ early Roman period. For example, none were encountered in the excavations at Stanway (Colchester), Folly Lane (St Albans) or Cobham (A2), in which chronologically and geographically they might have been anticipated. Instead, as we have seen, at Beckford, St Albans, Colchester, Chichester, Bures St Mary and Thérouanne they are present in more modestly-furnished grave groups. Never-the-less, the precocious use of brass for the manufacture of the St Albans King Harry Lane set (**Table 10**, complete set 436) might be taken to imply a Late Iron Age possession of considerable importance, even if not of the highest status.

Of the burials with cosmetic sets all save that at Beckford were located in urban cemeteries and an urban context is by far the most common, whether calculated for complete sets, all excavated finds or casual finds (**Table 20**). For towns the figures are 56% for sets and 31% for all excavated finds but when joined to figures for 'small towns' (6% and 24%) they yield an urban total of 62% for sets and 55% for all excavated finds. Set against the respective rural equivalents of 19% and 22% they imply a strong preference for centres of population, even if the margin of difference between a 'small town' and a 'village' or 'rural settlement' may sometimes be narrow and difficult to draw (Burnham 1995; Millett 1995; Mattingly 2006, 286–91). The situation is particularly striking in eastern England (combined excavated and casual finds): in Norfolk cosmetic grinders have been found at 9 of the 15 sites in the county characterized as Roman 'small towns' – Billingford, Brampton, Brettenham, Ditchingham, Fincham, Great

Walsingham, Hockwold, Saham Toney and Wicklewood/ Crownthorpe (Gurney 1995; Davies 2009, 173–86) – yielding between them a total of 44 components, with conspicuous concentrations at Brampton (5), Saham Toney (7), Hockwold (8), Great Walsingham (8) and Wicklewood/ Crownthorpe (10); while in Suffolk examples were found at 8 of the 9 sites characterized as 'small towns' – Coddenham, Felixstowe, Hacheston, Icklingham, Long Melford, Scole, Wenhaston and Wixoe (Plouviez 1995) – yielding a total of 20 components, with 4 from Hacheston, including a Type A mortar recorded on the PAS database (SF-1089C2) and a marked concentration at Wenhaston (eight). Together with an example from the town of Caistor St Edmund they comprise an essentially unbroken network of urban centres in the region of the Iceni and Trinovantes. Further finds of cosmetic grinders from 'small towns' are clustered in the zone adjacent to Norfolk and Suffolk, at Heybridge, Great Chesterford, Baldock, Cambridge, Stonea, Bourne and Sleaford, but dwindle beyond that with just two western outliers at Magiovinium and Wanborough (the latter a set from a disturbed burial) and two in the north, at Catterick and Carlisle.

Davies has noted that the 'small towns' in Norfolk, fairly regularly located at intervals of between 15 and 20 km and often strategically sited at route intersections, especially river-crossings, were 'the main infrastructure for the operation of the region' (Davies 2009, 173–4). As elsewhere, they appear to have been generally modest-sized and architecturally unpretentious settlements with, to a greater or lesser extent, commerce, markets, religious and industrial foci and, perhaps, some of the instruments of government at their heart, together with accommodation and services for travellers of all kinds. They would have been just the sort of place where you might buy or commission a cosmetic set from a bronzesmith. Equally, they were a place in which you met people – at the market, the temple, the fair – a forum for social intercourse, an opportunity, perhaps, for exhibiting and observing identity, whether through language, clothing and accoutrements, grooming practices or the use of cosmetics. In his recent consideration of the spread of Latin in pre-conquest Britain, Williams drew attention to the exceptional nature of tradition, as expressed in coinage, in the Norfolk and Suffolk region: 'The East Anglian tradition is exceptional in the extent to which it remains faithful to local traditional styles until very late. The evidence of the reception of classicizing motifs in adjacent traditions suggests strongly that this was a conscious expression of preference, rather than the outcome of ignorance' (Williams 2007, 9). It is possible that the concentration of cosmetic grinders in Norfolk and Suffolk is another manifestation of that preference, a continuing allegiance by the Iceni to British ways after the conquest, perhaps, an acceptable, non-confrontational way of expressing a different identity, and maybe specifically by women.

Within the excavated sample of cosmetic grinders from 'small towns' there are very few with meaningful specific contexts. Most were found in general levels or cut features – surfaces, layers, and the fills of ditches, pits and wells. More illuminating are those from Brampton (38) – in a disturbed level in a bath house – and from Baldock (16) – in the rectilinear enclosure ditch of Building V, a circular wooden structure, perhaps a domestic roundhouse, although several of the finds

indicate religious activity (Stead and Rigby 1986, 86, figs 4; 39A, 2; 60, 378–80; 66, 523). The mortar from Thistleton (506), too, has a context suggestive of a connection to religious activity for, although a ploughsoil find in an area of infant burials and ovens, it was from within a building that lay immediately adjacent to the temple precinct. Amongst the casual finds, the majority of the Wicklewood examples are from the Crownthorpe temple (540, 542–4, 546–9), and it is probable that many if not all those from Great Walsingham (213–20) are also from a temple site. Similarly, the finds from Hockwold (261–7) include at least one from Leyland's Farm (265), raising the possibility that some or all of those, too, may have had a religious context.

Thus, there might be a tendency to presume that other casual finds from 'small towns' are also likely to have derived from temple contexts. However, the quite large assemblage of well-recorded excavated finds from the Elms Farm, Heybridge site (Atkinson and Preston forthcoming) cautions against such an assumption. For, although a temple complex was central to the site, none of the seven cosmetic grinders (246–52) was from a specific context within the temple or its precinct. While it is still feasible that they had had some connection to ritual activity they may alternatively be regarded as part of the general domestic debris. All are of somewhat unexceptional appearance and condition – four pestles and three fragmentary mortars, unelaborate and worn – but they are, nevertheless, of considerable interest, since their sheer numbers (they are parts of seven separate sets), which are also mirrored by another type of toilet implement at the site – tweezers (Eckardt and Crummy 2008, 100), imply a level of currency suggestive of widespread everyday usage of cosmetic sets at a relatively low-status settlement (Jackson forthcoming b).

A similarly varied picture emerges from an examination of the excavation contexts of those cosmetic grinders found in towns – 31% of all excavated finds. The end-looped set from Canterbury (73) was found within a temple precinct, although in a layer described as 'pre-phase I temple clearance' (Jackson forthcoming a), while an end-looped mortar (76) was found in a roadside occupation deposit in the town. The mortar from Kingsholm (295) came from a general layer, and nothing is known of the context of the two casual finds from Silchester (462–3), though an example found in the 2007 excavations (Silchester Town Life Project, SF 4834) came from an area of heavy occupation (Context 7947) with a provisional date of second half of the 1st century AD (Mike Fulford, Nina Crummy and Sandie Williams *in litt.*). At Cirencester one of the two components of a set (100) was found in an area of shops in Insula VI, although it is conceivable that it derived from a feature (possibly disturbed) in the underlying fort, and a similar uncertainty attaches to the three casually-found examples from Wroxeter (562–4), which may belong to the military rather than the civilian occupation of the site. At Leicester another shop or retail context is suggested by the discovery of a centre-looped pestle (305) in excavations on the west wing and south-west corner of the forum. The Lincoln mortar (308) was found in the earliest rampart levels at the West gate of the *colonia*, while a pestle from an extra-mural site at York (570) found its way into ditch fill, part of a levelling phase at a site comprising ditched enclosures, burials and mausolea and rubbish dumping. There are burial contexts at

Chichester (92) and Thérouanne (501) as also at Colchester where, in addition to the Garrison set and a mortar excavated at the Butt Road cemetery (113), the majority of the numerous casual finds from the town are clearly or probably from cemeteries. Other Colchester contexts include a centre-looped pestle from a pit in the area of houses and temples flanking the street outside the Balkerne Gate (118) and a centre-looped mortar from the native industrial settlement at Sheepen (115). A mortar from Chichester (93) was found in the construction slot for a timber tank but was probably residual, while at Caistor St Edmund a Type E mortar (65) is recorded as coming from Building 4, kiln 3. Much more revealing is the context of the carefully recorded set from St Albans (438/439) found in the excavation of part of Insula II (Niblett *et al.* 2006, 142–4, fig. 42, no. 15). The two components were found in a levelling deposit which provided a base for a tile-built hearth, part of a complex of hearths, conduit and gravel surfaces associated with a timber building on masonry footings that preceded the construction of Building II, 1. The associated finds comprised, in addition to pottery, a relatively large number of small personal items – bone pins and phallic amulets, bronze brooches, seal box and metal fittings. As observed (Niblett *et al.* 2006, 73), these are unlikely to relate to metal-working or other hearth activity, and, in view of the construction sequence revealed (*ibid.* 55, 60), it is distinctly possible that most if not all the material, including the cosmetic set, derived from a disturbed burial group.

London provides by far the largest number of excavated contexts for cosmetic grinders from a single town (318–23, 325, 327a–8a) and, interestingly, all are linked to domestic occupation, whether from buildings, alley surfaces, drains, ditches, pits or dumps in open areas. Like those from Heybridge, the London finds appear to demonstrate the prevalence of the type, its widespread use and its longevity. In contexts dating from the 1st to 3rd century AD, cosmetic sets or their components come from sites throughout the occupied area – to west (319–21, 328) and east (325, 328a) of the Walbrook valley and from Southwark (318, 322–3, 327a) – and they are joined by casually-found examples from the Thames (324) and from the Walbrook (326–7), the latter raising the possibility of a ritual context. In fact, London is geographically at the heart of the distribution of cosmetic grinders from towns, a distribution focused on towns in the south-east: London's 13 finds (including 1 set) are exceeded only by the 21 from Colchester (1 set, 3 excavated examples and 17 casual finds); St Albans' total of 5 finds includes the largest number of complete sets (3); there are 4 finds from Canterbury, including 2 sets; 4 finds from Chichester, including 1 set; and 3 examples from Silchester. As we have seen, the set from Cirencester and the three components from Wroxeter are of uncertain status and may relate to either the urban or the earlier military occupation at those sites, while the other town finds – Caistor St Edmund, York, Lincoln, Leicester, and Gloucester – comprise only a single example each. This distribution, in conjunction with the evidence from dated contexts, suggests a focus of use or production of cosmetic sets in the towns of south-eastern Britain in the 1st century AD, perhaps starting in Colchester. Certainly, following the sparse and widespread distribution of cosmetic grinders in the Late Iron Age, the majority of (the admittedly modest number of) 1st century AD contexts is

accounted for by sets or components in Colchester, London, St Albans, Canterbury and Chichester (**Fig. 25**) Whether this represents manufacture in those places or a movement there of people who used cosmetic sets is at present impossible to say.

Twenty-two percent of the excavated finds of cosmetic grinders are from sites categorized as rural, comprising villages, small rural settlements, villas, farmsteads and, in one instance, a cave site. The villages and rural settlements are geographically widespread and varied in character, from the enigmatic settlement at Meols (341) to a domestic and industrial site near Whitchurch (535) to more generic agricultural settlements, which increase in density in the east. Notable is the very small number recorded from villas (five), and it may be significant that most of those – Beddington (24), Keston (292), Fishbourne (191) and Barton Farm (Cirencester) (102–3) lie in the hinterland of towns. There is frustratingly little specific contextual information, with the great majority of finds coming from topsoil, ploughsoil, residual or unstratified contexts. This is especially vexing at sites like Dragonby, where an end-looped set (154) and an end-looped mortar (155) might have derived from either the Iron Age or the Romano-British phase of this nucleated settlement. Similarly, the set from Fengate (187) is very likely to have been associated with Late Iron Age ritual activity at the site but confirmation is lacking because the original given context proved to be insecure. Potentially ritual contexts are also present at Brenley Corner (50), a roadside settlement that included a possible shrine, and at Lakenheath, where the fine zoomorphic mortar (301) was deposited (virtually intact and still functional) in the upper layer of a well. In the cave-system at Ogof-yr-Esgyrn (Dan-yr-Ogof) an end-looped pestle (400) may belong with either occupation debris or graves, and as such is paralleled by toilet implements from equivocal contexts at several Romano-British cave sites (Eckardt and Crummy 2008, 104). It has a broader regional context, for two more end-looped pestles (48–9) were excavated at the nearby fort at Y Gaer, Brecon, an end-looped mortar (536) was found in the excavations of the farmstead at Whitton, and a centre-looped set (62) and centre-looped mortar (63) were excavated in the legionary *canabae* at Caerleon.

Military contexts account for 19% of excavated finds of cosmetic grinders. At the fortresses of Caerleon and Chester they have been found only in the extra-mural *canabae*, but at fort sites they have been found both within the fort (Brecon, Castleford, Hod Hill, Richborough and Caister-on-Sea) and outside in the *vici* or garrison settlements (Brecon, Doncaster, Burgh Castle and Kirkby Thore). Like all those found within forts the closely-dated Castleford mortar (80), from a midden within the first fort, begs the question why was it there: had it been used by a soldier or is it evidence for women in the fort? Both are possible, but the evidence for the presence of women, even in the annexe of the second fort at Castleford, is at best ambiguous (Cool and Philo 1998, 357). Two of the mortars from Richborough (415, 418) may have derived from disturbed burials of the later 2nd century AD in the north-west quadrant of the stone fort but most, if not all, are from within the Shore fort, and there is another example from the Shore fort of Burgh Castle (58) and the associated fort at Caister-on-Sea (64). Otherwise, all of the military sites, including the industrial and supply depots at Wilderspool and Walton-le-Dale, are located in the west or north. The northernmost cosmetic grinder recorded to date, a broken end-looped mortar, was found near the fort at High Rochester (PAS NCL-627676), but as yet none has been found at the Hadrian's Wall forts. Dating evidence is good for the military finds but there are relatively few secure and informative specific contexts. The possible disturbed burial context at Richborough has already been mentioned and there is another potential burial find at Chester (91), where an idiosyncratic mortar was found in ditch fill at the Bedward Row cemetery site. A second mortar from Chester (90) came from domestic occupation debris in the area of strip buildings on the extra-mural settlement site at Priory Place. The set from Caerleon (62) was found with a 3rd century coin in a context associated with a phase of abandonment or demolition, and an end-looped mortar from Walton-le-Dale (515) was also found in an abandonment horizon, though the end-looped set and pestle from the same site were both unstratified (514, 516). The mortar from the depot at Wilderspool (550), found beneath a hearth 'in the vicinity of the bronze-founder's and enameller's workshop', may represent a finished product or a source of bronze for re-cycling. But perhaps the most intriguing of the military contexts is that of the end-looped pestle from the Roman fort at Hod Hill (268), found in the foundation trench of one of the timber buildings (Building A, identified as possible stabling or veterinary quarters) and with a likely date of deposition somewhere between AD 45 to 55. The form of the pestle is idiosyncratic and, coupled with the fact that there is wear on the tip of the rod, it seems very probable, though incapable of proof, that the pestle was a residual find from the Iron Age occupation of the hillfort, part of a pre-conquest Iron Age cosmetic set.

Significantly, all the cosmetic grinders from hillforts or Iron Age settlements are end-looped and several of them are not far distant from Hod Hill: mortars from the hillfort sites at Ham Hill and Wylye Camp (Bilbury Rings), and a pestle from the enclosed settlement at Gussage All Saints. Nothing is known of the context of the Wylye Camp find (565) and little of that from Ham Hill (231), but the Gussage pestle (226) was found in the uppermost layer of a pit and assigned a date within the bracket c. 100 BC–AD 80. The end-looped set from a Late Iron Age burial at Beckford (22) has already been discussed. In addition, there is a casual find from the hillfort at Hunsbury (275), the form, manufacture and composition of which are strongly suggestive of a Late Iron Age date; and an excavated pestle from a backfilled ditch of the Iron Age and Romano-British enclosure system at Normanton-le-Heath (391), a Late Iron Age context that may be no later than the mid-1st century BC (Hill 1997, 105; Thorpe, Sharman and Clay 1994, 48–9). Taken together these finds are indicative of widespread (though perhaps restricted) use in Britain in the Late Iron Age.

Long after cosmetic sets had gone out of use as two-piece kits a few examples of the more impressive component, the mortar, found their way into the hands and lives of Anglo-Saxon people. One centre-looped mortar (273) took on a new existence as part of a bag collection, which was buried at Horton Kirby in a female grave of the early 6th century AD. At another early Anglo-Saxon cemetery, on Chessell Down, an un-contexted end-looped mortar (89), found in 19th century excavations, is also likely to have been a curio in a 'bag collection'. Less certainty attaches to a fragmentary mortar

from Faversham (184), which may have derived from a burial in the rich Anglo-Saxon cemetery in the King's Field or from nearby Roman burials. Other finds include a centre-looped mortar found as a residual object in a Saxon or later feature in excavations at Repton (414) and a possibly re-worked mortar found beneath St Augustine's Abbey, Canterbury (Rigold 1970).

In addition to the broad context categories (Level 1: **Tables 16 and 18**) there are two specific types of context which may be found within and across those categories, namely sepulchral (cemeteries/ burials) and religious (temple/ shrine/ religious site) contexts. To avoid double counting – because the cosmetic grinders belonging to those groups have been included in the statistics for the Level 1 categories (for example set no. 73 from a temple site in the town of Canterbury, hence a town find) – the figures have been calculated as percentages of the whole sample totals (n = respectively 16, 95 and 111) and presented separately (Level 2: **Tables 17 and 19**).

To the complete sets from burials which have already been discussed can be added five components from excavated sepulchral contexts giving a total for burials of 13% for all excavated contexts (though that includes the post-Roman burial from Horton Kirby). Like the set from Wanborough (517) the mortars from the extra-mural cemeteries at Chester (91, from Bedward Row) and Colchester (113, from Butt Road) and the pestle from cave occupation at Ogof-yr-Esgyrn (400) are not specifically from burial contexts but are probably to be interpreted as grave goods from disturbed burials. Less certainly (and thus not included in the sepulchral statistics) components from Richborough (418) and York (570) and a set from St Albans (438/ 439) may also have derived from disturbed burials. Contemporary with another burial find from St Albans (set 436) is the diminutive (probable) pestle, probably selected as an amulet, which was part of a large array of grave goods, including toilet articles and perfume bottles, accompanying an adult female inhumation of about AD 40–50 in a stone sarcophagus from Saintes, France (444). The evidence of the individual components from excavated contexts tends to support that of the sets (arguably the least equivocal source), which indicates a minimum period of usage of cosmetic sets from the Late Iron Age (Beckford, King Harry Lane) to the late 2nd/ early 3rd century AD (Chichester, Thérouanne). The excavated finds from sepulchral contexts are supplemented by a number of casual finds: four from Colchester (109, 117, 119, 126), have recorded findspots located within the area of known Roman cemeteries; one from Newport (354) was found in association with human burials, coins and brooches of 1st to 3rd century AD date; one from St Albans (440) is thought to have come from a cremation grave; and a Type F mortar from Laddus Grove, Elm, tantalisingly described as having been found 'on the arm of a skeleton' (Trett 1983, 228, no. 4) was presumably from an inhumation burial.

Cosmetic sets were especially individual and intimate possessions often selected as grave goods, but they also appear to have been among the classes of object sometimes chosen for dedication at temples. Though not as ubiquitous as coins and brooches they were quite common, and included simple, inexpensive pieces as well as more elaborate examples, added to which their personal nature and apparent association with well-being and identity may have given them particular significance as religious gifts. As a consequence, perhaps, 11%

of the total of all excavated finds come from temples, shrines and religious sites, but that number is substantially increased by casual finds. Both urban and rural settings are represented and the geographical spread is quite wide, ranging from Canterbury to Lydney to Coleshill, Thistleton and Great Walsingham, while dated contexts span the period late 1st to 4th century AD. The Canterbury find (73) was an end-looped set from a temple precinct, in a layer described as pre-phase 1 temple clearance. At nearby Brenley Corner an idiosyncratic zoomorphic mortar (50) was found with other votive material suggestive of a shrine at this roadside settlement on Watling Street. More significantly, the religious centre at Springhead has yielded several examples: in addition to the catalogued mortar and pestle from Harker's excavations (472–3) another pestle was found in a pool channel context in recent excavations by Wessex Archaeology (SPH 00, SF 9154: J. Schuster *in litt.*) and there is another mortar and pestle from earlier excavations at the site in the Gravesham Museum Collection. At the Gosbecks theatre-temple complex an end-looped mortar (203) was found in the turf of the *cavea*-mound, while at Thistleton another end-looped mortar (506) was discovered in Building 6, just south of the temple precinct. Of the two components from the temple at Grimstock Hill, Coleshill (131–2), the pestle was unstratified but the mortar was found in temple demolition debris of the 4th century AD. Single examples are also recorded from the early excavations at Lydney (332) – more likely from the temple complex than from the hillfort or ironworking debris – and from Fison Way, Thetford (505), a topsoil find in excavations of the multiple ditched enclosure interpreted as a shrine. Amongst the casual finds there are single examples from the temple site at Brigstock (53) and from the temple site (or Iron Age occupation) at Woodeaton (560). But most importantly there are eight examples (540, 542–4, 546–9) recorded from the site of the temple at Crownthorpe, Wicklewood (Davies 2009, 179–80; Davies and Gregory 1991, 70, 75, fig. 3), together with another two likely to derive from the same site (541, 545); eight examples from Great Walsingham (213–20), many, if not all, of which are probably connected to a temple site (Gurney 1995, 57–9; Davies 2009, 181–4; Davies and Gregory 1991, 70, 75, fig. 3; Bagnall-Smith 1999); and another eight examples from Hockwold (260–7), at least one of which (265, from Leylands Farm), and probably more, conceivably derived from a religious context (Davies 2009, 184–5; Gurney 1986).

In summary, interrogation of context (social distribution) demonstrates that cosmetic sets 1) appear to have been widespread, though probably not numerous, in pre-conquest Britain, 2) were sometimes selected for a particular purpose, especially as grave goods and religious gifts, 3) circulated widely and freely in urban, rural and military settings in Roman Britain and 4) seem to have been especially prevalent after the Roman conquest in the south-east towns and in the 'small towns' and related settlements of Icenian territory. Furthermore, the evidence of associated finds places them firmly in the realm of personal ornament, body care and identity (Hill 1997; Eckardt and Crummy 2008, 91–107). To these may be added the evidence of geographical distribution and contextual dating which cast light on issues of origins, period of use and regionality.

Distribution (Maps 1–15)

The geographical distribution of cosmetic sets is based here on the parallel datasets of excavated and casual finds, with totals respectively of 104 and 366 provenanced examples. To a degree the two datasets represent test and control groups and it has been useful in some instances to plot them separately, as for the 'all finds', 'end-looped' and 'centre-looped' categories (**Maps 1–7**). For other categories, especially where the sample numbers are small, it has been more appropriate to combine both datasets in one map (**Maps 8–15**). Just as the categorisation of sites for the purpose of assessing social distribution tends to result in somewhat artificial groupings and rather un-satisfactory or invidious divisions between them, so the interpretation of the geographical spread of chosen categories of object may be fraught with uncertainty or, worse, may be potentially misleading. Nevertheless, the initial assessment of spatial distribution, the observation of patterning – whether foci, wider concentrations, trends or lacunae – is, at least, a relatively objective process and there are certainly some distinctive patterns in the distribution of cosmetic sets.

The first observation is that a comparison between the 'all sources' distribution (**Map 1a**, n = 366) and that for the excavated examples only (**Map 2**, n = 104) shows that both reveal the same geographical spread, as, in attenuated form, does that for the complete sets (**Map 3**, n = 20). In each case the most apparent lacunae are highland areas in the north-west; west Wales; Devon and Cornwall; and the Weald of Kent and Sussex. While these areas often register low finds densities in distribution plots the relative dearth of cosmetic grinders in the region extending westwards from the Weald into Hampshire, Dorset, Wiltshire, Avon and Somerset is more notable, even allowing for five un-plottable examples provenanced only 'Dorset' as well as an additional end-looped mortar from Silchester (Silchester Town Life Project, 2007 excavation, SF 4834) and a few examples recorded on the PAS database which help to redress the balance a little in the Hampshire region (Worrell 2008, fig. 3). In the north, too, the distribution is very sparse, with the pestle from Carlisle and a mortar from High Rochester (PAS NCL-627676) as the northernmost finds, and none recorded from Hadrian's Wall sites.

Seen in terms of concentrations rather than lacunae the great majority of cosmetic set components are found in the zone south of the Humber, east of the Welsh Marches and north of the North Downs, with a strong bias to the eastern half of that zone and high densities of finds in northern Kent, Essex and, above all, in Norfolk and Suffolk (**Map 1b**). As is evident from a comparison of **Maps 1a, 1b and 2**, the overwhelming numbers in Norfolk and Suffolk are a result of casual finds. To a degree, they undoubtedly reflect current land use and access, together with a longstanding high level of detectorist activity and reporting of finds, but the sheer number and concentrations appear to represent a meaningful distribution, demonstrating a genuinely higher usage of cosmetic sets in the region than in other parts of Britain. This is borne out, to some extent, by the PAS data (Worrell 2008, fig. 3 – with more of a Suffolk than a Norfolk bias), while **Maps 2 and 3**, although displaying a more uniform distribution, have a greater concentration of multiple finds in eastern England than elsewhere. Furthermore, the extremely large number of

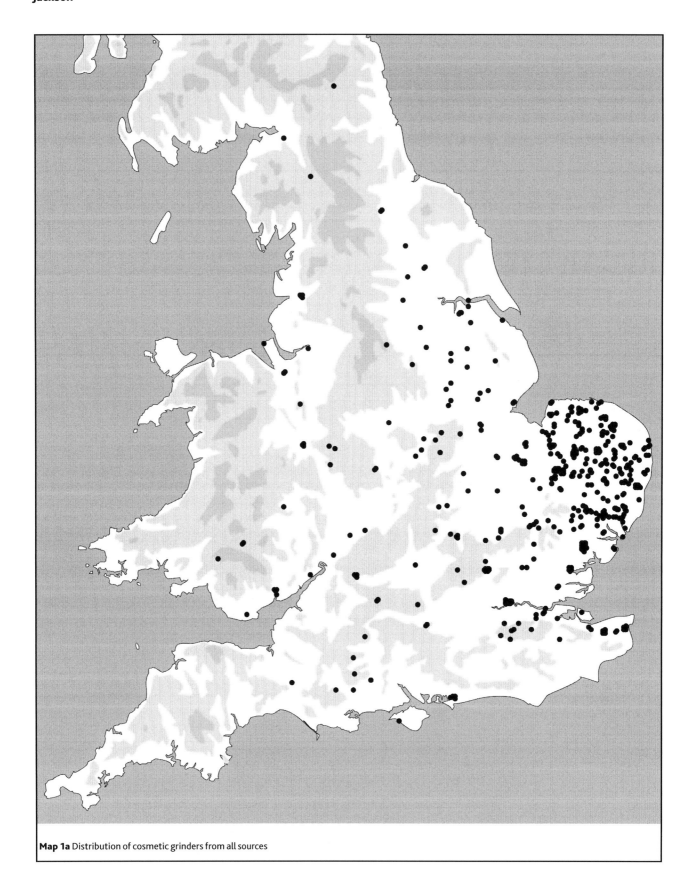

Map 1a Distribution of cosmetic grinders from all sources

findspots and their near-universal distribution in the region of the Iceni seem to indicate that they were in use at all types of site, including the many unexcavated small rural settlements and farms.

Despite the modest number of provenanced complete sets a number of observations may be made on their distribution (**Map 3**): the spread of end-looped sets broadly corresponds to that of the total sample of cosmetic set components; with one exception the centre-looped sets occupy the eastern part of the overall distribution; and mixed sets are currently restricted to Norfolk, Suffolk, St Albans and London, suggesting regional preference. The (un-mapped) centre-looped set from a grave at Thérouanne in France may, perhaps, be interpreted as the (most) personal belonging of a British émigrée. Turning to the finds of individual components, **Maps 4 and 5** show the distribution of end-looped components for, respectively, all sources (n = 214) and excavations only (n = 67). Both can be seen to conform to the distribution of end-looped sets as well as to each other and to the total sample distribution: the inference is that end-looped kits were current throughout the entire area of distribution of cosmetic sets. As if to underline that point, **Maps 6 and 7**, similarly showing the distribution of centre looped components for, respectively, all sources (n = 254) and excavations only (n = 37), display, with very few outliers, a contrasting and clear eastern distribution, concentrated above all in Norfolk, Suffolk and their margins: it may be inferred that there was a regional (eastern) appeal for, and corresponding manufacture of, centre-looped kits. The same relationship, if slightly less pronounced, can be discerned in the distribution patterns of the sample (n = 102 end; 75 centre) recorded on the PAS database (Worrell 2008, fig. 3).

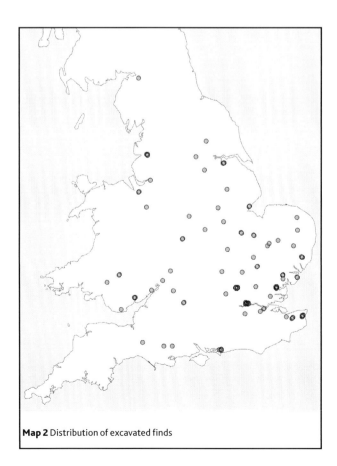

Map 1b Detail of Map 1a showing distribution in East Anglia and margins

Map 2 Distribution of excavated finds

Map 3 Distribution of complete sets

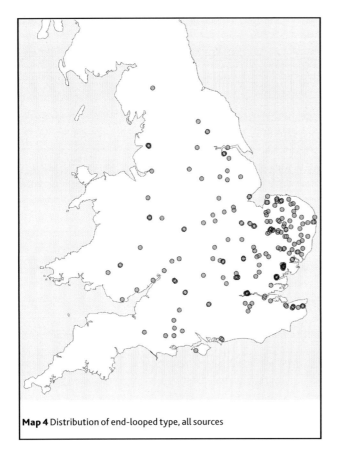

Map 4 Distribution of end-looped type, all sources

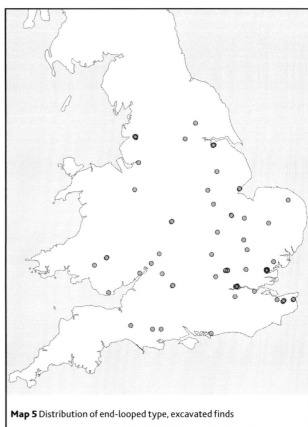

Map 5 Distribution of end-looped type, excavated finds

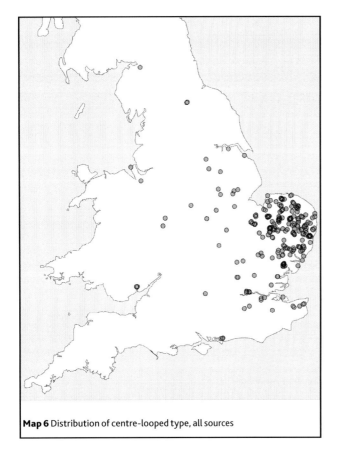

Map 6 Distribution of centre-looped type, all sources

Map 7 Distribution of centre-looped type, excavated finds

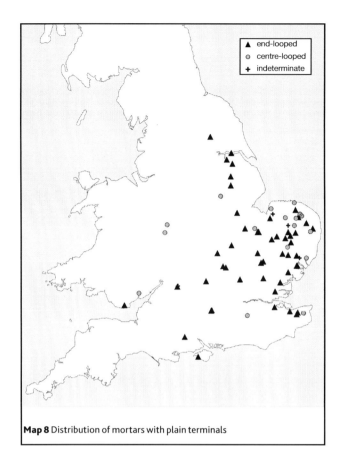

Map 8 Distribution of mortars with plain terminals

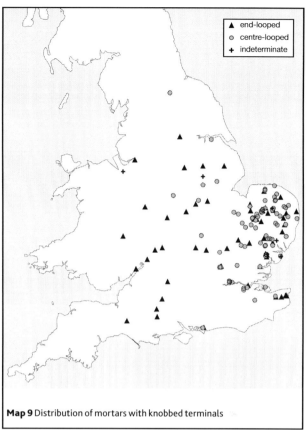

Map 9 Distribution of mortars with knobbed terminals

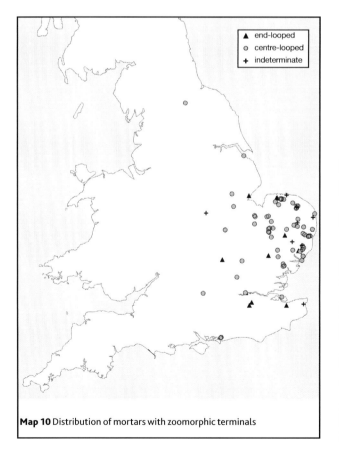

Map 10 Distribution of mortars with zoomorphic terminals

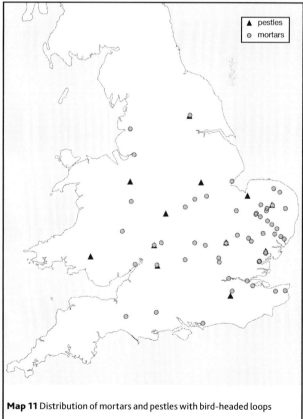

Map 11 Distribution of mortars and pestles with bird-headed loops

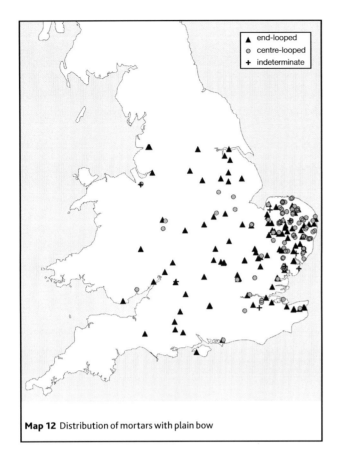

Map 12 Distribution of mortars with plain bow

Map 13 Distribution of mortars with incuse bow decoration

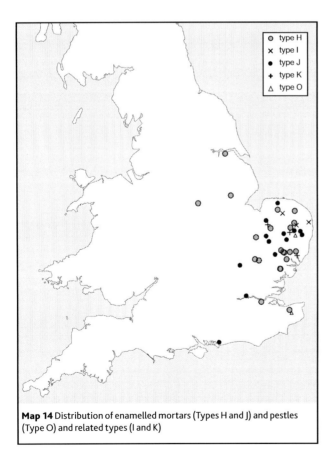

Map 14 Distribution of enamelled mortars (Types H and J) and pestles (Type O) and related types (I and K)

Map 15 Distribution of mortar types A, D and E

Interestingly, these two distributions, overall and eastern, persist when particular and distinctive features are plotted. Thus, **Map 11** demonstrates an overall distribution for bird-headed loops (n = 67), which are principally found on end-looped pestles and mortars; **Map 9** (knobbed mortar terminals, n = 141) reveals that end-looped mortars with a knobbed terminal were also a feature of choice throughout the overall distribution, while centre-looped mortars with knobbed terminals were concentrated in the east; **Map 8** shows an eastern preference for plain mortar terminals (n = 72), whether on end-looped or centre-looped mortars; and **Map 10** vividly illustrates that mortars (whether end-looped or centre-looped) with zoomorphic terminals (n = 79) are not only confined to the east but are mostly concentrated in Norfolk and Suffolk and their western and southern margins (a distribution that emerges from the PAS data, too (Worrell 2008, fig. 4). Perhaps unsurprisingly, mortars with a plain bow (n = 206), irrespective of their loop type, have an overall distribution (**Map 12**), but those with incuse decoration on the bow (again, irrespective of loop type) are restricted to the east (**Map 13**, n = 47).

Maps **14 and 15** reveal specific and restricted distributions for a number of the sub-types, most numerous of which are the enamelled mortars, Type H (with knobbed terminals) and J (with zoomorphic terminals). As can be seen on **Map 14**, Type J (n = 15) is heavily concentrated in Norfolk and Suffolk, a distribution reinforced by a mortar provenanced only 'Norfolk' (361), a finely-preserved uncatalogued example, with 19 cells of interspersed blue, red and green enamel, from Burgate, near Wortham, Suffolk (Ipswich Museum IPSMG: R.2007–4), which is closely similar to an unprovenanced example (578), and a mortar with about 20 cells of turquoise and blue enamel provenanced only 'Suffolk' recorded on the PAS database (SF-665921). The outliers comprise a broken example in London (322), a variant at Baldock (16), a set in the burial at Chichester (92) and another variant set found in the burial at Thérouanne (501). Type H (n = 20) is similarly concentrated in Norfolk and Suffolk but with a slightly wider distribution, with northern (South Ferriby – 469), western (Stapleford, Notts., uncatalogued) and southern (Canterbury – set 74) outliers. As with Type J, all the unplottable examples of Type H support this distribution – single examples from 'Suffolk' (487), 'Norfolk' (360), 'Lincolnshire' (311) and 'unprovenanced' (580) – as does the set from Battisford, Suffolk (Worrell 2008, 362–3). Type O enamelled pestles comprise one from Harleston, Suffolk (232), one in the set from Canterbury (74) and an unprovenanced example (586). It is interesting to note that all the examples of the related un-enamelled Types I and K lie within the Norfolk/ Suffolk 'heartland' of Types H and J.

Of even more restricted distribution (**Map 15**) are mortar Types A, D and E, albeit their numbers are small. A lead model for production of the Type A end-looped mortars was found in London (318), and catalogued examples of the type (n = 9) extend from Surrey through London into Suffolk and Norfolk, a distribution supported by an uncatalogued example from Hacheston (PAS database SF-1089C2). Even more localised are the equally distinctive centre-looped mortars Types D and E, with their sinuous strut-encircled loops and knobbed/ plain (Type D: n = 7) or bovid (Type E (n = 7)) terminals: both types

are focused in Norfolk, Type D with a variant outlier in Chester (90) and Type E with a variant outlier at Colchester (109). The Norfolk distribution of Type E is further underlined by an un-plotted example from 'Norfolk' (358) and by an uncatalogued mortar from Sall, Norfolk (Norfolk HER 50247), almost identical to an example from Great Walsingham (213). The four examples of the distinctive Type F mortar – from Wisbech, Elm, Brigstock and 'East Anglia' (53, 158, 174, 555) – have a similarly tight distribution (not mapped), perhaps reflecting localised production a little further west than Types D and E. The small number of examples of mortar Types B, G and M and pestle Type N (un-mapped) are all restricted to Norfolk and Suffolk, while mortar Type L, defined by slightly less distinctive traits, has a wider, though still eastern, distribution (un-mapped): from Norfolk through London to Kent and Sussex and westwards as far as Stevenage. The much more tightly-defined mortar Type C has a seemingly more localised eastern distribution (un-mapped), though it is represented by just four examples – London, St Albans, Norfolk (319a, 438, 357) and the uncatalogued example from Bures St Mary, Suffolk – all likely to have derived from the same archetype. Three are parts of complete sets and, significantly, they share the same pestle type, indicating that the pestle and mortar were made together.

In conclusion, despite the near-infinite variety in appearance of cosmetic grinders, implying a potentially very wide consumer choice, it has been possible to identify some distinctive groupings (sub-types: **Table 7**), in addition to the simple, overarching division between end-looped and centre-looped types, and to recognize patterns in their geographical distribution. In some instances the tightly-localized nature of the distribution, in combination with a small sample number, might be taken to represent the output of a single craftsman or workshop, while the occasional occurrence of near-identical components might suggest direct moulding from an existing mortar or pestle, either in a static workshop or by a peripatetic craftsman. The wider distribution of, for example, enamelled mortars or mortars with zoomorphic decoration or, indeed, centre-looped mortars and pestles, seems to indicate marketing zones and/ or regional preferences, served by more than one manufacturer or production centre. But what influenced those preferences is harder to interpret. The sheer overall number and the variety of decorated types concentrated in Norfolk and Suffolk and their margins might be seen to hint at special meaning attached to cosmetic sets by the Iceni (maybe by the Trinovantes and Cantiaci, too), perhaps a choice to continue – and to be seen to be continuing – a pre-conquest British mode of body care and self-presentation, even if in time some were adapted to Romanised taste by the incorporation of particular features or decorative motifs. Alternatively or additionally, however, they might be taken to reflect a wider social distribution within those groups of cosmetic sets and cosmetics, the use of which in other regions was rather more restricted, generally or socially. In sum, the impression is of a type that started with the end-looped variety in southern England in the Late Iron Age and, together with the centre-looped variety, became more widespread in Britain after the Roman conquest when it proved especially popular in eastern Britain, above all in the territory of the Iceni.

Table 13. Summary context of complete cosmetic sets

Total 21: 16 excavated, 5 casual; 9 end-looped, 7 centre-looped, 5 mixed.

Cat. no.	Provenance	Summary context
22	Beckford	End-looped. Excavated. Iron Age settlement. Burial. Late Iron Age. Close to upper chest of adult female inhumation. No other grave goods.
---	Bures St Mary	Mixed (as sets 319 and 438/439). Casual/ excavated. Burial. 1st/ 2nd cent. AD. Disturbed cremation (adult, sex indeterminate). Found with bronze, glass and pottery vessel fragments, casket fragments, mirror fragments and brooch.
62	Caerleon	Centre-looped. Excavated. Fortress extra-mural settlement. 3rd cent. AD. From abandonment/ demolition phase, with coin of Victorinus (269–271) but little else.
73	Canterbury	End-looped. Excavated. Temple. Late 1st/2nd cent. AD. Temple precinct, pre-phase I temple clearance.
74	Canterbury	Centre-looped. Casual. Brent Collection. Enamelled (both components).
92	Chichester	Centre-looped. Excavated. Burial. Late 2nd/early 3rd cent. AD. From box burial, cremation, sex and age not determined. Probably female according to associated finds – brooches, beads, ring, ligula, needles, glass vessels, samian, coarse pottery.
100/101	Cirencester	End-looped. Excavated. Town, *insula VI*, shops (or possibly earlier fort). From robber trench, presumably disturbed.
---	Colchester	Centre-looped. Excavated. Garrison site. Burial. Late 1st/ late 2nd cent. AD (provisional). From inhumation burial, tucked beneath skull. Adult, sex unknown. (Jackson 2006).
154	Dragonby	End-looped. Excavated. Iron Age and Romano-British nucleated settlement. Lower topsoil west of the East Road.
187	Fengate	End-looped. Excavated. Settlement complex. Ostensibly pre-200 BC, but problematic context.
192	Fishtoft	End-looped. Excavated. 'R-B agricultural site'. Context not known. Other finds included 3rd-4th cent. AD coins.
260	Hockwold	Centre-looped. Casual. Found 1980, circumstances unknown.
286	Itteringham (1)	Mixed. Casual. Hoard. Mid/late 2nd cent. AD. Associated finds comprise set 2 (below), key, ring, finger-rings, and 104 coins.
287	Itteringham (2)	Centre-looped. Casual. Hoard. Mid/late 2nd cent. AD. As 286 (above).
319	London	Mixed. Excavated. Town house near baths. AD 100–120. Associated objects (corroded together) were tweezers and nail-cleaner.
436	St Albans	End-looped. Excavated. Burial. AD 40–60. From cremation (adult, possibly male), in pottery flagon. Unlike associated iron toilet set, cosmetic set not burnt.
437	St Albans	Mixed. Excavated. Burial. Late 1st/early 2nd cent. AD. Adjacent to urned cremation (age and sex indeterminate but probably female), unburnt, with glass flask, apparently within a bronze-studded wooden casket.
438/439	St Albans	Mixed. Excavated. Town, Insula II. Early to mid-2nd cent. AD. Two components from same levelling context beneath tile hearth, preceding construction of Building II, 1. Probable original association with relatively large assemblage of small personal items – ?disturbed burial? Combination very similar to London set (319).
501	Thérouanne	Centre-looped. Excavated. Burial. Late 2nd/early 3rd cent. AD. Adjacent to urned cremation in pit, together with two pottery flagons and patera, glass bottle and flagon. Cremated bone not yet examined.
514	Walton-le-Dale	End-looped. Excavated. Probable military supply depot/industrial site. Unstratified (backfill of 1950s excavation). Site *floruit* early 2nd to mid–3rd cent. AD.
517	Wanborough	End-looped. Excavated (watching brief). Burial. Probably later 2nd/early 3rd cent. AD. From area of disturbed Roman cemetery.

Table 14. Summary context of excavated finds (excluding sets)

Cat. no.	Provenance	Summary context
5	Amersham	Roman settlement
16	Baldock	Roman 'small town'; building enclosure ditch. *c.* AD 180–220
23	Beck Row	LIA to Roman rural site
24	Beddington	Roman villa; rubble layer. Late 2nd – late 3rd cent. AD
38	Brampton	Roman 'small town'; bath house; disturbed level
48	Brecon	Roman fort; extra-mural area
49	Brecon	Roman fort (*floruit c.* AD 70–120)
50	Brenley Corner	Roman roadside settlement on Watling Street; possible shrine; range of votives; coins 2nd – late 4th cent. AD
63	Caerleon	Roman fortress; extra-mural settlement
65	Caistor St Edmond	Roman town; Building 4, Kiln 3
66	Cambridge	Roman 'small town'
76	Canterbury	Roman town; occupation on road-side metalling. *c.* AD 50–130
79	Carlisle	Roman 'small town'. Probably 4th cent. AD
80	Castleford	Roman fort; gravel/ midden. AD 70–86
89	Chessell Down	Early Anglo-Saxon cemetery, 5th–6th cent. AD; residual
90	Chester	Roman fortress; extra-mural settlement, strip buildings. Mid 2nd–3rd cent. AD
91	Chester	Roman fortress; extra-mural cemetery area, ditch fill. 3rd cent. AD
93	Chichester	Roman town; probably residual in timber foundation slot. Late 3rd-late 4th cent. AD
94	Chichester	Roman town
95	Chichester	Roman town. Flavian–late 1st cent. AD

Table 14 cont. Summary context of excavated finds (excluding sets)

Cat. no.	Provenance	Summary context
102–3	Cirencester	Roman villa (Barton Farm)
113	Colchester	Roman town; extra-mural cemetery (Butt Rd). 2nd–mid-5th cent.AD
115	Colchester	Iron Age and Roman industrial settlement (Sheepen). Probably 1st cent.BC–1st cent.AD
118	Colchester	Roman town; extra-mural area (Balkerne Lane), street, houses, temples, defences; pit. c.AD 100/125–250
131	Coleshill	Romano-Celtic temple and settlement; temple demolition layer. 4th cent. AD
132	Coleshill	Romano-Celtic temple and settlement
148	Doncaster	Roman fort; extra-mural settlement
155	Dragonby	Iron Age and Roman nucleated settlement; lower topsoil, south of R-B building 6
191	Fishbourne	Roman villa complex
203	Gosbecks	Romano-Celtic temple precinct; theatre, *cavea* mound. AD 150–250
208–9	Great Chesterford	Roman 'small town'
226	Gussage All Saints	Iron Age enclosed settlement; pit. 1st cent. BC–1st cent. AD
227–9	Hacheston	Roman 'small town'; unstratified
231	Ham Hill	Iron Age and Roman settlement
234	Harlow	Agricultural settlement; ditch fill. Late 3rd – 4th cent. AD, possibly residual
246–8, 252	Heybridge	Roman 'small town'/ temple complex; undated contexts
249	Heybridge	Roman 'small town'/ temple complex; prepared surface. Early to mid–2nd cent. AD
250	Heybridge	Roman 'small town'/ temple complex; make-up layer. Later 1st to mid-3rd cent. AD
251	Heybridge	Roman 'small town'/ temple complex; well. Later 2nd to mid-4th cent. AD
268	Hod Hill	Roman fort; timber building foundation trench. c AD 45–55, but probably residual
273	Horton Kirby	Anglo-Saxon cemetery; female grave, bag collection. Early 6th cent. AD
295	Kingsholm	Roman town; extra-mural settlement; general layer. 2nd–4th cent. AD
301	Lakenheath	Roman rural settlement; well, upper layer. 4th cent.AD
305	Leicester	Roman town; forum
308	Lincoln	Roman town; west gate, earliest rampart level. Late 2nd or early 3rd cent. AD
318	London	Roman town, Southwark; domestic occupation; open area, boundary ditch, upper fill. 3rd cent. AD
320	London	Roman town, west margin of Walbrook; domestic occupation; roadside drain. AD 65–95
321	London	Roman town, west margin of Walbrook; domestic occupation; open area. 4th cent. AD, residual
322	London	Roman town, Southwark; domestic occupation; alley surface. AD 120–160
323	London	Roman town, Southwark; domestic occupation; open area, dump – pre-house channel fill. AD 70–100. Apparently fused to an iron slide key (loop to loop)
325	London	Roman town, east; domestic occupation; building. AD 100–140
327a	London	Roman town, Southwark; domestic occupation; building, dump. 3rd cent. AD
328	London	Roman town, west; domestic occupation. Probably late 2nd/ 3rd cent. AD
328a	London	Roman town, east; domestic occupation; open area, dump. AD 100–150
332	Lydney	Roman temple complex and ironworking site
335	Magiovinium	Roman 'small town'; extra-mural settlement and cemeteries, ditch. Early 2nd cent. AD
391	Normanton-le-Heath	Late Iron Age and early Roman small agricultural settlement. Pre-conquest context, possibly no later than mid-1st cent. BC
399	Oakley	Roman 'small town' (Scole)
400	Ogof-yr-Esgyrn	Roman graves and occupation in cave system. Probably 2nd cent. AD
414	Repton	Early medieval ecclesiastical site; residual find in a Saxon or later feature
415–6	Richborough	Roman fort
417, 419	Richborough	Roman fort. c. AD 280–400+
418	Richborough	Roman fort; pit. 2nd cent. AD
444	Saintes	Roman burial; female inhumation in stone sarcophagus. c. AD 40–50. Other grave goods include mirror, perfume bottles, 'stirring rod', toilet articles
472	Springhead	Roman religious centre. *Floruit* 100 BC–AD 300
473	Springhead	Roman religious centre; pit. Mid-late 2nd cent. AD
476	Stevenage	Roman farmstead
477	Stevenage	Roman small agricultural settlement.*Floruit* 1st-2nd cent. AD
480	Stonea	Roman settlement
484	Stonea	Roman rural settlement. 2nd–3rd cent. AD
505	Thetford	Late Iron Age and Roman multiple ditched enclosure (?shrine)
506	Thistleton	Roman 'small town' and temple complex; within building, just outside temple precinct in area of ovens and infant burials
515	Walton-le-Dale	Roman military depot/industrial site; abandonment horizon. Early to mid-3rd cent. AD
516	Walton-le-Dale	Roman military depot/industrial site. Site *floruit* early 2nd to mid-3rd cent. AD
535	nr. Whitchurch	Roman domestic and industrial settlement. 1st–3rd cent. AD
536	Whitton	Late Iron Age and Roman farmstead
537	Wickford	Iron Age and Roman farmstead
550	Wilderspool	Roman military industrial site; beneath hearth, 'in the vicinity of the bronze-founder's and enameller's workshop'

Table 15. Summary actual or potential broad context of casual finds

Cat. no.	Provenance	Summary context
27	Billingford	Roman 'small town'
30	Boughton Monchelsea	Region of Roman bath house
31	Bourne	Roman 'small town'
32	Bower Chalke	Roman settlement
34–37	Brampton	Roman 'small town'
51	Brettenham	Roman 'small town'
53	Brigstock	Romano-Celtic temple complex
58	Burgh Castle	Roman fort; extra-mural
64	Caister-on-Sea	Roman fort. 3rd-4th cent. AD
81–2	Catterick	Roman 'small town'
106–7	Coddenham	Roman 'small town'
109, 117, 119, 126	Colchester	Roman town; cemetery area, outside Balkerne Gate
110–12, 114, 116, 120–5, 127–8	Colchester	Roman town (/fortress)
134	Congham	Roman villa area
146	Ditchingham	Roman 'small town'
174	Elm	Burial; 'on the arm of a skeleton'
185	Felixstowe	Roman 'small town'
188–90	Fincham	Roman 'small town'
213–20	Gt. Walsingham	Roman 'small town' and temple site
258	Hitcham	Roman rural settlement
261–7	Hockwold	Roman 'small town' and temple site
275	Hunsbury	Iron Age hillfort
278–9	Icklingham	Roman 'small town'
292	Keston	Roman villa area
300	Kirkby Thore	Roman fort and extra-mural settlement
317	Little Houghton	Iron Age and Roman settlement complex
324, 326–7	London	Roman town
330	Long Melford	Roman 'small town'
334, 336	Magiovinium	Roman 'small town'
341	Meols	Roman settlement
354	Newport	Roman burials. Late 1st-late 3rd cent. AD
420	Richborough	Roman fort
427	Rushall Down	Large Roman village
429–35	Saham Toney	Roman 'small town' and fort
440	St Albans	Roman town; ?Ins. XXIV; ?cremation burial
441	St Albans	Roman town
449–50	Scole	Roman 'small town'
462–3	Silchester	Roman town
465	Sleaford	Roman 'small town'
469	South Ferriby	Roman site
479, 482–3	Stonea	Iron Age and Roman settlement
522–9	Wenhaston	Roman 'small town'
540–9	Wicklewood	Roman 'small town' and Romano-Celtic temple site (Crownthorpe)
558	Wixoe	Roman 'small town'
560	Woodeaton	Iron Age and Romano-Celtic temple site
562–4	Wroxeter	Roman town and military site
565	Wylye Camp	Iron Age hillfort (Bilbury Rings)

Table 16. Context categories: excavated finds, Level 1 (sets in bold)

Town	**73, 92, 100/101, Colchester (Garrison), 319, 436, 437, 438/439, 501,** 65, 76, 93, 94, 95, 113, 115, 118, 295, 305, 308, 318, 320, 321, 322, 323, 325, 327a, 328, 328a, 570
'Small town'	**517,** 16, 38, 66, 79, 208, 209, 227, 228, 229, 246, 247, 248, 249, 250, 251, 252, 335, 399, 472, 473, 480, 506
Village/ rural settlement	**154, 187,** 5, 23, 50, 155, 234, 301, 477, 484, 505, 535
Villa/ farmstead/ cave	**192,** 24, 102, 103, 191, 400, 476, 536, 537
Military site (fortress, fort, canabae, vicus, military depot)	**62, 514,** 48, 49, 63, 80, 90, 91, 148, 268, 415, 416, 417, 418, 419, 515, 516, 550
Iron Age settlement/ hillfort	**22,** 226, 231, 391 (plus 268?)
Post-Roman site	89, 273, 414

Table 17. Context categories: excavated finds, Level 2 (sets in bold)

Burial/ cemetery	**22, 92, Colchester (Garrison), 436, 437, 501, 517,** 91, 113, 273, 400, 444
Temple/ shrine/ religious site	**73,** 50, 131, 132, 203, 332, 472, 473, 505, 506
Bath house	38

Table 18. Context categories: casual finds, Level 1 (sets in bold)

Town	**74,** 109, 110, 111, 112, 114, 116, 117, 119, 120, 121, 122, 123, 124, 125, 126, 127, 128, 324, 326, 327, 440, 441, 462, 463, 562, 563, 564
'Small town'	**260,** 27, 31, 34, 35, 36, 37, 51, 81, 82, 106, 107, 146, 185, 188, 189, 190, 213, 214, 215, 216, 217, 218, 219, 220, 261, 262, 263, 264, 265, 266, 267, 278, 279, 330, 334, 336, 429, 430, 431, 432, 433, 434, 435, 449, 450, 465, 479, 482, 483 522, 523, 524, 525, 526, 527, 528, 529, 540, 541, 542, 543, 544, 545, 546, 547, 548, 549, 558
Village/ rural settlement	32, 258, 317, 341, 427, 469
Villa	134, 292
Military site (fort, vicus)	58, 64, 300, 420
Iron Age settlement/ hillfort	275, 565

Table 19. Context categories: casual finds, Level 2 (sets in bold)

Burial/ cemetery	**Bures St Mary,** 109, 117, 119, 126 (and probably more), 174, 354, 440?
Temple/ shrine/ religious site	53, 540, 542, 543, 544, 546, 547, 548, 549, 560, (and probably all or some of 213, 214, 215, 216, 217, 218, 219, 220 as also **260,** 261, 262, 263, 264, 265, 266, 267)
Bath house	30

Table 20. Cosmetic grinders in context

Context, level 1	Excavated, sets		Excavated, all		Casual finds	
	no.	%	no.	%	no.	%
Town	9	56	29	31	28	25
'Small town'	1	6	23	24	69	62
Village/ rural settlement	2	13	12	13	6	5
Villa/ farmstead	1	6	9	9	2	2
Military site	2	13	18	19	4	4
I A settlement/ hillfort	1	6	4	4	2	2
TOTALS	16	100	95	100	111	100
Context, level 2						
Burial/ cemetery	7	44	12	13	8	8
Temple/ shrine	1	6	10	11	10 (28)	9 (25)

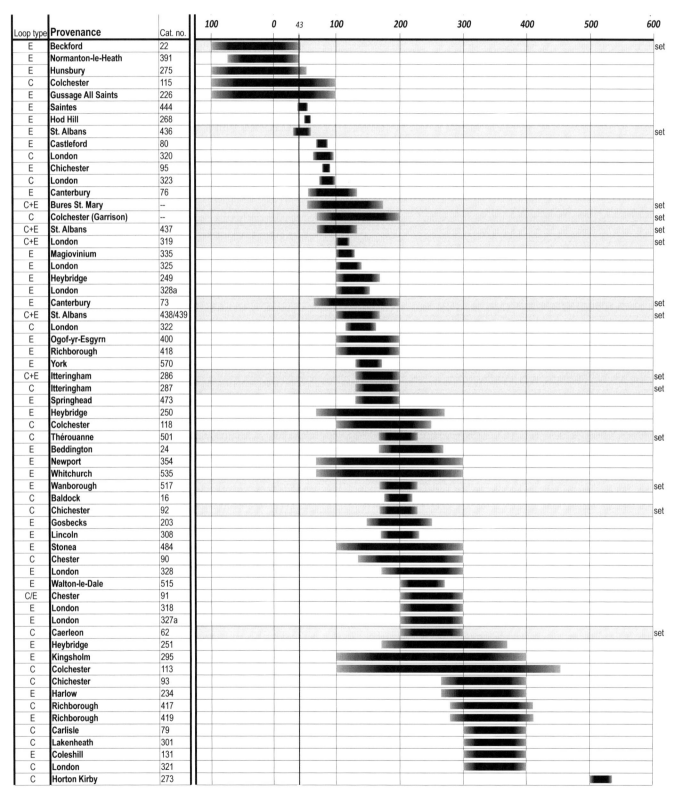

Figure 25 Cosmetic grinders from dated contexts (n = 61, including 14 sets)

7. Dating and Summary

Dating

Cosmetic sets are an entirely British phenomenon, an insular type with its origin in the pre-Roman Iron Age: 625 components are catalogued here; 178 were recorded by the Portable Antiquities Scheme up to 2007; the current overall total is likely to be in the region of one thousand; but just five finds have been recorded outside Britain, two immediately across the English Channel in the Pas-de-Calais, one in Saône-et-Loire, one in Puy-de-Dôme and one in Charente-Maritime (Cat. nos 501 and 444 and Guillaumet and Eugène 2009, 241–3). Some cosmetic sets display overtly Celtic-style decoration and several have been found in contexts showing that they were already in use at the time of the Roman conquest of Britain. Nevertheless, secure and precisely-dated pre-Roman Iron Age contexts have been vexingly elusive for an artefact type that is seldom intrinsically datable.

Of the 104 catalogued components or complete sets from excavations just 61 (including 14 sets) were found in dated contexts. These have been graphically illustrated in **Figure 25**. Using the 14 sets as an index of currency it can be seen that the likely minimum period of usage of cosmetic sets as small grinding kits extends from the Late Iron Age to the later 3rd century AD: one set has a Late Iron Age context (Beckford, 22), one is conquest-period (St Albans, King Harry Lane, 436), eight date to the later 1st or 2nd century AD (Bures St Mary, uncat., Colchester, uncat., St Albans, 437, London, 319, Canterbury, 73, St Albans, 438/ 439, Itteringham, 286–7), three to the late 2nd or early 3rd century (Thérouanne, 501, Chichester, 92, Wanborough, 517) and just one was found in a context which certainly post-dates the end of the 2nd century AD (Caerleon, 62). Taking the end first, the latter date is provided by the context of the set from Caerleon (62), which is dated by a single coin of Victorinus (AD 269–71). Even if the dating is accurate (a nearby hoard of 51 coins also ending with an issue of Victorinus suggests it is) the context is one of demolition or abandonment which might be taken rather to imply disuse than usage of the cosmetic set. In fact, the evidence of individual components tends to support the possibility of a reduction in usage of cosmetic sets starting, perhaps, as early as the late 3rd century, for several of the 3rd and 4th century contexts indicate or imply residuality (93, 234, 321) (though residuality is notoriously difficult to assess) or are connected to phases of abandonment, demolition or dumping (131, 327a, 515).

At all events, excepting the Caerleon find, the latest contexts for complete sets are the sepulchral finds from Thérouanne (501), Chichester (92) and Wanborough (517), all of which are late 2nd/ early 3rd century AD, and the majority of dated sets and individual components combine to suggest a heyday for the type of later 1st to early 3rd century AD. That relative intensity of use is fairly clearly demonstrated (33 of the dated contexts) and differs markedly from the results of Eckardt and Crummy's (larger) sample of toilet implements from dated contexts, which register strongly in the 4th century (Eckardt and Crummy 2008, 62). However, we should be cautious over the interpretation (from a modest-sized sample) of the negative evidence for the later 3rd and 4th centuries, not least on account of those cosmetic mortars with ring-and-dot decoration (53, 301, 393, 483, 597), indicative, though not diagnostic, of a late Roman date, and of the presence of components at Saxon Shore forts which flourished at that time (58, 64, 415–20). A single find could change the picture, for it is possible that the kits were still in use and that we simply lack the proof. Alternatively, it is conceivable that the mortar and pestle components found in later Roman contexts at Shore Fort and other sites were no longer in use as kits but as individual objects fulfilling amuletic, religious, symbolic or decorative roles. Certainly, the combination of suspension loop, compact size and visual attraction made cosmetic mortars and pestles especially suitable for re-use, as underlined by finds from two early Anglo-Saxon cemeteries: the centre-looped mortar in a 'bag collection' with a female burial of the early 6th century AD at Horton Kirby (273); and the end-looped mortar from the 5th – 6th century AD cemetery at Chessell Down (89). The implication is that in whatever way cosmetic grinders were functioning in the later 3rd and 4th centuries sufficient were still in circulation in some places at the end of the Roman period to enable acquisition by early Anglo-Saxon people.

Returning to origins, there are eight significant finds (two sets and six single components): Beckford (22), Normanton-le-Heath (391), Hunsbury (275), Colchester (115), Gussage All Saints (226), Saintes (444), Hod Hill (268) and St Albans (436). The set from Beckford was found with a Late Iron Age inhumation (Wills and Dinn forthcoming); the pestle from Normanton-le-Heath came from an Iron Age and Romano-British enclosure system in a Late Iron Age context that may be no later than the mid-1st century BC (Thorpe, Sharman and Clay 1994, 48–9; Hill 1997, 105); the Hunsbury mortar was brought to light as a result of 19th century iron-stone quarrying, part of a large collection spanning the whole of the La Tène Iron Age with virtually no Roman material (Fell 1936) –and its copper-rich composition, comparable to the sets from Beckford and King Harry Lane (**Table 10** and Cat. nos 22, 275), is also indicative of a pre-conquest date; the Colchester mortar came from the industrial settlement at Sheepen, in the Region 3 sand-pit, from which the finds are mostly of 1st century BC–1st century AD date (Hawkes and Hull 1947, 33); the same date bracket applies to the pestle found in a pit at the Iron Age enclosed settlement at Gussage All Saints (Wainwright 1979, 111–13); the tiny pestle from Saintes was part of a large group of grave-goods with a rich female inhumation in a stone sarcophagus dated c. AD 40–50; more significantly, the mortar from Arras is reported as coming from an Augusto-Tiberian context (Guillaumet and Eugène 2009, 242–3, fig. 2); the pestle from Hod Hill was already worn at the tip when it was deposited in the foundation trench of a building in the Roman fort some time between AD 45–55 (Richmond 1968, 113); and the set from St Albans in Grave 203 in the King Harry Lane Late Iron Age and Roman cemetery was part of a grave group with a cremation assigned to site Phase 3 and dated AD 40–60 by the excavators (Stead and Rigby 1989, 84, 96, 104, 324, 326) but re-dated by Mackreth to AD 35–55 on the strength of the brooch (see, e.g., Mackreth 1994, 50 and Mackreth 2009a, 134). Whichever chronology is accepted for the deposition of the cremation in King Harry Lane Grave 203 it is virtually certain that the manufacture and initial use of the cosmetic set preceded the Roman conquest, as indicated, too, by the distinctive looped hanger for the associated iron toilet set which is closely-paralleled by an Augustan type in the Moselle region (Miron 1989, 51, Typ E, Abb. 7. Eckardt and Crummy 2008, 20). Similarly, the Hod Hill pestle is best interpreted as a residual object, part of a (used) pre-conquest set belonging with the assemblage from the Iron Age hillfort, and, if the object from Saintes is indeed a tiny cosmetic pestle it, too, is likely to have been of British pre-conquest manufacture.

These finds from early contexts are strikingly widespread throughout the zone to the south and east of the Severn – Trent line or, seen in terms of Late Iron Age tribal areas, in the territories of the Dobunni, Durotriges, Corieltavi, Catuvellauni and Trinovantes, though at present, none is from the region of the Iceni, the area of greatest concentration of cosmetic grinders. Noticeable, too, is the concentration of end-looped sets and components at the start of the series – seven of the eight examples. Thus, while there is currently no clear evidence for an area of origin of the type more specific than southern Britain it seems likely that the genesis of cosmetic sets was in the end-looped variety, the use of which spread quite widely and rapidly and was soon followed by centre-looped examples that proliferated in the east, especially in the territory of the Iceni and Trinovantes, the focus, also, for the majority of the most elaborate and ornate examples. The context dates of complete sets of end-looped type span much of the perceived whole period of use of cosmetic sets – Late Iron Age (22), probable pre-conquest (436), late 1st/ 2nd century (76) and late 2nd/ early 3rd century (517); those of centre-looped type begin and end a little later – late 1st to 2nd century (Colchester (Garrison)), mid- to late 2nd century (287), late 2nd/ early 3rd century (92, 501) and late 3rd century (62); while the mixed sets (end-looped pestle with centre-looped mortar) are tightly clustered in the main *floruit* – late 1st to 2nd century (Bures St Mary and 437, 319, 438/439 and 286). The mixed sets are not only chronologically and spatially restricted – late 1st to 2nd century in Norfolk, Suffolk, St Albans and London – but three are of near-identical form combining a Type C mortar with an equally distinctive pestle (Bures St Mary, London (319) and St Albans (438/439), and present indications are that they are the product of a single craftsman or regional workshop.

Perhaps significantly, too, the three earliest dated contexts (1st century AD or earlier) for the centre-looped type – Colchester, Sheepen (115), London, No. 1 Poultry (320) and London, Borough High Street, Southwark (323), are all for centre-looped mortars of closely similar form. The No. 1 Poultry example is classed as a Type L mortar for which there is

just one other dated context, the find from the Butt Road cemetery in Colchester (113), which is no more specific than 2nd to mid-5th century. For Type D mortars only the variant from Chester (90) provides a dated context – mid-2nd to 3rd century, while Type A has two dated contexts in London – c.AD 100 – 140 for mortar 325 and c.AD 200 – 300 for the lead archetype 318. More informative are the three dates for Type C mortars – late 1st to 2nd century for the Bures St Mary find; c.AD 100 – 120 for the London, Blossom's Inn set (319); and early to mid-2nd century for the St Albans Insula II set (438/439) – giving a likely range for the type of late 1st to early 2nd century AD. With just four dated examples the Type J zoomorphic enamelled mortars nevertheless provide the best contextual dating evidence – c.AD 120 – 160 for the broken mortar from London, Borough High Street, Southwark (322); late 2nd century for the variant in the set at Thérouanne (501); c.AD 180 – 220 for the variant from Baldock (16); and late 2nd century/ early 3rd century for the set from Chichester (92) – indicating a probable date range for the type of 2nd to early 3rd century AD.

Finally, an opportunity to consider the particular circumstances of a single find is provided by the secure and unusually closely-dated military context of the end-looped mortar from Castleford (80), found within the first fort in a gravel/ midden spread of c. AD 71/4 to c. 86. This was a period of active campaigning in the conquest of northern Britain, spanning the governorships of Petilius Cerealis, Julius Frontinus and Julius Agricola. The principal garrison at Castleford at this time is thought to have been the Fourth Cohort of Gauls, a quingenary auxiliary unit largely comprised of infantry but with a contingent of cavalry (Holder 1982, 117; Jarrett 1994, 60, 75). It is believed that the unit was probably quite recently-arrived in the province (Cool and Philo 1998, 356) which prompts the question how did the cosmetic mortar find its way into the fort? There is little evidence for metalworking in Fort 1 (in contrast to the manufacture debris of enamelled vessels in Fort 2), so it is unlikely that the mortar was made on site. If we presume that it formed part of a set then the user, logically, should either have been a soldier of *cohors IIII Gallorum equitata* or a woman associated with the garrison. However, Cool found nothing in the material remains from Fort 1 to indicate the presence of women in the fort (Cool and Philo 1998, 357), so if not an acquisition in Britain by a serving soldier of the cohort perhaps the most likely explanation is that the cosmetic set was part of the belongings of a British man who had been recruited into the unit. If Mackreth is correct in his extrapolations from the demise of the essentially Icenian Rearhook brooch-type and the distribution of its hinged-pin derivative, the Castleford cosmetic set may even have arrived in the fort with a drafted contingent of Icenian men as part of the 're-structuring' which followed the suppression of the Boudican revolt (Mackreth 2009b). For, at least seven of the derivatives (late Fantails) together with an inscribed and enamelled Knee brooch (which names a *regio*), come from or near Castleford, prompting him to propose continuity of the Icenian brooch-making trade and a transfer to the Castleford region – 'a kind of enforced diaspora' – of skilled metalworkers from amongst the disaffected Iceni (*Ibid* 146–7). The particular combination of well-contexted and closely-dated material remains at Castleford – cosmetic mortar, Icenian brooch type and enamel-working debris (see p. 25) –

permit the creation of a fascinating scenario, though one not yet capable of full resolution. Appropriately, therefore, the Castleford mortar and its context demonstrate both how little we still know of the use of the objects termed cosmetic sets and how great the potential is for a progressively fuller understanding of the type.

Summary

Copper-alloy cosmetic sets are a distinctively British type which, like nail-cleaners, appear to reflect a particularly British social practice, as also, perhaps, regional and local identities (Eckardt and Crummy 2008, 118). They were made as two-piece crescent-shaped kits comprising a grooved mortar and a solid rod-like pestle with a suspension loop at the end or centre. Far from being the rare and exotic amulets once thought, it is now clear that they were widely-used Romano-British toilet implements that had their origin, and what seems to have been a more restricted use, in the British Late Iron Age. Some 600 are catalogued here and their distribution is almost exclusively within Britain. As well as East/ West trends there are concentrations at the south-east towns and in the 'small towns' of Norfolk and Suffolk. Most have been found as individual components by metal-detectorists, but over 100 come from archaeological excavations, which have also yielded 16 complete sets.

Traces of wear are often found on the working face of both components, and there is strong circumstantial evidence that they were kits used for the preparation and application of powdered mineral cosmetics, most likely colourings for the eyelids and face. There is great variety in size, form and decoration, and the mortars are often elaborated, especially at the terminals: animal heads, principally bovids, were a favoured motif in Eastern Britain but moulded knobs or plain terminals were more common and widespread. A frequent device was to model the loop of end-looped components into the form of a bird's head. An association with fertility is indicated by the crescent shape, by a few overtly phallic mortars and by the occasional twinning of male and female animal heads.

Most cosmetic grinders were cast bronzes but no two are identical because much of the decoration was applied at the finishing stage. This individuality was probably a consequence of the personal nature of cosmetic sets – they were especially intimate possessions which could be customized through the choice of décor and design. In view of the fact that they co-existed in Roman Britain with the more universal Roman paraphernalia of cosmetic preparation – stone palettes, bronze or bone scoops and spatulas, and metal, glass and ceramic *unguentaria* – it is possible that they were used by those who wished to express or emphasize a British or Romano-British rather than a Roman identity. Not surprisingly, therefore, cosmetic sets were also selected as grave-goods and appear to have been among the classes of object sometimes dedicated at temples.

Dated contexts range from the 1st century BC to the 4th century AD, with re-use of some components in Anglo-Saxon 'bag collections' of the 5th–6th century AD, but the majority of finds indicate a heyday in the 1st to 3rd century AD with a particular intensity of use in the late 1st to 2nd century AD.

8. Catalogue

Catalogue entries: format

Number. Provenance, County.
Length mm. Weight g.

Loop type, mortar/ pestle, sub-type, patina and condition. Description.

Circumstances of discovery.
Context date.
Published references.

Present location.

1. Alderford, Norfolk
L. 66 mm. Wt. 21.3 g.

Centre-looped mortar, with strongly-curved bow, low, plain, convex walls and bulbous knobbed terminals. The broken loop assembly, mounted on a low keel, probably comprised a strutted ring surmounting a triangular aperture.

Metal detector find. In private hands.

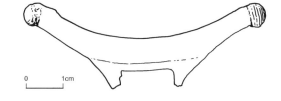

2. Alderford, Norfolk (Unillustrated)
L. *c.* 24 mm. Wt. 6.5 g.

?Centre-looped mortar fragment, comprising one end of the bow with coiled terminal knob.

Metal detector find. In private hands.

3. Alderton, Suffolk
L. 57.5 mm.

Centre-looped mortar, very abraded, with lightly-curved bow, plain, steeply-sloping walls, worn-down rims and U-sectioned groove. The terminals are in the form of a stylized head, probably a bird head. They are similar but not identical. Only the stub of the loop survives.

Metal detector find. In private hands.

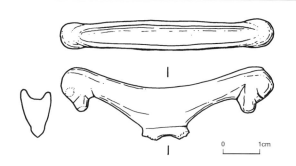

4. Aldworth, Berks
L. 73 mm. Wt. 44.5 g.

Centre-looped mortar, with olive green and mid-green patina. A heavy casting, quite heavily worn which has erased some details of the incuse decoration. The crescentic bow has convex walls with inturned rim. Traces of a lightly incised line below the rim are preserved at each end of the bow, more clearly at the smaller terminal. On the walls adjacent to the larger terminal is an arrangement of punched dots, progressively more worn towards the centre of the bow. The broad U-sectioned groove is capacious, with a broad basal wear facet. It runs over both terminals. The larger terminal is in the form of a bull's head, with inturned horns (the tip of one broken), a long blunt-ended muzzle, and a dewlap formed by extending the underside of the bow. The eyes are rendered with a punched circle and a further three circles occupy the flat space between brow and muzzle tip. The smaller terminal appears to be an unhorned bovid (?cow) or a dog. The short muzzle is tapered, lightly hollowed and ridged, with a rounded end. The ears are low and the eyes are rendered with a small

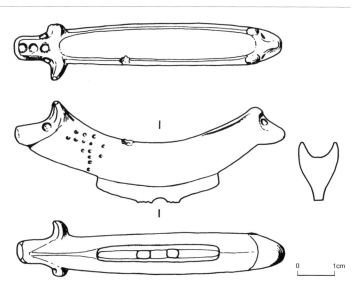

punched circle. There is no dewlap. The centre-loop was mounted on a low keeled plate. It is broken across the circular eye but was probably of plain discoidal form.

Metal detector find. Formerly in private hands, via the antiquity market.

British Museum, 1999,0802.1

5. Amersham, Bucks
L. *c.* 41 mm.

End-looped mortar, fragmentary, lacking the terminal and much of the bow. The remaining part of the bow shows little curvature and has apparently plain walls and a narrow groove. The ring-like loop has a sub-circular eye.

From archaeological investigations, 1983–9, of Roman site at Mantles Green (I, U/S. SF 1197).

Records of Buckinghamshire 34, 1992, 160, fig. 29, no. 10.

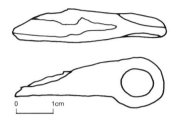

6. Ashby Folville, Leics
L. *c.* 70 mm.

End-looped mortar, with crescentic bow, apparently plain convex walls, knobbed terminal and rounded V-sectioned groove. The elaborate loop is based on a tendril and volute motif, giving the impression of a highly stylized bird's head, with the tip of the dished everted bill scrolled back onto the prominent crown.

Metal detector find. In private hands.

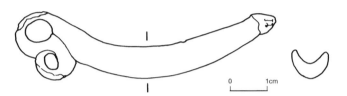

7. Ashill, Norfolk
L. 52.5 mm. (orig. *c.* 60 mm.) Wt. 5.6 g.

Centre-looped pestle, with mid-grey-green patina, the surface denuded in places. A large well-made example. The rod, with rounded keel, is broken at both ends. The large collar-like D-shaped loop is also broken across its circular eye.

Metal detector find. In private hands.

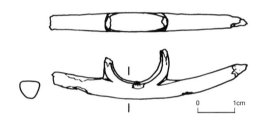

8. Ashill, Norfolk
L. 31 mm.

Centre-looped pestle. A very small example, with short, stout, circular-sectioned rod, one tip seemingly broken. The D-shaped loop has a circular eye.

Metal detector find. In private hands.

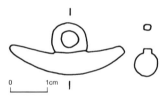

9. Ashwell, Herts
L. 51.5 mm. Wt. 10.6 g.

End-looped mortar, with green-grey patina. A small example, with crescentic bow, angular keel, plain steeply-convex walls, a globular knobbed terminal with neat neck-moulding, and a shallow U-sectioned groove, with wear polish on base and sides, that runs over the loop. The loop is in the form of a neatly-rendered stylized bird's head, with dished bill and circular eye.

Metal detector find. In private hands.

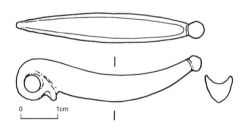

10. Ashwell, Herts
L. 55.7 mm. Wt. 7.8 g.

End-looped pestle, with lightly-pitted orange-brown (ferrous) patina. An elegant, well-finished example. The elliptical circular-sectioned rod swells towards the up-turned tip, which has a marked wear-facet on its underside. The slender loop, in the form of a stylized bird's head with prominent brow and everted bill, has a large tear-shaped eye.

Metal detector find. In private hands.

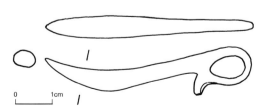

11. nr. Ashwell, Herts
L. 75 mm.

End-looped mortar, with dark brown-black patina, lacking only the terminal. A well-finished example with an elliptical bow, angled keel, steeply-sloping, lightly-convex, plain walls, and a shallow U-sectioned groove. The projecting terminal is broken, and its original form cannot be predicted. The proportionately large slender loop is in the form of a highly-stylized bird's head, with a large tear-shaped eye and a neatly-wrought, prominent, everted bill.

Metal detector find. In private hands.

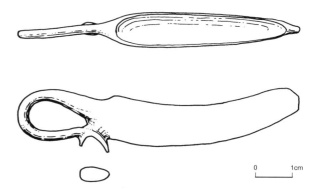

12. Ashwicken, Norfolk
L. 75 mm.

End-looped pestle, with dull metallic brown patina (cleaned). A long example, with tapered, crescentic, lentoid-sectioned rod demarcated from the oval-sectioned 'handle' by a simple ring moulding. There is a second ring moulding at the junction of the handle and loop. Wear polish is present in the circular eye and on the convex face of the rod. For the moulded bipartite form of the rod see no. 603, and for the 'latch-lifter' profile see nos 207 and 387.

Circumstances of discovery unknown.

Kings Lynn Museum, KL 1993.701.

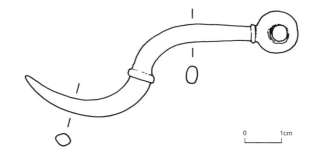

13. Attlebridge, Norfolk
L. 38.5 mm. Wt. 16.8 g.

Centre-looped mortar, with mid-green pitted patina. A small, very short, but heavy casting. The bow has deep plain convex walls with virtually straight rim. The deep U-sectioned groove has a high wear polish. Its asymmetric wear facet has encroached on the rim at either end. The terminals are plain. The plump D-shaped loop has a circular eye.

Metal detector find. In private hands.

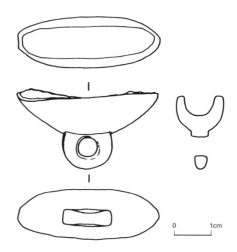

14. Badingham, Suffolk
L. 37 mm.

End-looped mortar, broken at both ends. The bow has low plain walls, a smoothly-rounded keel, and a shallow U-sectioned groove partly blocked with a ferrous soil concretion.

Metal detector find. In private hands.

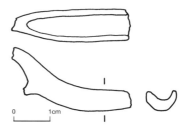

15. Badingham, Suffolk

L. *c.* 29 mm. (orig. *c.* 40 mm.)

Centre-looped pestle, with large ovoid suspension loop. The rod, of round cross-section, is broken at one end.

Metal detector find. In private hands.

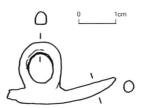

16. Baldock, Herts

L. 68 mm. Wt. 17.5 g.

Centre-looped mortar, Type J variant, with broad, thin-walled bow. Adjacent to the loop on both walls is a line of three sub-triangular cells, their apex pointing towards the loop. They are filled with coloured enamel, red flanked by light turquoise in both cases. The groove is deep and broad, its squared-off V-section the result of a basal wear facet. The terminals comprise two small bovid heads, with protuberant horns. One has a blunt-ended muzzle with slit mouth, the other has a small pointed muzzle with slightly gaping mouth. The collar-like D-shaped loop has a large heart-shaped eye.

From excavation, 1970, of Iron Age and Roman settlement. Area A1, western enclosure ditch of Building V.

Context date *c.* AD 180–220.

Jackson 1985, no. 73; I.M. Stead and V. Rigby, 1986, *Baldock* 136–8, fig. 60, no. 377.

Letchworth Museum

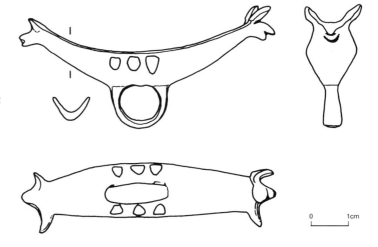

17. Barham, Suffolk

L. *c.* 62 mm.

Centre-looped mortar, of idiosyncratic form. The bow has near-vertical walls, with only gently curving rim. The carination of both walls and the angular keel are flanked by two rows of dot punched decoration which extends onto one of the terminals. The groove is quite deep and of narrow U-shaped cross-section. It is open at one end, where it passes through the square spout-like terminal. The other terminal is pointed and down-turned. The loop, a near circular ring, is very large.

Metal detector find. In private hands.

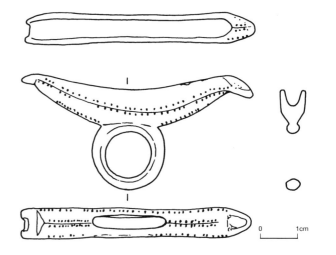

18. Barham, Suffolk

L. *c.* 31 mm.

Centre-looped pestle. A small example, with short stumpy arms, only slightly curved, and a high projecting loop plate, broken at the top across the tiny eye.

Metal detector find. In private hands.

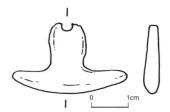

19. Barking, Suffolk
L. *c.* 47 mm, (orig. *c.* 67 mm.)

Centre-looped mortar, lacking one end of the bow. The near-vertical walls are plain, but the angular keel is decorated with a series of short cross-cuts. The groove is shallow, of broad U-shaped cross-section. The remaining terminal is knobbed, with an incuse rayed design. The loop is large, nearly circular, and of diamond-shaped cross-section.

Metal detector find. In private hands.

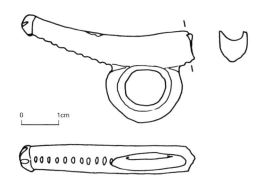

20. Bawburgh, Norfolk
L. 19.8 mm. Wt. 4 g.

Centre-looped pestle, with lightly-pitted and accreted olive-green patina. A fragment, comprising the central zone of the lightly-curved twin-tapered rod and the lower part of the elongated loop-plate, which is relatively narrow with bevelled edges.

Metal detector find. In private hands.

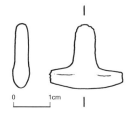

21. Baylham, Suffolk
L. *c.* 45 mm.

Centre-looped pestle. The circular-sectioned rod is thin, and one of the tapered arms is distorted. The loop, which surmounts a short pedestal, has a large circular eye.

Metal detector find. In private hands.

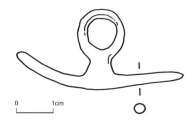

22. Beckford, Heref. and Worcs
L. mortar *c.* 72 mm. pestle *c.* 66 mm.

Set, comprising an end-looped mortar and an end-looped pestle. The mortar has a plain, thin-walled bow, with angular keel, capacious, broad V-sectioned groove and a knobbed terminal. The chunky loop, almost identical to that of the pestle, is in the form of a stylized aquatic bird's head, with prominent brow and everted bill. Both show signs of wear in the ovoid eye. The pestle has a very stout rod of pear-shaped cross-section, which clearly complements the profile of the groove in the mortar. Its reported 'silvered' finish is probably a surface tin-enrichment.

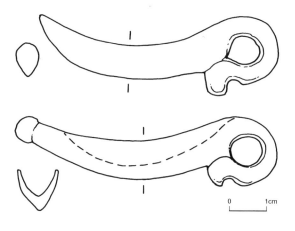

From a Late Iron Age burial, in excavations, 1975–9, of Iron Age settlements, by J. Wills. J.D. Hurst in J. Wills and J.L. Dinn (eds.), *Excavations at Beckford, Worcester, 1972–9*, CBA Research Report, forthcoming. The mortar was found close to the upper chest of an adult female skeleton which had been inhumed in a partially in-filled boundary ditch without a visible grave. The pestle was found just 15 cm apart in a disturbed layer above the inhumation. No other objects were found with the burial.

Metal analysis of the two components by Peter Northover (Northover in Wills and Dinn forthcoming) yielded the following results (in percent):
Mortar: 94.8 Cu; 4.39 Sn; tr.Zn; 0.04 Ni; 0.25 As; 0.43 Sb; 0.07 Ag; 0.02 Bi
Pestle: 84.9 Cu; 13.81 Sn; 0.12 Pb; 0.03 Zn; 0.59 Fe; 0.09 Ni; 0.21 As; 0.11 Sb; 0.08 Ag; 0.02 Bi.

23. Beck Row, Mildenhall, Suffolk

L. 91 mm.

Centre-looped mortar. The smooth, dark brown, slightly tin-
enriched surface is extensively overlain with sand-encrusted
corrosion products, but where they are absent, notably on
the keel, the original fine file-finishing marks are visible. The
long, slender elliptical bow has a flat keel, low, plain carinated
walls and knobbed terminals with neatly-cut mouldings.
Viewed from above the narrow, relatively shallow groove the
bow tapers from one end to the other, a size differential also
reflected in the terminal knobs. The loop is a small D-shaped
plate with a tiny unworn circular eye.

From archaeological excavation, 1999, of Late Iron Age to
Roman rural site, at Beck Row, Mildenhall, by Suffolk County
Council Archaeological Service.

Unstratified.

E. Bales, 2004, *A Roman maltings at Beck Row, Mildenhall,
Suffolk*, East Anglian Archaeology Occasional Paper no. 20, 30–1, fig. 21, 16.

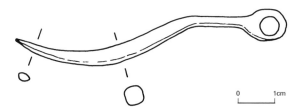

24. Beddington, Surrey

L. *c.* 71 mm.

End-looped pestle, with an atypically elongated neck. The crescentic,
tapered rod has an upturned faceted tip of lentoid cross-section. The
plate-like loop has a circular eye.

From excavations, 1981–7, of Roman villa site, by L. and R.A. Adkins.
Rubble layer, period 6, late 2nd–late 3rd cent. AD.

I. Howell (ed), 2005, *Prehistoric landscape to Roman villa. Excavations at
Beddington, Surrey 1981–7* (MoLAS Monograph 26), 94–5, fig. 76, M46.

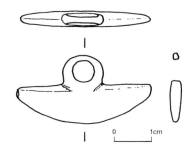

25. Beeston, Norfolk

L. 35.3 mm. Wt. 7.2 g.

Centre-looped pestle, with mixed green-grey patina, lacking most of
the original surface. A small light example, with deep, blunt-tipped,
unusually flat, twin-tapered rod, and a D-shaped ring with circular eye.

Metal detector find. In private hands.

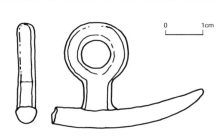

26. Besthorpe, Norfolk

L. 41 mm. (orig. *c.* 57 mm.) Wt. 10.9 g.

Centre-looped pestle, with flaking olive-grey patina, lightly encrusted
on one face with a pale brown ferrous deposit. One arm of the lightly
elliptical rod is broken, the other has a plump D-shaped cross-section and
a blunted tip. The loop, a large ring with a circular eye, surmounts a stout
pedestal-like stem. Both loop and pedestal have neatly chamfered angles.

Metal detector find. In private hands.

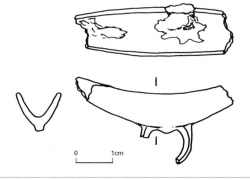

27. Billingford, Norfolk

L. 42 mm. Wt. 9.1 g.

Centre-looped mortar, Type I, with light green-grey patina. Both
terminals and part of the loop are lacking (all ancient fractures). The
bow has an angular keel, plain, thin, sloping walls and a capacious
groove of broad, deep, rounded V-shaped cross-section. The thin rims
are intact but both terminals are broken. The fragmentary loop is a
slender D-shaped ring with a large heart-shaped eye.

Metal detector find. In private hands.

28. Blakeney, Norfolk
Ht. 12 mm. Wt. 5.1 g.

Mortar fragment, with fine mid-green patina. Form uncertain, but more probably centre-looped than end-looped. Only one terminal and a short stretch of the adjacent bow survive. The bow has a marked keel, is relatively thin-walled, and has an asymmetric, rounded V-sectioned groove, which runs over the terminal. The terminal is a medium-sized, well-modelled bovid head. The ears are unusually clearly-rendered, the horns are small with rounded tips; the face is carefully wrought, though without any indication of eyes; and the tapered muzzle is slightly bulbous.

Metal detector find. In private hands.

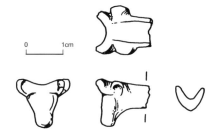

29. Blyth, Notts
L. 39.6 mm. Wt. 9.8 g.

Centre-looped pestle, with a mid-green patina, though lacking most of the original surface. A small, heavy boat-shaped example with V-sectioned rod and an ornate suspension loop with scrolled ends and a small arched eye.

Metal detector find. In private hands, via the antiquity market, through which it acquired the spurious provenance of Owmby, Lincs.

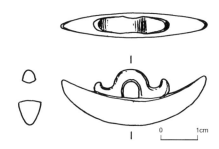

30. Boughton Monchelsea, Kent
L. 71 mm.

Centre-looped mortar, Type L variant. The deep sloping bow walls are decorated with an incuse triple chevron motif, slightly irregularly applied. The capacious groove has a rounded V-shaped cross-section and signs of a longitudinal wear facet. The terminals are knobbed, and the plate-like D-shaped loop has a circular eye.

Metal detector find in the area of the Roman bath-house at Brishing.

Archaeologia Cantiana 105, 1988, 305–7. fig. 6,3.

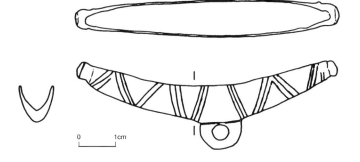

31. Bourne, Lincs
L. 40 mm (orig. *c.* 42 mm.) Wt. 5.4 g.

End-looped pestle, with mid-green smooth patina. The maximum and marked swelling of the circular-sectioned rod is set a little beyond the midpoint towards the fragmentary tip. The circular loop, set above the end of the rod, would originally have been larger: corrosion has removed the original surface.

Metal detector find. In private hands, via the antiquity market.

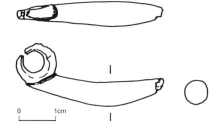

32. Bower Chalke, Wilts
L. *c.* 73 mm. (orig. *c.* 80 mm.)

End-looped mortar, with plain low-walled bow, slender groove, and simple knobbed terminal. The slender broken loop is in the form of a very devolved bird's head, with everted bill.

Metal detector find from an extensive area of Roman settlement. The site has yielded a diverse range of finds dating from the Late Iron Age to the Late Roman period. In private hands.

33. Bradfield Combust with Stanningfield, Suffolk

L. 39 mm. Wt. 4.63 g.

End-looped mortar, lacking the loop and part of the bow. The low-walled, plain, lightly-elliptical bow has a worn and corroded rim, a broad, shallow, U-sectioned groove, a rounded keel and a simple blunt-pointed terminal.

Metal detector find. In private hands.

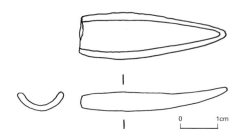

34. Brampton, Norfolk

L. 64.5 mm. Wt. 31.6 g.

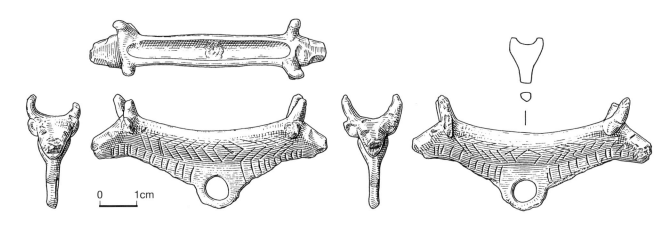

Centre-looped mortar with green patina. The relatively short bow has a shallow, and only lightly-curved, broad, U-sectioned groove. The two bovid terminals vary a little in detail. Both are horned, with ears, eyes, nostrils and mouth depicted as well as elongated stylized dewlaps, which extend to the slightly asymmetrically-placed D-shaped loop plate with circular eye. The rather irregularly-incised decoration on the walls and dewlaps may have been intended as a simplified depiction of the animals' coat.

Metal detector find. In private hands.

35. Brampton, Norfolk

L. 28.9 mm. Wt. 5.9 g.

(?) Centre-looped mortar, fragment only, with mid-green patina, lightly accreted with pale brown soil. All that survives is one terminal and a short section of the adjacent bow. The zoomorphic terminal is in the form of a stylized bovid, with triangular head, tapered muzzle, in-turned horns (one tip broken), and prominent everted ears. On both walls of the bow is a series of deeply-incuse hatched lines, perhaps intended to represent the stylized shaggy coat of the animal. The groove, which runs over the head, has a capacious U-shaped cross-section.

Metal detector find. In private hands.

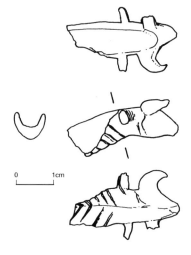

36. Brampton, Norfolk
L. 71 mm. Wt. 45.7 g.

Centre-looped mortar, Type E, with strongly-curved plump bow. The apparently plain convex walls have an in-turned rim. The groove is comparatively slender, of modest capacity and of rounded V-shaped cross-section. The terminals are zoomorphic, presumably very devolved bovids, with bulbous head, tapered face and flared, flat-ended muzzle. One terminal has a small raised dot on each side of the head giving the appearance of an eye. Each terminal is joined to the centre loop by an indented openwork strut, which begins at the muzzle and ended on the now broken lower perimeter of the large crescent-shaped loop. Both struts are fragmentary but their form is clearly the same as those of no. 213. Unlike that one, however, the openwork panels are all perforate. Nevertheless, the form, size and weight of these two mortars are so similar that they could have been made from the same mould. Such differences as there are reflect the type and degree of cold working after casting.

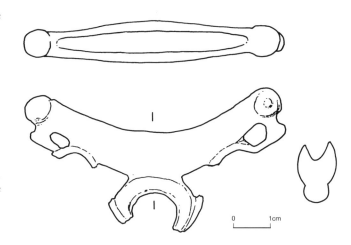

Metal detector find. Formerly in private hands, via the antiquity market.

British Museum, 1999,0802.2.

37. Brampton, Norfolk
L. 47.1 mm. Wt. 7.6 g.

Centre-looped mortar, Type H, with pitted and ferrous-encrusted pale green patina. Both terminals, part of the bow and much of one wall rim are lacking, as also the loop. The crescentic bow has a rounded keel ridge and thin convex walls with chipped rim. At the centre of both walls, adjacent to the loop base, is an arc of incuse tiny triangular cells, their apex pointing towards the loop: three cells on one wall, four narrower cells on the other wall. One of the three appears to have held green enamel, but all other cells are either empty or of indeterminate colour. The relatively capacious groove has a broad U-shaped cross-section. The loop base appears to have been re-worked following breakage of the loop. It has been filed smooth to a sort of low plinth and four incuse lines marked on it.

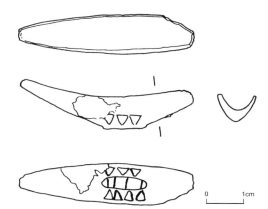

Metal detector find. In private hands.

38. Brampton, Norfolk
L. 60 mm.

End-looped mortar, with dark green smooth patina. The bow has plain, sloping, slender-rimmed walls and a capacious V-sectioned groove. The terminal is a small knob with a neck moulding. The loop is a stylized bird's head with elongated bill.

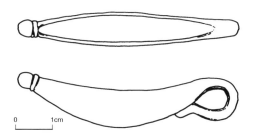

From excavation, 1970, of Roman settlement site. Found in a disturbed level during excavation of the bath house.

Jackson 1985, no. 16; Trett 1983, no. 11. For site see A.K. Knowles, 'The Roman settlement at Brampton, Norfolk', *Britannia* 8, 1977, 209–21.

On loan to Norwich Castle Museum, L1975.16.

39. Brandon, Suffolk
L. 69 mm. Wt. 29.5 g.

Centre-looped mortar. Cleaning of the exterior has revealed the golden brown colour of the body metal beneath a pale grey-green and patchy liver-red patina. The lightly-encrusted whitish-green corrosion products remain intact in the groove. An atypical and ornate example with a broad and deep crescentic bow, rounded angular keel and convex walls, with a symmetrical moulded decor. The tiny, ambiguous zoomorphic terminals, with hollowed eyes, prominent brow and upturned pointed bill were probably intended as highly-stylized aquatic birds' heads, and the same is probably true of the two adjoining ends of the D-shaped loop, which have a marked brow ridge and dished bill. The broad, very capacious groove has a deep V-shaped cross-section, with a light, axially asymmetric, basal wear facet which runs onto the terminals.

Metal detector find. Formerly in private hands, via the antiquity market.

British Museum, 1999,0802.3.

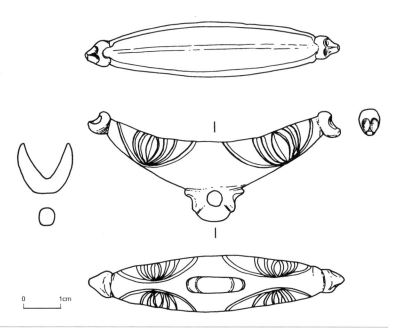

40. Brandon, Suffolk
L. 61 mm. Wt. 32.4 g.

Centre-looped mortar, with surface-depleted, irregular, variable green, oiled patina. A rather heavy inelegant casting, with lightly elliptical bow, flattened keel, plain, lightly-convex walls, and chipped rims. The U-sectioned groove has a marked basal facet and wear polish which runs onto the bulbous, neck-moulded terminals. The large, thick, ovoid loop has a circular eye.

Metal detector find. Formerly in private hands, via the antiquity market.

British Museum, 1999,0802.4.

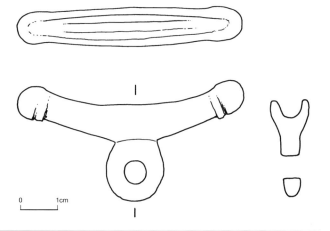

41. Brandon, Suffolk
L. 59 mm. Wt. 5.2 g.

Centre-looped pestle, with metallic green-grey (tin-enriched) patina. Both arms of the slender, softened diamond-sectioned rod are distorted. There is a little wear on the underside at the centre. The neatly formed D-shaped loop has a heart-shaped eye.

Metal detector find. Formerly in private hands, via the antiquity market.

British Museum, 1999,0802.6.

42. Brandon, Suffolk
L. 39.3 mm. Wt. 14.1 g.

Centre-looped pestle, with mid-green dusty patina. A large example of 'rocking-horse' type, with plump, lightly curved rod and tall prominent struts supporting a discoid loop with small circular eye. There was little post-casting work, and quite rough filed facetting is visible, especially on the margins of the triangular aperture.

Metal detector find. Formerly in private hands, via the antiquity market.

British Museum, 1999,0802.7.

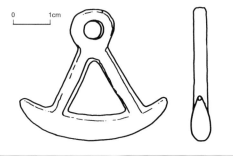

43. Brandon, Suffolk
L. *c.* 54 mm.

End-looped mortar. An elegant design, with plain sloping walls, a lightly flattened keel, a broad, U-sectioned groove and a small knobbed terminal. The fine loop is in the form of a stlyized aquatic bird's head, with a pronounced ridged everted bill. The eye is ovoid, possibly due to wear.

Metal detector find. In private hands.

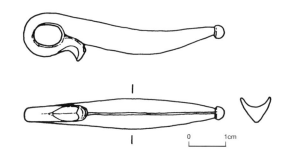

44. Brandon, Suffolk
L. 61. 5 mm.

End-looped mortar, with smooth olive-brown patina. A heavy, competent casting. The bow has plain sloping walls and a flattened keel. The capacious squared V-sectioned groove ends with a neatly formed pouring lip. There is wear in the eye of the circular loop, which has a squarish cross-section.

Metal detector find, donated to Moyses Hall Museum, Bury St Edmunds, no. 1985–35A.

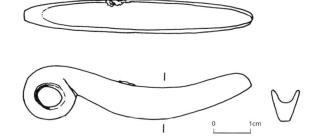

45. Brandon, Suffolk
L. 56.6 mm. Wt. 8.5 g.

End-looped pestle, with smooth grey (tin-enriched) patina, lightly-pocked and encrusted in a few places, notably at the tip. The lightly-elliptical rod is swollen just beyond its midpoint and has a wear facet on the two lower sides of the upturned tip. The collar-like loop, with tubular eye, has a neatly-cut rim-moulding on both sides.

Metal detector find. Formerly in private hands, via the antiquity market.

British Museum, 1999,0802.8.

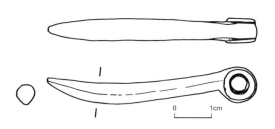

46. ?Brandon, Suffolk
L. 71.2 mm. (orig. *c.* 80 mm.) Wt. 12 g.

Centre-looped mortar, Type H, with pale mottled grey-green patina. The crescentic bow has an angular keel, thin sloping walls and a capacious groove of broad V-shaped cross-section with a marked basal wear facet. One terminal is lacking. The survivor is a tiny simple knob. The loop is a D-shaped ring with heart-shaped eye. On both walls adjacent to the loop is an arc of four tiny triangular cells, their apex pointing away from the loop. Remains of the enamel inlay are present in most of the cells. The colour cannot now be determined but the residue has a uniform appearance implying that all were filled with the same colour.

Metal detector find. Formerly in private hands, via the antiquity market. The given provenance is suspect because a mortar acquired from the dealer on the same occasion, and also said by him to come from Brandon, was actually from Melton Mowbray (no. 340). Other examples from the same dealer also proved to be falsely provenanced (nos 211, 481, 485).

British Museum, 1999,0802.5

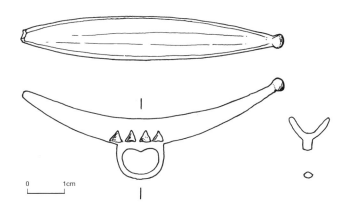

47. nr. Breamore, Hants
L. 52 mm.

End-looped mortar, of atypical form. A very diminutive example, with near-straight, very thin, plain, low-walled bow, very slender V-sectioned groove, plain blunt terminal, and a suspension loop formed by a tiny circular perforation. Above the perforation is a short zone of fine, crimped, 'pie-crust' decoration, similar to that sometimes seen on Late Iron Age metalwork.

Metal detector find. In private hands.

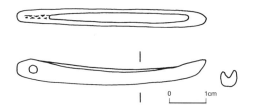

48. Brecon, Powys
L. *c.* 71 mm.

End-looped pestle. A large example, with strongly curved D-sectioned stem. The centrally mounted circular loop is separated from the stem by a series of neat ring mouldings.

From excavations, 1924–5, of the Roman fort. Found to the north of the fort.

Jackson 1985, no. 44; R.E.M. Wheeler, 1926, *The Roman Fort near Brecon* 116, fig. 58, no. 11.

Cardiff, National Museum of Wales.

49. Brecon, Powys
L. 56 mm.

End-looped pestle. A simple, unadorned, roughly-made example. The turned-over loop has a free end. The lower stem has a lightly curved facet on its convex edge. The tip is broken.

From excavations, 1924–5, of the Roman fort. Unstratified. *Fort floruit c.* AD 70–120.

Jackson 1985, no. 54; R.E.M. Wheeler, 1926, *The Roman Fort near Brecon* 116, fig. 58, no. 12.

Cardiff, National Museum of Wales.

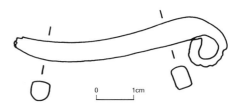

50. Brenley Corner, Kent
L. 97.8 mm. Wt. 46.9 g.

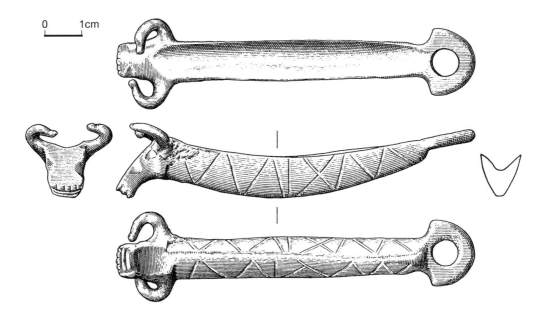

End-looped mortar, of distinctive, idiosyncratic, form, with a good mid-green patina. A heavy casting with lightly-elliptical bow and an axially asymmetric, angular, keel. The sloping thin-rimmed walls (cf. no. 292) are decorated with an incuse linear design, comprising an irregular zig-zag motif with a near-central X framed by a pair of verticals. The broad, shallow V-sectioned groove, with marked basal wear facet, runs onto the loop and over the terminal. The terminal is a large stylized bovid head, with very prominent strongly-inturned horns, their tips knobbed, and a broad, flattened, angular face with chamfered muzzle and incuse mouth and nostrils. The loop is a shouldered D-shaped plate which, like no. 73, is set, atypically, in a different plane to the bow walls. There is a little wear in the circular eye.

From excavation, 1972, of Roman roadside settlement on Watling Street, at Brenley Corner, near Faversham, by Frank Jenkins, for Canterbury Excavation Committee and the Dept. of the Environment. Remains included a possible shrine, with a range of votives – *dea nutrix* type seated mother goddess figurine, pottery face urn, two 'triple vases', and a high concentration of coins ranging in date from the 2nd century to later 4th century AD.

Royal Museum, Canterbury. BC 73.141.

51. Brettenham, Norfolk
L. 77 mm. Wt. 11.3 g.

End-looped mortar, with smooth dark green patina. A light
example with only gently curved low, thin-walled bow,
plain except for a pair of incised lines which run along the
lightly flattened keel; and a single incised line which runs
round the lower edge of the terminal pouring lip. The bow
is lightly distorted axially, and is distinctly asymmetric
to the loop. The U-sectioned groove is capacious, with a
distinct basal wear facet and an open end. The loop is of
turned-over form, the tip butted against the underside of
the bow, and is elaborately decorated with a pair of deeply-
incised lines running around the perimeter to the point
where they meet a deeply-moulded four-leaf design, which
is rather reminiscent of the zoomorphic terminals of some
penannular brooches.

Metal detector find. In private hands.

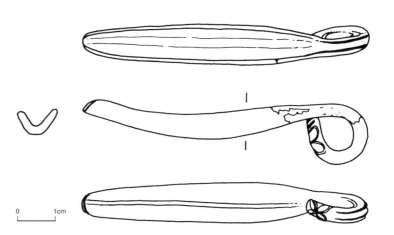

52. Brigg, Humberside
L. 42 mm. Wt. 11.7 g.

End-looped mortar, 'cleaned' and with an artificially induced (green-
painted) patina. A simple, very idiosyncratic, example, with short
straight bow, rounded angular keel, plain sloping walls and lightly-
convex rim. The groove, of relatively capacious U-shaped cross-section
with basal facet, runs out of the plain open-spouted terminal. The loop
is no more than a tiny roughly-countersunk hole passing through the
wedge-shaped end.

Metal detector find. In private hands.

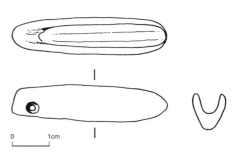

53. Brigstock, Northants
L. c. 75 mm.

Centre-looped mortar, Type F, of heavy ornate
form. The bow walls are sharply carinated. Their
upper section is near-vertical and is decorated
with a central incised ridged moulding flanked
by a raised ring-and-dot motif and a raised
rib. The lower sloping section is plain, but the
angular keel is incised with a line of chevrons. The
rounded V-sectioned groove is relatively shallow.
The terminals are bovids with strongly moulded
muzzles and inturned horns. The appreciable
difference in size and shape of the heads may have
been a deliberate feature intended to show the
twinning of bull and cow. The loop is a circular
ring, the pedestal base of which is integrated
with the central moulding. For a near-identical
example, see no. 158.

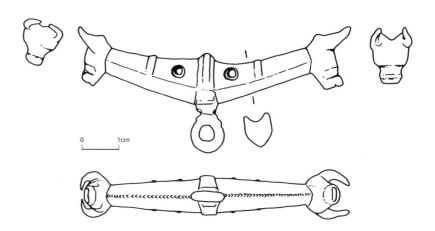

From surface collection, Brigstock temple site. In private hands.

B. Dix, 'Some further Roman bronzes from Brigstock, Northamptonshire', *Antiquaries Journal* 66, 1986, 126–130, fig. 2, no. 6.

54. Brisley/ Stanfield, Norfolk
L. 57.5 mm. Wt. 7.55 g.

End-looped pestle, with slender, strongly-angled rod and simple loop
with tiny, circular, countersunk eye.

Metal detector find. In private hands.

55. Bromeswell, Suffolk

L. *c.* 47 mm.

Centre-looped mortar, badly corroded. The bow is a simple crescent, with apparently plain walls and plain terminals. Corrosion and surface depletion may have destroyed the rim of the walls, but the U-sectioned groove must always have been shallow. The suspension loop is broken, but the projecting plate, on which it was mounted, remains. It is a low rectangle and is set back slightly from the keel of the bow, giving the object a distinct asymmetry.

Metal detector find. In private hands.

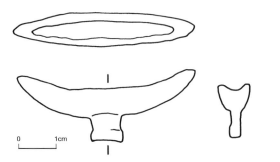

56. Broome, Norfolk

L. 73 mm.

Centre-looped mortar, badly corroded. The bow has plain sloping walls and a rounded V-sectioned groove. One of the terminals is knobbed, the other lipped. The loop is a large ring with circular eye.

Jackson 1985, no. 84; Trett 1983, no. 25.

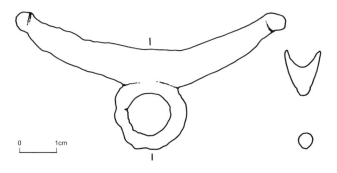

57. near Brough, Nottinghamshire

L. 31.2 mm. Wt. 6.6 g.

Mortar fragment, with exposed green corrosion products beneath a dark brown patina. The fragment comprises one end of the bow, with a rounded keel, plain sloping walls, a small knobbed terminal, and a relatively broad shallow groove, of rounded V-shaped cross-section, with a marked basal wear facet.

Metal detector find. In private hands, via the antiquity market.

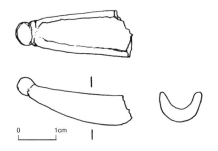

58. Burgh Castle, Suffolk

L. 65 mm. Wt. 12.1 g.

Centre-looped mortar, Type I, badly damaged, with mid-green patina, black-green (tin-enriched?) in places. The strongly curved bow has an angular keel, and sloping, plain, thin walls, their rims chipped and broken. The broad U-sectioned groove is capacious and worn. Both terminals are broken, but this distinctive mortar type had two varieties of terminal, small knobs or small bovid heads. In this case, since one of the terminals is broken very close to the tip, we can confidently predict that they must have been of the knobbed variety rather than the slightly thicker-necked bovid form. Only the stub of the loop survives, but sufficient to show that it was a slender D-shaped ring, with large heart-shaped eye. It is set at a distinct angle to the keel of the bow.

Metal detector find. In private hands.

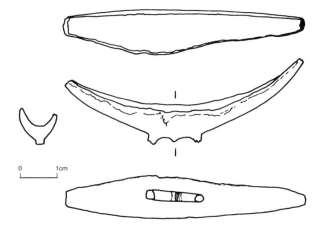

59. Burgh Castle, Suffolk

L. 45.3 mm. Wt. 11.2 g.

Un-looped mortar, with dark grey-black patina. A diminutive neatly-made example with relatively broad crescentic bow, chamfered keel, plain sloping walls, carinated below the in-turned rim, a shallow U-sectioned groove with wear polish, and zoomorphic terminals apparently in the form of 1) a highly stylized bird's head, with dished, everted, broad-ended bill, 2) a ?very devolved bovid head, the tip of its muzzle damaged. In place of a loop is a small central plinth with flat tongue-like projection with which the mortar is very readily held between thumb and forefinger.

Metal detector find. Formerly in private hands, via the antiquity market.

British Museum, 1999,0802.9

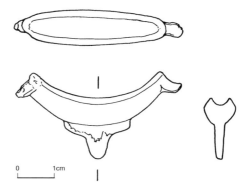

60. Burlingham, Norfolk

L. 57 mm. Wt. 10.5 g.

Centre-looped mortar, with green patina, the original surface preserved only in the groove. The bow is slender, with plain, low, sloping walls and inturned rim. The capacious U-sectioned groove runs over the terminals. Wear polish is visible on the basal facet, and the distinct axial asymmetry of the groove may also be a product of wear. The prominent spherical knobbed terminals have a simple neck moulding. The loop is broken, but the angle of the remaining stumps, and their extended keel-like junction with the bow, suggest that the loop was originally strutted.

Metal detector find. In private hands.

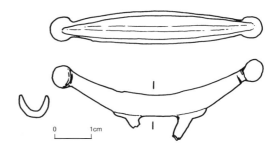

61. Buxhall, Suffolk

L. 62 mm. Wt. 8.26 g.

A large example, with long crescentic rod of circular cross-section turning to a thick lentoid section towards the tip. The eye of the circular loop is blocked with ferrous corrosion products.

Metal detector find. In private hands.

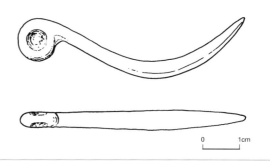

62. Caerleon, Gwent

L. mortar c. 45 mm, pestle c. 35–45 mm.

Set, comprising a centre-looped pestle corroded in the groove of a centre-looped mortar. This set, now missing, was recorded in 1986. From the record sketch it is evident that both components were small. No decoration was noted (nor is visible) on the mortar (but corrosion could easily have hidden any incised ornament on the walls), and the terminals appear plain and simple. The simple loop has a circular eye. The pestle has a relatively large D-shaped or heart-shaped loop.

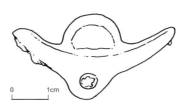

From excavations, 1984–6, of Roman fortress extra-mural settlement, at Mill Street, Cambria House site, by Dr. Edith Evans for Glamorgan-Gwent Archaeological Trust.

From an abandonment/demolition phase of the site in a context which produced a coin of Victorinus (AD 269–271), but little else. That the coin date may be meaningful is implied by the nearby discovery in a drain of a hoard of 51 coins, the latest of which are also issues of Victorinus. Besly dated the hoard to AD 269 (E. Besly in R. Bland (ed.), 1992, *Coin Hoards from Roman Britain,* vol. IX, 101–3).

E. Evans, 2000, *The Caerleon* canabae. *Excavations in the civil settlement 1984–90*, Britannia Monograph Series no. 16 (London), 344, no. 81.

63. Caerleon, Gwent

L. *c.* 38 mm.

Centre-looped mortar, lacking both terminals and much of the bow and loop. The bow walls are plain, the groove capacious U-sectioned, and the loop in the form of a flat D-shaped plate with small ovoid eye.

From excavations, 1984–6, of Roman fortress extra-mural settlement, at Mill Street, Allotments site, by Dr. Edith Evans for Glamorgan-Gwent Archaeological Trust.

Unstratified.

E. Evans, 2000, *The Caerleon* canabae. *Excavations in the civil settlement 1984–90*, Britannia Monograph Series no. 16 (London), 343–4, fig. 81, no. 80.

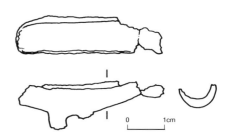

64. Caister-on-Sea, Norfolk

L. 49 mm.

Centre-looped mortar. The small, short bow has plain sloping walls and a capacious V-sectioned groove, with marked basal facet. One terminal is moulded (bird-headed?), the other is in the form of a small lipped spout. The loop, mounted on a simple projecting pedestal, is a large ring with ovoid eye.

Found on the Roman fort site, 1936, with material of mainly 3rd- and 4th-century, but also 2nd-century date, together with stone building debris.

Journal of Roman Studies 26, 1936, 253 fig. 27; Jackson 1985, no. 85; M.J. Darling and D. Gurney, 1993, *Caister-on-Sea. Excavations by Charles Green 1951–55* (East Anglian Arch. Rep. no. 60) 89, fig. 57, no. 294.

Norwich Castle Museum, 155. 948.

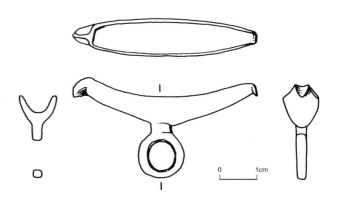

65. Caistor St Edmund, Norfolk

L. 61 mm.

Centre-looped mortar, Type E variant, with remnants of the pale green patina which has mostly been removed to reveal the dull golden brown metal surface. An elegant and very finely crafted example. The plump bow has convex walls, plain except for an arc of punched inverted crescents below the thin upright rim. The shallow U-sectioned groove, completely encircled by the rim, has a slightly faceted base. The identical terminals are in the form of a stylized down-turned swan's head, with pronounced bill. A very slender sinuous strut links the tip of each bill to the centre loop via the keel of the bow. They have a neat ridge-and-groove moulding on their underside at the point of contact with the bow, and continue as a slender ridge moulding round the lower perimeter of the large circular loop.

From excavation, 1929, by D. Atkinson. Building 4, kiln 3. Unpublished.

Norwich Castle Museum 152.929.

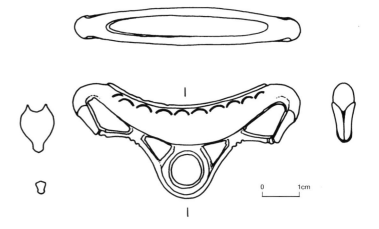

66. Cambridge, Cambs

L. *c.* 61 mm.

End-looped mortar, with crescentic bow, rounded keel, low plain walls, shallow, rounded, V-sectioned groove and plain blunt-pointed terminal. The loop is coiled.

From archaeological excavations, 1956–1988, on Castle Hill. RGS Ia, 109 45 Pit.

J. Alexander and J. Pullinger, 2000, *Roman Cambridge: Excavations on Castle Hill 1956–1988* (= *Proceedings of the Cambridge Antiquarian Society* vol. LXXXVIII, 1999, ed. Alison Taylor), Cambridge Antiquarian Society, Cambridge, 88, 97, pl. XII, no. 104.

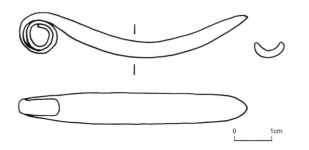

67. Cambridge area
L. 69.4 mm. Wt. 15.2 g.

Centre-looped mortar. The mid-green patina has suffered badly from recent cleaning. The bow has thin, sloping walls, with damage to one rim. There is an engraved elliptical line adjacent to the loop, and another flanks the junctions of loop and bow. The groove, of rounded V-shaped cross-section, is deep and capacious, with a basal facet. Both terminals are plain, one a little damaged. The large D-shaped loop is roughly-formed and appears to have been cast-on to the completed bow. A casting blemish on the interior was probably a result of incorrect heat control in this process.

Metal detector find. Formerly in private hands, via the antiquity market.

British Museum, 1999,0802.10.

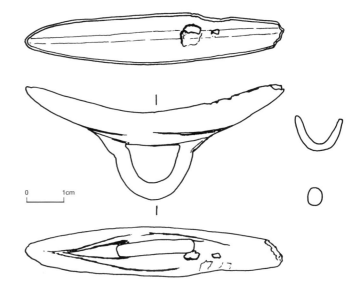

68. Cambridgeshire, south, unprovenanced
L. 37.9 mm. (orig. *c.* 39 mm.) Wt. 8.6 g.

Centre-looped pestle, with brown patina. The twin-tapered rod is short, elliptical and quite stout, of plump, chamfered, D-shaped cross-section, and lacks one tip (probably recent damage). The loop is a large circular ring surmounting a double-moulded pedestal. The relatively thick patina precludes an assessment of wear on the rod.

Metal detector find. Formerly in private hands, via the antiquity market.

British Museum, 1999,0802.14.

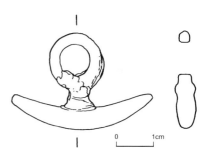

69. Cambridgeshire, unprovenanced
L. 66.6 mm. Wt. 15.4 g.

End-looped pestle, with pitted and eroded olive-green patina. A large example with quite thick rod of lentoid cross-section. Its markedly angular 'heel' demarcates the end of the working face. The disproportionately bulky loop, though badly denuded of its surface in several places, was evidently in the form of a stylized aquatic bird's head, with projecting brow and everted bill. The eye is small and circular.
Metal detector find. Formerly in private hands, via the antiquity market.

British Museum, 1999,0802.12

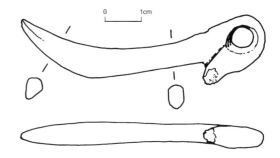

70. Cambridgeshire, unprovenanced
L. 56 mm. Wt. 9.1 g.

End-looped pestle, with lightly pocked and flaked olive-green patina. A well-proportioned and well-finished example, with crescentic rod, of plump lentoid cross-section, which swells near the upturned blunt tip. The neatly-wrought loop, with tear-shaped eye, is in the form of a stylized aquatic bird's head, with everted dished bill. A wear facet is visible on the convex face of the swollen section of the rod.

Metal detector find. Formerly in private hands, via the antiquity market.

British Museum, 1999,0802.11.

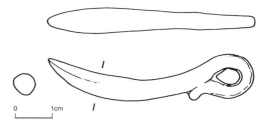

71. Cambridgeshire, unprovenanced

L. 55.2 mm. Wt. 5.6 g.

End-looped pestle, with fine brown patina and underlying golden-coloured metal. A simple elegant pestle with slender, circular-sectioned, elliptical rod, lightly wear-polished on the 'belly'. The simple ovoid loop has a little wear polish in the oval eye.

Metal detector find. Formerly in private hands, via the antiquity market.

British Museum, 1999,0802.13.

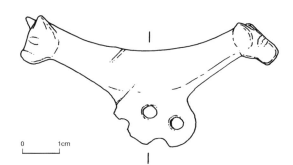

72. Campsey Ash, Suffolk

L. *c.* 70 mm.

Centre-looped mortar, with steeply-sloping walls, a U-sectioned groove and zoomorphic terminals in the form of stylized bovid heads, both slightly different, with muzzle, eyes and ears/ horns quite simply rendered. The idiosyncratic large loop plate, now partly broken, had at least three small circular perforations.

Metal detector find. In private hands.

73. Canterbury, Kent

L. mortar 87.2 mm, pestle 66.1 mm. Combined Wt. 54.3 g.

Set, in fine condition, with lightly-encrusted, smooth, olive to mid-green patina, comprising an end-looped pestle corroded in the groove of an end-looped mortar. The mortar has a strongly-curved, very narrow bow with lightly-rounded keel and deep, plain, near-vertical walls. The groove, as far as can be discerned, is of very narrow V-shaped cross-section, and runs onto the loop and the large spherical knobbed terminal. The simple plate-like loop, divided from the bow by a band of four crudely executed incuse lines, is set, exceptionally, in a different plane to the bow. It has a small circular eye, slightly off-centre. Both these features recur on the pestle, which also has a band of incuse mouldings at either side of the loop/ rod junction and a further band on top of the loop plate. The rod itself, to judge from optical examination and radiography, is of blunt knife-like form and fits snugly into the groove of the mortar. It is markedly curved, slender and very deep, with a thin triangular cross-section and sharply-pointed, upturned tip. Both the tip and loop, as viewed from above the concave edge, are skewed to one side, perhaps to aid grinding. A slight amount of wear is visible in the eye of both loops.

From excavation, 1981, of Cakebread Robey site, temple precinct, Layer 617. Pre-phase I temple clearance.

Context date, late 1st or 2nd century AD.

Jackson 1985, no. 3; P. Bennett, *Excavations in the Castle Street and Stour Street areas*, The Archaeology of Canterbury, Vol. VI, forthcoming.

Canterbury Museum, CBR IV: 713.

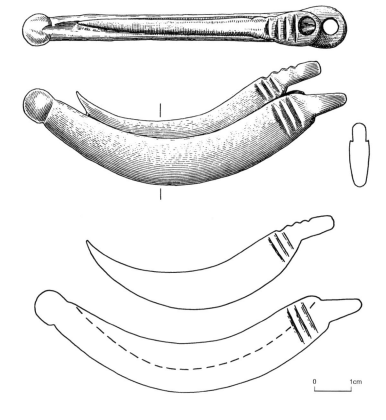

74. Canterbury, Kent

L. mortar 88.2 mm. (orig. *c.* 108 mm.), pestle 79.8 mm. (orig. *c.* 82 mm.)
Wt. Mortar 12.9 g. Wt. Pestle 11.9 g.

Set, comprising a centre-looped mortar, Type H, lacking one terminal, and a centre-looped pestle, Type O, lacking one tip. Both components have been heavily stripped, revealing the dull brown-golden metal at the expense, in most places, of the original surface. Thus, the loops, mortar walls and terminal, and one pestle tip are attenuated, split and eroded, and the mortar, in particular, has suffered some loss in weight. The strongly-curved bow has an angular keel and thin steep walls, with an arc of six hollow-based triangular cells adjacent to the loop on both faces. The cells, whose apex points away from the loop, are completely devoid of enamel inlay or its remains. The broad, capacious groove has a rounded V-shaped cross-section with basal wear facet. The remaining emaciated terminal is a simple small knob. The slender, ring-like, D-shaped loop has a relatively small heart-shaped eye. The large, ornate pestle has a rhomboid-sectioned rod with remains of a light, slightly asymmetric wear-facet on the keel. The two non-functional (concave) faces of the rod are decorated with two arcs of three small triangular cells flanking the junction of loop and rod. The cells, whose apex points away from the loop, are now empty. The large loop is a D-shaped ring with heart-shaped eye. For a near-identical pestle see no. 586.

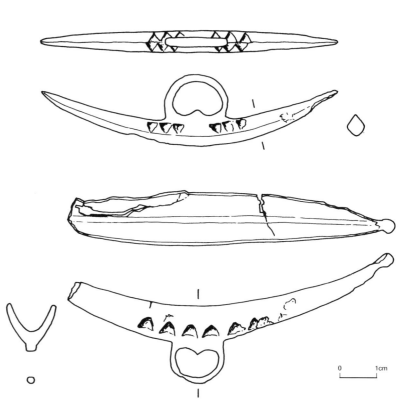

This set, from the Brent Collection, was seen by Reginald Smith in Oct/Nov. 1918, when his paper was at proof stage. He regarded the components as two separate pendants and inserted a reference (but no illustration) to the mortar only (Smith 1918,60, Fn.1). As the photograph that Smith had made at the British Museum (PRB Dept. neg. no. SUB.5.44) shows, the set was then un-cleaned and lightly encrusted, and Smith seems to have been unaware of the enamel inlay cells. Thus, he likened it to a knobbed example from Colchester (no. 116). His correspondence on the objects with Mr. Mead of the Royal Museum, Canterbury, on 2nd October and 15th November 1918, is preserved in the archives of that Museum.

Jackson 1985, no. 92.

Royal Museum, Canterbury, 2247 and 2248.

75. ?Canterbury, Kent

L. 64.2 mm. Wt. 15.5 g.

End-looped mortar, badly crushed and distorted, with mid-green patina. The bow was slender and lightly-curved with low, convex walls, a smoothly rounded keel, and a plain blunt-pointed terminal. The walls are decorated with incuse lines which follow the curvature of the bow, one line immediately beneath each rim, one along the keel, and a pair in between. What is visible of the groove shows it to have been of rounded V-shaped cross-section, with wear-polish in the base. The crook-like loop with tapered, scrolled tip and small circular eye, may have been intended as a stylized bird's head.

Royal Museum, Canterbury, 6948.

76. Canterbury, Kent

L. *c.* 70 mm.

End-looped mortar, with only very lightly elliptical parallel-sided bow, very low, plain, sloping walls, a rounded keel, and a broad rounded V-sectioned groove, which runs through the simple open, spout-like terminal. The broken loop appears to have been a simple circular ring.

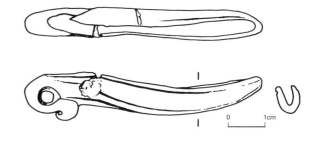

From excavation, 1990, of Longmarket site by Canterbury Archaeological Trust. 1990–11. SF 5368. From Context 6103, an occupation deposit on a large spread of flint and pot metalling flanking the south-western side of the major Roman road running from Westgate to near Burgate.

Context date, *c.* AD 50–130.

77. Carleton Rode, Norfolk
L. 45 mm. Wt. 8.9 g.

End-looped mortar, with brown and green pitted and puffy patina. A small example, broken at both ends. The short elliptical bow has plain walls with nearly straight rim, a rounded keel, and a U-sectioned groove partially blocked with corrosion. The broken terminal was probably plain, and the broken loop probably large and simple.

Metal detector find.

Norwich Castle Museum, 378.985 (402).

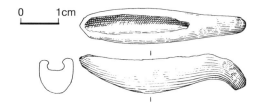

78. Carleton Rode, Norfolk
L. 32.5 mm. Wt. 5 g.

Centre-looped pestle, with pitted olive-brown patina, partially covered with a brown accretion. A small simple example, with slender twin-tapered rod (tips eroded), elongated loop plate and small circular eye, now blocked by corrosion products.

Metal detector find. In private hands.

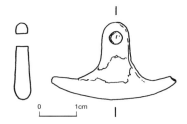

79. Carlisle, Cumbria
L. 39 mm. (orig. *c.* 58 mm.)

Centre-looped pestle. A large example lacking one end of the rod and part of the loop. The surviving arm is slender with an ovoid cross-section. The loop is a D-shaped ring.

From excavations at the Lanes site, by Carlisle Archaeological Unit. Context KLA D 81.

Context date, late Roman, probably 4th century AD.

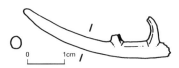

80. Castleford, West Yorkshire
L. 80 mm.

End-looped mortar, with plain deep walls, rounded keel, relatively capacious groove, and a plump knobbed terminal. The loop is neatly crafted, with a sub-circular eye, slightly elongated by wear facets. A simple rim-moulding embellishes the upper and outer edges of the loop and, in conjunction with a cross-moulding at the junction with the groove, forms a reserved, plain, cambered triangular field on the perimeter of the loop.

From excavations by West Yorkshire Archaeological Service. Trench N (15V), context N1145, gravel/ midden.

Context date, Phase Ic = *c.* AD 71/4–*c.* AD 86 (Fort I).

H.E.M. Cool and C. Philo (eds.), 1998, *Roman Castleford. Excavations 1974–85, Volume I: The small finds*, Yorkshire Archaeology 4, West Yorkshire Archaeology Service (Wakefield), 85, 90, no. 421.

The results of Energy Dispersive X-ray Fluorescence (EDXRF) analysis of the mortar (by David Dungworth) are included in Cool and Philo 1998, table 18, p. 119, no. 421, where they are expressed as Cu 84.55, Zn 0.37, Pb 4.79, Sn 10.20, Fe 0.09, Ni nd, Mn nd, As nd, and the alloy characterised as leaded bronze.

Wakefield Museum, cat.no. 1719, S.F. 824.

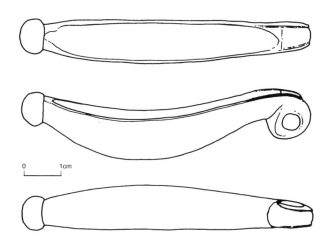

81. nr. Catterick, North Yorkshire
L. 72.8 mm. Wt. 16.9 g.

Centre-looped mortar, with very irregular green patina. A poorly-preserved example which has suffered recent heavy abrasion/ attrition of the corrosion products ('cleaning') and extensive re-colouring of the resulting highly uneven surface. The bow is slender and near parallel-sided, with angular keel, steeply-sloping walls, damaged rims and narrow, relatively shallow, V-sectioned groove, which runs over both terminals. One terminal is in the form of a zoomorphic head, probably a highly-stylized bovid, with low horns/ ears, simply-rendered eyes, and a tapered, slender, blunt-ended muzzle. The other terminal, which is tapered and down-turned and lacks its tip, may have been intended to represent the beast's tail. Only the corroded stub of the centre loop remains.

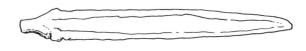
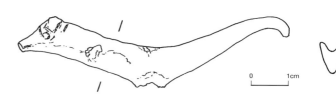

Metal detector find. Formerly in private hands, via the antiquity market.

P.R. Wilson, 2002, *Cataractonium: Roman Catterick and its hinterland. Excavations and research, 1958–1997. Part II*, CBA Research Report 129, (English Heritage, London), 149, no. 3.

British Museum, 1999,0802.15.

82. nr. Catterick, North Yorkshire
L. 55.4 mm. (orig. *c.* 66 mm.) Wt. 13.7 g.

Centre-looped mortar, with irregular green patina, poorly-preserved and incautiously 'cleaned', with some re-colouring of the resulting uneven surface. The elliptical bow, markedly swollen at the centre and tapered near the terminals, has a rounded keel, convex walls, damage-flattened rims and a partially-cleaned corrosion-blocked groove, the profile and capacity of which cannot be ascertained. The complete terminal is a prominent domed knob; the other, undoubtedly its pair, is broken at the slender neck. Only very vestigial remains of the centre loop, or, more probably, a low-ridged strut-and-loop assembly, survive, having been apparently ground away recently.

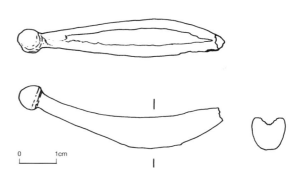

Metal detector find. Formerly in private hands, via the antiquity market.

P.R. Wilson, 2002, *Cataractonium: Roman Catterick and its hinterland. Excavations and research, 1958–1997. Part II*, CBA Research Report 129, (English Heritage, London), 149, no. 4.

British Museum, 1999,0802.16.

83. Charsfield, Suffolk
L. *c.* 46 mm.

Centre-looped mortar, Type H, lacking both terminals and part of the loop. The bow has thin sloping walls with an arc of three hollow based triangular cells adjacent to the loop on both walls. The cells, whose apex points away from the loop, contain traces of their enamel inlay, but the colour cannot be determined. The deep, capacious groove has a broad U-shaped cross-section. The loop was a large D-shaped ring with heart-shaped eye.

Metal detector find. In private hands.

84. Charsfield, Suffolk
L. 46.5 mm (orig. *c.* 68 mm).

Centre-looped pestle, lacking one arm. A large example with slender rod of rhomboid cross-section and a large ring-like D-shaped loop.

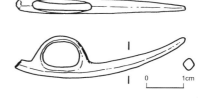

Metal detector find. In private hands.

85. Charsfield, Suffolk

L. 50.7 mm.

Centre-looped pestle, with asymmetric twin-tapered rod of plump D-shaped cross-section. Only the stub of the loop remains.

Metal detector find. In private hands.

86. Charsfield, Suffolk

L. 41 mm.

Centre-looped pestle, with short, stout, strongly-curved twin-tapered rod of rounded bi-conical cross-section. The small basal-moulded loop is broken across its circular eye, and the rod tips are eroded.

Metal detector find. In private hands

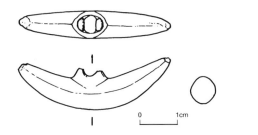

87. Chediston, Suffolk

L. 51.3 mm. Ht. 44 mm. Wt. 22.9 g.

Centre-looped mortar, of most unusual form, completely adapted to the shape of a stylized bird. Thus, the bow is short and deeply hollowed, and the terminals stand much higher than normal. The bow walls are plain. The groove is short and shallow with a broad U-shaped cross-section. One terminal is in the form of a bird's head with short pointed bill, the other comprises the tail, which is slightly fanned. The loop is a comparatively large near-circular plate with a medium-sized round eye.

Metal detector find. In private hands.

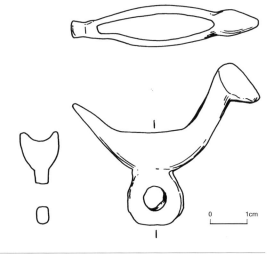

88. Chelsham, Surrey

L. 71 mm.

End-looped mortar, Type A, with light green corroded surface (most of the original surface now lacking). The long, slender, elliptical bow has an angular keel, steeply-sloping walls and a shallow U-sectioned groove. The remnants of surviving original surface at the terminal and near the loop demonstrate that the walls were originally ornamented with an incuse double zig-zag motif. The terminal is in the form of a very devolved bovid head, with tapered muzzle, prominent brow and vestigial horns. The loop, with sub-triangular eye, lies beneath the end of the bow. It was probably intended to give the appearance both of the beast's folded tail and of the stylized head of a water bird.

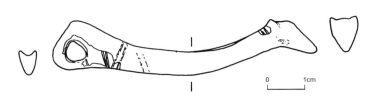

Metal detector find. In private hands.

89. Chessell Down, Isle of Wight

L. 71 mm.

End-looped mortar. Very slender bow, with low, convex, plain walls, broad, gently rounded keel, and very shallow groove of squared U-shaped cross-section. The terminal is plain and pointed, the loop a slender ring with large circular eye.

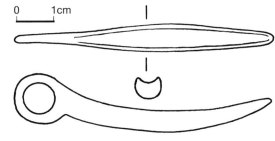

An un-contexted find from 19th-century excavations at the early Anglo-Saxon cemetery (5th–6th century AD) on Chessell Down. Probably a grave good, perhaps a curio in a 'bag collection'. There is a Roman villa at Rock, some 2.5 km. to the S.E. of the site.

G. Baldwin Brown, 1915, *The arts in early England*, vol. IV, 419, pl. XCIX,3; Smith 1918, 57–8, fig. 7; C.J. Arnold, 1982, *The Anglo-Saxon cemeteries of the Isle of Wight*, 41, 68, fig. 27, no. 26 (a 1:2 drawing, where the size is wrongly given as 3.6 cm); Jackson 1985, no. 23.

British Museum, 1867,0729.125.

90. Chester, Cheshire
L. *c.* 65 mm.

Centre-looped mortar, Type D variant, with partial surface erosion and encrustation. The convex walls are plain except for an incuse line below the rim. The groove, of rounded V-shaped cross-section is quite capacious. The moulded terminals, which may be very devolved bovid heads, are linked to the loop by gently curved struts. The loop is a circular ring mounted on a tall, tapered pedestal.

From excavation, 1989, at Priory Place.

Context date, mid-2nd–3rd century AD.

Chester, Grosvenor Museum.

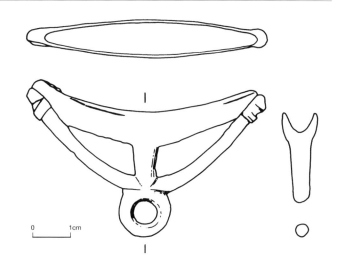

91. Chester, Cheshire
L. 68.5 mm.

Mortar, with both centre loop and end loop. The bow has plain, steep, lightly-carinated walls, an angular keel, and a V-sectioned groove. The knobbed terminal has a lightly engraved line at its base. Both loops are of similar size with a tiny circular eye.

From excavation, 1977, of Bedward Row site. From the cemetery area, ditch fill.

Context date 3rd century AD.

Jackson 1985, no. 98.

Chester, Grosvenor Museum.

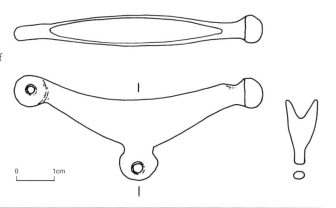

92. Chichester, West Sussex
L. mortar *c.* 78 mm. pestle *c. c.* 62 mm.

Set, comprising a centre-looped mortar, Type J, and a centre-looped pestle. The mortar has a rounded keel, and thin convex walls, with an arc of six small triangular cells adjacent to the loop on both faces. The cells, whose apex points towards the loop, are now devoid of the coloured enamel inlay they once contained. The capacious groove is of broad, deep, U-shaped cross-section. The terminals are in the form of small highly stylized bovid heads with lightly inturned horns and blunt-ended muzzles. The loop is a D-shaped ring. The pestle is a slender twin-tapered rod with faceted tips and a D-shaped loop.

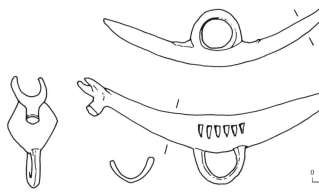

From excavation, 1965, of St Pancras Roman cemetery, Trench E, Burial Group 228, box burial, cremation. The associated finds, mostly items of personal adornment, include brooches, beads, ring, ligula, needles, glass vessels, Antonine samian and coarse ware pottery. The finds are suggestive of a female burial, but, unfortunately, the cremated bones were not examined.

Context date, late 2nd/early 3rd century AD.

A. Down and M. Rule, 1971, *Chichester I*, 115, fig. 5.18; Jackson 1985, no. 57.

93. Chichester, West Sussex
L. 62 mm. Wt. 10.5 g.

?Centre-looped mortar. The deep bow has plain steeply-sloping walls, an angular keel, and a rounded V-sectioned groove, partially blocked with corrosion. The terminals are enigmatic in appearance. Though the initial impression is of small, simple bovid heads, the prominent point above the muzzle and between the horns/ears is only with difficulty explained as the brow ridge. There is no trace of the centre-loop, perhaps a casualty to damage, corrosion and heavy cleaning, though it is not impossible that one of the terminals is a broken end-loop.

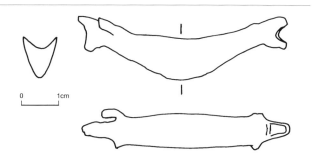

From excavation, 1981, of the Cattlemarket site. From a rectangular timber slot (A34) for a timber tank.

Context date, late 3rd–late 4th century AD, but probably residual.

Jackson 1985, no. 66. A. Down, 1989, *Chichester 6*, 200–1, fig. 27.5, no. 72.

94. Chichester, West Sussex
L. 66 mm.

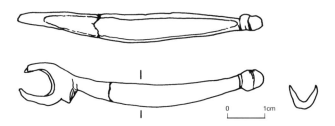

End-looped mortar. A fractured, distorted and corroded example with slender elliptical bow. The convex walls appear to have been plain and the keel flattened, and there is a marked basal facet in the V-sectioned groove. The knobbed terminal appears to have had a neck and girth moulding. The loop, partially worn through in antiquity or corroded away in the ground, has an angular stepped junction with the bow, perhaps intended as the bill of a very devolved bird's head.

From the garden of Mr. Frederick Sadler, Little London, Chichester.

Jackson 1985, no. 15, where it was unavailable for study. Re-located in 1993.

Chichester District Museum, CHCDM 2034.

95. Chichester, West Sussex
L. 54 mm. (orig. *c.* 57 mm.)

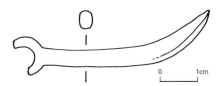

End-looped pestle. The oval-sectioned stem has a facet on the swollen, upturned, tapered tip. The broken loop was a circular ring.

From excavations, 1968–75, of N.W. Quadrant, Area 2 (Not Area 5, as stated in Down 1978), J84.

Context date, Flavian–late 1st century AD.

A. Down, 1978, *Chichester 3*, 293, fig. 10.32, no. 36; Jackson 1985, no. 45.

96. near Chichester, West Sussex
L. 50 mm. Wt. 6.2 g.

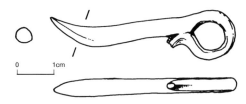

End-looped pestle, with pitted grey (tin-enriched?) patina. An elegant example with a lightly sinuous rod. The underside of its swollen up-turned tip bears a marked wear facet. The quite large loop is cast in the form of a stylized aquatic bird's head, with prominent brow and everted bill, the tip of which is broken. Wear marks are visible in the near-circular eye.

For metal composition see Scientific Analyses.

Said to have been found in 1993, from the South Downs a little to the north of Chichester.

Donated to the British Museum, 1994,0701.1.

97. near Chichester, West Sussex.
L. 47.5 mm. Wt. 7.1 g.

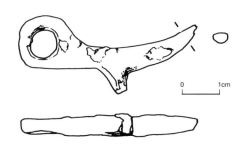

End-looped pestle, with a mid-olive-green shiny patina. The small rod has an upturned tip, a projecting spur, and a large ovoid suspension loop. The original surface, as preserved by the shiny patina, is very irregular, and this is evidently not a product of post-depositional agencies. It would appear that this was a casting that underwent no finishing work, and this might account for the spur, which could then be interpreted as a sprue on the uncleaned, possibly failed/rejected casting. Alternatively, though less likely, the spur may have been a simple decorative feature, akin, perhaps, to the struts on some mortars, for it would not have impeded use of the tip.

Purchased on the antiquity market, and donated to the British Museum, 1995,0502.1.

98. Chipstead, Surrey
L. *c.* 65 mm.

Centre-looped mortar, evidently quite badly corroded with apparent loss of surface. The crescentic bow is slender, with ridged keel, steeply-sloping plain walls, unusually pronounced rim projection, plain blunt-tipped terminals and a narrow shallow groove of rounded V-shaped cross-section. The loop, now broken, is also of unusual form: its large, apparently circular, eye is deeply recessed into the bow, which is notched either side of the ring-like loop.

Metal detector find. In private hands.

J. Bird, 'A Romano-British cosmetic mortar from Chipstead', *Surrey Archaeological Collections* 86, 1999, 206–7.

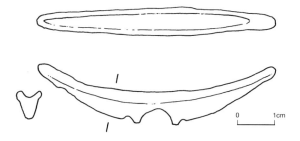

99. Church End, nr. Saffron Walden, Essex
L. 70.5 mm. Wt. 11.5 g.

Centre-looped mortar, Type H, with olive and green patina. A slender, light example with crescentic bow, angled keel, thin steeply-sloping walls, fine rim, relatively capacious groove of rounded V-shaped cross-section with basal wear facet, and simple, small knobbed terminals. On both walls is a panel of five tiny triangular cells, placed symmetrically either side of the loop, their apex pointing towards the keel. No trace of the enamel inlay survives. The loop is a relatively large D-shaped ring with heart-shaped eye.

Metal detector find. In private hands.

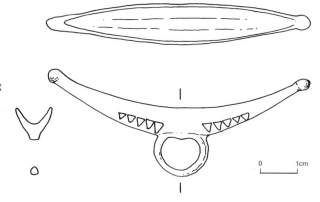

100. Cirencester, Glos
L. 66 mm.

End-looped mortar, forming a set with no. 101. An elegant well-made example, with slender elliptical bow. The low convex walls are plain; the groove is of V-shaped cross-section with a basal facet, and the terminal is a simple tapered point. The loop has a large circular eye and a 'stepped' junction with the bow, perhaps a version of the devolved bird's head seen on other examples.

In 1985 attention was drawn to the possibility that nos 100 and 101 comprised a set (Jackson 1985, nos 24 and 43). A careful examination of the pieces subsequently, together with a more general consideration, permits greater certainty: the pestle fits snugly in the groove of the mortar, and both profiles, as well as the distinctive stepped loop, match so closely that it may be considered virtually certain that the two were made as a set.

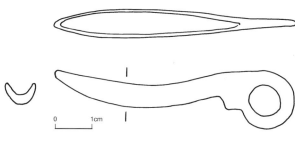

From excavations, 1974–7, at St Michael's Field. Robber trench, i.e. within town, southern half, Insula VI, shops, but also within the Leaholme fort or its annexe.

J. Wacher and A. McWhirr, 1982, *Cirencester Excavations I*, 111–12, fig. 37, no. 104; Jackson 1985, no. 24; A. McWhirr, 1986, *Cirencester Excavations III*, 247–8, fig. 162.

Cirencester, Corinium Museum.

101. Cirencester, Glos
L. 57 mm.

End-looped pestle, forming a set with no. 100. A simple well-cast example with a curved wear facet on the convex edge of the upturned tip. The stepped loop may have been intended as a highly devolved bird's head. There is wear in the ovoid eye. So similar to no. 100 that there is little doubt that they were made as a set.

From the Cripps Collection.

Jackson 1985, no. 43.

Cirencester, Corinium Museum, C46.

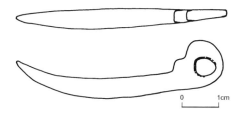

102. Cirencester, Glos

L. 46.5 mm.

Mortar, with smooth dark grey patina. The anomalous suspension device comprises a crescentic strut in place of a loop. A small example with plain sloping walls, angular keel, and a relatively capacious V-sectioned groove with marked wear polish. The plain terminals and slender strut, like the bow, appear quite rudimentarily made, with little post-casting work.

From the Barton Gravel Pits, i.e. from the site of the Barton Farm Roman villa.

Jackson 1985, no. 99.

Cirencester, Corinium Museum, B433.

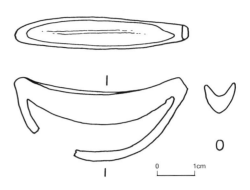

103. Cirencester, Glos

L. 61 mm.

End-looped pestle. A good casting, with a facet on the convex face of the upturned tip and traces of wear in the circular eye of the neatly 'coiled' loop.

Provenance as no. 102.

Jackson 1985, no. 47.

Cirencester, Corinium Museum, B432.

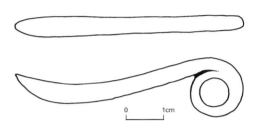

104. Claydon, Suffolk

L. c. 50 mm.

Centre-looped pestle, with slender, sub-lentoid-sectioned, twin-tapered rod, one tip of which is bent, and a ring-like D-shaped loop with heart-shaped eye.

Metal detector find. In private hands.

105. Cockfield, Suffolk

L. 58 mm. Wt. 12.56 g.

End-looped mortar, poorly preserved and lacking part of its loop. The unevenly curved bow has an angular keel, steeply-sloping plain walls with chipped rims, a narrow U-sectioned groove, and a simple knobbed terminal. The loop, broken across the eye, appears to have been in the form of a highly-stylized bird's head.

Metal detector find. In private hands.

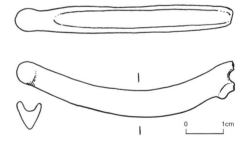

106. Coddenham, Suffolk

L. 36 mm.

Centre-looped mortar, Type H, lacking both terminals, part of the bow, the top of one wall, and most of the loop. A small example, with an angular keel, and low, sloping, thin walls decorated with an arc of four triangular cells adjacent to the loop. The cells, whose apex points away from the loop, contain traces of their enamel inlay, which has discoloured to a pale green. The capacious groove has a deep V-shaped cross-section. Only the stub of the D-shaped loop remains.

Metal detector find. In private hands.

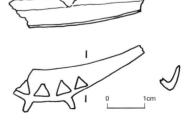

107. Coddenham, Suffolk
L. *c.* 73 mm. (orig. *c.* 76 mm.)

End-looped mortar, with slender, lightly-curved bow, plain low walls, a comparatively capacious groove and a simple terminal The loop, though broken, was clearly in the form of a devolved bird's head, and the slightly everted bill terminal remains. The eye would have been large and tear-shaped.

Metal detector find. In private hands.

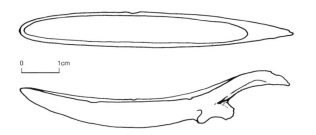

108. Codsall Wood, Staffordshire
L. *c.* 47 mm.

Centre-looped mortar with apparently plain walls and terminals and a small D-shaped loop with circular eye.

Metal detector find. In private hands.

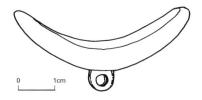

109. Colchester, Essex
L. 96 mm.

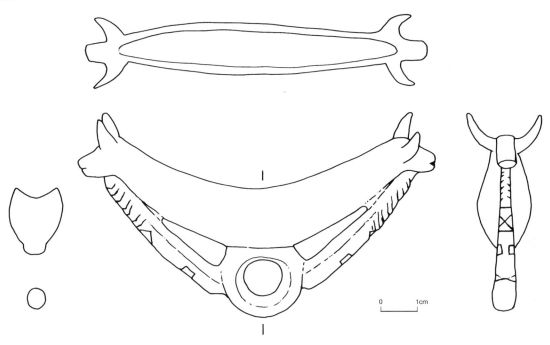

Centre-looped mortar, Type E variant. A large, very heavy and elaborate example. The strongly curved bow has deep plain convex walls with an upright rim, and a broad, shallow groove of rounded V-shaped cross-section. The bovid-head terminals have long everted horns and a blunt-ended muzzle with slit mouth. A stout strut links the throat of each head to the side of the suspension loop, the end closest to the throat, with incuse and notched decoration, giving the appearance of dewlaps. The loop, a large thick ring with circular eye, shows no sign of wear.

From the garden of 13, Rawstorn Road, i.e. within the Roman cemetery area outside the Balkerne Gate.

Colchester Museum Report 1930, 42, pl. XII no. 5; Jackson 1985, no. 61.

Colchester Museum, 446.29.

110. Colchester, Essex
L. 55 mm.

Centre-looped mortar, Type G, heavily cleaned, revealing
a golden brown pitted patina. The bow has steep, lightly
convex walls, plain except for a pair of incuse lines
at each end. The U-sectioned groove is narrow and
extremely shallow. Both zoomorphic terminals are small
and simplified. One has a triangular head, with pointed
muzzle and low horns or ears, and was probably intended
as a bovid. The other has a narrow head with rounded
blunt muzzle and a single projecting ?horn. The incuse
lines could be construed as neck halters or collars, cf. no.
241. The loop is a large circular ring.

Found in Colchester, 1856.

Colchester Museum Report 1930, 43, pl. I, fig 2; Jackson
1985, no. 67.

Colchester Museum, 237.47.

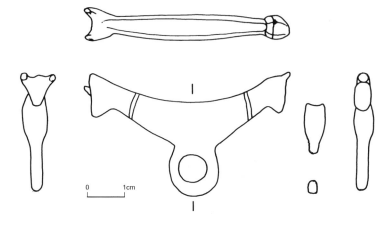

111. Colchester, Essex
L. 65 mm. (orig. *c.* 92 mm.)

Centre-looped mortar, Type H, with metallic grey (tin-enriched) patina,
lacking one end of the bow and most of the loop. A large example, with
an angular keel, thin sloping walls and an arc of triangular cells adjacent
to the loop. Corrosion at the broken end obscures some detail, but on
one face there are at least three cells filled with ?red enamel, on the
other face probably five cells, of which the outer two on one side bear
traces of ?green enamel and the centre one a different colour enamel,
perhaps red or orange. The apex of the cells points towards the loop. The
capacious groove has a rounded V-shaped cross-section with basal wear
facet. The remaining terminal is a small simple knob. Only the stub of
the large D-shaped loop remains.

Joslin Collection.

Smith 1918, 60–61, fig 14. *Colchester Museum Report* 1930, 43, no. 3, pl. XII, no. 2; Jackson 1985, no. 75.

Colchester Museum, JOS. 1057.

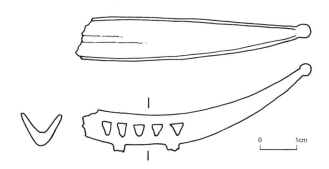

112. Colchester, Essex
L. 65 mm. (orig. *c.* 75 mm.)

Centre-looped mortar, Type H, with a light coating of green corrosion
over the olive patina, lacking one terminal. The bow is slender and
strongly-curved, with an angular keel, low, sloping, thin walls and a
capacious groove of rounded V-shaped cross-section. Corrosion partially
obscures the bow, but there is an arc of at least three small triangular
cells adjacent to the loop on both walls. Their apex points away from the
loop and they retain their ?green enamel inlay. The remaining terminal
is a tiny simple knob. The loop is a D-shaped ring with a lightly heart-
shaped eye.

Circumstances of discovery unknown.

Jackson 1985, no. 76.

Colchester Museum.

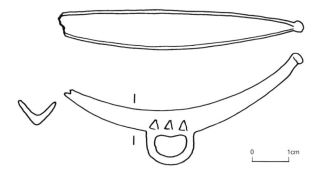

113. Colchester, Essex.
L 69 mm

Centre-looped mortar, Type L variant, of markedly asymmetric design. The lightly-curved bow has a rounded keel, and convex walls with a rather roughly-applied incuse diagonal triple line motif flanking the loop on both faces. The groove is very capacious, of deep, U-shaped cross-section. The loop, a D-shaped plate with off-centre sub-circular eye, is set well to one side of the centre point. The quite crudely-modelled terminals comprise a highly stylized bovid head and a bulbous knob, both with neck grooves. This may have been a conscious attempt to twin a bull's head with a phallus.

From excavations, 1976–9, of the Butt Road Roman cemetery.

Context date, Periods 1–2, = 2nd–mid-5th century AD.

N. Crummy, 1983, *Colchester Archaeological Report 2*, 146–7, fig. 180, no. 4288; Jackson 1985, no. 69.

Colchester Museum.

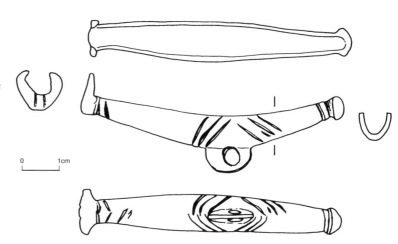

114. Colchester, Essex
L. 42 mm.

Centre-looped mortar, Type L, with mid-green encrusted corrosion over an olive patina. The slender bow, with angular keel, is corroded and distorted and both terminals are broken. The low sloping walls are decorated with an incuse diagonal triple line motif flanking the loop, and part of a repeat of this motif at one broken end. The groove is narrow, with a V-shaped cross-section. The loop is in the form of a flat D-shaped plate with an off-centre circular eye, almost worn through.

Circumstances of discovery unknown.

Colchester Museum Report 1930, 43, no. 5; Jackson 1985, no. 80.

Colchester Museum, 405.29.

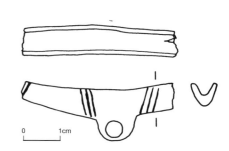

115. Colchester, Essex
L. 69 mm.

Centre-looped mortar, cleaned, with dull, golden brown, corrosion-pitted patina. The slender, lightly-curved bow has a rounded keel, low, plain walls, a deep U-sectioned groove with marked basal wear facet, and knobbed terminals with a simple neck moulding. The small, plate-like, D-shaped loop, quite crudely-made, is unworn.

From Sheepen, Region 3, sand-pit, i.e. native industrial settlement. Finds from the sand-pit are mostly of 1st century BC–1st century AD date.

Colchester Museum Report 1930, 43, no. 6; C.F.C. Hawkes and M.R. Hull, 1947, *Camulodunum* 33, pl. C, 18; Jackson 1985, no. 81.

Colchester Museum, 145.31.

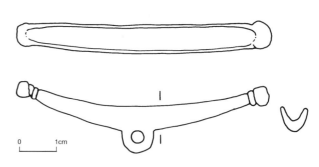

116. Colchester, Essex
L. 66 mm.

Centre-looped mortar, with pitted and encrusted green patina. The bow has plain, sloping walls (one dented and broken), a gently angled keel, a deep groove, of rounded V-shaped cross-section, with slight basal facet, and simple, compressed knobbed terminals. The ring-like loop has a slightly worn sub-circular eye.

Circumstances of discovery unknown.

Smith 1918, 60, fig. 12; *Colchester Museum Report* 1930, 41, no. 2, pl. XII, no. 3; Jackson 1985, no. 83.

Colchester Museum, Jos. 1057.

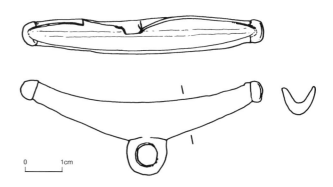

117. Colchester, Essex
L. 38.7 mm. (orig. *c.* 52 mm.)

Centre-looped mortar. A small example, further reduced by corrosion and heavy cleaning. The slender, strongly-curved bow has an angular keel and low, sloping, plain walls, lacking their rim. The groove, of shallow V-shaped cross-section, runs over the remaining terminal which is a simple knob. The thin, ring-like loop, mounted on a short keel plate, is broken across its ovoid eye.

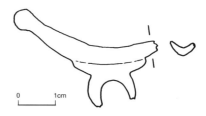

From 'The Union', i.e. within the Roman cemetery area outside the Balkerne Gate.

Jackson 1985, no. 86.

Colchester Museum, 237.02.

118. Colchester, Essex
L. 61.5 mm.

Centre-looped pestle. The slender, twin-tapered rod has a low D-shaped loop with tiny circular eye.

From excavations, 1973–6, in Balkerne Lane.

Context date, Period 5, a and b = *c.* AD 100/125–250.

N. Crummy, 1983, *Colchester Archaeological Report* 2, 145–7, fig. 180, no. 4287; Jackson 1985, no. 94.

119. Colchester, Essex
L. 75 mm.

End-looped mortar, with smooth green-brown patina. A very heavy casting with a very broad bow and large, flat, button-like knobbed terminals. The lightly convex thick-rimmed walls are decorated with an incuse zig-zag motif, heavily worn near the centre. The broad U-sectioned groove displays wear polish. The relatively small loop is in the form of a stylized bird's head, with everted bill and circular eye. It is mounted on a squared keel ridge with other cast projections.

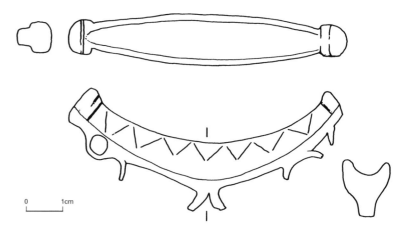

Provenance as no. 117.

Colchester Museum Report 1930, 43, no. 7, pl. XII, no. 4; Jackson 1985, no. 8.

Colchester Museum, 735.30.

120. Colchester, Essex
L. 60 mm. (orig. *c.* 62 mm.)

End-looped mortar, with lightly encrusted green patina. The strongly-curved bow has plain sloping walls, a rounded keel, and a very small lightly-knobbed terminal. The groove, of deep V-shaped cross-section with basal wear facet, has a marked axial asymmetry, probably a product of wear. The slender ring-like loop is broken across its small circular eye.

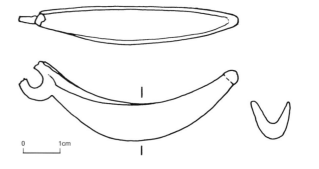

From the 'Bowling Green in Castle Park'.

Colchester Museum Report 1937, pl. XIII, 8; Jackson 1985, no. 17.

Colchester Museum, 621.35.

121. Colchester, Essex
L. 64 mm. (orig. *c.* 68 mm.)

End-looped mortar, with encrusted green patina. The lightly-curved bow has low, plain, gently carinated convex walls, a large, spherical, knobbed terminal, and a V-sectioned groove. Only the broken stub of the apparently simple loop remains.

Circumstances of discovery unknown.

Smith 1918, 58–9, fig. 8; *Colchester Museum Report* 1930, 41, no. 1; Jackson 1985, no. 11.

Colchester Museum.

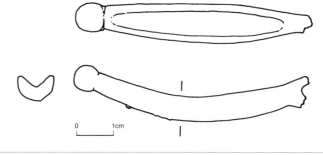

122. Colchester, Essex (Unillustrated)
L. 56 mm.

(?) End-looped mortar. A fragment, consisting of one knobbed terminal and part of the very lightly-curved, plain, low-walled bow. This is probably the missing part of no. 123.

From Culver Street, 1936, i.e. within fortress, and *colonia*.

Jackson 1985, no. 38.

Colchester Museum, 1175.36

123. Colchester, Essex
L. 30.5 mm.

End-looped mortar, with dull metallic brown (cleaned) patina. A fragment, comprising the damaged loop and part of the bow. The almost straight bow has low, plain, sloping walls, a rounded, asymmetric keel, and a capacious, rounded V-sectioned groove, which runs over the loop. The loop, a simple, tapered ring, is broken across (or worn through) its circular eye. This is probably the missing part of no. 122.

Provenance as no. 122.

Jackson 1985, no. 39.

Colchester Museum, 1174.36.

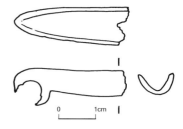

124. Colchester, Essex
L. 48 mm. (orig. *c.* 50 mm.)

End-looped mortar, with lightly-encrusted green patina. The bow is short, with a virtually straight rim, plain sloping walls, and an asymmetric rounded keel. The broad deep groove has a rounded V-shaped cross-section and deep basal wear slot. The terminal is plain. The loop, an apparently simple ring, is broken across the circular eye.

Circumstances of discovery unknown.

Colchester Museum Report 1930, 43, no. 4, pl. XII, no. 1.

Jackson 1985, no. 36.

Colchester Museum, 683.29.

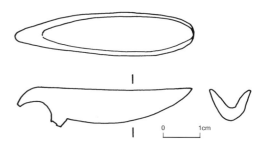

125. Colchester, Essex
L. 59 mm.

End-looped pestle. A strongly-curved tapered rod with a curved facet on the convex edge of its upturned tip. The loop has a tiny circular eye and a slender bill-like extension, giving the impression of an aquatic bird's head.

Provenance as no. 120.

Colchester Museum Report 1937, pl. XIII, 10 (where provenance and register number have been transposed with those of no. 126); Jackson 1985, no. 41.

Colchester Museum, 622.35.

126. Colchester, Essex

L. 64 mm. (orig. *c*. 66 mm.)

End-looped pestle. A large example, with curved facet on the convex edge of the upturned tip, the end of which is broken. The plain ring-like loop has an ovoid eye.

Provenance as no. 117.

Colchester Museum Report 1937, pl. XIII, 9 (where provenance and register number have been transposed with those of no. 125); Jackson 1985, no. 48.

Colchester Museum, 515.36.

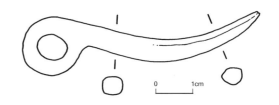

127. Colchester, Essex

L. 76.3 mm. Wt. 25.1 g.

End-looped pestle, with a lightly-encrusted metallic green-grey (tin-enriched) patina. An atypical example in the form of a miniature latch-lifter (as no. 133). The rod comprises two distinct parts, a straight handle stem of lightly-chamfered rectangular cross-section and a strongly-curved working end, of sub-hexagonal cross-section, with upturned tapered tip. A simple incuse moulding frames both ends of the handle, while the loop rim is ornamented with small incuse triangles. There is a little wear in the circular eye and on the convex edge of the tip of the rod.

Circumstances of discovery unknown.

British Museum, Pollexfen Collection, 1870,0402.250.

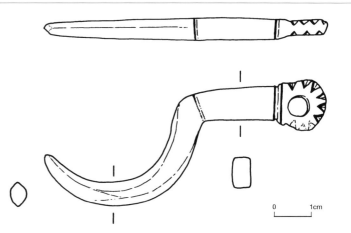

128. Colchester, Essex

L. 65.9 mm. Wt. 5.9 g.

End-looped pestle, with fine dark green matt patina. Both rod and loop are a little distorted and the tip of the rod slightly chipped. This pestle, with its long, chamfered, square-sectioned rod and 'shepherd's crook' coiled loop, has been worked from a rod, not cast – a working seam/striation is visible along the underside at the tip, near the centre and at the loop. The end of the rod is heavily worn through use, so much so that the thin tip is almost worn away. The slightly-distorted coiled loop has a rectangular cross-section.

Metal detector find. In private hands, via the antiquity market.

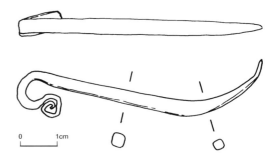

129. (?) near Colchester, Essex

L. 75.3 mm. Wt. 16.0 g.

Centre-looped mortar, Type J, with lacquered, lightly-pitted dark green patina. The strongly-curved bow has steeply-sloping walls and an angular keel. The walls, one thinner than the other, are decorated with an arc of enamel-inlaid small triangular cells, which extend almost to the terminals. Their apex points towards the loop. Three colours of enamel are used, red, light green and blue, in 20 cells on each wall, with a similar but not identical, and not quite symmetrical arrangement. The fine preservation of one wall reveals, from left to right, 2 blue, 2 green, 2 blue, 2 green, 3 red (centre), 3 green, 2 blue, 2 green, 2 blue. On the other wall the surviving traces reveal (left to right): 1 blue, 3 green, 2 blue, 3 green, 3 red (centre), 2 green, 2 blue, 2 green, 2 blue.

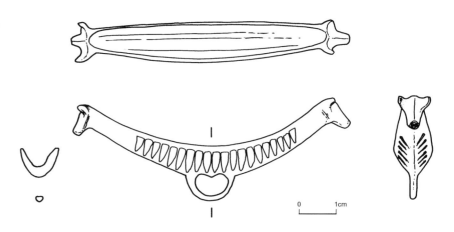

The capacious V-sectioned groove has wear polish, a basal wear slot and a wear 'ledge', on the thicker wall. The small, neatly-formed, bovid head terminals have inturned horns and a ridged, lightly-bulbous muzzle. The loop is a slender D-shaped ring with a heart-shaped eye.

Metal detector find. In private hands via the antiquity market. Thought to have been found in the Colchester region, this mortar and pestle no. 130 were spuriously described as a set on the antiquity market, by which time, also, their provenance had been overlooked.

130. (?) near Colchester, Essex
L. 56.8 mm. Wt. 6.6 g.

Centre-looped pestle, with lacquered green patina. A slightly asymmetric, crescentic, twin-tapered rod of rhomboid cross-section, with a D-shaped loop. There is an off-centre wear facet on the keel near one tip.

Metal detector find. In private hands via the antiquity market. For further details see mortar no. 129.

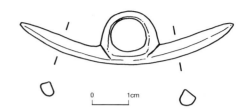

131. Coleshill, West Midlands
L. 57 mm. (orig. *c.* 60 mm.)

End-looped mortar. The strongly-curved bow has plain convex walls, a capacious groove of rounded V-shaped cross-section, and a tiny knobbed terminal. The large ring-like loop is broken across its circular eye.

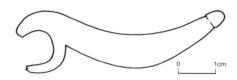

From excavation, 1979, of the Romano-Celtic temple and settlement at Grimstock Hill, by J. Magilton. From context A4 1284, SF 618, a 4th century AD temple demolition layer.

Jackson 1985, no. 18; J.Magilton, 2006, 'A Romano-Celtic temple and settlement at Grimstock Hill, Coleshill, Warwickshire', *Transactions Birmingham and Warwickshire Archaeological Society* 110, 175–6, fig. 71, no. 62.

Warwick, Warwickshire Museum, A7617.

132. Coleshill, West Midlands
L. 39 mm.

End-looped pestle. A small example, of blunt knife-like form, with deep, slender, rectangular-sectioned stem and upturned tapered tip. The loop has a tiny eye and a bill-like projection, giving the appearance of an aquatic bird's head.

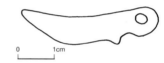

Provenance as no. 131. A US, SF 95, unstratified.

Jackson 1985, no. 42; J. Magilton (publication reference as no. 131), fig. 71, no. 63.

Warwick, Warwickshire Museum, A7618.

133. Colkirk, Norfolk
L. 45 mm.

Centre-looped mortar, Type H, lacking both ends of the low-walled elliptical bow and most of the loop. Adjacent to the loop on both walls is an arc of five (originally six) triangular cells, their apex pointing away from the loop, containing decayed greenish-coloured enamel inlay. The fragmentary loop was a D-shaped ring with a heart-shaped eye.

Metal detector find. In private hands.

134. Congham, Norfolk
L. 34.6, 34. 5 and 34.1 mm. Wt. 21.7 g.

Triple mortar, Type M, with central triangular aperture. In some places the metallic grey (?tin-enriched) patina is blistered and pitted with corrosion. All three units are virtually identical, with plain rounded terminals, smoothly convex plain walls and keel, and thin rims. The grooves, of rounded V-shaped cross-section, all display wear polish. The points of contact of the three units are neatly finished. It is hard to see that there would be any advantage in the provision of three mortars, and the design may be regarded as a novelty, though there was probably significance in the religious and magical power of the number three. Perhaps from the same mould as no. 139.

Metal detector find, 1994, from the area of the Congham Roman villa. In private hands.

135. Corpusty, Norfolk

L. 57 mm. (orig. *c.* 60 mm.) Wt. 6.7 g.

End-looped mortar, with pale green patina. The lightly-elliptical bow is exceptionally slender, with a rounded keel, very low plain sloping walls, and a simple tapered blunt point. The groove is extremely shallow, really only a light depression which runs from loop to tip. The proportionately slender loop is broken across its tear-shaped eye. It appears to have taken the form of a highly-devolved bird's head with elongated bill.

Metal detector find. In private hands.

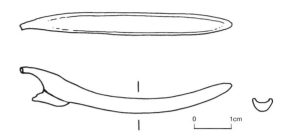

136. Cossington, Leics

L. 61 mm.

Mortar fragment, probably centre-looped, consisting of one end of the bow with large bovid terminal. The walls are steep and apparently plain, but the lightly flattened keel in the region of the terminal has an incuse design comprising a line of tiny lozenges – perhaps a stylized representation of the bull's dewlap. The groove is deep, of narrow V-shaped cross-section. It runs onto the bull's brow, terminating in an open 'spout' between the beast's horns. The head is large and striking, with prominent inturned horns (one broken). A line of incuse zig-zag decoration runs down the centre of the neatly-modelled face, from brow to muzzle. Projecting from the muzzle tip is a small circular ring, now partly broken. In view of its relatively diminutive size and atypical plane it is unlikely to have been the suspension loop, and it is tempting to regard it as a depiction of the bull's nose-ring. Another novel feature is the hollow-cast head with flat base and perforated circular eyes. It is possible that the hollow underside and eyes were filled with a packing material that contrasted with the colour of the metal. A zoomorphic terminal of this size and elaboration is more likely to have been one of a pair on a centre-looped mortar than a singleton on an end-looped mortar.

Metal detector find. In private hands.

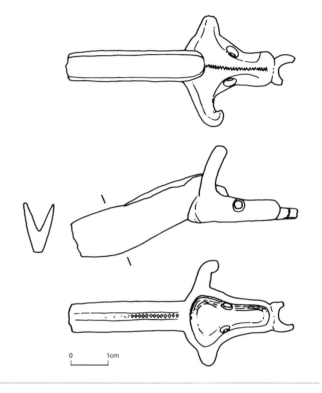

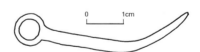

137. Costessey, Norfolk

L. 48 mm. Wt. 2.13 g.

End-looped pestle. A slender example with simple circular loop, set on the mid-line of the rod, and strongly-angled tip.

Metal detector find. In private hands.

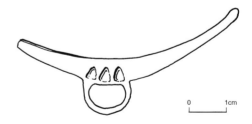

138. Cranwich, Norfolk

L. 60 mm. (orig. **c.** 70 mm.) Wt. 9.1 g.

Centre-looped mortar, Type H, with crescentic low-walled bow. One terminal is broken, the other has a gently swollen knob. Adjacent to the loop on both walls is an arc of three triangular cells, their apex pointing away from the loop. No trace of their enamel inlay survives. The loop is a D-shaped ring with D-shaped eye.

Metal detector find. In private hands.

139. Cranworth, Norfolk

L. 41, 40 and 39 mm. Wt. 19.6 g.

Triple mortar, Type M, with central triangular aperture. The smooth dark brown/black patina is pitted in a few places. The three units are very similar in form, and the slight variation in size is probably fortuitous. All have plain pointed terminals, lightly carinated walls, and very thin rims. The grooves, of rounded V-shaped cross-section, are capacious, with a high wear-polish in their base. The points of contact of the three units are less neatly finished than those of no. 134.

Metal detector find. In private hands.

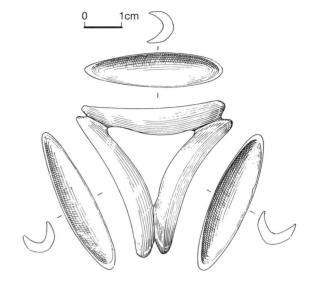

140. Darenth, Kent

L. 70.5 mm. Wt. 19.3 g.

Centre-looped mortar, recently cleaned, in consequence of which little of the original surface survives. Thus, although the steep, lightly-convex walls appear plain, the incuse triple neck moulding behind the small spherical knobbed terminals may be the remnants of a once more extensive engraved design. The narrow groove has a shallow U-shaped cross-section. The ring-like D-shaped loop has a circular eye with signs of wear.

Metal detector find, 1989 or 1990, at Old Mill Farm. Formerly in private hands, via the antiquity market, through which it had become divorced from its full provenance.

British Museum, 1999,0802.17.

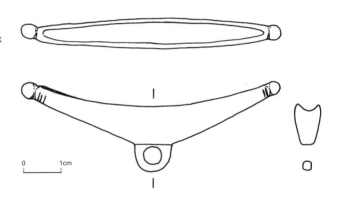

141. Deal/Canterbury, Kent

L. 47.6 mm. Wt. 24.8 g.

Centre-looped mortar, with a smooth dark green patina which preserves most of the original surface. A small, heavy example with a deep-bellied bow. The plain, sloping walls have a gently-inturned, thick, rounded rim. The groove, of rounded V-shaped cross-section, has wear polish and a marked basal wear facet. It runs over the terminals, which are in the form of small, flattened, button-like knobs. The atypical loop comprises a tiny circular eye within a slight expansion at the centre of the angular keeled bow.

Metal detector find. In private hands, via the antiquity market.

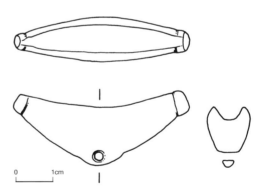

142. Debenham, Suffolk

L. 57 mm.

End-looped mortar, lacking the terminal end. The lightly-elliptical bow has an angular keel, steep convex plain walls, and a groove of rounded V-shaped cross-section. The loop is in the form of the stylized head of a water bird, with elongated dished bill.

Metal detector find. In private hands.

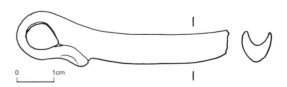

143. Denton, Norfolk

L. 32.4 mm. Wt. 4.5 g.

(?) End-looped mortar, fragment only, with badly-pitted dark grey-brown patina. What survives is one end of the slender elliptical bow, with flattened keel, plain steep walls, and a proportionately deep V-sectioned groove with basal facet, partially blocked with a ferrous concretion. The terminal is a small plain knob with slight neck constriction. Breakage of the bow appears recent.

Metal detector find. In private hands.

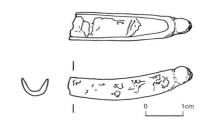

144. Diss, Norfolk

L. 57.6 mm. Wt. 16.8 g.

Centre-looped mortar, with a lightly-pocked smooth brown patina. An elegant casting, with strongly-curved crescentic bow, rounded keel, plain lightly-convex walls, gently-inturned rims, tiny plain terminal knobs, and a U-sectioned groove with markedly asymmetric basal wear facet, which has worn away the wall at diagonally opposite ends. The loop is omega-shaped, with a worn circular eye.

Metal detector find. Formerly in private hands, via the antiquity market.

British Museum, 1999,0802.18.

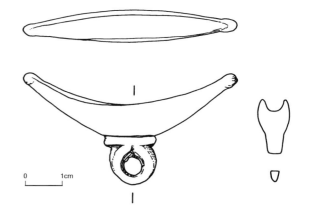

145. Diss, Norfolk

L. 34.3 mm. (orig. *c.* 57 mm.) Wt. 6.8 g.

Centre-looped mortar, with irregular dark brown patina, revealing underlying green corrosion products where chipped. Part of the loop and almost half of the bow are missing. The slender crescentic bow has an angular keel, plain sloping walls with chipped rims, and a U-sectioned groove with marked wear polish. The remaining blunt-pointed terminal is chipped but may once have been lightly knobbed. The loop is a small D-shaped ring broken across its circular eye.

Metal detector find. In private hands.

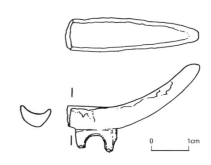

146. Ditchingham, Norfolk

L. 34 mm. Wt. 7.25 g.

Centre-looped pestle, small, with short deep crescentic rod (both tips missing) and D-shaped loop with circular eye.

Metal detector find. In private hands.

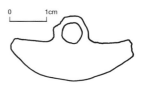

147. near Ditchingham, Norfolk

L. 57.5 mm. (orig. *c.* 66 mm.) Wt. 7.4. g.

Centre-looped mortar, Type J, with a smooth green-grey patina, which preserves the original surface in most places. One terminal, most of the loop, and much of one wall are broken, the latter also distorted. The lightly curved bow has an angular keel and thin convex walls, with an arc of six small triangular cells adjacent to the loop on the complete wall. The tips of just four of the cells remain on the broken wall. The cells, whose apex points towards the loop, retain remnants of their enamel inlay, but the colour is now indeterminate. The base of the capacious V-sectioned groove is set a little to one side of the longitudinal axis. The surviving zoomorphic terminal is a small, highly-devolved horned bovid, with only the blunt-ended rhomboid muzzle and simplified crescent-shaped horns rendered. Only the stub of the large, thin, D-shaped loop survives.

For metal composition see Scientific Analyses.

Metal detector find, from 'a Roman/Saxon site between Bungay and Ditchingham'. Formerly on the antiquity market.

British Museum, 1993,0901.1.

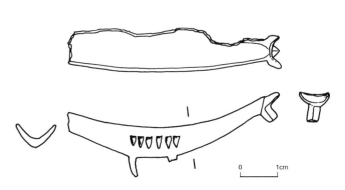

148. Doncaster, South Yorkshire

L. 52 mm.

Centre-looped pestle, with a strongly-curved, stout circular-sectioned, twin-tapered rod, its tips broken. The loop is a simple ovoid ring.

From rescue excavations, 1966, at Frenchgate, site DG. Unstratified.

P.C. Buckland and J.R. Magilton, 1986, *The Archaeology of Doncaster: 1. The Roman Civil Settlement*, British Archaeological Reports, Brit. Ser. 148, 85–6, fig. 19, 4.

149. Dorset, unprovenanced

L. 55 mm. (orig. *c.* 63 mm.) Wt. 9.7 g.

End-looped mortar, with slightly pitted olive-brown patina, lightly coated in places with a mid-green encrustation. A small example with only gently-curved slender bow. The convex walls are plain and very low with inturned rim, the keel smoothly-rounded. The groove, of U-shaped cross-section has wear polish on the basal facet. The terminal has a small, flat-ended, button-shaped knob. The loop is broken but appears to have been simple, undecorated and circular.

Metal detector find. Formerly in private hands, via the antiquity market.

British Museum, 1999,0802.19.

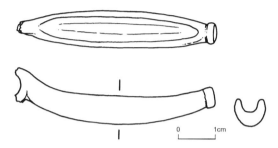

150. Dorset, unprovenanced (Unillustrated)

L. *c.* 60–70 mm.

End-looped mortar, with apparently low plain walls, large knobbed terminal, and a simple loop.

Seen on antiquity market, but not available for study. Present whereabouts unknown.

151. Dorset, unprovenanced

L. 81 mm. Wt. 16.4 g.

End-looped pestle. A very large example, with smooth green patina. The neatly-formed ring-like loop is circular, of rounded square cross-section, with a large round eye, at the back of which suspension wear is very evident, both as a distinct shine and as a rounding-off of the angle. The rod is very long, with a pillow-sectioned proximal end and an expanded, keeled, distal end. The keel displays wear polish and a single facet a short distance before the raised tip. Recent damage, comprising a dent and two scrapes, has bent the tip sideways and caused stress marks in the patina around the point of impact. The profile is probably little changed, but the sideways turn seen in the top view may be entirely due to the damage.

For metal composition see Scientific Analyses.

Metal detector find, formerly on the antiquity market.

British Museum, 1994,0405.4.

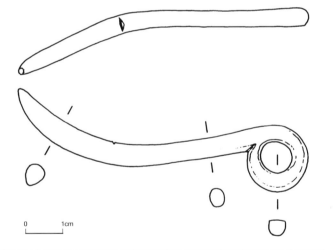

152. Dorset, unprovenanced

L. 57 mm. Wt. 16. 9 g.

End-looped pestle, with slightly pitted brown-black surface revealed by recent cleaning. The rod is of deep-bellied, blunt, knife-like form with a flattened top, near-vertical sides, and thin V-shaped cross-section. Removal of the patina has destroyed any trace of wear on the rod, but wear polish is visible on the remnants of green patina in the elongated eye of the simple discoidal loop.

For metal composition see Scientific Analyses.

Metal detector find, formerly on the antiquity market.

British Museum, 1994,0405.3.

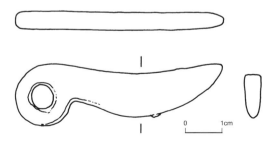

153. Dorset, unprovenanced
L. 68.5 mm. Wt. 15 g.

End-looped pestle, with extensively-pitted, light grey-green patina, the original surface preserved in only a few places. A large thick, relatively straight rod of sub-lentoid cross-section, with upturned blunt-ended tip, and an ovoid ring-like loop, with worn ovoid eye, set on the mid-line of the rod.

Metal detector find. Formerly in private hands, via the antiquity market.

British Museum, 1999,0802.20.

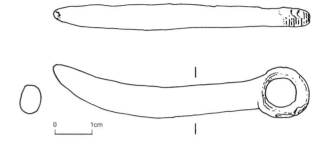

154. Dragonby, Humberside
L. mortar *c.* 79 mm, pestle *c.* 75 mm.

Set, comprising an end-looped mortar and an end-looped pestle. Both are plain, with a circular, ring-like loop. The mortar has plain, steeply-sloping walls, a rounded keel, plain, slightly constricted terminal, and a V-sectioned groove with pronounced basal flattening. The long pestle has a circular-sectioned rod swollen towards the tip.

From excavations, 1964–73. DR 66 CZ, from Site 2, lower topsoil west of the East Road (F229).

J. May, 1996, *Dragonby. Report on Excavations at an Iron Age and Romano-British Settlement in North Lincolnshire, Volume 1*, 276,278, fig. 11,25, no. 77.

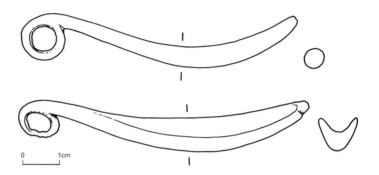

Analysis, by EDXRF (May 1996, 288, Table 11.1) yielded the following results, mortar: Cu 97.55, Pb 1.19, Sn 0.65, Fe 0.04, As 0.12. pestle: Cu 96.35, Pb 2.18, Sn 0.87, Fe 0.14, As 0.11.

155. Dragonby, Humberside
L. *c.* 48 mm.

End-looped pestle, with an oval-sectioned rod and an ovoid ring-like loop, its eye elongated through wear.

From excavations, 1964–73. DR67 PA, from Site 1, lower topsoil south of Romano-British Building 6.

J. May (publication reference as no. 154), 276, 278, fig. 11.15, no. 78.

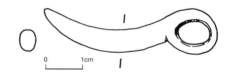

Analysis, by ED XRF (May 1996, 288,Table 11.1) yielded the following result: Cu 99.62, Pb 0.32, Fe 0.06.

156. Dungworth, South Yorkshire.
L 75 mm

End-looped mortar, with plain sloping walls, smoothly-rounded keel and capacious groove of broad V-shaped cross-section. The terminal may have been vestigially-knobbed though this may simply be a consequence of the damaged rim in that region. The loop is a circular ring with large ovoid eye.

Found 1921, at Hall Broom reservoir, in clay, 5 ft below surface level. Donated by finder.

Sheffield City Museum, L.1921.79.

157. Durham County, unprovenanced
L. 55 mm. Wt. 27.3 g.

Centre-looped mortar, with patchy green corrosion over a dark brown patina. A heavy, rather rudimentarily-made example. The asymmetric bow has a rounded V-shaped keel, steeply-sloped plain walls with virtually straight rims (one damaged in antiquity), a V-sectioned groove, and tiny knobbed terminals. The sub-triangular loop, slightly asymmetric to the axis of the bow, has a lentoid knop at its apex.

Metal detector find. In private hands, via the antiquity market.

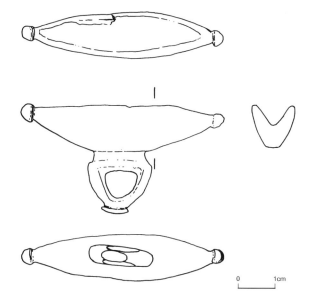

158. East Anglia, unprovenanced
L. *c.* 75 mm.

Centre-looped mortar, Type F, of heavy ornate form. The sharply carinated bow walls are decorated with ridged mouldings, the terminals are bovids with strongly moulded muzzles and prominent horns, and the loop is a projecting circular ring, the pedestal base of which is integrated with the central moulding. Its circular eye is markedly off-centre. Although varying slightly in details and finish this example is so similar to no. 53 that it is quite probable that both emanate from the same archetype if not the same mould.

Metal detector find. On the antiquity market.

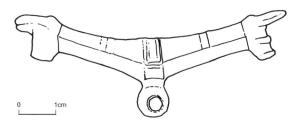

Unavailable for study, but a single photographed view (with scale) was illustrated in *Treasure Hunting* magazine, for May 1992, p. 7, pic. 13, where it is misleadingly referred to as a 'Celtic woad grinder'.

159. East Anglia, unprovenanced
L. *c.* 87 mm.

Centre-looped mortar, with long elliptical bow, apparently plain convex walls, simple pointed terminals, and a small D-shaped loop with circular eye.

Metal detector find. On the antiquity market.

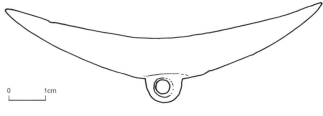

Unavailable for study, but a single photographed view (with scale) was illustrated in *Treasure Hunting* magazine, for May 1992, p. 7, pic 12, where it is misleadingly juxtaposed with a centre-looped pestle (no. 160) (the two are not a set) and described as a 'Celtic bronze woad grinder'.

160. East Anglia, unprovenanced
L. *c.* 61 mm.

Centre-looped pestle, with stout twin-tapered rod and ornate loop, in the form of a prominent neatly moulded plate with circular eye.

Metal detector find. On the antiquity market.

Unavailable for study, but a single photographed view (with scale) was illustrated in *Treasure Hunting* magazine for May 1992, p. 7, pic 12, where it is misleadingly juxtaposed with a centre-looped mortar (no. 159) (the two are not a set) and described as a 'Celtic bronze woad applicator'.

161. East Anglia, unprovenanced
L. 34.2 mm. Wt. 6.7 g.

Centre-looped pestle, with light grey-green patina. 'Anchor' type, with neatly-formed twin-tapered rod, and crisply-angled loop, with circular eye, surmounting a tall pedestal, the edges of which are neatly chamfered.

Metal detector find. In private hands.

162. East Anglia, unprovenanced
L. 43.8 mm. Wt. 10.9 g.

Centre-looped pestle, with partial mid-brown patina eroded in many places disclosing the underlying pitted porous pale green corrosion products. The twin-tapered crescentic rod has a plump lentoid cross-section. Corrosion has removed the tips and most of the underside surface. The large loop has a tear-shaped eye, scrolled terminals (also lacking their tip) and a small triangular piercing, now blocked with a ferrous concretion.

Metal detector find. Formerly in private hands, via the antiquity market.

British Museum, 1999,0802.22.

163. East Anglia, unprovenanced
L. 92 mm. Wt. 27. 8 g.

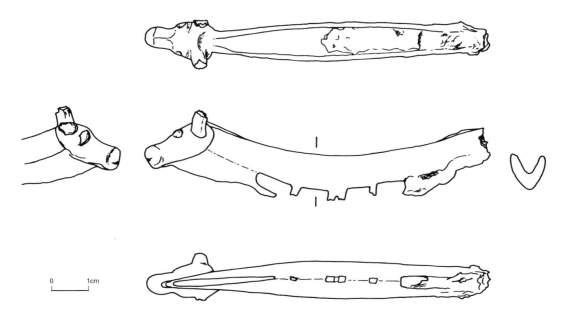

End-looped mortar, Type A variant, damaged, with dark brown and green encrusted patina, the original surface visible in only a few restricted areas. The bow is very long and gently curved, with low convex walls, which appear to have been plain, and an angular keel. The capacious groove, of rounded V-shaped cross-section is partially blocked with corrosion products. The bovid terminal is large, and, though corroded, was clearly finely-modelled. There are upturned horns (both fragmentary), a naturalistically depicted face with well-rendered eyes, and a tapered muzzle with bulbous end, on which was shown the mouth and, probably, the nostrils. Beneath the head is a marked dewlap. Fragmentary thin struts occupy the space between the dewlap and the loop. Most of the loop is broken away, but it was evidently of the type which lay below the end of the bow, with an elongation giving the appearance both of the bull's folded tail and of a stylized bird's head (cf. nos 236, 325, 380, 394, 422, 495 and 558).

For metal composition see Scientific Analyses.

Metal detector find, formerly on the antiquity market.

British Museum, 1992,1201.2.

164. East Anglia, unprovenanced
L. 58.7 mm. Wt. 14.5 g.

End-looped mortar, heavily cleaned, revealing a pitted, dull golden-coloured metal surface. The surface of the groove is better preserved. A smallish example, with lightly elliptical bow, rounded keel, plain convex walls, a simple, plain, blunt-pointed terminal, and a relatively capacious U-sectioned groove with wear-polished surface. The chunky loop is in the form of a bird's head, with marked brow ridge and dished bill.

Metal detector find. Formerly in private hands, via the antiquity market. Purported to be a 'pair' with no. 167 by the trade vendor, but unlikely to be so.

British Museum, 1999,0802.21.

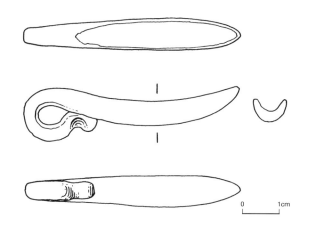

165. East Anglia, unprovenanced
L. 83.7 mm. Wt. 33.1 g.

End-looped mortar, with quite extensively-pitted mid-green patina. A relatively heavy casting, with lightly curved bow, rounded keel, plain convex walls, thick rims, a simple projecting round-knobbed terminal, and a capacious groove of broad, slightly asymmetric, V-shaped cross-section. The loop was evidently originally a large ring with circular or sub-circular eye, but after breakage and/ or heavy wear at the distal end the upper part of the ring was roughly cut and hammered down to close the break and permit continued suspension. In that way the size of the loop was reduced and the shape of the eye changed to its present sub-pear shape.

Metal detector find. In private hands, via the antiquity market.

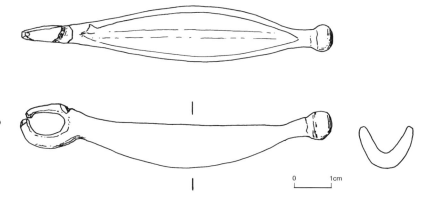

166. East Anglia, unprovenanced
L. 43.6 mm. Wt. 6.6 g.

End-looped mortar, with brownish patina, very heavily abraded and facetted through insensitive cleaning. The tip, apparently plain, may once have been longer. Only the stub of the apparently simple end loop survives. A small simple example, with angular keel, steep, apparently plain, walls, chipped rims, and a groove of rounded V-shaped cross-section with wear shine and a slightly asymmetric wear facet.

Metal detector find. In private hands.

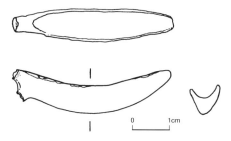

167. East Anglia, unprovenanced
L. 70.2 mm. Wt. 9.9 g.

End-looped pestle, with grey-green patina, rather pitted at the loop. A large, very finely-made example. The long sinuous rod has a marked centre ridge and side carinations and swells towards the tip. The underside of the swelling displays wear polish which extends as far as the tip. The loop is very elegantly formed in the shape of a bird's head, with marked brow ridge and everted ridged bill.

Metal detector find. Formerly in private hands, via the antiquity market. Although the pestle would fit in the groove of mortar no. 164 there is neither close similarity nor other intrinsic reason to indicate that they were made or used as a pair, despite the claim of the trade vendor.

British Museum, 1999,0802.23.

168. East Anglia, unprovenanced
L. 41.4 mm. Wt. 2.3 g.

End-looped pestle, with smooth mid-green patina. A tiny, light example, with slender elliptical rod, upturned tip, and a very small, partially-fractured, loop with tiny circular eye. There is slight wear polish and a wear facet on the base of the swollen area of the rod near the tip.

Metal detector find. Formerly in private hands, via the antiquity market.

British Museum, 1999,0802.24.

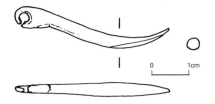

169. East Anglia or Cambridgeshire, unprovenanced
L. 81 mm. Wt. 21.5 g.

Centre-looped mortar, with olive-brown patina pitted and encrusted in many places with active corrosion. The crescentic bow has plain, steeply-sloping, lightly-convex walls, an angular keel, thick rims, and a U-sectioned groove, which runs onto the moulded, knobbed terminals. Only the stub of the loop survives, and corrosion obscures the adjacent wall area on both faces of the bow which appear to have been decorated with an engraved (or enamelled?) inverted V-shaped motif or large triangular cell.

Metal detector find. Formerly in private hands, via the antiquity market.

British Museum, 1999,0802.25.

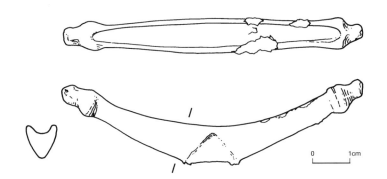

170. East Anglia or Cambridgeshire, unprovenanced
L. 65.2 mm. Wt. 9.8 g.

End-looped mortar, with cleaned, very extensively and heavily pitted mixed green patina. A simple, elegant example with quite strongly-curved, slender parallel-sided bow, angular keel, low, apparently plain, lightly-convex sloping walls, thin badly chipped rims, a narrow, relatively capacious U-sectioned groove with basal wear facet, and a very small understated knobbed terminal. The corrosion-emaciated, simple, ring-like loop has a large circular eye.

Metal detector find. Formerly in private hands, via the antiquity market.

British Museum, 1999,0802.26.

171. East Bilney/ Stanfield borders, Norfolk
L. 49.3 mm. (orig. *c.* 58 mm.) Wt. 4.9 g.

Centre-looped pestle, with pale brown-green patina. An example of very standard form, with elliptical twin-tapered rod (one tip broken), of D-shaped cross-section, and a large ring-like loop with ovoid eye, much of which is broken.

Metal detector find. In private hands.

172. Edwardstone, Suffolk
L. *c.* 68 mm.

Centre-looped mortar, with lightly curved bow, plain sloping walls, smoothly-rounded keel and capacious U-sectioned groove. The knobbed terminals are neatly formed, with a triple-groove neck moulding. The loop is a simple sub-rectangular plate with a small circular eye.

Metal detector find. In private hands.

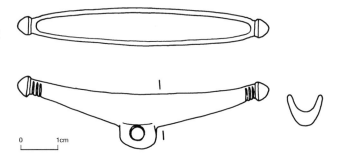

173. Edwardstone, Suffolk
L. *c.* 52 mm.

Centre-looped mortar. A small example with strongly-curved bow, plain steep walls, and a narrow U-sectioned groove. The terminal knobs are simple and quite rudimentarily finished. The loop is a discoidal plate with a circular eye.

Metal detector find. In private hands.

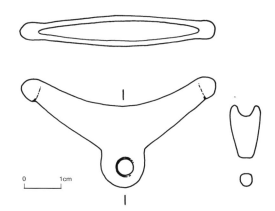

174. Elm, Cambs
L. 73 mm.

Centre-looped mortar, Type F, badly corroded and damaged. The bow walls are thin and sharply carinated, with a near-vertical upper section. Remains of a central ridged moulding and a flanking rib can be discerned. The deep U-sectioned groove is very capacious. As on no. 53, the two bovid terminals appear to differ slightly in size and form. They seem less well rendered, but that may be a consequence of corrosion. The broken loop was evidently a circular ring on a pedestal base linked to the central moulding.

Found 1945, at Laddus Grove, apparently in association with a burial ('...on the arm of a skeleton...').

Trett 1983, no. 4; Jackson 1985, no. 65.

Donated to Wisbech Museum.

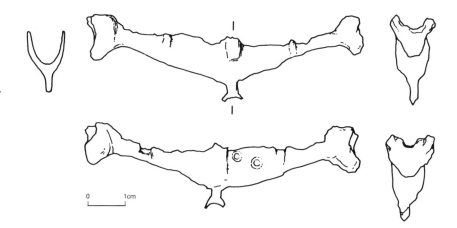

175. Elmton, Derbyshire
L. 69 mm.

End-looped mortar, with plain, convex walls, smoothly-rounded keel, capacious groove of broad U-shaped cross-section, simple knobbed terminal, and ring-like loop with circular eye.

Metal detector find, 1986. Donated by finder.

Sheffield City Museum, 1986.47.

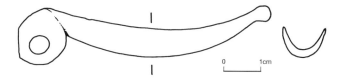

176. Ely, Cambs
L. 60.4 mm. (orig. *c.* 78 mm.) Wt. 12.1 g.

Centre-looped mortar, Type H, with a mottled mid-to dark-green smooth patina, covered in places with a light coating of pale brown soil. One terminal and most of the loop are lacking and both walls and the loop are distorted, all of which appears to be ancient damage. The strongly-curved bow has thin lightly-convex walls with an arc of three small elongated triangular cells on each face adjacent to the loop. Their apex points towards the loop and they retain their decayed enamel inlay, though the original colour is now indeterminate. The groove is capacious, of slightly asymmetric rounded V-shaped cross-section. The surviving terminal is a small neat knob on the end of the finely-tapered bow. The loop was evidently of the heart-shaped variety.

Metal detector find. Formerly in private hands, via the antiquity market.

British Museum, 1999,0802.27.

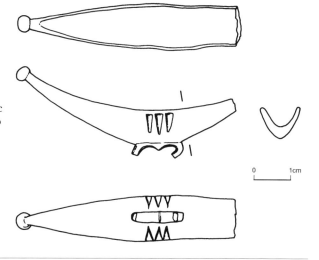

177. Enderby, Leics

L. *c.* 90 mm.

End-looped mortar, with long elliptical bow, angular keel, steeply-convex, apparently plain walls, a bulbous knobbed terminal, and a narrow, deep, V-sectioned groove. The large loop is in the form of a stylized bird's head, with marked brow and elongated everted bill. The form and size are very similar to those of the pestle from Normanton-le-Heath (no. 391).

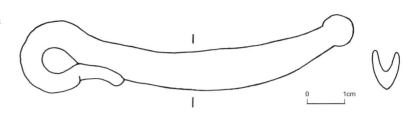

Metal detector find from a rally, on a site that appears to be exclusively of 1st–2nd century AD date. In private hands.

178. Essex, unprovenanced

L. 58.2 mm. Wt. 17.3 g.

Centre-looped mortar, with recently cleaned brown patina. The very lightly curved, near parallel-sided bow has low, plain, steeply-sloping walls, with quite thick rim, and a rounded V-sectioned groove, which runs over the terminals. The rounded terminals have a pair of tiny knobs, one projecting from each side. If other than abstract they are marginally more phallic than zoomorphic! The proportionately large discoidal loop has a lemon-shaped eye, elongated by wear.

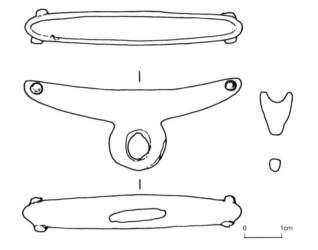

Metal detector find. Formerly in private hands, via the antiquity market.

British Museum, 1999,0802.28.

179. Essex, unprovenanced

L. 58 mm. Wt. 14.6 g.

Centre-looped pestle, with smooth grey-green patina. The stout, twin-tapered rod has a lozenge-shaped cross-section, chamfered at the sides adjacent to the loop, and worn on the keel. The arms are markedly unequal and one appears to have been intentionally truncated in antiquity. Both have blunt tips. The comparatively large collar-like loop has a plump D-shaped eye and a sharply moulded base.

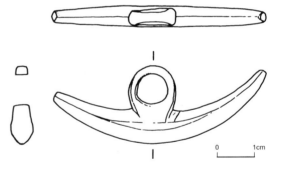

For metal composition see Scientific Analyses.

Metal detector find, formerly on the antiquity market.

British Museum, 1986,0802.2.

180. Essex, unprovenanced

L. 47 mm. Wt. 9.6 g.

Centre-looped pestle, with strongly-curved twin-tapered rod. The keeled edge shows signs of wear, especially near the centre. The small circular loop has a sharply moulded plinth.

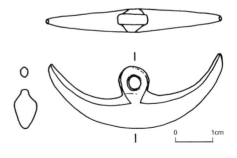

For metal composition see Scientific Analyses.

Metal detector find, formerly on the antiquity market.

British Museum, 1986,0403.1.

181. Essex, unprovenanced
L. 67.5 mm. Wt. 19 g.

End-looped mortar. A finely crafted example with smooth green patina. The gently elliptical bow has low, plain, carinated walls, a flattened keel, a simple shouldered knob terminal, and a shallow groove, of broad U-shaped cross-section with an asymmetric wear facet. The finely cast and finished loop is in the form of an aquatic bird's head, with ridged everted bill and prominent brow. A little wear is visible in the circular eye.

For metal composition see Scientific Analyses.

Metal detector find, formerly on the antiquity market.

British Museum, 1986,0802.1.

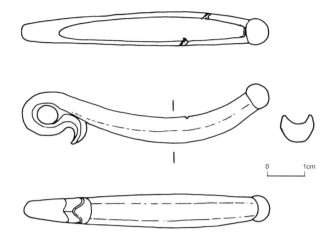

182. Essex, unprovenanced
L. 53.3 mm. Wt. 4.6 g.

End-looped pestle, with mid-green patina. A slender, elegant, crescentic rod of round cross-section, with swollen, sub-lentoid-sectioned working zone and tapered up-turned tip. The slender loop is now broken across its apparently small eye.

Metal detector find. Formerly in private hands, via the antiquity market.

British Museum, 1999,0802.29.

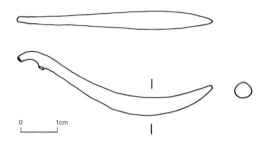

183. Eyke, Suffolk
L. 50.1 mm. Wt. 26.8 g.

Centre-looped mortar, with mid-olive-green patina gouged and abraded in many places. A heavy casting, with plump elliptical bow, plain convex walls, shallow, flattened U-sectioned groove, and simple down-turned terminals, which form a rib and merge with the now broken strutted loop. The terminals were doubtless intended as very devolved bird heads with elongated bills.

Metal detector find. Formerly in private hands, via the antiquity market, by means of which it acquired the erroneous and spurious provenance of 'from Norfolk, ??Brandon area' !!

British Museum, 1999,0802.30.

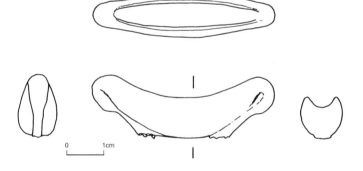

184. Faversham, Kent
L. 55 mm. Wt. 7.7 g.

End-looped mortar, with encrusted green patina, lacking the loop and part of the bow. The remaining part of the bow has low, plain, sloping walls, a narrow V-sectioned groove with basal wear facet, and a simple pointed terminal.

For metal composition see Scientific Analyses.

From the Gibbs Collection, most of which came from the King's Field. In addition to the rich Anglo-Saxon cemetery Roman burials are known in the area.

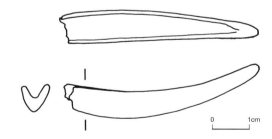

C. Roach Smith, 1871, *A Catalogue of Anglo-Saxon and Other Antiquities Discovered at Faversham....* (London), 16, where it is described as 'the end of a strigil; or part of the case of some curved instrument'; Smith 1918, 58–9; Jackson 1985. no. 27.

British Museum, 1260.70 (Gibbs Bequest).

185. (?) Felixstowe, Suffolk
L. 64 mm.

Centre-looped mortar, with smooth dark
grey patina. The bow has carinated walls,
their upper part near-vertical. Rim and
carination are marked by a simple dot-
punched line. The shallow groove has a
rounded V-shaped cross-section. The stylized
zoomorphic terminals depict two different
animals; the larger one a bovid, with ears,
inturned horns and blunt-ended muzzle; the
other, with dot-punched decoration on the
pointed muzzle, slighter, and without horns,
perhaps intended as a cow to complement
the bull. The loop, a thin plate, with dot-
punched border and circular eye, is markedly
asymmetric.
A 19th-century find in the Fitch Collection.

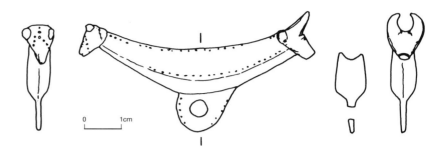

Trett 1983, no. 2; Jackson 1985, no. 64.

Norwich Castle Museum, 76.94 (698).

186. Felthorpe, Norfolk
L. 55.6 mm. Wt. 10.5 g.

End-looped mortar, with heavily-lacquered brown and green patina. A
small example with only very lightly
curved bow, plain, very low, near-vertical walls, a broad lightly rounded
keel, and a shallow V-sectioned groove, with basal facet, which runs over
the plain, blunt-pointed terminal. Atypically, the loop is a coil of rather
irregular gauge wire, originally tucked below the end of the bow, but
now distorted out of position.

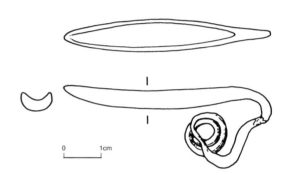

Metal detector find. In private hands.

187. Fengate, Cambs
L. mortar 61 mm. pestle 61 mm.

Set, comprising an end-looped mortar and an end-looped pestle. The
mortar has plain convex walls, a smoothly-rounded keel, a simple
pointed terminal, and a capacious, very broad U-sectioned groove.
The loop is a thin circular ring with ovoid eye and a neat grooved
moulding at the junction with the bow. The pestle has a long, sinuous
stem with wear on the convex face of the swollen upturned tip. The
simple ovoid loop has a lemon-shaped eye.

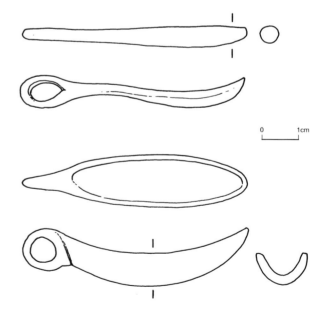

From excavation, 1989, of the Power Station site, by F. Pryor.
The context, originally thought to pre-date 200 BC, proved to be
problematic, and the set is more likely to belong with the small
number of Late Iron Age and Roman finds than to any earlier period.
In the final report (Pryor 2001) Coombs gives the context for both
components as 'from spoil heap'.

D. Coombs, 1992, 'Flag Fen platform and Fengate Power Station post
alignment – the metalwork', *Antiquity* 66, 514–15, fig. 8, no. 14;
F. Pryor, 1994, 'Flag Fen', *Current Archaeology* 137, 179–84; F. Pryor,
2001, *The Flag Fen basin: archaeology and environment of a Fenland
landscape*, English Heritage Archaeological Reports, 281, fig. 10.11, nos
274–5, 282 (where the metal analysis is mistakenly placed with the
entry for the pestle, no. 275, rather than the mortar, no. 274 – see 304,
table 10.2, penultimate entry), 294 , 299, fig. 10.20 , 301. The given
analysis (by Peter Northover) for the mortar is Fe 0.07, Co 0.01, Ni
0.21, Cu 97.98, Zn 0.00, As 0.00, Sb 0.16, Sn 1.35, Ag 0.07, Bi 0.06, Pb
0.07, Au 0.00, S 0.02. The low tin content is noteworthy.

188. Fincham, Norfolk
L. 33.7 mm. Wt 4.4 g.

Centre-looped mortar, Type J variant, fragment, with slightly friable green patina over paler green powdery corrosion products. Only one terminal and part of the adjacent bow survives. The curved bow has a ridged asymmetric keel and thin, lightly-convex, steeply-sloping walls with chipped rims. Both walls are decorated with a long arc of enamel-inlaid, slender, incuse cells in the form of an ornate floral (?highly-stylized lotus bud) motif, their apex pointing towards the keel. On one wall are six cells filled with blue enamel, the seventh with red enamel and the eighth, of which part survives at the break, retaining a trace of red enamel, too. On the other wall are seven cells filled with blue enamel and part of an eighth cell at the break, now devoid of inlay. The relatively capacious groove is of rounded V-shaped cross-section. The remaining terminal is a (for this type) relatively large bovid head, with long, ridged, flaring, square-ended muzzle and tiny ears/ horns (one broken).

Metal detector find. In private hands.

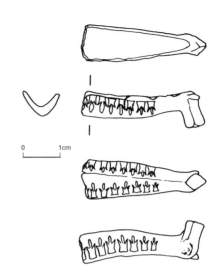

189. Fincham, Norfolk
L. 38.1 mm. Wt. 7.7 g.

Centre-looped pestle, with pale grey-green patina. A neatly-made example, with an equal-armed rod of plump D-shaped cross-section and a tall-stemmed round suspension loop with a small circular eye.

Metal detector find. In private hands.

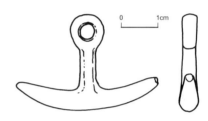

190. Fincham, Norfolk
L. 39.2 mm. Wt. 9.2 g.

Centre-looped pestle, with pale green-grey dusty, slightly uneven patina, retaining soil traces in crevices. A lightly elliptical twin-tapered rod with a circular loop mounted on a tall pedestal and integral swag-like struts linking the tips of the rod to the junction of loop and pedestal. Extensive flashing remains in the eye of the loop, in the two sub-triangular apertures flanking the pedestal, and on the outer edges of the struts – clear evidence that no finishing work took place after casting. Although the loop shows no sign of use it is not possible to ascertain whether or not the grinding face of the rod is worn.

Metal detector find. In private hands.

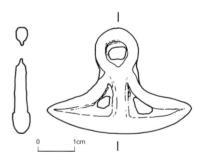

191. Fishbourne, West Sussex
L. 80 mm.

Centre-looped mortar, Type L. The slender, gently-curved bow has a narrow V-shaped groove and low, sloping, thin walls, which are decorated with an incuse diagonal triple line motif flanking the loop. The shouldered knob terminals and neck mouldings are neatly-formed. The D-shaped loop plate has a small circular eye.

From excavation of villa complex. Ploughsoil.

B. Cunliffe, 1971, *Fishbourne II*, 121, fig. 50, 141; Jackson 1985, no. 79.

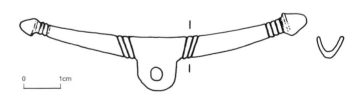

192. Fishtoft, Lincs

L. mortar *c.* 88 mm. pestle *c.* 61 mm.

Set, comprising an end-looped mortar and an end-looped pestle. The elaborate mortar has a strongly-curved, near parallel-sided bow, with convex walls and a deep, narrow, V-sectioned groove. The walls are decorated with a simple linear dot-punched motif. The large bovid terminal is finely – and quite naturalistically-moulded, with prominent inturned horns, upturned ears, deep-socketed round eyes, and a broad, flared blunt-ended muzzle with slightly gaping mouth. The large loop, with lemon-shaped eye, has a bill-like extension and was probably intended both as the bull's tail and as a stylized aquatic bird's head, the small projecting knob perhaps representing some form of crest or plumage. The neatly moulded stud at the centre of the convex underside of the bow was probably held to steady the mortar when in use. The pestle is a slender crescentic rod of blunt knife-like form, with pronounced side facets on the upturned end. Its simple ring-like loop has a circular eye.

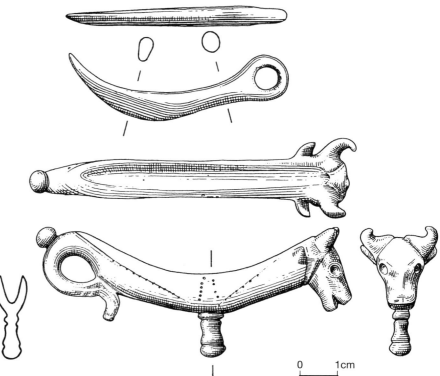

This set, which was submitted to an auction house in 1977 (Christies Sale Catalogue, Fine Antiquities, Tues. 12 July 1977. Lot 208, plate 54), but was withdrawn before the sale, was then stated only to have come from Lincolnshire (Jackson 1985, no. 4). Some years subsequently it was discovered to have come from excavations in 1970 on a site at Fishtoft, near Boston, Lincs., by Mr. G. Bullivant. Unfortunately, the notice of the excavation (*Lincolnshire History and Archaeology* 6, 1971, 7, fig. II, 8) did not include a reference to the context of the find; nor is it known how the set came to be on the antiquity market. Sadly, its whereabouts is still unknown. The site yielded a rectangular wattle-and-daub building with a hearth and oven. The finds included coins of the 3rd to 4th centuries AD, an iron plough coulter, and objects of worked jet and bone (*Britannia* 6,1975,244; 7,1976,324; 8,1977,388).

Jackson 1985, no. 4.

193. Forncett, Norfolk

L. *c.* 62 mm.

Centre-looped mortar, Type K, lacking one terminal, part of the bow and most of the loop. The lightly-crescentic bow has a rounded angular keel, sloping plain walls and a capacious V-sectioned groove. The remaining terminal is a stylized bovid head with prominent everted horns and a slender angular muzzle with grooved mouth. What remains of the loop suggests it was a D-shaped ring with large eye.

Metal detector find. In private hands.

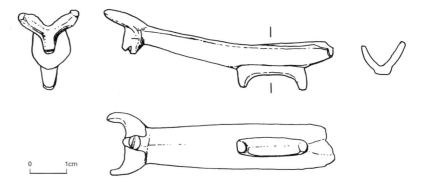

194. Foulden, Norfolk
L. 69.8 mm.

Centre-looped mortar, with brown patina. The bow is very slender, with low, parallel-sided, steeply-sloping walls (the rim of one a little lower than the other), decorated with an incuse paired-V motif either side of the loop. The very shallow U-sectioned groove, partially blocked with a ferrous encrustation, runs over the terminals. The stylized bovid-head terminals are near-identical, with only the everted horns, ears and tapered muzzle depicted. The D-shaped loop is broken across its circular eye.

Metal detector find, donated to Kings Lynn Museum.

Trett 1983, no. 5; Jackson 1985, no. 63.

Kings Lynn Museum, KL 75.981 (A1626).

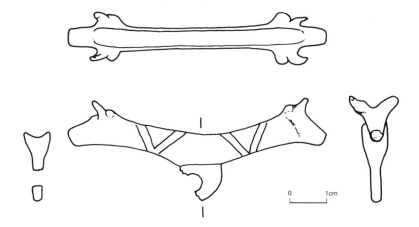

195. Fressingfield, Suffolk
L. 58 mm.

End-looped mortar, its exterior surface destroyed by ruthless post-discovery 'cleaning' (abrasion). Only the groove and terminal knob are as found. The elliptical bow has a rounded keel, apparently plain convex walls, a moulded, flat-ended, terminal knob, and a very shallow groove of broad U-shaped cross-section. The badly-damaged loop was apparently plain, with an ovoid eye.

Metal detector find. In private hands.

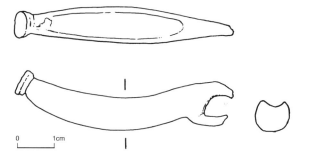

196. Fring, Norfolk
L. 33 mm. Wt. 9.5 g.

Centre-looped pestle, with mid-green patina. An anchor-shaped example, slightly asymmetric and rather rudimentarily made with little finishing after casting. The strongly curved rod has a rounded keel. The flat circular loop is supported on a pedestal with simple step-moulding.

Metal detector find. In private hands.

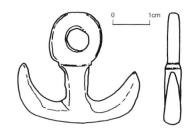

197. Garboldisham, Norfolk (Unillustrated)
L. c. 45 mm. Wt. 8.6 g.

Centre-looped pestle, with triangular-sectioned, elliptical, twin-tapered rod and thin-walled collar-like loop with large sub-circular eye.

Metal detector find. In private hands.

198. Gate Burton, Lincs
L. 51 mm. Wt. 12.1 g.

Centre-looped pestle, with brown patina. A stout example, with wear facet on the keeled rod, most noticeably at the centre. The large, thin, flat ring-like loop has only a vestigial stem. There is wear in the circular eye.

Metal detector find, from the north side of the Roman road half a mile east of Littleborough (*Segelocum*). In private hands.

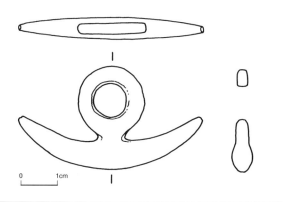

199. Gisleham, Suffolk

L. 54 mm. Wt. 11.6 g.

Centre-looped mortar, with recently abraded pocked green patina, the original surface surviving in only a few places. The bow is very strongly-curved, with plain steeply-sloping walls and prow-like, small simple knobbed terminals. The V-sectioned groove, with basal wear facet, has been almost worn through the wall at diagonally opposed ends. Only the stub of the D-shaped loop survives, with an arc of the circular eye.

Metal detector find. In private hands.

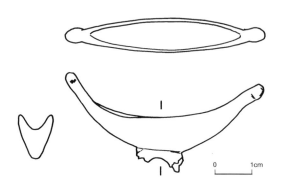

200. Gloucestershire area

L. 42.2 mm. Wt. 8.4 g.

End-looped pestle, with light green patina and mid-orange-brown soil accretion in the mouldings and eye. A small, stout example, the thick curved, circular-sectioned rod of which swells and turns lightly to one side near the blunt tip. There is a wear facet beneath the tip and a small casting blemish to one side. The D-shaped loop with circular eye is elaborately moulded, and has the appearance of a stylized aquatic bird's head with prominent brow and everted bill. Working marks are clearly visible, but not obtrusive, both on the rod and loop.

Metal detector find. Formerly in private hands, via the antiquity market.

British Museum, 1999,0802.31.

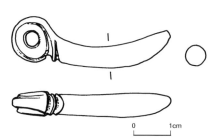

201. Gloucestershire area

L. 52.6 mm. Wt. 9.9 g.

End-looped pestle, with patchy olive and dark grey patina. The oval-sectioned elliptical rod is markedly worn on the keel of its mid-section and, less so, on the convex face of the upturned tip. The small loop is in the form of a stylized aquatic bird's head, with marked brow and everted bill. There is wear in the sub-circular eye.

Metal detector find. Formerly in private hands, via the antiquity market.

British Museum, 1999,0802.32.

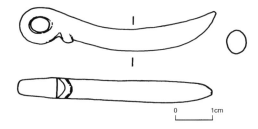

202. Godstone, Surrey

L. 27.2 mm. Wt. 8.6 g.

End-looped pestle, lacking most of the rod, with light olive-green patina, the original surface surviving only inside the loop and on concave curves. The rounded-rectangular-sectioned rod has a looped terminal in the form of a stylized bird's head, with tear-shaped eye and everted bill.

Metal detector find during field survey.

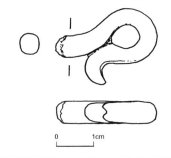

203. Gosbecks, Essex

L. 70 mm. (orig. *c.* 73 mm).

End-looped mortar, with green patina. The bow has steeply-sloping plain walls, an angular keel, and a broad, shallow, V-sectioned groove with basal wear facet, partly obscured by corrosion. The broken terminal was probably a plain point. The large loop is in the form of a stylized bird's head with everted bill. There is wear at the back of the circular eye.

From excavation 1967, of Roman theatre. Turf of *cavea*-mound, Trench 18, Phase 2.

Context date, AD 150–250.

R. Dunnett, 1971, 'The excavation of the Roman theatre at Gosbecks', *Britannia* 2, 44–5, fig. 6,1; Jackson 1985, no. 30.

Colchester Museum.

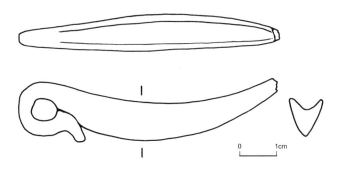

204. Grandford, Cambs
L. 71 mm. Wt. 18.8 g.

Centre-looped mortar, with corroded light brown patina, retaining some soil coating. The bow has plain, convex walls, an angular keel, a groove of rounded V-shaped cross-section, simple knobbed terminals, and a very small ring-like loop broken across its tiny circular eye.

Metal detector find. In private hands.

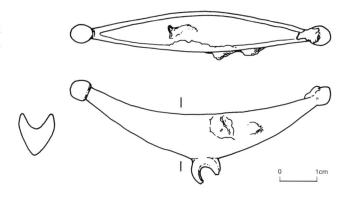

205. Grandford, Cambs
L. 68 mm.

Centre-looped mortar. The crescent-shaped bow has plain, convex walls, an angular keel, a U-sectioned groove, simple pointed terminals, and a ring-like loop with small circular eye.

Metal detector find 'on the west side of the line of a Roman road'.

Trett 1983. no. 6; Jackson 1985. no. 90.

Donated to Wisbech Museum, 145.1979.

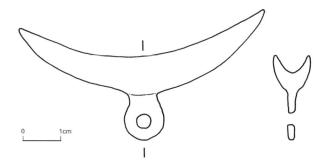

206. probably Grandford, Cambs
L. 53.1 mm.

End-looped mortar, with mid-green patina, lightly accreted with pale brown soil and corrosion products. The gently curved bow, broken at one end, has a rounded angular keel, plain, sloping walls, and a deep, capacious, V-sectioned groove with slightly asymmetric basal facet. The unusual 'pinched', prow-like terminal, which reinforces the boat-like appearance of the bow, has a chipped end and may once have been more elaborate. It seems unlikely that it was the loop plate, which was probably at the broken end.

Metal detector find.

Donated to Wisbech Museum, 1991.49, 263.

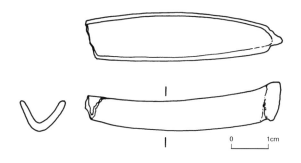

207. probably Grandford, Cambs
L. 57.5 mm.

End-looped pestle, with mid-green patina, lightly accreted with pale brown soil, which also blocks the eye of the loop. An atypical example in the form of a miniature latch-lifter. Thus, the rod comprises two distinct parts, a straight handle stem of chamfered rectangular cross-section, and a strongly-curved working end of sub-oval cross-section with upturned tapered tip. The loop plate, which is in a different plane to normal, has a sub-circular eye, elongated through wear, and a pair of simple, neatly-wrought mouldings at the junction with the handle stem. For the bipartite form, cf. nos 12 and 387; and for the atypical loop plane, cf. nos 73 and 473.

Metal detector find.

Donated to Wisbech Museum, 1991.49, 262.

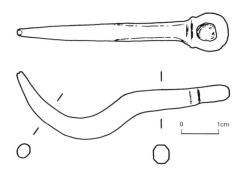

208. Great Chesterford, Essex

L. *c.* 74 mm.

Centre-looped mortar, Type H. The broad, strongly-curved bow has an angular keel and low, thin, carinated walls with two arcs of six contiguous, small triangular cells flanking the loop on both faces. Their apex points towards the loop. The capacious groove has a broad U-shaped cross-section. The terminals are small simple knobs. The ring-like loop is large, with a D-shaped eye.

From excavations in advance of gravel extraction, 1948–9, at the northern end of the Roman walled town, by Major J.G.S. Brinson.

For site see *VCH* Essex, vol. 3, 1963, 72–88.

Cambridge, Museum of Archaeology and Anthropology.

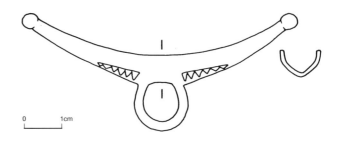

209. Great Chesterford, Essex

L. *c.* 62 mm.

End-looped mortar. The broad, lightly-curved bow has plain walls, broad groove, simple pointed terminal, and simple loop with circular eye.

From the excavations of Lord Braybrooke (R.C. Neville) between *c.* 1845–1860.

A. Way, 1869, 'Bronze relics of the late Celtic period', *Archaeological Journal* , XXVI, 77; Smith 1918, 59; Jackson 1985, no. 29.

In 1950 Neville's collection was transferred from Audley End to the Cambridge University Museum of Archaeology and Anthropology.

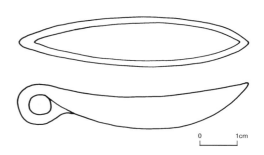

210. nr. Great Chesterford, Essex

L. 69.9 mm. Wt. 18.2 g.

End-looped mortar, with a mid-green patina, heavily abraded on the exterior but preserving the original surface in the groove. The bow is simple, with a rounded keel, apparently plain gently-sloping walls, thick rims and a plain rounded terminal. The very capacious groove is broad and deep with a U-shaped cross-section, slight basal wear facet, and marked wear polish. Too little of the loop survives to indicate its form.

Metal detector find. In private hands.

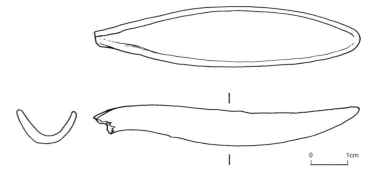

211. Great Cornard, Suffolk

L. 64.7 mm. Wt. 38.5 g.

Centre-looped mortar, with brown-olive patina. The tips of most of the projecting parts lack their patina and are reduced to a corroded green metal giving those parts a misleadingly emaciated or spindly appearance. A heavy example with short, lightly-curved bow, plain convex walls, a flattened keel and a broad, deep, capacious V-sectioned groove, with marked basal wear facet. The large bovid terminals are not identical. Both have prominent inturned horns (one with a bulbous tip) and simply rendered muzzles, but one is slightly less sturdy that the other, with a triangular muzzle and a more slender neck, and it seems probable that a pairing of bull and cow was intended. The D-shaped loop, heavily attenuated by corrosion, is flanked by a pair of short stubby struts, and a further pair of knobs project from the wall rims adjacent to the loop. Their purpose/significance is unclear, but the arrangement is not dissimilar to that on no. 261.

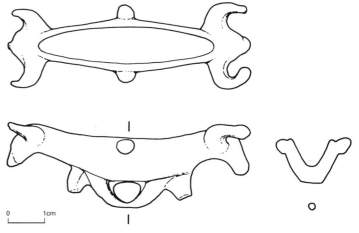

Metal detector find. Formerly in private hands, via the antiquity market, through which it acquired the spurious provenance of 'Stonea'.

British Museum, 1999,0802.33.

212. Great Sturton, Lincs
L. 70 mm. Wt. 15 g.

End-looped mortar, with dark grey-green patina. The lightly-curved bow has low, plain, sloping walls, with thin rim, an angular, slightly asymmetric, keel, a large spherical knobbed terminal, and a moderately deep and capacious V-sectioned groove, with basal wear facet, which encroaches on the loop and terminal. The small, tapered loop has a tiny circular eye, slightly elongated through wear.

For metal composition see Scientific Analyses.

Metal detector find, formerly in private hands.

British Museum, 1991,1101.1.

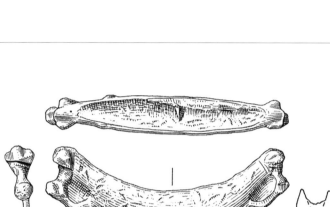
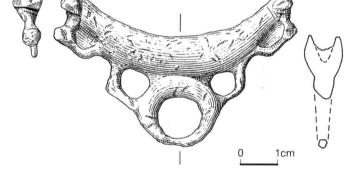

213. Great Walsingham, Norfolk
L. 67 mm. Wt. 40.3 g.

Centre-looped mortar, Type E, with black-brown patina extensively encrusted with mid-green, bright green and maroon corrosion. The modest-sized bow and groove are strongly-curved. The bow walls are plain with an inturned rim. The rounded V-sectioned groove is partly filled and obscured by corrosion products. The large crescent-shaped loop has a circular eye. It is flanked by indented openwork struts, which link the loop to the two zoomorphic terminals. If intended as specific animals, rather than mythical or fabulous beasts, the terminals are probably bovid, though heavily stylized. They have vestigial horns/ears, with a distinctive crest between, a marked brow ridge, tapered face with bulbous muzzle, and dewlaps formed by the end of the sinuous strut, the openwork panel of which is here imperforate. Corrosion has obscured and degraded the surface preventing a proper appreciation, but this looks like a fine piece of casting and craftsmanship. For a near-identical mortar see no. 36.

Metal detector find. In private hands.

214. Great Walsingham, Norfolk
L. 92 mm. Wt. 43.3 g.

Centre-looped mortar, with recently cleaned brown-green patina. A large example with very long, slender bow, plain, convex walls, a smoothly-rounded keel, V-sectioned groove with basal wear facet, and a large plain ring-like loop with circular eye. One terminal is a neatly-formed shouldered knob; the other is a stylized bovid head with simply rendered short horns (one broken), ears (one damaged), brow ridge, and slightly flared, flat-ended muzzle with slit mouth.

Metal detector find. In private hands.

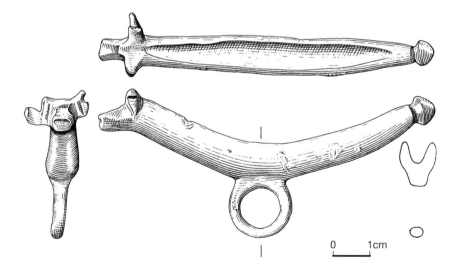

215. Great Walsingham, Norfolk

L. 49 mm. (orig. *c*. 82 mm.) Wt. 8.1 g.

Centre-looped mortar, Type J, with smooth pale grey-green patina, lightly coated with light brown soil on the terminal and in the groove. The bow is broken to one side of the loop, of which only the stub survives. The strongly-curved bow has steeply-sloping, thin walls and a rounded keel. Eight of the original 12 small elongated triangular cells remain on both faces, in an arc adjacent to the loop. Their apex points towards the loop, and all are now devoid of their enamel inlay. The capacious, broad, V-sectioned groove has a marked, slightly asymmetric, longitudinal wear-facet near the base of one wall. The small, highly-stylized bovid terminal has tiny everted horns and a thick, ridged, blunt-ended muzzle. The broken loop was evidently a D-shaped ring.

Metal detector find, reputedly near to no. 220. In private hands.

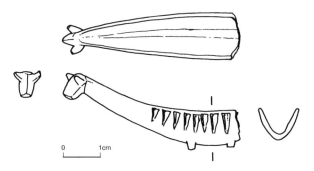

216. Great Walsingham, Norfolk

L. 43 mm. (orig. *c*. 73 mm) Wt. 27.5 g.

Centre-looped mortar, with pale grey-green patina, lightly accreted with pale buff soil in the groove and crevices. The bow is broken to one side of the loop, of which only the stub survives. A very bulky casting with deep, very lightly-curved bow, plain, carinated, inturned walls, a rounded keel and a narrow groove of asymmetric V-shaped cross-section, probably a product of wear. The remaining terminal knob is a lightly-domed button with volute-type neck-mouldings. The broken, probably ring-like, loop was mounted on an asymmetrically orientated low oval plinth.

Metal detector find. In private hands.

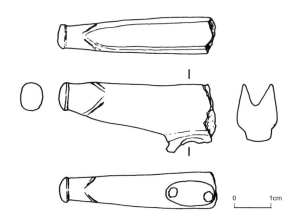

217. Great Walsingham, Norfolk

L. 50 mm. Wt. 6.1 g.

Centre-looped pestle, with thin, dark-green patina. The crescent-shaped rod has a triangular cross-section, with a wear-polished facet along the full length of the keel, but slightly more marked at the tips, where the sides and end also display wear marks. The upper face of the rod retains file-finishing marks. The loop is a D-shaped, thin-walled collar, with a large sub-circular eye. The distinct narrowing of its upper part is probably a product of wear.

Metal detector find. In private hands.

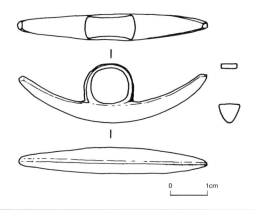

218. Great Walsingham, Norfolk

L. *c*. 61 mm. Wt. 11.6 g.

End-looped mortar, with broad lightly-elliptical bow, rounded keel, convex walls, an incuse line-and-dot-punched moulding beneath the rim, a capacious V-sectioned groove (partially filled with corrosion products), a small knobbed terminal with simple neck moulding, and a ring-like loop (fractured at the top) with a large circular eye.

Metal detector find. In private hands.

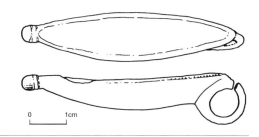

219. Great Walsingham, Norfolk

L. 47 mm. Wt. 5.9 g.

End-looped pestle. A simple, well-cast example with grey (tin-enriched) patina. The strongly-curved rod, of rounded rectangular cross-section is very heavily worn, with a marked 23 mm long polished wear facet on the convex edge of the attenuated upturned tip. The plain ring-like loop has a simple junction with the rod. Its lemon-shaped eye is elongated through wear.

Metal detector find. In private hands.

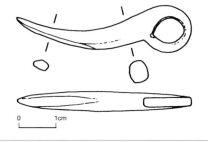

220. Great Walsingham, Norfolk

L. 30.5 mm. Wt. 4.9 g.

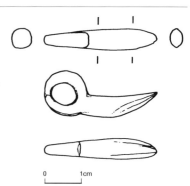

End-looped pestle, with smooth pale grey patina. The circular-sectioned rod is extremely short, but was undoubtedly originally longer, probably much longer. The oblique truncation of the tip and three wear facets on its underside attest to long and heavy usage. The neatly-made tapered ring-like loop has a sub-circular eye elongated through wear.

Metal detector find, reputedly near to no. 215. In private hands.

221. Great Yarmouth, Norfolk

L. 33.6 mm. Wt. 7.4 g.

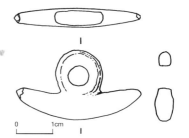

Centre-looped pestle, with mid-brown patina, chipped at one rod tip revealing underlying powdery light blue corrosion. A small example, with relatively stout, short, twin-tapered rod and large ring-like loop with circular eye.

Metal detector find. Formerly in private hands, via the antiquity market.

British Museum, 1999,0802.34.

222. near Great Yarmouth, Norfolk

L. 55 mm. Wt. 9.5 g.

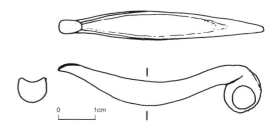

End-looped mortar, recently over-cleaned and re-patinated with a light coat of blacking. A small example, with a slender, sinuous bow, low, plain, lightly-carinated walls (their thin rim abraded away in the cleaning process), a smoothly-rounded keel, and a very shallow, broad V-sectioned groove. The plain, downturned loop has a circular eye. Uniquely, the everted terminal is in the form of a small solid, curved platform. It is possible that this was used to break up the substance coarsely before reduction to a powder in the groove using the pestle.

Metal detector find. In private hands, via the antiquity market.

223. Great Yeldham, Essex

L. 44 mm (orig. *c.* 57 mm)

Centre-looped pestle, lacking one arm and part of the ring-like D-shaped loop. The rod, of modified rhomboid cross-section, has a rounded keel.

Metal detector find. In private hands.

224. Grimsby, Humberside

L. 56 mm. Wt. 20.6 g.

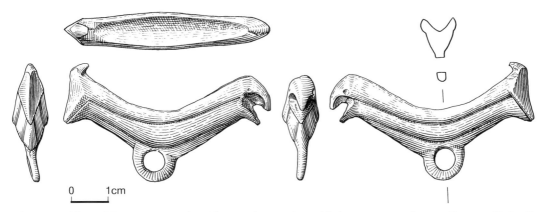

Centre-looped mortar, with rough brown-green patina. A heavy, robust casting, with short, very strongly-curved bow, profiled walls, angular keel and V-sectioned groove. The two very stylized zoomorphic terminals appears to be: 1) a bird's head, with open beak – the down-turned upper bill suggests a corvid (crow or raven); 2) a goat's head or the head of a fabulous beast, with pointed muzzle and single, central, back-swept horn. Alternatively, it may be a crested bird or fowl. The D-shaped, plate-like loop, with circular eye, is markedly off-centre.

For metal composition see Scientific Analyses.

Metal detector find. Formerly on the antiquity market.
British Museum, 1990,0702.3.

225. Grundisburgh, Suffolk (Unillustrated)
L. *c.* 42 mm.

End-looped mortar, lacking about half of the bow, with apparently plain walls and a loop apparently set beneath the end of the bow. Few details available.

Metal detector find. In private hands.

226. Gussage All Saints, Dorset
L. 59 mm.

End-looped pestle, with very lightly curved stem, upturned tip, and simple loop with circular eye.

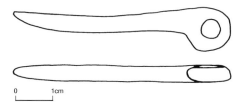

From excavation, 1972, of Iron Age enclosed settlement. Found in Pit 348, near the centre of the enclosure.

Context date (Phase 3), 1st century BC–1st century AD.

G. Wainwright, 1979, *Gussage All Saints* 111–13, fig. 87, no. 3051.

Dorchester, Dorset County Museum, 1985.30. SF 3051.

227. Hacheston, Suffolk
L. 29 mm. Wt. 20.9 g.

Mortar fragment, with smooth dark green patina. One terminal and the end of the bow of a large, heavy, highly-ornamented mortar, broken and gashed in antiquity. The bow is deep and markedly V-sectioned with, at this point, a slender, shallow U-sectioned groove. The terminal is in the form of a bovid head, with inturned horns (the tip of one broken) and clearly-depicted eyes, nostrils and mouth. The head and muzzle are quite naturalistically portrayed, as are the rippled dewlap (keel) and the shaggy, curly coat, which is rendered by modelling and by punching with a multiple overlapping ring-and-dot motif, both on the brow and on the neck (bow walls). The lower-most punched motif on the beast's face is a ring without a central dot. Other than the eyes this is the only such example on the surviving fragment and suggests it was intended to depict a pendant disc or ring rather than a hairlock or curl.

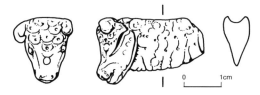

From excavations, 1973–4, of Roman small town. Unstratified. Field 1 south. Found metal detecting roadworks spoil. SF 2311.

T. Blagg, J. Plouviez and A. Tester, 2004, *Excavations at a large Romano-British settlement at Hacheston, Suffolk in 1973–4*, East Anglian Archaeology Report no. 106, 119–20, fig. 79, no. 118.

228. Hacheston, Suffolk
L. 68.5 mm. Wt. 18.1 g.

Centre-looped mortar, stripped and lacquered, revealing a good casting, with smooth surface, now golden-brown in appearance. The bow is fractured and glued, the rims are chipped, and the plumper terminal has suffered from partial surface erosion and lacks its tip. The strongly-curved bow has plain, sloping, lightly-convex walls and a capacious, deep, rounded V-sectioned groove, which runs onto the terminals and has a marked basal wear facet. The walls are subtly asymmetric, both in depth and contour, to complement the respective terminals – the plumper terminal has a slightly deeper flanking bow (= neck). Both terminals appear to have been intended as stylized birds' heads. The plumper one, with simple pointed bill, is of uncertain family or order; the other, with a ridged, dished, blunt-ended bill looks like a water-bird. The D-shaped ring-like loop had a circular eye, now elongated through wear.

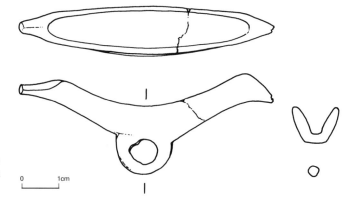

Provenance as no. 227. Unstratified. Field 1 south. SF 2608.

Publication as no. 227: 119–20, fig. 79, no. 116.

229. Hacheston, Suffolk
L. 71.9 mm. (orig. *c.* 85.4 mm.?) Wt. 22.5 g.

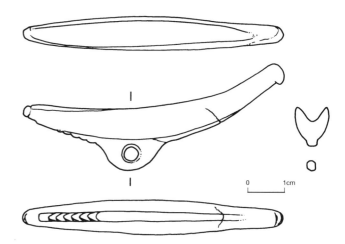

Centre-looped mortar, with a mid-green patina, slightly pocked and flaking in places. In its present form, a distinctly asymmetric and rather heavy, ungainly example, but it is very probable that it was broken and re-worked in antiquity. The bow is slender with plain, low, convex walls. Near the knobbed terminal is a casting flaw – a partial fissure. The D-shaped, plate-like loop, with small circular eye, merges into the raised rib, which runs along the keel of the bow. To the knobbed terminal side the rib appears plain, but to the other side it has an incuse herring-bone motif. The knobbed terminal is lightly downturned and, in combination with the raised rib, gives a distinctly phallic appearance to that end of the bow. The other terminal is formed by a filed ledge on the underside, which truncates the ridged keel. Other indications that this end is re-worked are the ground-away wall and rim on one side and the strong asymmetry of overall design. It is possible that the breakage occurred at a casting blemish similar to that at the other end of the bow. That the mortar was, nevertheless, well used is indicated by the very distinct wear polish and basal facet in the V-sectioned groove.

Provenance as no. 227. Unstratified. Field 1 south. SF 2310.

Publication as no. 227: 119–20, fig. 79, no. 117.

230. Haddiscoe, Norfolk
L. 68 mm. Wt. 7.4 g.

Centre-looped pestle. A large example, with smooth mid-brown patina. The slender rod is ridged on the concave edge and rounded on the functional convex edge, where there is a distinct wear-polish in the central zone. The large ring-like D-shaped loop is broken.

For metal composition see Scientific Analyses.

Metal detector find. Formerly on the antiquity market.

British Museum, 1993,0901.2.

231. Ham Hill, Somerset
L. 69 mm.

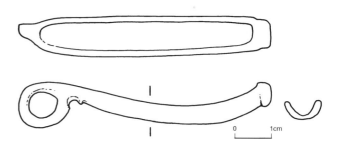

End-looped mortar. The elliptical bow is unusually parallel-sided, with plain, low, sloping walls, a flattened keel, and a broad, capacious groove with flattened V-shaped cross-section and a squared end. The simple knobbed terminal is also square-ended when viewed from above. The loop, with large sub-circular eye, is neatly undercut at its junction with the bow, and was evidently intended as a stylized bird's head with everted bill.

From excavations, 1930, by H. St George Gray. Find no. E.43 in cutting XVII, on 'the top of black layer'. Described by Gray as a 'heavy bronze ear-dropper'.

Taunton, Somerset County Museum, H.H. 1930, E.43.

232. Harleston, Norfolk
L. 51.5 mm. Wt. 8 g.

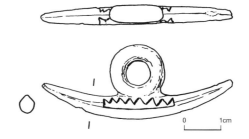

Centre-looped pestle, Type O variant, with partially pitted and iron-stained grey-green patina. An ornate example, with large, chunky, circular loop and rhomboid-sectioned twin-tapered rod, inset with a panel of contiguous small triangular cells adjacent to the loop on both faces. One face is poorly-preserved, but the other reveals a row of eight cells, their apex pointing towards the loop, with traces of the red enamel they once contained. There is wear polish and a light wear facet on the keel of the rod.

Metal detector find. Formerly in private hands, via the antiquity market.

British Museum, 1999,0802.35.

233. Harlow, Essex

L. 56 mm. Wt. 8.2 g.

Centre-looped mortar, quite heavily encrusted with mid-green corrosion.
A small example, with low, plain, convex walls, knobbed terminals, and
a capacious rounded V-sectioned groove with basal wear facet which,
as so often, is slightly diagonal to the axis. In consequence the rim of
both walls is worn down at one diagonally opposite end. The small loop,
mounted on a short, low, neatly moulded keel plate, is broken across its
tiny circular eye.

Metal detector find. In private hands, via the antiquity market.

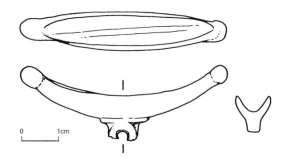

234. Harlow, Essex

L. *c.* 63 mm.

End-looped pestle, a large, heavy, idiosyncratic example. The very stout,
strongly-curved rod has a rounded keel, shield-shaped cross-section and
up-turned pointed tip. The large, coiled loop, with sub-circular eye, has
incuse linear decoration on its outer edge.

From excavation, 1993, at Old House, Harlow. The site, which comprised
pits, ditches and surfaces, was thought to be part of a larger, probably
agricultural, settlement. The pestle was found in a late 3rd–4th century
AD ditch context but may have been residual.

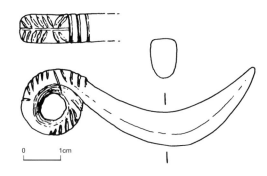

235. Harpenden, Herts

L. 61 mm. Wt. 13.4 g.

End-looped mortar, with green-grey patina. The strongly-curved
bow has plain, steeply-sloping walls, a lightly-rounded keel,
V-sectioned groove and simple blunt-tipped terminal. The loop is
in the form of a stylized aquatic bird's head, with everted bill. On
the forward zone of the keel is a very marked wear facet as though
this part of the mortar had been used (?re-used) for ?burnishing.

Metal detector find. Formerly in private hands.

St Albans, Verulamium Museum.

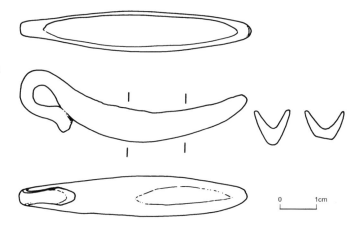

236. Hasketon, Suffolk

L. *c.* 70 mm.

End-looped mortar, Type A. The long, deep, parallel-sided bow has an
angular keel, a narrow U-sectioned groove and steep, convex, thin-
rimmed walls with incuse quadruple zig-zag decoration. The terminal
is in the form of a very devolved bovid head, with blunt-ended muzzle,
grooved mouth, slit-like eyes and simply-rendered horns (one broken).
The loop, with circular eye, lies beneath the end of the bow. It has an
elongation and was probably intended to give the appearance both of
the beast's folded tail and of a stylized bird's head.

Metal detector find. In private hands.

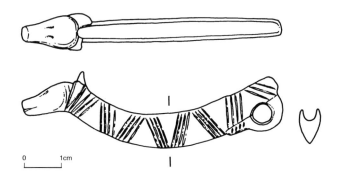

237. Hatfield Broad Oak, Essex
L. 48.5 mm Wt. 9.3 g.

End-looped mortar, with oiled, pocked, corroded, rather poorly-preserved mottled green patina, with a spot of active corrosion. A small example with lightly-elliptical bow, rounded angular keel, and low, plain, convex walls, each of which has a poorly-preserved, corroded, small projecting knob near its mid-point. The very shallow groove is of broad, flat V-shaped cross-section; the terminal is a plain blunt point; and the loop, set at a right-angle to the normal plane, is a simple round ring broken across the circular eye.

Metal detector find. Formerly in private hands, via the antiquity market.

British Museum, 1999,0802.36.

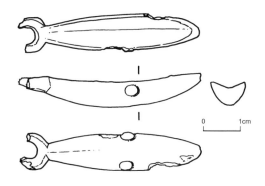

238. Helperby, North Yorkshire
L. c. 65 mm.

End-looped mortar, with lightly-curved elliptical bow and apparently plain walls. The broken tip may once have terminated in a knob. An unusually long neck extends between the bow and the simple sub-circular loop.

Metal detector find. In private hands.

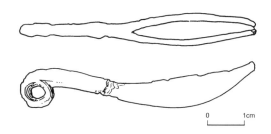

239. Henham, Essex
L. 55 mm. (orig. c. 62 mm.) Wt. 16. 9 g.

End-looped mortar, recently cleaned, with dark green-grey surface beneath patchy, pale green-buff patina. The lightly-curved bow has low, plain sloping walls, a rounded keel, and a rounded V-sectioned groove with basal wear facet. The broken terminal was probably plain. The neatly-formed ovoid loop has an off-centre, wear-elongated eye and a simple moulding. This was not a perfect casting, and flaws are visible within the groove near the broken end, on one rim at the angle change, and in the incompletely tidied grooved flash on the keel at the junction with the loop.

Metal detector find. In private hands.

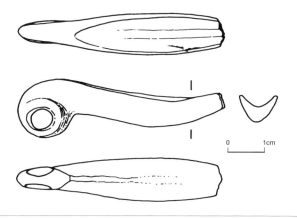

240. Henley, Suffolk (Unillustrated)
L. c. 50 mm.

Mortar fragment, unavailable for study. The Suffolk County Council Sites and Monuments Record photo shows part of the bow with a knobbed terminal. The missing terminal was probably an end loop as no trace of a central one is visible.

Metal detector find. In private hands.

241. Henstead (with Hulver Street), Suffolk
L. 53.3 mm. Wt. 14.5 g.

Centre-looped mortar, Type G, with lightly-pitted smooth metallic grey (tin-enriched) patina. A small, quite heavy example, with slender bow, plain, steep, convex walls, an angular keel, and a narrow V-sectioned groove, with basal wear-polish, which runs over the small zoomorphic terminals. Axial asymmetry of the wear in the groove has resulted in attrition of the rim at one end of each wall at diagonally opposite ends. One terminal is a stylized bovid or dog's head, with dished, tapered muzzle (the tip eroded), 'pin-point' eyes, and eroded horns/ears. The other is less well preserved, but was evidently different, with a bulbous, shield-shaped head, eroded ears, and 'pin-point' eyes quite low on the muzzle. It looks somewhat feline. Both terminals are separated from the bow by a pair of incuse lines, which might be construed as the animals' collar or halter, cf.. no. 110. Only the stub of the ring-like ?circular loop remains.

Metal detector find. In private hands.

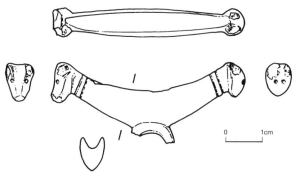

242. Henstead, Suffolk
L. *c.* 40 mm.

Centre-looped pestle, with lightly-curved, plump, twin-tapered rod and ring-like D-shaped loop with circular eye.

Metal detector find. In private hands.

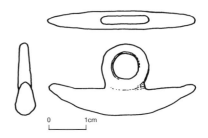

243. Hertfordshire, unprovenanced
L. *c.* 49 mm.

End-looped mortar, a small example with short elliptical bow, plain walls, plain blunt-pointed terminal, and a relatively broad groove. Only the stub of the thin ring-like loop survives. It has a large circular eye.

Metal detector find. In private hands.

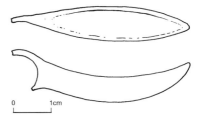

244. Hevingham, Norfolk
L. 64.2 mm. Wt. 33.05 g.

Centre-looped mortar, with good pale buff-green patina, lightly abraded at projecting points. A heavy casting, with only very lightly elliptical, parallel-sided bow, angular keel, steeply sloping walls lightly inturned at the rims (one rim markedly thicker than the other), and a broad U-sectioned groove, with basal facet, which runs onto the zoomorphic terminals. Each terminal is in the form of a bovid head, with prominent horns, blunt-ended muzzle and deep-socketed circular eyes. The loop is a projecting sub-rectangular plate, with small circular eye. Although the heads are hardly differentiated in type, it is very probable that they were intended to represent the twinning (union) of bull and cow, since the neck of one is markedly deeper than the other, and its brow rather more prominent (thick-set bull). A hint of further realism is revealed by a close inspection of the wall-preserved patina, which shows very lightly incised hatched 'texturing' of the walls (neck of the beasts) adjacent to the terminals.

Metal detector find. In private hands.

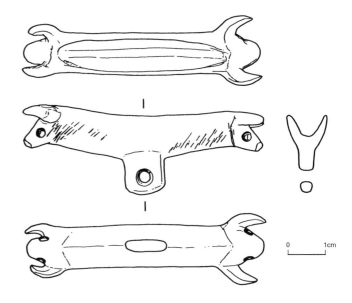

245. Hevingham, Norfolk
L. 66 mm.

Centre-looped mortar. A heavy example with elliptical bow, thick, plain, sloping walls, a U-sectioned groove, and two similar zoomorphic terminals. The animal type is enigmatic – one head has a pointed muzzle, the other a flat muzzle, and only the eyes are depicted. There is no sign of horns. Above each head is an incuse line. The loop is a large thick disc with circular eye.

Metal detector find. In private hands.

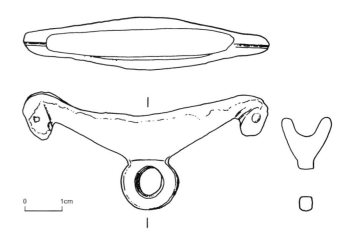

246. Heybridge, Essex
L. 45.7 mm. Wt 7 g.

Centre-looped pestle, with lightly-pitted olive-brown patina overlying light green corrosion products. The twin-tapered elliptical rod has a sub-triangular cross-section with a light wear facet along the keel. The loop is a large ring with circular eye.

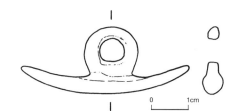

From excavation, 1994, of the Romano-British 'small town' at Elms Farm, Heybridge, by M. Atkinson for Essex County Council Field Archaeology Group. The settlement spanned the period from the Late Iron Age to early Anglo-Saxon times but appears to have had its heyday in the 1st century BC to 1st century AD. The focus appears to have been a temple complex.

Un-dated context (11000) on the east half of the site, SF 2872.

M. Atkinson and S.J. Preston, forthcoming, *Excavations at the Iron Age and Roman Settlement at Elms Farm, Heybridge, Essex 1993–5,* East Anglian Archaeology monograph.

247. Heybridge, Essex
L. 46.4 mm. Wt. 11 g.

End-looped mortar, with lightly-pitted green patina. A small example, with short elliptical bow, angular keel, plain, steep, lightly-convex walls, shallow U-sectioned groove, and flattened knob terminal with ring moulding. The broken end-loop was evidently in the form of a stylized bird's head, of which only the everted bill remains.

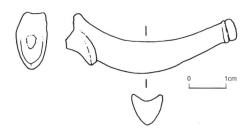

Provenance as no. 246. Area A, un-dated context (4000) on the west half of the site, SF 1050.

248. Heybridge, Essex
L. 23.9 mm. Wt. 3 g.

End-looped mortar, fragment, with pitted grey-green patina. Only the loop and a small section of the adjacent bow survive. The bow has a rounded keel and a U-sectioned groove. The loop, in the form of a neatly-wrought stylized bird's head with circular eye and dished bill, is enhanced by a moulded rib that runs around the perimeter from the back of the head/ loop to the brow above the bill. There is wear polish inside the eye.

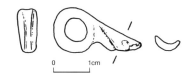

Provenance as no. 246. Area A, un-dated context (4000) on the west half of the site, SF 1867.

249. Heybridge, Essex
L. 37.8 mm. Wt. 7 g.

End-looped mortar, with pitted mid-green patina. A broken fragment comprising the greater part of the bow. The keel is rounded, the walls plain, steep and lightly convex, the narrow U-sectioned groove deep and capacious with a narrow basal wear facet, and the terminal simple, with a plain blunt point chipped at the tip.

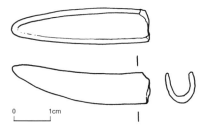

Provenance as no. 246. Area D, prepared surface, context 9645, SF 4917.

Context date (Period III B): early–mid-2nd century AD.

250. Heybridge, Essex
L. 55.7 mm. Wt. 5 g.

End-looped pestle, with pale green patina. The long, slender, elliptical rod is of ovoid cross-section tapering to a lentoid cross-section on the up-turned tip. The underside of the tip is worn and polished through use. The tiny loop has a D-shaped eye and a neat ring-moulding at the junction with the rod.

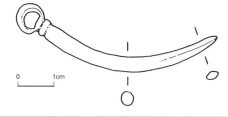

Provenance as no. 246. Area G, make-up layer, context 7636, SF 2443.

Context date (Period III–IV): later 1st–mid-3rd century AD.

251. Heybridge, Essex
L. 48.1 mm. Wt. 4 g.

End-looped pestle, with mid-green shiny patina. The lightly-curved, slender, circular-sectioned rod swells beneath the up-turned lentoid-sectioned tip. The loop is tiny and simple, with a tear-shaped eye.

Provenance as no. 246. Area L, well 14984, context 14985, SF 7345.

Context date (Period IV–V): later 2nd–mid-4th century AD.

252. Heybridge, Essex
L. 30.9 mm. Wt. 6 g.

(?)End-looped pestle, with brittle olive-green patina overlying powdery bright green corrosion products. The strongly-curved D-sectioned rod is unusually short and broad. Its collar-like loop preserves the remains of incuse decoration. The object is probably a pestle, though it may be a buckle pin.
Provenance as no. 246. Area D, un-dated context (9403) on the west side of the site, SF 3276.

253. Hillington, Norfolk
L. c. 47 mm.

Centre-looped pestle, with slightly asymmetric twin-tapered rod and tall D-shaped loop with circular eye.

Metal detector find. In private hands.

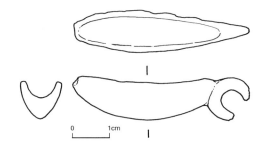

254. Hinderclay, Suffolk
L. 47 mm.

End-looped mortar, with badly corroded exterior surface. The lightly-curved bow has a rounded angular keel, apparently plain convex walls, chipped rims, a capacious U-sectioned groove, and a broken circular end-loop. The damaged terminal was probably a simple blunt point.

Metal detector find. In private hands.

255. Hindringham, Norfolk
L. 84 mm.

Centre-looped mortar, of novel design, in the form of a stylized fish/dolphin. The smoothly-curved, quite slender, bow has convex walls and a narrow groove. The tapered, rounded head terminal has horizontal slit mouth, tiny ovoid eyes, and gills depicted, together with stylized scales on the underside of the neck. The other terminal is a flattened plate with profiled edge (now chipped), which represented the creature's tail fin, with small punched circles, presumably intended as scales, on the underside. The loop, an asymmetric plate with tiny circular eye, is also adapted to the creature's anatomy, in this case the ventral fin.

Metal detector find. In private hands.

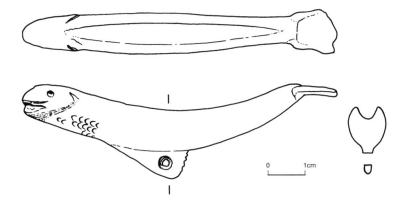

256. Hintlesham, Suffolk
L. c. 48 mm (orig. c. 60 mm).

Centre-looped mortar, Type H, lacking one end of the bow and most of one wall. The crescentic bow has thin, steeply-sloping walls decorated with an arc of small triangular cells, five on each wall, their apex pointing towards the loop. Some contain traces of orange enamel. The U-sectioned groove is capacious; the surviving terminal appears to have been a plain rounded point; and the D-shaped loop, now distorted, has a heart-shaped eye.

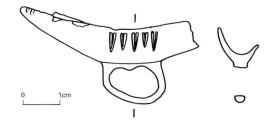

Metal detector find, 1996, from a site which has yielded a metalwork scatter including 1st century brooches and 2nd–4th century coins. In private hands.

257. Hitcham, Suffolk

L. 63.5 mm.

Centre-looped mortar, with elliptical bow, plain convex walls, U-sectioned groove and simple knobbed terminals. The loop-plate, mounted on a low keel, has a small circular eye.

Metal detector find. On antiquity market. Illustrated in dealer's catalogue, 2000, lacking its provenance. Present whereabouts unknown.

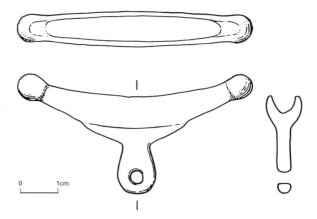

258. Hitcham, Suffolk

L. *c.* 35 mm.

Centre-looped mortar, Type H, fragment only, lacking both terminals and the loop. The remaining part of the bow has thin, steeply-sloping, lightly convex walls and a capacious broad U-sectioned groove. The central zone of both walls is decorated by a row of three hollow-based triangular cells, their apex pointing away from the loop. All of the cells are now empty. The remaining straight basal ridge of the loop suggests it was of the D-shaped ring-like form rather than the heart-shaped type.

Metal detector find. In private hands.

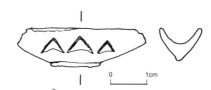

259. Hitcham, Suffolk

L. 56 mm. Wt. 11.64 g.

End-looped mortar, worn, with crescentic bow, angular keel, apparently plain steep walls, a shallow narrow groove, broken loop and simple blunt terminal, possibly originally with incised decoration.

Metal detector find. In private hands.

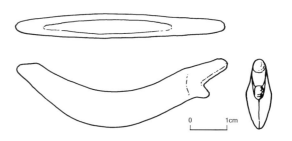

260. Hockwold, Norfolk
L. mortar 106 mm. pestle 70 mm. Wt. mortar
62.4 g. pestle 9 g.

Set, comprising a centre-looped mortar and a
centre-looped pestle. Both components have
been stripped and are now light golden brown
in colour, except the groove which is shiny and
golden. A few small remnants of the original
dark green patina survive. The mortar is a very
large and heavy casting. Its deep bow has an
angular keel, steep convex walls, decorated with
an incuse paired chevron motif adjacent to the
loop, and large, bulbous knobbed terminals. The
U-sectioned groove is polished smooth through
wear and runs deeply over the terminals. The
large collar-like loop has a circular eye. The
pestle, a crescentic twin-tapered rod, with
collar-like D-shaped loop, has a wear facet on
the convex edge, most distinctly in the central
zone.

For metal composition see Scientific Analyses.

Found 1980. Subsequently on the antiquity
market. Cleaning had taken place by 1986.
When acquired by the British Museum in 1990
the set had 'lost' its provenance.

Trett 1983, no. 26; Jackson 1985, no. 58.

British Museum, 1990,0702.1-2.

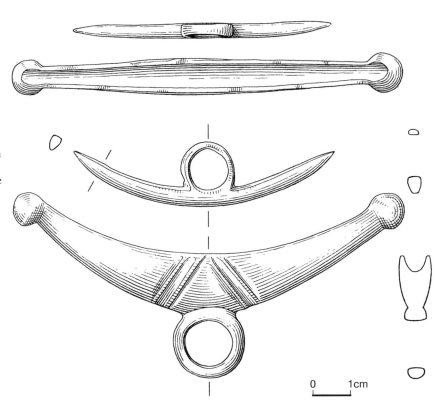

261. Hockwold, Norfolk
L. 103 mm. Wt. 80.3 g.

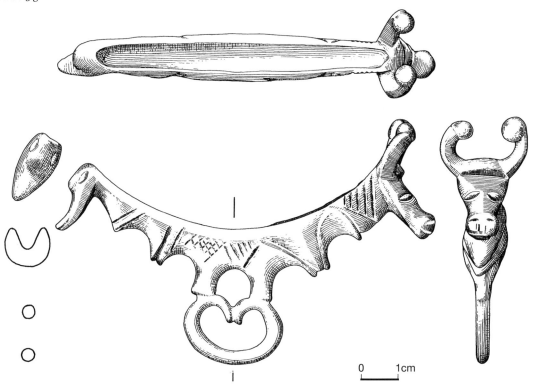

Centre-looped mortar, with green patina. A large, elaborate and finely crafted example, with strongly-curved bow, large heart-shaped loop and
two large, sensitively-modelled zoomorphic terminals. The greater one is a bovid head with stout inturned horns, their tips knobbed, prominent
ridged brow, raised lentoid eyes, and a lightly bulbous muzzle with mouth and nostrils depicted. The smaller terminal is a bird's head, almost
certainly a duck, with high crown, small raised lentoid eyes, and a long dished bill with lightly upturned tip. The intricate cast and incuse
decoration of the bow, deceptively asymmetric, is finely integrated with the zoomorphic terminals, representing in part the neck of the respective
animals. The V-sectioned groove has a flattened base, probably a longitudinal wear-facet, though light corrosion inhibits examination.

For metal composition see Scientific Analyses.

From garden of finder, Nursery Lane, '3–4 inches below surface', 1976. Donated to British Museum by finder.

Jackson 1985, no. 59.

British Museum, 1977,0403.1

262. Hockwold, Norfolk
L. 79.1 mm. Wt. 27.8 g.

Centre-looped mortar, with smooth olive-brown patina and partial light ferrous accretion. The slender lightly-elliptical bow has an angular keel and convex walls, one markedly lower than the other. Beneath each rim is a dot-punched incuse linear moulding which encircles the terminals. Beneath each terminal the bow is decorated with three moulded projections, which may have been intended to be seen as devolved bird heads. Similar mouldings flank the projecting keel-like loop-plate, which has a small circular eye. The long slender groove, of U-shaped cross-section, runs over the terminals.

Metal detector find. In private hands.

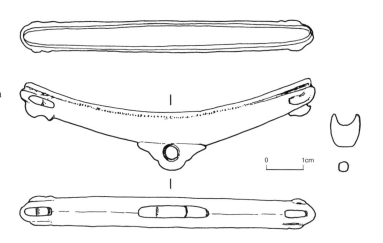

263. Hockwold, Norfolk (Unillustrated)
L. c. 57 mm.

(?)Centre-looped mortar, in brittle condition, about half surviving. The heavily-corroded broad groove terminates above the prominent bovid terminal, the long curved horns of which are distorted.

Metal detector find. In private hands.

264. Hockwold, Norfolk
L. c. 50 mm.

Centre-looped pestle, with asymmetric, circular-sectioned, strongly-tapered arms and a small D-shaped loop with circular eye on a tall, narrow pedestal.

Metal detector find, 'near Black Dyke' (probably Blackdyke Farm). In private hands.

265. Hockwold, Norfolk
L. 55 mm.

End-looped mortar, with pale green-brown patina. A small finely-made example, with an excessively slender, lightly elliptical bow, very low, finely carinated walls with thin rims, a flattened keel, and a proportionately large U-sectioned groove with a slight wear-polish. The tiny terminal knob has a neat neck-moulding. The loop is lightly 'coiled' with a circular eye.

Metal detector find from Leylands Farm. Lent by finder to Moyses Hall Museum.

Bury St Edmunds, Moyses Hall Museum, 1982-363.1.

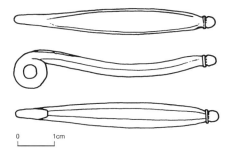

266. Hockwold, Norfolk (Unillustrated)
L. 40 mm. Wt. 8.55 g.

(?)End-looped mortar fragment, comprising part of the plain-walled elliptical bow. The groove is partially blocked with corrosion products. The terminal is a neatly-formed, flattened, bulbous knob.

Metal detector find/ field-walking survey. In private hands.

267. Hockwold, Norfolk (Unillustrated)

L. 77 mm. Wt. 22.5 g.

End-looped pestle. A large and heavy example, with a long, deep, elliptical rod of thick knife-like form. The loop may have been intended as a highly-stylized bird's head.

Metal detector find/ field-walking survey. In private hands.

268. Hod Hill, Dorset

L. 62 mm. Wt. 6.1 g.

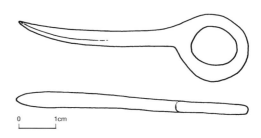

End-looped pestle, with smooth green patina. The upturned tip of the lightly elliptical rod has a very distinct asymmetric wear-facet on its convex face. The very large, flat ring-like loop has an ovoid eye,

For metal composition see Scientific Analyses.

From excavations, 1951–8, of Roman fort; from foundation trench of Building A (?Stabling/veterinary quarters?).

Fort dated c. AD 45–55.

I. Richmond, 1968, *Hod Hill II* 113, fig. 56, no. 6; Jackson 1985, no. 51.

British Museum, 1960,0405.466

269. Holme Hale, Norfolk

L. c. 27 mm.

Centre-looped mortar. Fragment only, from central part, comprising part of the steep, thin-walled bow and the stub of the loop. The damaged walls nowhere preserve their rim, but the U-sectioned groove was evidently capacious. The loop, apparently of large discoidal form (though possibly more complex), is mounted on a low pedestal.

Metal detector find. In private hands.

270. Holt, Norfolk

L. 32 mm. Wt. 2.17 g.

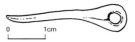

?End-looped pestle. A small example with relatively large loop. Possibly a buckle pin.

Metal detector find. In private hands.

271. Hopton-on-Sea, Norfolk

L. 55 mm.

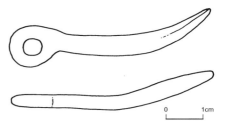

End-looped pestle, with pale green-brown patina. The distal end of the elliptical rod is atypically turned to one side as viewed from above. This appears to have been an intentional feature, rather than damage, and may have facilitated the grinding process. There is a marked wear facet on the convex face of the upturned tip. The simple ovoid loop with small circular eye saw little finishing work after casting.

Metal detector find from Valley Farm, with other objects of 1st–9th century AD date. In private hands.

272. Horsham St Faith, Norfolk

L. 32 mm.

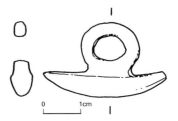

Centre-looped pestle, with shiny dark-green patina on the inner face of the loop and concave face of the rod; elsewhere light-green soft corrosion products. A short example, with relatively large sub-circular loop and short twin-tapered rod (one tip broken) of rounded triangular cross-section.

Metal detector find. In private hands.

273. Horton Kirby, Kent
L. c. 74 mm.

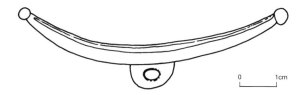

Centre-looped mortar, with slender plain-walled bow, spherical knobbed terminals and D-shaped loop plate with circular eye.

From Anglo-Saxon grave (no. 69), in a female bag collection. There is a nearby Roman villa, from whence the mortar may have derived.

Grave dated early 6th century AD.

A. Cumberland, 1938, 'Saxon cemetery, 'Riseley', Horton Kirby', *Trans. of Dartford and District Archaeol.Soc.* 8, 14–30; B. Ager, 1985, 'The smaller variants of the Anglo-Saxon Quoit brooch', in S.C. Hawkes, D. Brown and J. Campbell (eds.), *Anglo-Saxon Studies in Archaeology and History 4,* 1–58, esp. 21, no. 17, 52, fig. 22, 17d; R.H. White, 1988, *Roman and Celtic Objects from Anglo-Saxon Graves* B.A.R. Brit. Ser. 191, 147 and 348, fig. 92,3.

Dartford Borough Museum.

274. Humberside, unprovenanced
L. 65.4 mm. Wt. 21.5 g.

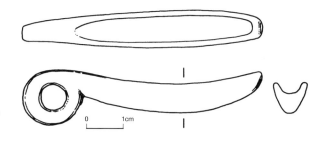

End-looped mortar, with pale to mid-green lightly pocked patina. A simple example, with small lightly-elliptical bow, plain sloping walls, chamfered keel, shallow, broad U-sectioned groove with light wear-polish, and plain terminal with lightly-upturned, square-ended tip. The relatively large loop is a simple, thick ovoid disc with a circular, lightly-worn eye.

Metal detector find. Formerly in private hands, via the antiquity market.

British Museum, 1999,0802.37.

275. Hunsbury, Northants
L. 62.6 mm. Wt. 6.9 g.

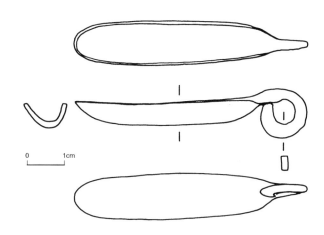

End-looped mortar, with smooth brown-green patina. A very light, simple example, with virtually straight bow, apparently hammered out from a single rod of metal. The sloping walls and rim are very thin and plain, the rounded keel markedly off-centre, and the terminal plain with an upturned base and simple rounded end. The asymmetry of the capacious groove corresponds to that of the keel. The thin circular loop is quite crudely made. It is flattened, has a free end, and is asymmetric to the bow.

From hillfort, finds made without proper record at the end of the 19th century during ironstone-quarrying. The large collection of metalwork, pottery etc. spans the whole of the La Tène Iron Age but contains almost no Roman material.

Smith 1918, 57, fig. 3; C. Fell, 1936, 'The Hunsbury Hillfort, Northants', *Archaeological Journal* XCIII, 57–100, esp. 65, pl. 1, no. 2; Jackson 1985, no. 33.

The analysis of a drilled sample from the loop (using a CAMEBAX automated electron probe micro-analyser in the Dept. of Metallurgy and Science of Materials, University of Oxford) is given in I. Barnes, 1985, 'The Non-Ferrous Metalwork from Hunsbury Hillfort, Northants.' (Univ. of Leicester, Post-graduate Diploma in Post-excavation Studies, 1984/5. p.32, cat.no. 40), where the elemental composition is expressed thus: 98.6% Cu; 0.95% Sn; 0.06% As; 0.15% Sb; 0.05% Pb; – Co; 0.04% Ni; 0.04% Fe; 0.07% Ag; – Au; t Zn; 0.04% Bi.

Northampton Museum, D.284.1956-7.

276. Hunston, Suffolk
L. 50 mm.

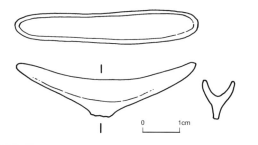

Centre-looped mortar. A modest-sized example, with gently-curved bow, low, plain, convex walls, ridged keel, a relatively deep groove of keeled U-shaped cross-section, and simple rounded terminals. The loop, mounted on a projection of the keel ridge, is broken. For its probable form see no. 299.

Metal detector find. In private hands.

277. nr. Huntingdon, Cambs
L. 51.3 mm. Wt. 8.4 g.

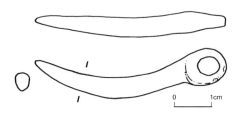

End-looped pestle, with slightly uneven mid-green patina. A simple, quite rudimentary example, with crescentic tapered rod of plump triangular cross-section, and a simple oval loop with sub-circular eye. Viewed from above, the loop is offset to one side of the rod.

Metal detector find, from a 'meadow towards M11', south-east of Huntingdon. Formerly in private hands, via the antiquity market.

British Museum, 1999,0802.38.

278. Icklingham, Suffolk
L. 78 mm. Wt. 18.4 g.

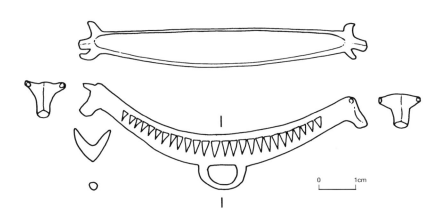

Centre-looped mortar, Type J, with smooth, light green patina. The strongly-curved bow has steeply-sloping walls and an angular keel. The walls are decorated with an arc of enamel-inlaid small triangular cells, which extend almost to the terminals. Their apex points towards the loop. Two colours of enamel are used, red and light blue, in 26 cells on each wall, with a similar, but not identical, arrangement. On one wall five central blue cells are flanked by two pairs of red cells and a further eight blue cells on one side nine on the other. On the second wall there are six central blue cells, flanked by two pairs of red cells and a further eight blue cells. The broad V-sectioned groove has a basal wear-slot towards one terminal. The small bovid-head terminals have inturned horns and a ridged, lightly bulbous muzzle. The loop is a simple D-shaped ring.

For enamel and metal composition see Scientific Analyses.

Found 1947, on field surface, north of Canada Belt. Donated by finder to British Museum.

Jackson 1985, no. 71.

British Museum, 1957,1003.6.

279. Icklingham, Suffolk
L. c. 53 mm.

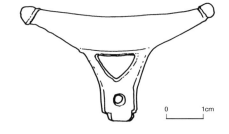

Centre-looped mortar. The small, lightly elliptical bow has plain walls and simple, shouldered, knobbed terminals. The loop is an elaborate, disproportionately large, keeled and strutted plate, with a triangular opening and tiny circular eye.

Formerly in the Warren collection. Smith based his record on a pencil drawing, with details, in one of Sir Augustus Wollaston Franks' sketch books, (Drawings, Book A, p. 13) but the object was not available, and its whereabouts is still unknown.

Smith 1918, 61, fig. 15; Jackson 1985, no. 87.

280. Ilketshall St John, Suffolk
L. 30 mm.

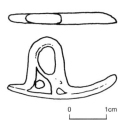

Centre-looped pestle, with crescentic rod, incomplete at one end, and an arched loop with ovoid eye, beneath which are two voids. A poor or failed casting, which may, nevertheless, have been used, in view of the apparent wear facet at the end of the longer surviving arm of the rod.

Metal detector find. In private hands.

281. Ilketshall St Margaret, Suffolk
L. 39.3 mm. Wt. 6.3 g.

Centre-looped mortar, Type J, with unstable brown patina. A fragment only, comprising some two-thirds of the bow, with the stub of the broken loop, but lacking both terminals. The elliptical bow has an angular keel and steeply-sloping walls with badly-chipped and eroded rims. The walls are decorated with a continuous arc of small triangular cells, their apex pointed towards the keel. Sixteen survive on one wall, 15 on the other, from which it can be calculated that the original number on each wall totalled at least 24 and probably 25 cells. Just four retain remains of their enamel inlay – an adjacent pair on one wall filled with blue enamel, and single examples with traces of red enamel and light turquoise enamel separated by an empty cell on the other wall. These are sufficient to indicate an arrangement identical or similar to that on cat. nos 578 and 278, namely five central turquoise cells flanked by two red cells and a further eight blue cells. It is probable that the missing terminals were small stylized bovid heads, as on nos 578 and 278. The rounded V-sectioned groove is lightly encrusted with corrosion products. Only the stub of the D-shaped loop remains.

Metal detector find. In private hands.

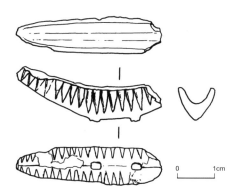

282. Ingoldisthorpe, Norfolk
L. 29 mm. Wt. 5.4 g.

Centre-looped mortar, with brown and pale green dusty patina. The apparently plain bow, with straight-rimmed walls, was always tiny, the U-sectioned groove shallow and the capacity very small, but the original dimensions cannot now be ascertained exactly owing to the severely denuded and chipped surface. The merest stub of the loop survives.

Metal detector find. In private hands.

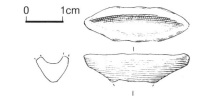

283. Ingoldisthorpe, Norfolk
L. 43 mm. Wt. 7.8 g.

End-looped mortar, with grey-green patina. The terminal and parts of the bow and loop are missing. The bow has plain, steep, thin walls, a rounded keel, and a capacious groove of rounded V-shaped cross-section, with a slight basal wear facet. The loop, now broken and distorted, appears to have been large, circular and neatly 'coiled'.

Metal detector find. In private hands.

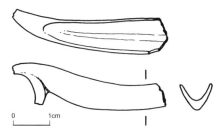

284. Ingoldisthorpe, Norfolk (Unillustrated)
L. 82 mm. Wt. 21.7 g.

End-looped mortar, in poor condition (corrosion-eaten), lacking part of the loop, the terminal and the wall rims. The elliptical bow appears to have been plain and the loop of simple form, turned downward.

Metal detector find. In private hands.

285. Ingoldisthorpe, Norfolk
L. 56.8 mm. Wt. 10.4 g.

End-looped pestle, with poorly-preserved green-grey heavily pitted patina (cleaned and lacquered). The slender crescentic rod, of blunt knife-like form, has a markedly swollen upturned end with pronounced side-facets. The simple thick ring-like loop has a small circular eye.

Metal detector find. In private hands.

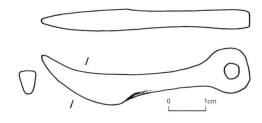

286. Itteringham, Norfolk
L. mortar 96 mm. pestle 55 mm. Wt. mortar 82 g. pestle 9 g.

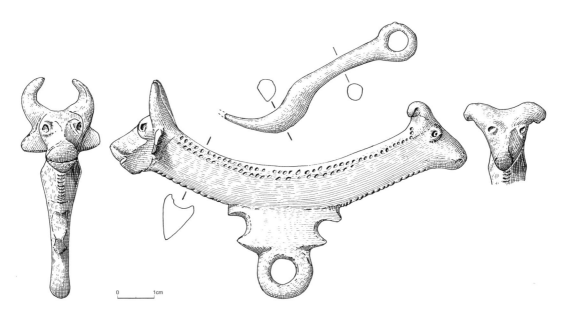

Set, comprising a centre-looped mortar and an end-looped pestle. The large and ornate heavy mortar has a crescentic bow, angular keel, steeply-sloping walls with in-turned rims, and prominent zoomorphic terminals. There is a line of punched decoration beneath each rim and on either side of the keel. The terminals are large and well-modelled, one in the form of a stylized bull's head, with in-turned horns, ears, eyes, muzzle and mouth rendered, the other in the form of a stylized ram's head, with out-turned horns, eyes and muzzle depicted. The groove, which runs over both terminals, displays a little sign of wear. The circular loop, the eye of which is slightly worn, projects from a large moulded plinth, in one side of which are two small casting flaws. The pestle, a variant of the 'latch-lifter' type, has a small circular loop, set on the midline of the straight circular-sectioned stem, and a strongly-curved rod of lentoid cross-section, its tip recently chipped. The end of the rod is precisely adapted to the size and profile of the groove in the mortar.

Metal detector find. Part of a Treasure hoard, which also comprised a second cosmetic set (no. 287), 2 silver finger-rings, a base silver ring, a copper-alloy key, 62 silver *denarii*, 42 copper-alloy coins, and parts of 3 pottery vessels

The finger-rings, coins and pottery indicate a date of deposition of the hoard in the 2nd century AD (latest coin: AD 141–161).

R.P.J. Jackson and I. Leins 'Itteringham', in *Treasure Annual Report 2000* (DCMS, London, 2002), 24–5; I. Leins 'Itteringham, Norfolk', in R. Abdy, I. Leins and J. Williams (eds.), *Coin hoards from Roman Britain, Volume XI* (Royal Numismatic Society, London, 2002), 77–83.

British Museum, 2001,0801.1-2.

287. Itteringham, Norfolk
L. mortar 60 mm. pestle 51 mm. Wt. mortar 27 g. pestle 12 g.

Set, comprising a centre-looped mortar and a centre-looped pestle. The mortar has a crescentic bow, angular keel, lightly-convex, steeply-sloping, plain walls, thick rims, and simple knobbed terminals. The relatively capacious groove is of rounded V-shaped cross-section, with basal wear and an asymmetric wear facet near one terminal. The distinctive loop is large and D-shaped. It is rather rudimentarily finished and shows no sign of wear. The pestle has a crescentic twin-tapered rod, with a lightly-worn keel and blunt-pointed tips. The distinctive large D-shaped loop is virtually identical to that of the mortar, and they were evidently made as a matching set.

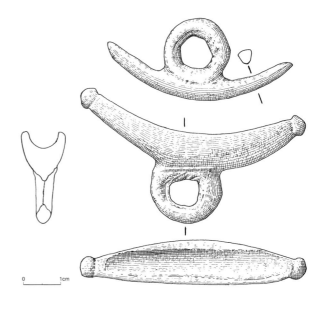

Metal detector find. Provenance, date and publication details as no. 286.

British Museum, 2001,0801.3-4.

288. Kelling, Norfolk
L. 51 mm, Wt. 11.5 g.

Centre-looped mortar, with green patina, the surface eroded and chipped in some places. The slender, slightly asymmetric bow has plain, steep walls (the rim of one broken), a capacious groove of slender U-shaped cross-section, and simple rounded terminals. An asymmetric basal wear facet slightly across the axis of the groove has worn away the rim of both walls at diagonally opposite ends. The large, plump, D-shaped loop has a worn circular eye.

Metal detector find. In private hands.

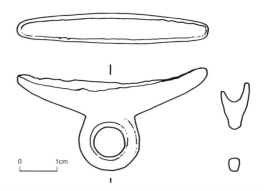

289. Kenninghall, Norfolk
L. 58.8 mm. (orig. *c.* 70 mm.) Wt. 11.6 g.

Centre-looped mortar, Type J, with sparsely pitted and lightly abraded dark green patina, lacking the loop and one terminal. The elliptical bow has an angular keel and thin, quite deep, steeply-sloping walls decorated with an arc of enamel-inlaid elongated triangular cells adjacent to the loop. The symmetrical arrangement of nine cells (their apex pointing towards the loop) is the same on both walls: The three central cells, filled with red enamel, are flanked by three cells with blue enamel. The colours are still quite vivid, and only a few tiny fragments are missing. The capacious V-sectioned groove has a light basal wear facet. The surviving terminal is a small, well-formed and neatly-finished bovid head, with ridged, flat-ended muzzle, a slight brow-ridge and in-turned horns, the tips damaged. Only the base of the loop remains.

Metal detector find. Donated by finder to the British Museum.

British Museum, 2010,8005.1.

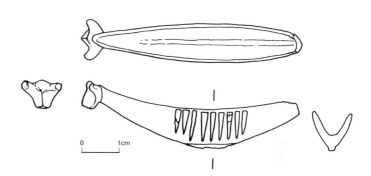

290. Kent, unprovenanced
L. 52.1 mm. Wt 26.6 g.

Centre-looped mortar, with fine brown patina. A carefully-finished, relatively heavy, example in good condition. The crescentic bow has a flat keel, plain carinated walls with neatly-moulded rims, and flattened knobbed terminals, also neatly moulded. The relatively capacious, broad U-sectioned groove, with marked wear polish and broad basal wear facet, runs over both terminals. The small loop has a circular eye.

Metal detector find. Formerly in private hands, via the antiquity market.

British Museum, 1999,0802.39.

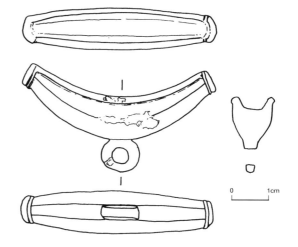

291. Kent, unprovenanced
L. *c.* 36 mm.

Centre-looped pestle. A small example, with stout, twin-tapered rod and plump D-shaped loop with circular eye.

On antiquity market. Seen (illustrated) in dealer's catalogue, 1993. Present whereabouts unknown.

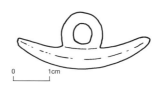

292. Keston, Kent

L. 65 mm. Wt. 26.1 g.

End-looped mortar, with smooth brown metallic patina,
the surface badly pitted in places. The short elliptical bow
has plain convex walls with sharp rim (like no. 50), a lightly
angular keel and a V-sectioned groove, partly obscured by
corrosion. The bovid head terminal has inturned horns,
small button-like ears, and a ridged tapered muzzle
with bulbous end, on which the mouth is depicted. The
shape and angle of the adjacent part of the bow were
accommodated to the form of the beast's neck. The ovoid
loop has suffered badly from corrosion, but may also have
been blemished in the casting process.

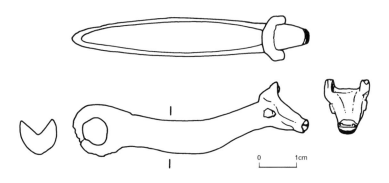

For metal composition see Scientific Analyses.

British Museum Accessions Register records that it was 'Found near Roman remains at Keston, Kent', but no further details are known.

Jackson 1985, no. 5.

British Museum, 1927,1011.1.

293. Keswick, Norfolk

L. 65 mm. Wt. 12.86 g.

Centre-looped mortar, Type H, lacking both terminals and most of the
loop. The slender elliptical bow has an angular keel, sloping walls (the
rims chipped), and a deep groove of broad V-shaped cross-section.
Adjacent to the loop on both walls is an arc of four hollow-based
triangular cells, their apex pointing away from the loop, inlaid with
black enamel. The fragmentary loop was a D-shaped ring with heart-
shaped eye.

Metal detector find. In private hands.

294. Keswick, Norfolk (Unillustrated)

L. 28 mm. Wt. 3.18 g.

Centre-looped mortar, lacking much of the bow and most of the loop. The walls appear plain.

Metal detector find. In private hands.

295. Kingsholm, Glos

L. *c.* 56 mm.

End-looped mortar, with virtually straight-rimmed bow, apparently plain
walls, small knobbed terminal, and thick ovoid loop with tiny circular
eye and a grooved moulding centrally recessed around the perimeter.
The groove was not drawn or described in the published account, and
the object was unavailable for study in 1991.

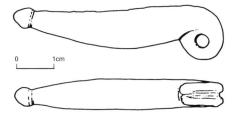

From excavations, 1972, at 72 Deans Way; from layer II, 7 = general layer
= phase 4.1 = 2nd–4th century AD.

H.R. Hurst, 1985, *Kingsholm*, 102, fig. 36, no. 6.

Gloucester Museum.

296. King's Lynn, Norfolk

L. 54 mm. Wt. 13.4 g.

Centre-looped pestle, with a smooth grey (tin-enriched), patina. A quite large,
well-made and ornate example. The neatly crescentic rod has a plump D-shaped
cross-section. One tip is a little blunter than the other. Asymmetric wear facets
are present on the convex face of the rod near both tips, more strongly-marked
at the blunter tip. The discoidal loop, which projects from a tapered pedestal, is
surmounted by a tiny cone-like finial. There is a little wear in the circular eye,
which is intentionally set a little above centre of the loop.

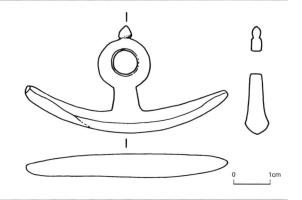

Metal detector find. Formerly in private hands, via the antiquity market.

British Museum, 1999,0802.41.

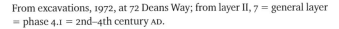

297. King's Lynn, Norfolk
L. 27 mm. Wt. 6.73 g.

Centre-looped pestle, Type N. The loop plate, in the form of a stylized sitting or swimming water bird, above a rectangular perforation, is placed centrally on the concave edge of a short crescentic rod with blunt-pointed tips.

Metal detector find. In private hands.

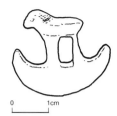

298. King's Lynn region, Norfolk
L. 58 mm. Wt. 19.6 g.

Centre-looped mortar, with traces of green patina in angles and crevices and in the groove. Elsewhere recent ruthless cleaning has removed the original surface with the patina, revealing the rather pitted coppery-looking body metal. The slender bow has apparently plain, low, lightly-carinated walls, an angular keel, and a V-sectioned groove with a slight basal facet. The terminals are large bulbous knobs which, in conjunction with two further globular protuberances from the keel, give the object a distinctive and phallic appearance. The small loop, with its tiny off-centre eye, is more correctly comma-like than circular. What appears to be a fracture or butted join is probably a casting flaw.

Metal detector find. Formerly in private hands, via the antiquity market.

British Museum, 1999,0802.40.

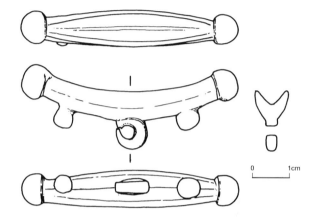

299. Kirby Cane, Suffolk
L. 60 mm. Wt. 18.7 g.

Centre-looped mortar, with dark green-black, rather pitted surface, recently waxed or oiled. The slender bow has low, plain, near-vertical, lightly convex walls with inturned rim, a ridged keel, a shallow U-sectioned groove with very marked wear polish, and simple rounded terminals. The ovoid loop, which projects from the keel ridge, has a simple notched moulding (worn) and a small circular eye. The casting and workmanship appear quite rudimentary.

Metal detector find. In private hands.

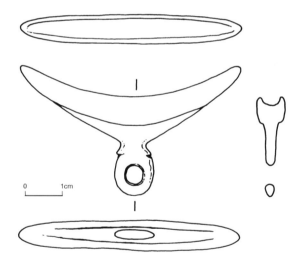

300. Kirkby Thore, Cumbria
L. 52 mm.

End-looped pestle. The strongly-curved rod has a deep, thick, blunt, knife-like upturned tip and a small loop with a tiny circular eye.

The Roman fort and *vicus* at Kirkby Thore flourished 1st-4th century AD.

Jackson 1985, no. 55.

Carlisle, Tullie House Museum, 63.1951 (Cumpston Bequest).

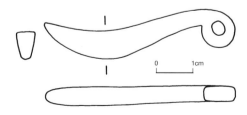

301. Lakenheath, Suffolk
L. 123.5 mm. Wt. 103.2 g.

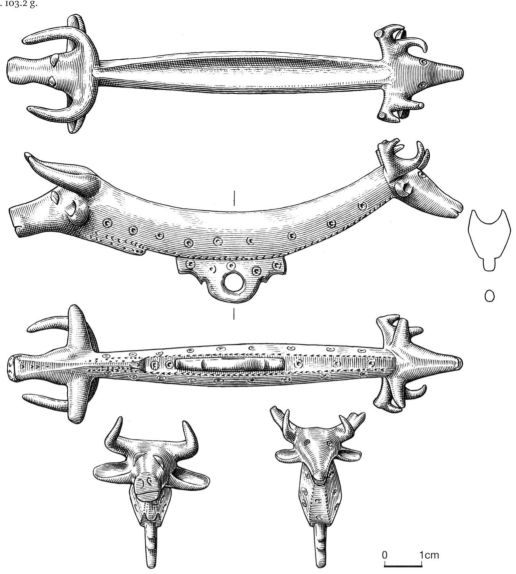

0   1cm

Centre-looped mortar, cleaned and conserved, with olive-green patina and localized areas of green and livery-red corrosion products. The largest and most elaborate example yet known, complete, except for the upper part of the stag's antlers. An unblemished casting with extensive subsequent working, this is a small masterpiece of design and manufacture. There is a fine sense of balanced asymmetry between the two zoomorphic terminals which extends to a subtle distinction between the necks of the animals – the bull has a deep, stolid neck and stylized dewlap, while the very slightly more acute upward curve of the opposite end of the bow gives to the stag's neck an appropriately more delicate, graceful form. The bow is large and elliptical with a sharp carination on both walls. Above this carination the walls are plain, with a thin rim; below they are decorated with an arc of slightly irregularly-disposed incuse ring-and-dot motifs, nine on each wall. The flattened keel is also decorated with this motif, three on the stag's side of the centre-loop, but just two closely-spaced examples on the bull's side, where the greater part of the keel is occupied by the beast's dewlap. Both of the angled edges of the keel are ornamented with a closely-spaced V-punched motif, the line of which continues along the sides of the dewlap, and the same punch was used to highlight the lower margin of the dewlap, and the underside of the bull's muzzle. The U-sectioned groove is relatively shallow and slender.

Both zoomorphic terminals are sensitively modelled in the round, and in their combination of naturalism and stylisation they encapsulate the essence of the animals depicted. The bovid head is the heavier, bulkier terminal (though the size and bulk of the stag's head would originally have been greatly enhanced by the complete antlers). Viewed from the front, the bulls' head is skewed slightly downwards to the right, and there is a similarly marked asymmetry to ears, horns, and eyes all of which are a little out of alignment with their partner. The horns are pointed, but not sharp, the ears large, elongated and neatly hollowed, the almond-shaped eyes in relief, with incised rim, and the head and muzzle sensitively contoured, with incised mouth and nostrils on the flattened muzzle end. The stag is altogether more delicate, with smaller ears (though of the same form), a smaller head, and a finely-rendered, tapered muzzle, with mouth and nostrils on the rounded end. As with the bovid head there is a distinct asymmetry to the ears and eyes, and the basal tines of the antlers are also awry. Both antlers are broken above the second tine. The incuse dot-and-ring eyes give the animal an appropriately startled expression. The suspension loop takes the form of an ornate plate projecting from the keel. There is a relatively small circular eye, and a zig-zag row of five incuse ring-and-dot motifs, on each face.

For metal composition see Scientific Analyses.

From excavation, 1993, of Roman rural settlement at RAF Lakenheath, by A. Tester for Suffolk County Council. Found in an upper layer of a 1st/2nd century AD well.

Context date, 4th century AD.

Bury St Edmunds, Moyses Hall Museum, on loan from RAF.

302. Lakenheath, Suffolk
L. 71 mm.

Centre-looped mortar, Type J, with a smooth green-grey (tin-enriched) patina. The lightly-elliptical bow has an angular keel and thin, steep walls, with an arc of seven small triangular cells adjacent to the loop on both faces. The cells, whose apex points towards the loop, are filled with red enamel. The capacious, rounded V-sectioned groove runs over the stylized bovid-head terminals. They are small, with short flattened muzzles and prominent everted horns. The loop is a slender D-shaped ring.

Found in or before 1965 during ploughing. Donated by finder to Moyses Hall Museum.

Trett 1983, no. 3; Jackson 1985, no. 72.

Bury St Edmunds, Moyses Hall Museum, 1981–57 (OS).

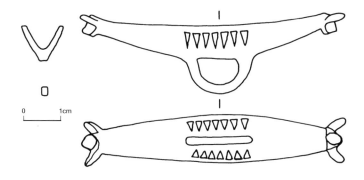

303. Lakenheath, Suffolk
L. 55.5 mm.

End-looped pestle, with smooth grey-green patina. A fine casting. The slender, circular-sectioned rod has a strongly-curved tip with marked facet on the convex face. The eye of the simple circular loop is elongated through wear.

Metal detector find from 'Roman field'.

Bury St Edmunds, Moyses Hall Museum, 1982-363.2, on loan from finder.

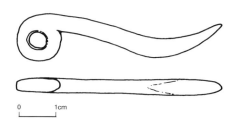

304. Laughterton, Lincs
L. 50.5 mm. Wt. 9.5. g.

End-looped mortar, with green-brown patina. A small, elegantly-cast example, with slender strongly-curved bow, plain, near-vertical walls, a smoothly rounded keel, small, bulbous knobbed terminal, and very shallow U-sectioned groove with marked wear-polish. The carefully profiled loop has a heart-shaped eye, with traces of wear.

Metal detector find. In private hands.

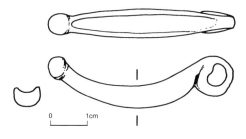

305. Leicester, Leics
L. 43 mm. (orig. *c.* 55 mm.)

Centre-looped pestle, encrusted with green and light brown corrosion products. One arm of the slender, twin-tapered rod is broken. The other, complete except for the tip, has a lozenge-shaped cross-section, but the corrosion is too severe to determine whether or not there are wear-facets. Only the stub of the D-shaped loop survives.

From excavations, 1963–4, on the west wing and south-west corner of the Roman forum, at St Nicholas Street.

For the site, see M. Hebditch and J. Mellor, 1973, 'The forum and basilica of Roman Leicester', *Britannia* 4, 1–83, esp. 6–19.

Leicester, Jewry Wall Museum, 365.1964/121.

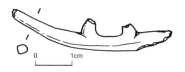

306. Leiston, Suffolk
L. 62 mm. Wt. 15.2 g.

Centre-looped mortar. The elliptical bow has steep plain walls, a worn U-sectioned groove, and simple, worn, blunt terminals, perhaps originally lightly knobbed. The worn D-shaped loop is broken across its circular eye.

Metal detector find. In private hands.

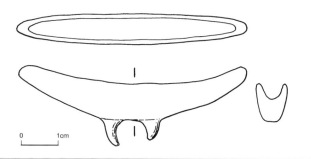

307. Lillingstone Dayrell, Bucks
L. *c.* 85 mm.

End-looped mortar. A large example, with apparently plain, carinated walls, an angular keel and a knobbed terminal. The loop is in the form of a stylized aquatic bird's head, with prominent brow and elongated bill. The groove was not visible in the single photograph available.

Metal detector find. In private hands.

308. Lincoln, Lincs
L. 61 mm. Wt. 8.5 g.

End-looped mortar, cleaned and conserved, with mid-green-brown corrosion-pitted patina. A simple, light example, with virtually straight bow, low, plain, convex walls, a lightly-angular keel and a rounded V-sectioned groove with basal facet. The groove runs over the slender, pointed, lightly-drooped, spout-like terminal. The loop is a sub-circular ring with ovoid eye.

From excavations, 1970–2, in the *colonia*, site of west gate, at the Park. P 70, small find Ae 133, from the earliest rampart levels.

Context date, late 2nd or early 3rd century AD.

J. Mann, 1983, *Archaeology in Lincoln 1982–3* 33, fig. 11d; Jackson 1985, no. 22.

Lincoln, City and County Museum.

309. Lincolnshire, unprovenanced
L. 70 mm. Wt. 13.5 g.

Centre-looped mortar, Type K, with dark brown-grey patina, a little damaged and distorted at a recently repaired fracture midway between one terminal and the loop. An elegant, well-proportioned casting, with low, plain, thin sloping walls, an angular keel, and a deep, capacious bowed V-sectioned groove, with a distinct narrow basal wear facet, which runs over the terminals. The terminals are simple, stylized, well-made bovid heads, comprising broad inturned horns and a flat triangular head, one with a slightly more pointed muzzle than the other. Neither eyes nor mouth are depicted. The loop is a simple D-shaped ring with a circular eye set a little off-centre.

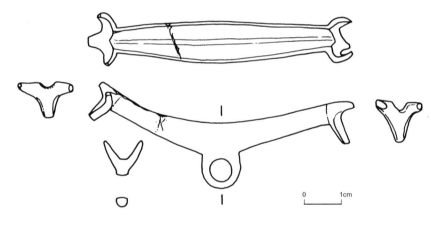

For metal composition see Scientific Analyses.

Metal detector find, formerly in the collection of Richard Hattatt. Ostensibly found with no. 310, and the two are described as a set by Hattatt. (R. Hattatt, 1989, *Ancient Brooches and Other Artefacts* 448, 451, fig. 19, no. 122.) However, their form and patina mitigate against this. They were evidently not made as a set and probably were not even used together. More likely is either that they were found in the same general vicinity, or that the finder/former owner simply put together two stray finds as a 'set'.

British Museum, 1990,0502.1.

310. Lincolnshire, unprovenanced
L. 43 mm. Wt. 9 g.

Centre-looped pestle, with pale grey patina. The keeled crescentic rod has a slight wear-facet near the tip of one arm; the other is obscured by a casting flaw. The loop is plate-like, with a small knobbed finial set a little off-centre, and a tiny ovoid eye. The loop plate is rather rudimentarily made, and file-finishing marks are visible in most places.

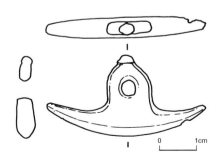

For metal composition see Scientific Analyses.

Circumstances of discovery unknown – see no. 309.

British Museum, 1990,0502.2.

311. Lincolnshire, unprovenanced
L. 82 mm. Wt. 14.7 g.

Centre-looped mortar, Type H, with lightly-pitted green corrosion where the olive-brown patina is lacking. The crescentic bow has an angular keel, low thin convex walls, a deep capacious V-sectioned groove with basal wear slot, and small knobbed terminals. Adjacent to the loop on both walls is an arc of three tiny triangular cells, their apex pointing towards the loop. All six retain their orange enamel inlay. The surviving stub of the loop reveals that it was a D-shaped ring with heart-shaped eye.

Metal detector find. In private hands, via the antiquity market.

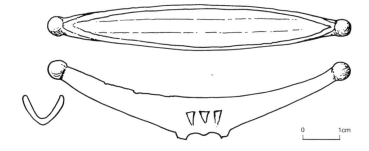

312. Lincolnshire/East Yorkshire
L. 65.4 mm. Wt. 14.1 g.

End-looped mortar, with pocked grey-green patina lacking most of the original surface (except in the groove). The bow is only lightly elliptical, with a flattened keel, very low carinated plain walls, a large plain terminal knob, and a U-sectioned groove with wear polish and basal wear facet. The loop, in the form of a devolved aquatic bird's head with elongated bill, is broken across the eye, damage which probably occurred in antiquity.

Metal detector find. In private hands via the antiquity market.

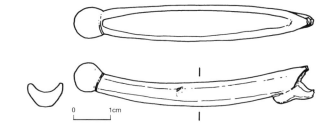

313. ?Lincolnshire/Leicestershire, unprovenanced
L. 49 mm. Wt. 13.3 g.

Centre-looped mortar, with mid-green dusty patina, heavily abraded at the rim and around the eye of the suspension loop. The small, lightly-curved bow is slightly asymmetric. It has plain, low, convex walls, a shallow groove of broad V-shaped cross-section with a basal wear facet, and plain rounded terminals. The loop comprises a thick pear-shaped projection with small circular eye, now partially blocked with soil. The wall/loop junction is marked by an incised cross on both faces.

Metal detector find. Formerly in private hands, via the antiquity market.

British Museum, 1999,0802.42.

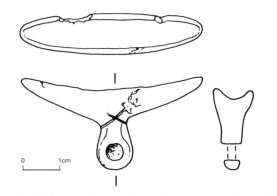

314. Linton, Cambs
L. 36.4 mm. Wt. 11.9 g.

Centre-looped mortar, with smooth pale green-grey patina. A very small but heavy example with short, broad bow, steep, lightly-convex plain walls with straight rim, and plain terminals. The terminals may once have been more elaborate (and there is a trace of ribbing or moulding at one end), but they have been truncated by very considerable wear in antiquity. This wear has partially flattened the rims and has produced a deep straight narrow, U-sectioned groove, which has worn through the base of the original broad shallow groove. The D-shaped loop, broken in antiquity, has a circular eye elongated through wear.

Metal detector find. In private hands, via the antiquity market.

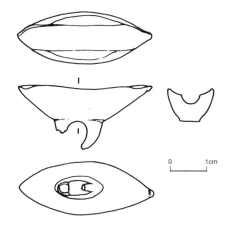

315. Little Finborough, Suffolk
L. c. 35 mm.

Centre-looped mortar, Type H, fragment, comprising part of the bow. Both terminals, part of the bow and the centre loop are missing. The thin-walled bow has sloping walls and a rounded V-sectioned groove, evidently originally capacious. Both walls retain four triangular incuse cells, their apex pointing away from the loop. Only slight traces of their enamel inlay survives, its colour indeterminate. It would appear that four cells on each wall was the likely original full complement.

Metal detector find. In private hands.

316. Little Finborough, Suffolk

L. 77.5 mm.

End-looped mortar. The elliptical bow has a rounded keel, seemingly plain steeply-sloping walls with narrow rim, a broad U-sectioned groove, and a probably plain blunt-ended terminal (its tip now lacking). The simple loop has an ovoid eye.

Metal detector find, said to have been found in association with a lock bolt and a sherd of Antonine samian. In private hands.

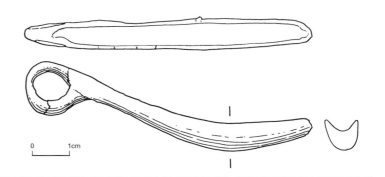

317. Little Houghton, Northants

L. 51. 9 mm. (orig. *c.* 70 mm).

Centre-looped mortar, heavily corroded, with irregular mid-green patina. One terminal and part of the narrow bow, are lacking, the loop is broken and one wall is dented. The steep-sided walls have a moulded vertical rib between the terminal and the loop. The companion rib is in the missing section. The keel is angular and the groove deep, of narrow V-shaped cross-section. The remaining terminal is poorly-preserved but was evidently a rounded knob with a pair of recessed pelleted mouldings around its girth. The relatively small, broken, D-shaped loop had a circular eye.

From Pylon Field, circumstances of discovery unknown. For the location – Site 9 or 10, Iron Age and Roman buildings and kilns, part of the East Houghton Iron Age and Roman complex – see *RCHM Northampton vol.II*, 1979, 85–9, and fig. 80.

Jackson 1985, no 82.

Northampton Museum, D.100. 1958-9.

318. London

L. 81 mm. (undistorted, 98 mm.) Wt. 72.3 g.

Archetype, for Type A end-looped mortar(s), made of lead or lead alloy, with a brown-cream patina. The bow has been bent out of shape and there are several scrapes and dents in the soft metal, but the original surface detail is generally well-preserved in the patina. The long, slender elliptical bow has deep, plain, steep, carinated walls, an angular keel, and a narrow, shallow, rounded V-sectioned groove, which retains its manufacturing score marks and runs over both terminals. The loop, positioned below its plain tapered terminal, is in the form of a stylized bird's head, with prominent brow and elongated, lightly everted, bill, but it was also probably intended to represent the folded tail of the bull at the other terminal. The small circular eye is completely unworn. The zoomorphic terminal is a very rudimentarily-finished bovid head, with working facets and file marks especially noticeable on the brow, upper muzzle and horns. As on the bow and the loop, additional detail and decoration were undoubtedly to be worked into the copper-alloy castings. For example, the muzzle may then have been filed flatter, the horns modified, and eyes, nostrils, dewlap detail, and bow-engraving added. For the products of this type of archetype, perhaps cast in a 'lost lead' process, see nos 88, 236, 325, 380, 394, 422, 495 and 558.

For metal composition see Scientific Analyses.

From excavations, 1988, by Dept. of Greater London Archaeology, at Skipton Street, near the Elephant and Castle. Site 90, open area, period 8; found in the upper fill of the probable boundary Ditch 340 (Small find 60, context 338. Trench XI, Grid 115/220, Area B. Site archive, text section 35). No significant associated finds.

Context date 3rd century AD.

Jackson 1993, 167–9, fig. 3 (in which the now superseded provisional context date of *c.* AD 130/140–200 was cited).
C. Cowan, F. Seeley, A. Wardle, A. Westman and L. Wheeler, 2009, *Roman Southwark settlement and economy. Excavations in Southwark 1973–91*, MoLA monograph 42, 110, <S99>, fig. 89, 237.

Museum of London.

319. London
L. mortar 64 mm. pestle 63 mm. Wt. mortar 18.5 g. pestle 3.7 g.

Set, comprising a centre-looped mortar, Type C, and an end-looped pestle, both rather badly corroded, with a pitted mid-green patina, the original surface lacking in some places. The mortar has a lightly-elliptical bow and steeply-sloping walls, their upper part decorated with two series of incuse, irregularly-hatched lines centred upon a vertical line at the loop, and bordered by a line which follows the contour of the keel. The capacious, rounded V-sectioned groove, with signs of wear in the base, runs onto both terminals. One is a small simple knob, its surface now denuded. The other is a neatly-formed bovid head, with prominent horns, marked brow-ridge, pointed muzzle and simply-rendered mouth. The D-shaped plate-like loop has a small circular eye partly blocked with corrosion. For very similar mortars see nos 357 and 438. The broken-tipped pestle is a slender, sinuous rod with an atypical swelling adjacent to the plate-like circular loop. It fits comfortably in the groove of the mortar.

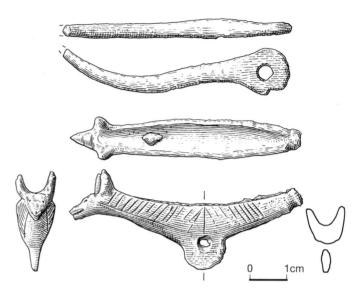

From excavation, 1955, of a timber and clay house at Blossoms Inn, near the Cheapside Roman baths, by W.F. Grimes. Found in an iron-pan concretion, fused together with a small looped tweezers and a looped nail cleaner (WFG 41, context 63, site acc. no. 51), all no doubt originally strung together on the same cord or thong.

Context date (pottery) *c.* AD 100–120.

Jackson 1993, 165–167, fig. 2. For the site, see W.F. Grimes, 1968, *The Excavations of Roman and Mediaeval London* 131–4; and J.D. Shepherd, 1987, 'The pre-urban and Roman topography in the King Street and Cheapside areas of the City of London', *Trans. London and Middlesex Archaeol.Soc.* 38, 11–58, esp.23–6.

Museum of London.

320. London
L. *c.* 64 mm.

Centre-looped mortar, Type L, with small knobbed terminals, D-shaped plate-like loop and incuse multiple chevron motif on walls.

From excavations, 1996, at No. 1. Poultry, Cheapside, by MoLAS. ONE 94<3142> [12229].

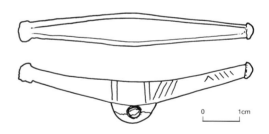

Period 3, phase 1, Flavian redevelopment AD 65–95, from roadside drain (Road 1).

J. Hill and P. Rowsome, in prep., *Roman London and the Walbrook stream crossing: excavations at 1 Poultry and vicinity 1985–96*, MoLA monograph series.

Museum of London.

321. London
L. *c.* 62 mm.

Centre-looped mortar, with large knobbed terminals, D-shaped ring-like loop, and apparently plain, near-vertical walls.

From excavations, 1996, at No. 1. Poultry, Cheapside, by MoLAS. ONE 94 <3492> [17661].

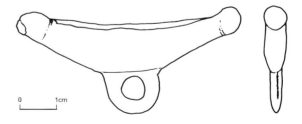

Period 6, phase 4, 4th century robbing, from Open Area 58, a much disturbed area which contained significant quantities of residual material, including 1st-century coins.

J. Hill and P. Rowsome, in prep., *Roman London and the Walbrook stream crossing: excavations at 1 Poultry and vicinity 1985–96*, MoLA monograph series.

Museum of London

322. London
L. 40 mm

Centre-looped mortar, Type J, badly corroded, with broken terminals and damaged D-shaped loop. There is an arc of six small enamel-inlaid triangular cells adjacent to the loop on both faces, the apex of the cells pointing towards the loop.

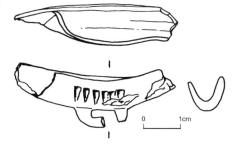

From excavations, 1995, at Borough High Street, Southwark (Jubilee Line Extension site), by MoLAS. BGH 95 <950> [3308].

Period 6, AD 120–160, from an alley surface.

J. Drummond-Murray and P. Thompson, 2002, *Settlement in Roman Southwark. Archaeological excavations (1991–8) for the London Underground Limited Jubilee Line Extension Project*, MoLAS monograph 12, 109 <R118>, fig 87; 224.

Museum of London.

323. London
L. *c.* 45 mm.

Centre-looped mortar, lacking one end. The complete end has a knobbed terminal. Full details not available at time of writing, but X-radiography appears to show the object in direct association with an iron slide key, as though the two had been strung together when deposited and had been fused together, loop to loop, by the corrosion products.

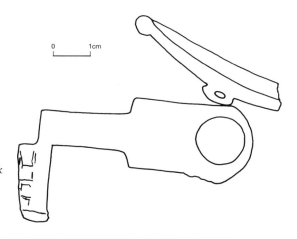

From excavations, 1989, at 179–91 Borough High Street, Southwark, by MoLAS. 179 BHS 89 <909> [390].

Period 4 dump (Open Area 3), (Flavian expansion) AD 70–100.

C. Cowan, F. Seeley, A. Wardle, A. Westman, L. Wheeler, 2009, *Roman Southwark settlement and economy. Excavations in Southwark 1973–91*, MoLA monograph 42, 133, <S37>, fig. 99, 232.

Museum of London.

324. London, River Thames
L. 54 mm. Wt. 7.7 g.

Centre-looped pestle, with brown-black Thames patina, and some concretion, especially in the eye of the loop. The lightly crescentic rod has D-sectioned arms of markedly unequal length, and a large neatly-made ring-like D-shaped loop with a heart-shaped eye.

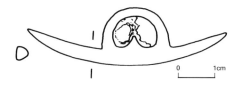

For metal composition see Scientific Analyses.

Part of a collection of objects from the River Thames, acquired in 1851. The other objects include bronze coins, needle, stylus, hairpin and ring, but there is no stated association.

British Museum, 1851,0228.7.

325. London
L. 74 mm. Wt. 19 g.

End-looped mortar, Type A, heavily corroded. The elliptical bow has an angular keel, steep convex walls, with part of the original incuse and dot-punched zig-zag decoration still visible, and a U-sectioned groove. The zoomorphic terminal is a devolved bovid head, with prominent horns, angled blunt-ended muzzle and slightly gaping mouth. The loop, set beneath the opposite plain terminal, is in the form of a stylized bird's head, which was probably also intended to represent the tail of the bull.

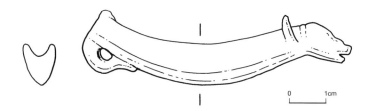

From excavation, 2001, of site at 60–63 Fenchurch Street, by Wessex Archaeology. Excav. code FNE 01, [1794], SF 3569.

Context 1794, Building 11, Period 5, *c.* AD 100–140.

[A fragment of another (plain) end-looped mortar was a residual find in a medieval pit (Context 1248, Pit 1136, Open Area 16, Period 8, 11th-12th century AD)]

V. Birbeck and J. Schuster, 2009, *Living and working in Roman and later London. Excavations at 60–63 Fenchurch Street*, Wessex Archaeology Report no. 25, 81–3, fig. 53, no. 3569.

Museum of London.

---

326. London. L. 70 mm

End-looped pestle. A large example with long, lightly-curved rod, characteristically swollen towards the upturned, plump D-sectioned tip, which has a marked facet on its convex face. The simple ring-like loop is worn through.

From London Wall. It appears to have a 'Walbrook patina' and is therefore probably of 1st–2nd-century AD date.

Jackson 1985, no. 49.

Museum of London, 3983.

---

327. London
L. 50 mm.

End-looped pestle. The slender, lightly-curved rod has an upturned tip of plump D-shaped cross-section, with a curved facet on its convex face. The small, circular, ring-like loop is centrally-set on the end of the rod.

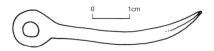

Found during redevelopment of Bucklersbury House, Walbrook. The 'Walbrook patina' is indicative of a 1st- to 2nd-century AD date.

Jackson 1985, no. 46.

Museum of London, 20770.

327a. London (unillustrated)
L. 54 mm.

End-looped pestle. Of near identical form and size to no, 327.

From excavations at Courage's Brewery site. COSE84 <515> [1469].

Period 3, building 15.2, 3rd century AD dump.

C. Cowan, 2003, U*rban development in north-west Roman Southwark*, MoLAS monograph 16, 157, <S44> fig. 111.

Museum of London.

---

328. London
L. 51 mm.

End-looped pestle. The circular-sectioned rod expands to a plump D-sectioned working zone (its surface obscured by an accretion of soil and corrosion products) and terminates in a strongly-upturned, blunt-pointed tip. The small, ovoid plate-like loop has a tiny, worn, circular eye.

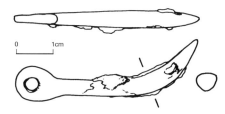

From excavation, 1988, of Gresham Street site, by the Dept. of Urban Archaeology. LSO 88, context 23.

Context date, probably late 2nd/3rd century AD.

Museum of London.

328a. London (unillustrated)
L. 45.5 mm.

End-looped pestle. The elliptical rod is comparatively short and broad, with a D-shaped cross-section and an up-turned blunt tip. The loop is slender with a circular eye.

From excavations at Lloyds Register, Fenchurch Street. FCC95 <575> [1332].

Open area 10 – dump. Period 3, AD 100–150.

R. Bluer and T. Brigham, 2006, *Roman and later development east of the forum and Cornhill. Excavations at Lloyd's Register, 71 Fenchurch Street, City of London*, MoLAS monograph 30, 25, <S11> fig. 21, 151.

Museum of London.

329. Long Bennington, Lincs
L. 65 mm. Wt. 23.7 g.

Centre-looped mortar, with mid-green patina. The very lightly-curved, parallel-sided bow has near-vertical, plain, carinated walls. One side is smoother than the other indicating the usual suspension position. The lower wall and squared-off keel still display quite coarse file-finishing marks, which may have had a decorative intent as the angled striations are symmetrical about the suspension loop. The broad, deep groove is very capacious, of V-shaped cross-section, with a very broad basal wear facet. A casting blemish at one end evidently did not impede its use. The neatly-knobbed terminals – a low compressed dome with a slender ring moulding – have a slightly phallic appearance. The D-shaped loop is faceted and has a circular eye.

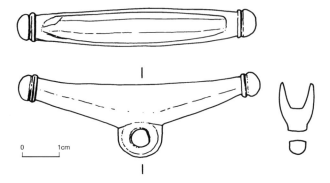

Metal detector find.

Lincoln, City and County Museum, LM 97-74.

330. Long Melford, Suffolk
L. 51 mm. Wt. 17.6 g.

Centre-looped mortar, with elliptical bow, steep walls, broad, worn, U-sectioned groove, and plump knobbed terminals, one larger than the other. Traces of incuse cross-hatched decoration survive in places on the walls. The thick ovoid loop has a slightly off-centre circular eye.

Metal detector find. In private hands.

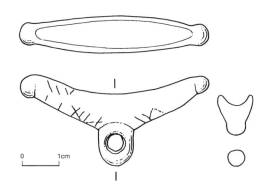

331. Lound, Suffolk
L. 59 mm. Wt. 16.91 g.

End-looped mortar, quite heavily corroded. The deep elliptical bow has plain walls, a prominent knobbed terminal with flanking moulded discs, and a simple round loop with circular eye.

Metal detector find. In private hands.

332. Lydney Park, Glos
L. *c.* 77 mm.

End-looped mortar. The slender bow has deep, plain, steeply-angled walls and a lightly-chamfered keel. Its end is tapered and up-turned, with a large, button-like, knobbed terminal The groove is narrow and V-sectioned. The loop, divided from the bow by a pair of mouldings, has an elongated, ovoid, eye and a prominent, everted bill-like extension giving the appearance of an aquatic bird's head.

From 'earlier excavations', before 1819. Thus not known whether from the hillfort, ironworking or temple complex.

S. Lysons, 1819, *Reliquiae Britannico-Romanae* Vol. II, pl. XXX, no. 6; Revd W.H. Bathurst, 1879, *Roman Antiquities at Lydney Park, Glos.*, pl. XXI, no. 8; Smith 1918, 58–9, fig. 10; R.E.M. and T.V. Wheeler, 1932, *Lydney*, 83, fig. 18, no. 65 (scale 1:2, not 1:1 as stated); Jackson 1985, no. 9.

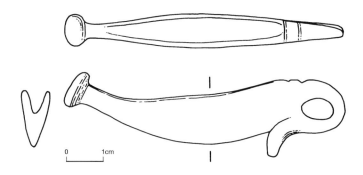

333. Lynford, Norfolk
L. 58 mm. Wt. 14.1 g.

Centre-looped mortar, with green-flecked mid-brown patina. The slender, strongly-angled bow has low, carinated walls, with traces of a lightly-incuse 'ribbed' decoration following the contours of the bow. The small, slender, V-sectioned groove has a basal wear facet. The neat, sub-spherical knobbed terminals have a simple neck moulding. Only the stub of the loop survives. It appears to have been large and mounted on a keeled plate

Metal detector find.

Norwich Castle Museum, 216.986.

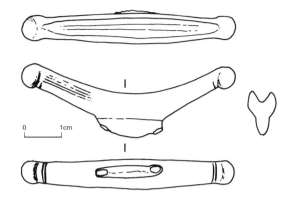

334. Magiovinium, Bletchley, Bucks
L. 76 mm.

End-looped mortar. The straight bow, now a little damaged and distorted, has plain, convex walls, a rounded V-sectioned groove, and a bulbous knobbed terminal with simple neck moulding. A pair of incuse lines flanking the angular keel link the terminal to the loop, which is elegantly-modelled in the form of an aquatic bird's head, probably a swan, with long, curved neck, small ring-and-dot eyes, a prominent crown and long, dished bill.

Metal detector find.

Jackson 1985, no. 6. D.S. Neal, 1987, 'Excavations at Magiovinium, Bucks. 1978–80', *Records of Buckinghamshire* 29, 45–6, fig. 24, no. 40.

Present location unknown.

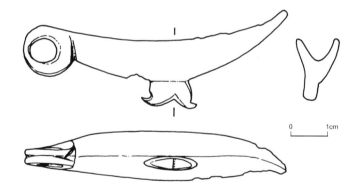

335. Magiovinium, Bletchley, Bucks
L. 71 mm.

End-looped mortar, with a broad curved bow, plain, steeply-sloping walls, a capacious, rounded V-sectioned groove, a plain, blunt-pointed terminal, now distorted to one side, and an angular keel with plate-like expansion of enigmatic ?bird-like shape. The thick disc-like loop has a central incuse line around its perimeter. The eye is elongated through wear.

From excavations, 1978–80, of extra-mural settlement and cemeteries. Site 17, fill of Ditch 2128, Phase 4.

Context date, early 2nd century AD.

Jackson 1985, no. 32. Publication details as no. 334, 45–6, fig. 24, no. 41.

Aylesbury, Bucks. County Museum.

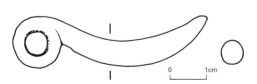

336. Magiovinium, Bletchley, Bucks
L. 53 mm.

End-looped pestle. The strongly-curved, plump, circular-sectioned rod has an upturned, blunt tip, and a ring-like loop with circular eye.

Metal detector find.

Jackson 1985, no. 53. Publication details as no. 334, 45–6, fig. 24, no. 42.

Present location unknown.

337. Maldon, Essex
L. 75.8 mm. Wt. 30.5 g.

Centre-looped mortar, with dark-green patina. The strongly-curved bow has plain, steep, lightly-convex walls with a thick rim, and a deep, capacious groove of rounded V-shaped cross-section. Wear in the groove was slightly oblique to the main axis, as evidenced by the rims. The slender terminals have a neatly-formed bulbous knob, somewhat phallic in appearance. Only the stub of the ring-like D-shaped loop remains. Metal detector find, said to have come from the northern outskirts of Maldon, a description that does not exclude the possibility that it was from the Roman site at Elms Farm, Heybridge.

In private hands, via the antiquity market.

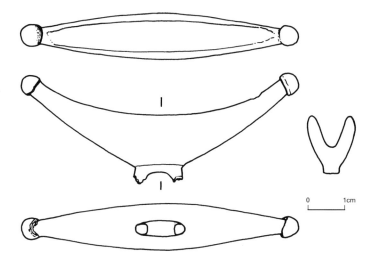

338. near March, Cambs
L. 48 mm. Wt. 13.9 g

Centre-looped pestle, with a dark brown (iron-stained) patina, lightly flaked and pitted. A heavy example with a stout crescentic rod of sub-circular cross-section at the centre. At the tapered ends, one of which has lost its tip, wear facets have modified the cross-section to a plump lentoid shape. The chunky loop, rather irregularly finished, has an asymmetric circular eye. Surface casting irregularities and filed finishing marks are present in several places, especially on the loop and on the rod at its junction with the loop.

Metal detector find. In private hands, via the antiquity market.

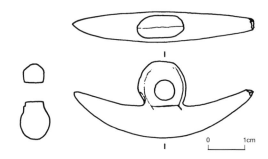

339. Marsham, Norfolk
L. *c.* 50 mm.

Centre-looped mortar. Not available for study, but the photograph shows a short deep lightly-curved bow with plain walls, simple, blunt-pointed terminals, a capacious groove, and a ring-like D-shaped loop expanded at its junction with the keel of the bow.

Metal detector find. In private hands.

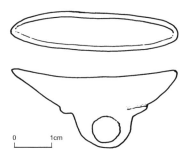

340. Melton Mowbray, Leics
L. 86.7 mm. Wt. 24.1 g.

Centre-looped mortar, with dark brown/ black patina, partially flaked away at the terminals and on the rims. The strongly-curved deep bow has an angular keel, steep plain walls with badly damaged rims, and a rounded V-sectioned groove with basal wear polish. The terminals have an elaborate and prominent baluster moulding. The damaged, plate-like, D-shaped loop, with small circular eye, is divided from the bow by a simple groove-and-ridge moulding.

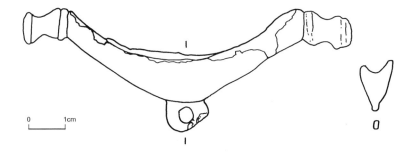

Metal detector find. Formerly in private hands, via the antiquity market, by means of which it acquired the false provenance of 'Brandon'.

British Museum, 1999,0802.43.

341. Meols, Cheshire

L. 45 mm.

Centre-looped pestle. A slender example, with asymmetric, crescentic rod, of ovoid cross-section at the centre, and a neat circular ring-like loop.

One of several hundred Roman objects found on this part of the north Wirral coast in the 19th century.

D. Griffiths, R.A. Philpott and G. Egan, 2007, *Meols. The Archaeology of the North Wirral Coast*, 49, 57, pl. 6, no. 202.

Chester, Grosvenor Museum, 391.R.1976.

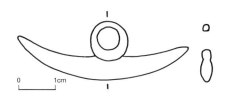

342. Metfield, Suffolk

L. 70 mm. Wt. 32.7 g.

Centre-looped mortar, with strongly-curved bow, plain walls, zoomorphic terminals, worn groove, and large ring-like loop with circular eye. The terminals are worn highly-stylized animal heads, probably intended as bovids, with flattened muzzles and drilled eyes. The difference in size is likely to have been intended to depict the twinning of a male and female animal.

Metal detector find. In private hands.

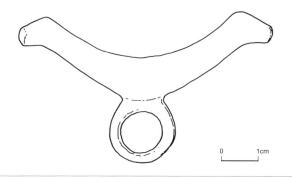

343. Metfield, Suffolk

L. 44 mm. Wt. 9.8 g.

Centre-looped mortar, lacking one terminal. The crescentic bow has low, plain, steep walls and a shallow, worn, U-sectioned groove. The surviving terminal is a worn oval knob, with a pair of slanting incuse lines at its junction with the bow. At the centre of the keel is a small triangular plate, perhaps part of a loop assembly.

Metal detector find. In private hands.

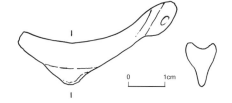

344. Middleton, Norfolk

L. *c.* 56 mm.

End-looped mortar, with stout, lightly-curved bow, plain, steep, carinated walls, flattened keel, capacious U-sectioned groove, simple blunt-pointed terminal, and D-shaped down-turned loop with circular eye.

Metal detector find. In private hands.

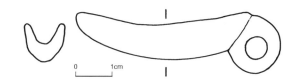

345. Mileham, Norfolk

L. 71.2 mm. Wt. 26.6 g.

Centre-looped mortar, with light grey-green dusty patina, lacking virtually the entire original surface except in the groove where it is mostly intact – a smooth dark green-black patina. Despite the surface depletion this was evidently a well-made example, with elliptical bow, apparently plain, steeply-sloping walls, lightly-inturned rims, a rounded angular keel, and well-formed, plump knobbed terminals with a simple ring moulding. The U-sectioned groove has wear polish and a basal wear facet which runs over the terminals. In the base of the groove are three symmetrically-placed small circular pits, one of which retains its silver-coloured metal inlay, its surface smoothed by the wear facet. The loop, a large circular ring, is broken across the eye.

Metal detector find. Formerly in private hands, via the antiquity market.

British Museum, 1999,0802.44.

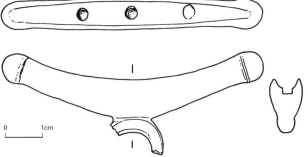

346. Mileham, Norfolk
L. 51.4 mm. Wt. 16.6 g.

Centre-looped mortar, with mid-grey patina. A simple plain example with mis-shaped bow, apparently a flawed casting. The plain sloping walls have eroded rims, and the simple, tapered, blunt-pointed terminals have eroded tips. The wear facet and wear polish in the rounded V-sectioned groove are asymmetric as a result of the casting flaw. The D-shaped loop is broken across its eye.

Metal detector find. In private hands.

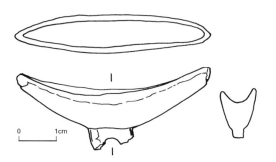

347. Mileham, Norfolk
L. *c.* 41 mm.

Centre-looped pestle, with crescentic, circular-sectioned, twin-tapered rod (one tip broken), and D-shaped plate-like loop with circular eye.

Metal detector find. In private hands.

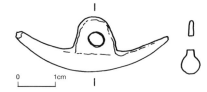

348. Minster-in-Sheppey, Kent
L. 91.5 mm. Wt. 64.8 g.

Centre-looped mortar, with partially abraded and iron-stained green and brown patina. The long, strongly-curved bow has plain bulbous walls, with upright lightly-hatched rims, a rounded keel, and a shallow U-sectioned groove, which runs over both terminals. The large bovid-headed terminal is well-modelled, with horns (both broken), ears, eyes and nostrils clearly depicted. There may originally have been more detail on the flared muzzle, but the patina is badly eroded in this region. The dewlap is complete, though a little chipped at the edges. The second terminal, also badly eroded, is a simple, ridged sub-rectangular knob. The loop is broken, but sufficient survives to show that it was originally a large, stout D-shaped plate with circular eye.

For metal composition see Scientific Analyses.

Beach find, probably as a consequence of coast erosion.

Donated by finder to British Museum; 1987,1004.1.

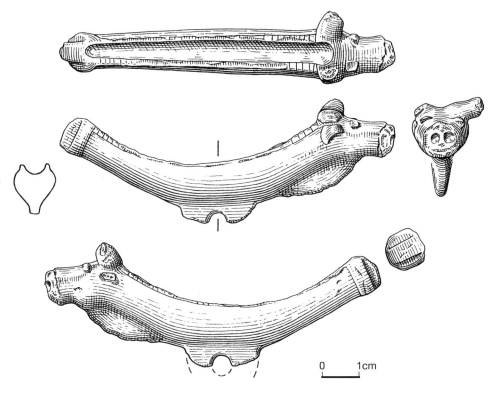

349. Morningthorpe, Norfolk
L. 71 mm. (orig. *c.* 80 mm.) Wt. 7.4 g.

Centre-looped mortar, Type L. A very light example, with pale green patina. One terminal is lacking, the loop is broken, the rims are chipped and the original surface is poorly-preserved in the central region. The bow is lightly-curved, with thin, steeply-angled walls and a capacious, deep V-sectioned groove, which retains low casting flashes at one end. The small, down-turned, knobbed terminal has a triple-grooved neck-moulding. The incuse hatched design on the walls adjacent to the loop is very irregular – two-and-two on one wall two-and-three on the other. The small, thin, plate-like loop, probably originally D-shaped, is broken across its circular eye.

Metal detector find. In private hands.

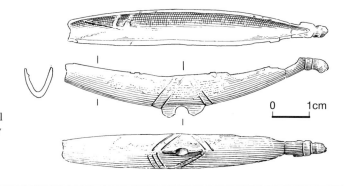

350. Morton, Lincs
L. 78 mm. Wt. 64.5 g.

Centre-looped mortar, with green-speckled mid-brown patina. A heavy example, with stout, strongly-curved bow, deep, plain, steep, convex walls, lightly-inturned rim, an angular keel, and a broad V-sectioned groove with basal wear facet. The large bovid-head terminal is finely and naturalistically modelled, with inturned horns, projecting simple ears, a broad flat brow, moulded eyes, a tapered, lightly rounded blunt-ended muzzle with slit mouth, and a simple plate-like dewlap which merges with the keel of the bow. The second terminal, smaller and much more highly-stylized, is in the form of a bird's head, rendered very simply, with a flattened crown and tapered, lightly-dished, blunt, round-ended bill. The small, plump, D-shaped loop has a circular hourglass eye with little sign of wear.

Metal detector find. In private hands.

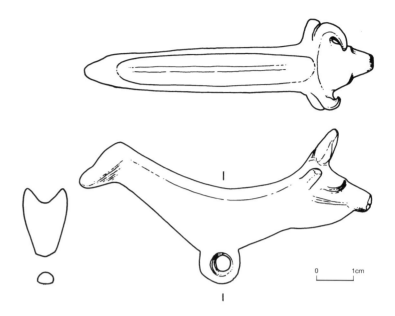

351. Morton, Lincs
L. 46 mm. Wg. 15 g.

End-looped mortar, with a mid-green patina. A small, light, well-made example, of very atypical form and proportion, the design of which combines utility with elegant decoration in miniature. The knife-shaped bow is very lightly domed and exceedingly narrow, with very thin, near-vertical walls and a rounded keel. The walls are plain except for a single incised line just above the keel. The straight, very slender, U-sectioned groove is relatively capacious and has a marked basal facet. It runs over the plain terminal, where the rim of one wall is partially worn away. Unusually, it is the end-loop, rather than the terminal or bow, that is the major decorative component. It comprises a highly-stylized, beautifully-rendered boar's head, optimally viewed with the object suspended by its loop or held with the groove upside down. For, to incorporate the suspension loop, which also comprised the grip, the head is turned below the groove. In consequence the animal's neck is 'stretched' to an elegant but unrealistic slender form. Nevertheless, it incorporates a stylized version of the characteristic bristle ridge, rendered by a pair of

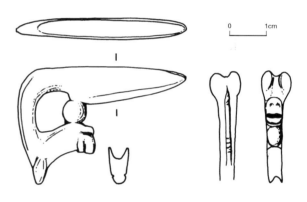

incised lines, flanking a low, slender, cross-cut ridge. The head itself has upright ears, a dished brow, and an upturned flattened muzzle with very lightly incised nostrils above the incised slit mouth. Two incised lines on top of the muzzle may be wrinkles or, less probably, very devolved tusks. A simple ball moulding fills the gap between the creature's chin and the underside of the bow and gives the eye of the loop a plump, comma-like shape. This is a common Roman device for the provision of zoomorphic looped terminals and may be compared, for example, with a bird-headed looped vehicle fitting from Trier (H. Menzel, 1966, *Die römischen Bronzen aus Deutschland II: Trier*, (Mainz), 111, no. 271, Taf. 82, 271).

Metal detector find. In private hands.

British Museum, 1996,1001.1.

352. Mundham, Norfolk
L. 66.7 mm. Wt. 30.8 g.

End-looped mortar, with partially-pitted, smooth, grey-green patina, preserving much of the original surface. A well-made, stout, heavy casting, with short, deep, elliptical bow, rounded angular keel, steep, convex, plain walls, a rounded V-sectioned groove with basal facet, and a small, ovoid, knobbed terminal. A single curved incuse line on each wall divides the bow from the large ovoid loop, which is in the form of a stylized swan's head, with strongly-curved neck, prominent crown and forehead, and long dished bill with everted tip.

Metal detector find. In private hands.

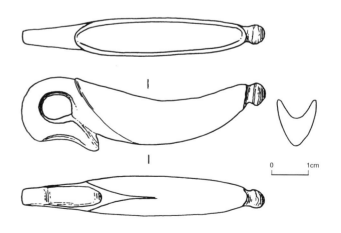

353. Newark-on-Trent area, Notts

L. 42.2 mm. Wt. 12.3 g.

Centre-looped mortar, with lightly-pitted, smooth, olive-green patina. A small un-elaborate example, with short broad bow, rounded ridged keel, plain, lightly-carinated, convex walls, simple blunt-pointed terminals, and a very capacious, broad, deep, rounded V-sectioned groove, which retains a greyish lump in the base and a little more adhering to the sides. The ring-like loop was worn through in antiquity.

Metal detector find. Formerly in private hands, via the antiquity market.

British Museum, 1999,0802.45.

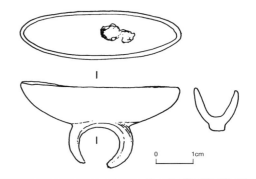

354. Newport, Gwent

L. 64 mm.

End-looped mortar, lacking one end of the bow and part of the loop. The bow has low, plain, convex walls, and a rounded keel with central, ridged expansion, which is plated with a white metal, probably tin. Remains of a similar coating are present in the broad, shallow U-sectioned groove, which has a basal facet and a marked ledge on one side, presumably products of wear. The loop appears to have been a simple, circular ring.

From quarrying at Liswerry, 1910. Apparently found in association with human burials and coins, brooches and other finds of late 1st-late 3rd century AD date.

V.E. Nash-Williams, 1924, 'Miscellanea', *Archaeologia Cambrensis* 79, 389, no. 7; Jackson 1985, no. 37.

Cardiff, National Museum of Wales.

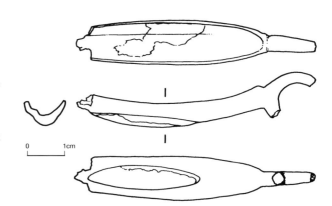

355. Newton Kyme, N. Yorkshire (Unillustrated)

Mortar, type and form unknown. Object not available for study. Neither illustration nor further written details forthcoming.

Probable metal detector find. On the antiquity market.

356. Norfolk, unprovenanced

L. 52.2 mm. Wt. 17.1 g.

Centre-looped mortar, Type G, with light-green patina, lacking most of the original surface. A small example, with slender crescentic bow, apparently plain steeply-sloping walls, with in-turned rim, and a narrow, shallow, rounded V-sectioned groove, with basal wear polish. One terminal is in the form of a very stylized bovid head, with tiny horns, triangular face and pointed muzzle. The other terminal, also zoomorphic, is smaller and more enigmatic: the head is narrow, with a rounded blunt muzzle and a pair of tiny upright ears (or horns?). The loop is a large D-shaped ring with circular eye.

Probable metal detector find. Formerly on the antiquity market.

British Museum, 1997,0101.3.

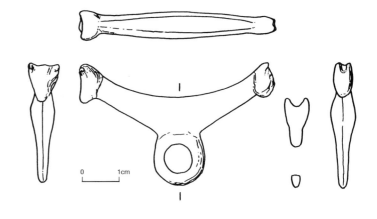

357. Norfolk, unprovenanced
L. 66.1 mm. Wt. 22.6 g.

Centre-looped mortar, Type C, lacking the entirety of its
original surface (except in the base of the groove) as a
consequence of cleaning by the finder. The resulting lightly-
pitted dark grey surface with sparse green patches thus
preserves little evidence of the original surface treatment,
but the last vestiges of incuse hatched lines are visible on
the keel to either side of the loop. It is likely that the original
bow decor was closely similar to that on mortar nos 319
and 438, since the form of bow, terminals and loop is also
very closely paralleled by those mortars. The bow is lightly
elliptical with a marked central swelling, a rounded angular
keel, steeply sloping walls and a capacious V-sectioned
groove with basal slot which runs onto the terminals. One
terminal is in the form of a highly-stylized, quite roughly-
rendered bovid head, with upright horns/ears, grooved
brow-ridge and pointed muzzle. The other terminal was in
the form of a tiny vestigial knob marked only by a very slight
waisting of the tip. The D-shaped loop with circular eye was worn through in antiquity.

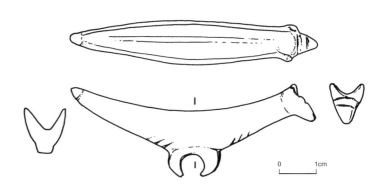

Metal detector find, said to be from the Norwich region. Formerly in private hands, via the antiquity market.

British Museum, 1999,0802.46.

358. Norfolk, unprovenanced
L. 67.7 mm. Wt. 21.7 g.

Centre-looped mortar, Type E variant, with light green-
grey patina. A formerly ornate but presently very worn
and damaged example, lacking its loop and strutting.
Chafing on both walls is recent, but other damage may
have occurred before deposition. The lightly-elliptical
plump bow has convex, apparently plain, walls with a thin
raised rim emphasized by an incuse line at its base. The rim
completely encircles the U-sectioned groove, which has a
basal facet and wear polish. Axially asymmetric wear has
abraded diagonally opposite ends of the walls. The matching
terminals are in the form of a stylized down-turned bird's
head, now eroded, but evidently always slender-billed. On
the adjacent part of the keel are the broken remains of a
slender sinuous strut, which originally encircled the missing
loop and linked it to the tip of the birds' bills via the keel.

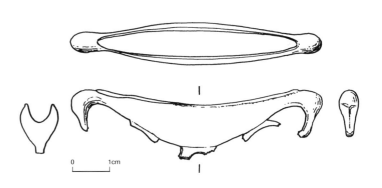

Probable metal detector find. Formerly on the antiquity market.
British Museum, 1997,0101.4.

359. Norfolk, unprovenanced
L. 49.8 mm. Wt. 19.5 g.

Centre-looped mortar, with fine green patina, lightly encrusted at one
end of the bow. A small, heavy casting with short, narrow, elliptical bow,
angular keel, very deep, plain facetted walls and a shallow U-sectioned,
wear-polished groove which runs onto the terminals. The quite simply
formed down-turned terminals appear to have been intended as stylized
birds heads, though a purely abstract design is equally feasible. The ring-
like loop was broken across its circular eye in antiquity.

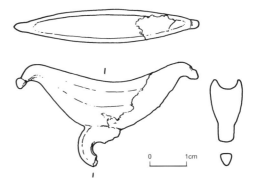

Metal detector find, said to be from the Norwich region. Formerly in
private hands, via the antiquity market.

British Museum, 1999,0802.47.

360. Norfolk, unprovenanced
L. 61 mm. (orig. *c.* 72 mm). Wt. 8.8 g.

Centre-looped mortar, Type H, with olive-brown patina. One end of the
bow is lacking and there is abrasion on one wall and rim. The slender,
crescentic bow has an angular keel and low, thin, convex walls with
an arc of three tiny triangular cells adjacent to the loop on both faces.
The cells, whose apex points away from the loop, are now devoid of
their enamel inlay. The capacious groove, of rounded V-shaped cross-
section, has a slight basal wear facet. The surviving terminal is a tiny
sub-spherical knob. The very slender D-shaped ring-like loop has a heart-
shaped eye.

Metal detector find. In private hands, via the antiquity market.

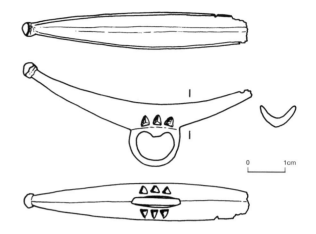

361. Norfolk, unprovenanced
L. 46.6 mm. Wt. 6.3 g.

Centre-looped mortar, Type J, with yellow-brown patina and underlying bright
green corrosion products, lacking both terminals and most of the loop. The lightly-
curved bow has an angular keel and thin convex walls, with an arc of six small
triangular cells adjacent to the loop on both walls. The cells, whose apex points
towards the loop, retain their enamel inlay, green in every case. The capacious
groove, partially blocked with a ferrous concretion, has a broad V-shaped cross-
section with basal wear facet. By comparison with more complete examples with
a similar arrangement of inlaid cells, the missing terminals are likely to have been
bovid rather than knobbed. Only the stub of the D-shaped loop survives.

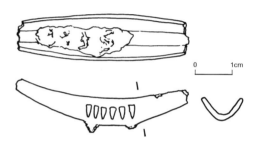

Metal detector find. Formerly in private hands, via the antiquity market.

British Museum, 1999,0802.51.

362. Norfolk, unprovenanced
L. 66 mm. Wt. 20.2 g.

Centre-looped mortar, with greyish patina. The slender elliptical bow has
convex walls with a heavily-worn, incuse zig-zag motif below the rim.
The narrow U-sectioned groove with pronounced basal wear facet, runs
onto the terminals, which are in the form of neat sub-spherical knobs.
The elegant, slender strutted loop, possibly intended as opposed stylized
dolphins, has a triangular piercing and a small circular eye.

For metal composition see Scientific Analyses.

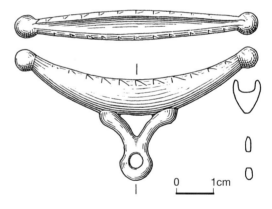

Metal detector find, formerly on the antiquity market. Said to have been
found about 20 years prior to 1986 'with' no. 372.

British Museum, 1986,0801.1.

363. Norfolk, unprovenanced

L. 75.8 mm. Wt. 34.7 g.

Centre-looped mortar, with dark green-black patina, which is eroded on most of the exterior, revealing underlying pitted green corrosion. The groove preserves a shiny green patina. A relatively heavy example, with elliptical bow, rounded angular keel, plain steeply-convex walls with thick rim, and a broad, deep, capacious, U-sectioned groove, with marked wear polish and an axially asymmetric wear slot, which has worn down the rim at one diagonally opposite end of each wall. The groove runs onto the two large, bulbous, knobbed terminals. Between each terminal and the loop another smaller knob hangs from the keel of the bow. In combination with the upward curve of the bow and the large terminal knobs these lesser knobs appear distinctly testicular, and there can be little doubt that a double-phallic motif was intended. The loop is a thick D-shaped ring with D-shaped eye.

Metal detector find. Formerly in private hands, via the antiquity market.

British Museum, 1999,0802.48.

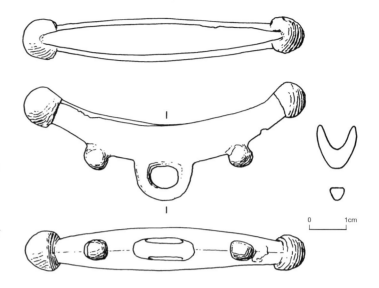

364. Norfolk, unprovenanced

L. 88.7 mm. Wt. 35.4 g.

Centre-looped mortar, with a dark grey-black patina. A large example, with long, slender, deep, crescentic bow, angular keel, very steeply-sloping walls, and a narrow, very shallow, U-sectioned groove. The walls are plain except for an incuse double hatched motif adjacent to the loop. The terminals comprise a prominent domed knob, one distinctly larger than the other and with grooved mouldings at the neck and round the girth. The slighter end was evidently re-worked in antiquity, the keel having been filed back and given a ridged, saw-like edge by the application of a series of cross-cuts. The ridging appears more functional than decorative. The D-shaped ring-like loop has a circular eye.

Metal detector find. Formerly in private hands, via the antiquity market.

British Museum, 1999,0802.49.

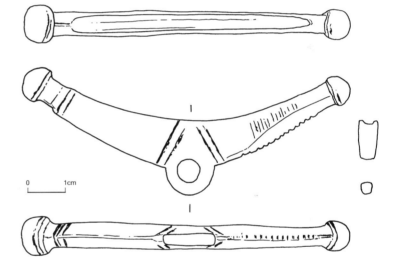

365. Norfolk, unprovenanced

L. 44.5 mm. Wt. 11.8 g.

Centre-looped mortar, with irregular, brown (iron-stained) patina, lightly accreted in places, and partially flaking to reveal the underlying pale green corrosion products. A small, rather poorly-preserved example, with short, lightly elliptical bow, apparently plain steeply-sloping walls (one higher than the other), a flattened keel, plain, blunt-pointed terminals, and a relatively capacious U-sectioned groove with axially asymmetric basal wear facet which runs over the terminals. The large disc-like D-shaped loop, with sub-circular eye, is markedly asymmetric to the longitudinal axis of the bow.

Metal detector find. Formerly in private hands, via the antiquity market.

British Museum, 1999,0802.50.

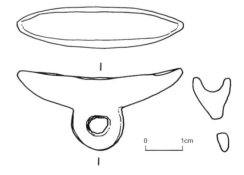

366. Norfolk, unprovenanced
L. 48.2 mm. Wt. 12.7 g.

Centre-looped pestle, Type N, with green-grey patina. A finely-wrought example, in good condition, with crescentic twin-tapered rod (one tip chipped) of rounded lozenge-shaped cross-section. On top of the slightly asymmetric, ovoid, ring-like loop, with circular eye, is the figure of a sitting (or swimming) duck, with bulbous head, projecting bill and folded wings, the feathers rendered in stylized form by simple incuse hatching.

Metal detector find. Formerly in private hands, via the antiquity market.

British Museum, 1999,0802.52.

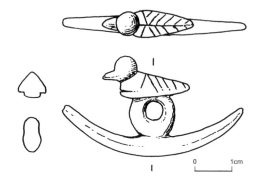

367. Norfolk, unprovenanced
L. 50.6 mm. Wt. 5.2 g.

Centre-looped pestle, with light, metallic, green-grey patina. The slender, elliptical, twin-tapered rod has a shield-shaped cross-section and blunt-pointed tips. The D-shaped ring-like loop has a large eye. There is a distinct wear shine over the whole of the convex lower face of the rod. Metal detector find. Formerly in private hands, via the antiquity market.

British Museum, 1999,0802.55.

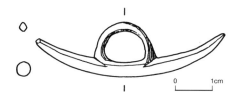

368. Norfolk, unprovenanced
L. 49.9 mm. Wt. 6.0 g.

Centre-looped pestle, with a stable, quite smooth, mottled pale green and brown patina. Recent in-ground disturbance has broken away the D-shaped loop and badly distorted the crescentic rod. The rod has a rounded triangular cross-section and a slight wear facet on its keel. It was always asymmetric, with one arm markedly longer than the other.

Metal detector find. Formerly in private hands, via the antiquity market.

British Museum, 1999,0802.56.

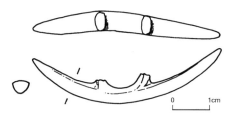

369. Norfolk, unprovenanced
L. 34.9 mm. Wt. 7.1 g.

Centre-looped pestle, with mid- to dark-green patina. In places a blackish patina seals the green corrosion products, beneath which the liver-coloured metal is partially revealed. This distinctive sequence recurs on mortar no. 377, with which this pestle was acquired, and the two may have been used as a set. A small, neatly-made example with short, lightly-curved rod of plump triangular cross-section. The large, round ring-like loop has a circular eye.

Metal detector find. Formerly in private hands, via the antiquity market.

British Museum, 1999,0802.53.

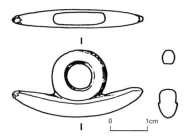

370. Norfolk, unprovenanced
L. 30.8 mm. Wt. 6.6 g.

Centre-looped pestle, with brittle, dark grey-green patina, mostly flaked away to reveal underlying irregular green corroded metal. A tiny example, with lightly-crescentic, short, stubby, twin-tapered rod, the corroded tips broken. The tiny corrosion-depleted loop, with circular eye, is mounted on a pair of angled struts which enclose a small triangular aperture.

Metal detector find. Formerly in private hands, via the antiquity market.

British Museum, 1999,0802.54.

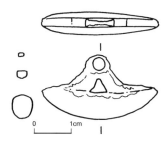

371. Norfolk, unprovenanced

L. 30 mm. Wt. 5.6 g.

Centre-looped pestle, with pale green patina. Both ends of the rod are broken, and the loop lacks most of its original surface. The strongly-curved plump rod has a sub-circular cross-section and preserves a distinct wear shine on its convex lower face, especially near the centre. The large ring-like loop has a heart-shaped eye.

Metal detector find. Formerly in private hands, via the antiquity market.

British Museum, 1999,0802.57.

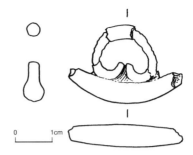

372. Norfolk, unprovenanced

L. 34 mm. Wt. 8 g.

Centre-looped pestle, with brown, sand-accreted patina. A small, quite crudely-made example, with short, slender, strongly-curved arms and a prominent loop, comprising a long tongue-shaped plate with tiny circular eye.

For metal composition see Scientific Analyses.

Metal detector find, formerly on the antiquity market. Said to have been found about 20 years prior to 1986, 'with' no. 362.

British Museum, 1986,0801.2.

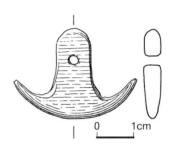

373. Norfolk, unprovenanced

L. 84.7 mm. Wt. 31.6 g.

End-looped mortar, with mid-grey-green smooth patina, lightly pitted in places, but preserving most of the original surface. A large flamboyant example, distinctly asymmetric, and quite rudimentarily-finished in places. The large, broad, crescentic bow has gently-carinated plain walls (one higher than the other) and a very capacious, broad, deep, rounded V-sectioned groove, with marked wear polish and basal facet, which runs over the loop and terminal. The angular keel is off-centre and lightly sinuous, apparently the result of grinding away a casting blemish. The terminal is a large bovid head, with very broad, in-turned asymmetric horns (one distorted), modelled head, round, empty, hollow-socketed eyes (perhaps originally inlaid with glass), and a lightly-flared rounded muzzle. The thick sub-discoid loop, with circular eye, is axially asymmetric.

Probable metal detector find. Formerly on the antiquity market.

British Museum, 1997,0101.1.

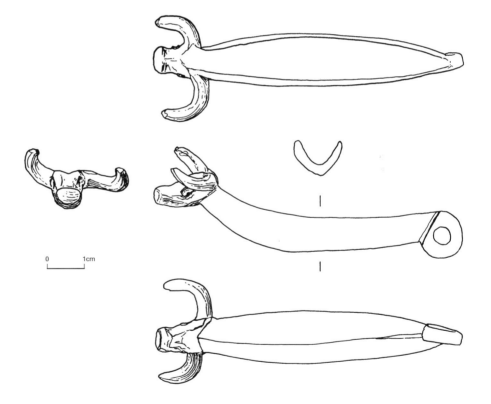

374. Norfolk, unprovenanced

L. 60.7 mm. (orig. *c.* 65 mm.) Wt. 28.7 g.

End-looped mortar, with pale green pitted and corroded metallic grey (tin-enriched) patina. A heavy example, with broad bow. The plump walls are plain, but the squared keel is raised and decorated with facets and with incuse chevron patterns below the terminal and the loop. The engraved line which edges the keel runs onto the imperforate terminal to end in a simple eyed scroll, and a pair of converging engraved marginal lines further embellish the perimeter of the terminal. The loop is too damaged to reveal its form which was, however, more than a simple ring. Both the terminal and the loop have the appearance of a stylized aquatic bird's head. The shallow groove, of broad, rounded V-shaped cross-section, has a marked wear-polish.

Metal detector find. Formerly in private hands, via the antiquity market.

British Museum, 1999,0802.60.

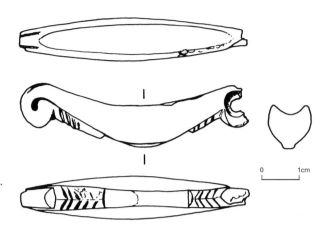

375. Norfolk, unprovenanced

L. 70.7 mm. Wt. 13 g.

End-looped mortar, with smooth mid-green patina, very lightly pitted on the loop and bow and more extensively corroded on the terminal knob. A finely-crafted, elegantly-designed example, with slender, elliptical, low-walled bow, ridged keel, plain steeply-convex walls, thin rims (now chipped), a knobbed terminal, and a slender, rounded, V-sectioned groove with marked wear polish. The loop is finely wrought in the form of a bird's head, with circular eye, brow ridge, and ridged everted bill. A neat moulding divides it from the bow, and a further slender channelled moulding runs around the perimeter of one side of the loop. There appears not to have been one on the other side.

Metal detector find. Formerly in private hands, via the antiquity market.

British Museum, 1999,0802.59.

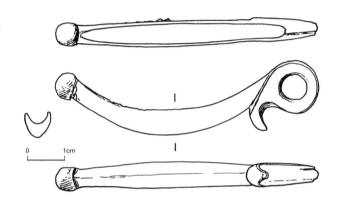

376. Norfolk, unprovenanced

L. 68.2 mm. Wt. 21.2 g.

End-looped mortar, with orange-brown iron-stained patina, chipped on one rim. The crescentic bow has an angular keel, plain convex walls with lightly in-turned rim, a knobbed terminal, and a V-sectioned groove with axially asymmetric wear facet. The loop is a slender ring in the form of a very stylized bird's head, with worn brow ridge and elongated dished bill, which extends onto, and merges into, the keel of the bow. The eye is elongated through wear.

Metal detector find. Formerly in private hands, via the antiquity market.

British Museum, 1999,0802.69.

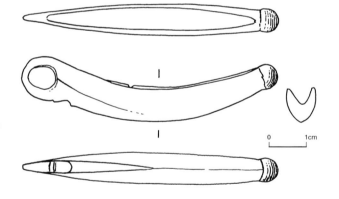

377. Norfolk, unprovenanced

L. 54 mm. Wt. 9.7 g.

End-looped mortar, with patina/corrosion products as pestle no. 369. The pestle fits snugly in the groove of the mortar and, although not described as such by the vendor, the two may have been used as a set. The bow is simple and short, with an angular keel, plain sloping walls, almost straight rims and a plain blunt-pointed terminal. Both walls have been dented by recent damage near their mid-point. The groove, of rounded V-shaped cross-section, is relatively capacious. The large loop, with pear-shaped eye, is in the form of a stylized aquatic bird's head, with marked brow ridge and elongated bill. It had worn through in antiquity.

Metal detector find. Formerly in private hands, via the antiquity market.

British Museum, 1999,0802.61.

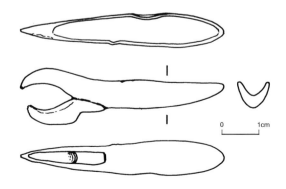

378. Norfolk, unprovenanced

L. 61 mm. Wt. 16 g.

End-looped mortar, with very fine, smooth, mottled brown-olive patina. A plain, simple, well-finished casting, with rounded keel, plain steeply-convex walls, a U-sectioned groove, with wear polish and basal facet, which runs onto the loop and terminal, and a plain blunt-pointed terminal. The loop is a simple chunky disc with sub-circular eye.

Probable metal detector find. Formerly on the antiquity market.

British Museum, 1997,0101.2.

379. Norfolk, unprovenanced

L. *c.* 60 mm.

End-looped mortar, lightly elliptical, with apparently plain-walled bow, lightly-knobbed terminal, and simple loop, the sub-circular eye elongated, perhaps through wear.

On the antiquity market. Not available for study.

See *Benet's artefacts of England & the United Kingdom, current values* (Cambridge 2000), p. 47, no. I14 – 0104, where the object is wrongly scaled, juxtaposed with a non-matching pestle (no. 385), erroneously classed as 'Celtic' and described as a 'woad-grinding set'.

380. Norfolk, unprovenanced

L. unknown.

End-looped mortar, Type A. Not available for study, this example was illustrated with a small, unscaled, photo in an antiquity sale catalogue in 1993. It is evidently of the type of archetype no. 318, and I have enlarged and redrawn the photo with reference to no. 558, which it most closely resembles. The long bow has carinated walls, a zoomorphic (probably bovid) terminal, and a loop apparently in the form of a stylized tail/bird's head.

Antiquity market/private hands. Probably a metal detector find.

381. Norfolk, unprovenanced

L. 81 mm. Wt. 11 g.

End-looped pestle, with a smooth mid-brown patina. Recent impact damage, probably at, or shortly before, the time of discovery, has distorted the rod just off-centre towards the loop and flaked away part of the patina. A very long, elegant, well-made, and well-finished example, comprising a long circular-sectioned rod, with up-turned, plump, D-sectioned, blunt-pointed tip, and a large slender loop in the form of a stylized bird's head, with large tear-shaped eye and elongated dished bill. There are distinct wear striations and wear polish on the convex underside of the tip.

Metal detector find. Formerly in private hands, via the antiquity market.

British Museum, 1999,0802.62.

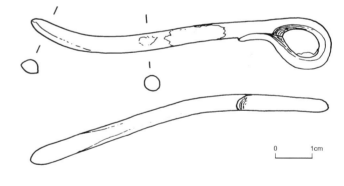

382. Norfolk, unprovenanced

L. 40.8 mm. Wt. 4.4 g.

End-looped pestle, with lightly-pitted and -accreted green patina. A small example, with a lightly-elliptical rod and a marked, unusually flat wear facet, which has probably truncated the original end. The neatly-made loop is in the form of a stylized aquatic bird's head, with small circular eye and strongly everted bill.

Metal detector find. Formerly in private hands, via the antiquity market.

British Museum, 1999,0802.65.

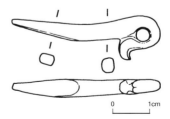

383. Norfolk, unprovenanced
L. 42.8 mm. Wt. 4.2 g.

End-looped pestle, with sparsely pitted smooth brown metallic patina. A small example, heavily worn, with a marked oblique wear facet, well to one side of the end of the rod, which probably truncated the tip. The slender loop, with large, lightly ovoid eye, is in the form of a very stylized aquatic bird's head with everted bill.

Metal detector find. Formerly in private hands, via the antiquity market.

British Museum, 1999,0802.64.

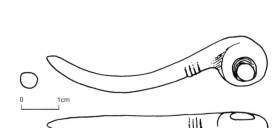

384. Norfolk, unprovenanced
L. 59.5 mm. Wt. 13.3 g.

End-looped pestle, lacking its original surface everywhere except a small area beneath the rod at the junction with the loop, where the dark green patina preserves traces of a simple ring moulding. The elliptical rod has a plump lentoid cross-section and a blunt-pointed up-turned tip. The circular eye of the chunky loop is positioned markedly off-centre.

Metal detector find. Formerly in private hands, via the antiquity market.

British Museum, 1999,0802.66.

385. Norfolk, unprovenanced
L. *c.* 55 mm.

End-looped pestle, strongly curved, with circular loop, moulded stem, and knife-like rod with pointed tip.

On the antiquity market. Not available for study.

See *Benet' artefacts of England & the United Kingdom, current values* (Cambridge 2000), p. 47, no. I14 – 0104, where the object is wrongly scaled, juxtaposed with a non-matching mortar (no. 379), and erroneously classed as 'Celtic' and described as a 'woad-grinding set'.

386. Norfolk, unprovenanced
L. 58.3 mm. Wt. 17.6 g.

End-looped pestle, with partially-pitted grey-green patina. A fine, quite heavy example, with deep angular rod of knife-like form, a lightly-rounded angular keel, and wear polish on both sides of the tip. The slightly scrolled loop has a neatly-cut rib between flanking grooves running all the way round its perimeter. It has a near-circular eye, with a little wear polish.

Metal detector find. Formerly in private hands, via the antiquity market.

British Museum, 1999,0802.63.

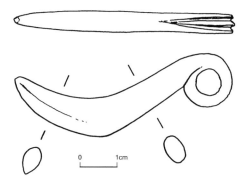

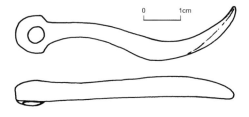

387. Norfolk, unprovenanced
L. *c.* 60 mm.

End-looped pestle, with long, sinuous, strongly-curved rod and neatly-moulded shouldered D-shaped loop with circular eye.

Metal detector find. In private hands.

388. Norfolk, unprovenanced
L. 49 mm. Wt.13.6 g.

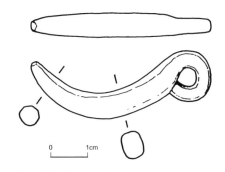

End-looped pestle, with partially corroded dark grey patina. A short, heavy, very strongly-curved example. The form is simple and the manufacture quite rudimentary, notably in the angular turn of the sub-circular loop, but the bar-like rod has been carefully finished on all its faces and at its blunt tip, on the convex face of which is a wear facet.

Metal detector find. Formerly in private hands, via the antiquity market.

British Museum, 1999,0802.67.

389. Norfolk, unprovenanced
L. 69 mm. Wt. 20.3 g.

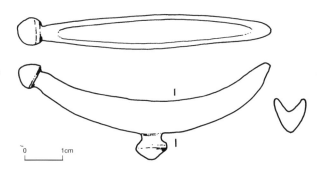

Mortar, unlooped. The strongly-curved bow has low, plain, convex walls, an angular keel, with central projecting knob, and a shallow V-sectioned groove with a slight basal wear facet. One terminal has a bulbous, shouldered knob, the other, more steeply upturned, is a plain blunt point. The latter may have been re-worked after breakage of an end-loop, but there is no conclusive evidence for this. [For a broken and re-worked loop see no. 392].

For metal composition see Scientific Analyses.

Metal detector find, formerly on the antiquity market.

British Museum, 1986,0301.1.

390. Norfolk, unprovenanced
L. 63.7 mm. Wt. 29.2 g.

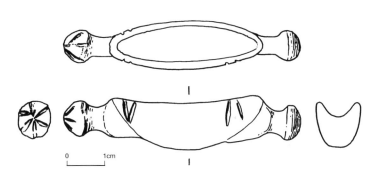

Un-looped mortar, with waxed dark brown-black patina, partially flaked revealing underlying dark green corrosion. A heavy casting, with short, deep, broad bow, rounded keel, convex walls, with simple incuse decoration at each end, and thick rims, which completely encircle the broad V-sectioned groove with basal facet and marked wear polish. At each end of the bow a large domed knob is mounted on a keel-like extension. The end of the knobs is decorated with an incuse six-rayed star motif, one badly affected by corrosion. There is no sign of any former attachment for a centre loop. A slight wear polish on the neck of the more prominent knobbed terminal is suggestive of attachment at that point.

Metal detector find. Formerly in private hands, via the antiquity market.

British Museum, 1999,0802.68.

391. Normanton-le-Heath, Leics
L. 69 mm.

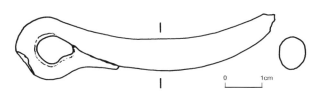

End-looped pestle. A large and heavy example, lacking the tip of its ovoid-sectioned, bar-like rod. The large loop is in the form of an aquatic bird's head, with elongated dished bill.

From excavation of Iron Age and Romano-British enclosure system.

Context date, Phase 3a (1088), apparently a pre-conquest context, possibly no later than the mid-1st century BC.

R. Thorpe, J. Sharman and P. Clay, 1994, 'An Iron Age and Romano-British enclosure system at Normanton-le-Heath, Leicestershire', *Trans. Leicestershire Archaeol.and Hist. Soc.* 68, 48–9, fig. 25,2.

In view of the proximity of the sites, shared Late Iron Age ceramic traditions and overall chronology (S. Elsdon in Thorpe *et al.* 1994, 38), it is interesting to note the similarity in form and size between the Normanton pestle and the mortar from Enderby (no. 177), even though the latter is not from the excavated site at Enderby.

Leicestershire Museums, Arts and Records Service Acc. no. A159.1990:901.

392. ?Northampton area
L. 80 mm. Wt. 22.1 g.

End-looped mortar, with mid-brown patina. The tapered, elliptical bow has plain convex walls, with lightly inturned rim, and a rounded keel. The groove, of U-shaped cross-section is capacious and unusually deep, in part a product of long and heavy wear. As is often the case the wear has caused a degree of asymmetry in the walls (one now lower than the other) and in the shape and alignment of the groove. The sub-spherical terminal knob is simple and plain. The loop, in the form of a devolved bird's head, with strongly-everted bill, was once circular, with a large eye, but it was worn through in antiquity and a simple repair effected by hammering together the fractured ends, filing down one face of the loop adjacent to the butted join and adding a metal repair patch or collar. The latter, now lost, is evidenced by the silver-grey remains of solder. In addition to this repair and the wear in the groove, prolonged usage is demonstrated by wear polish on knob, bill and loop.

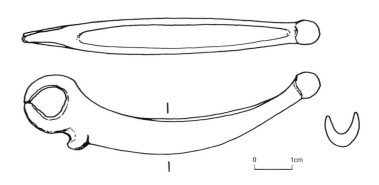

Metal detector find. Formerly in private hands, via the antiquity market.

British Museum, 1999,0802.70.

393. North Creake, Norfolk
L. 78 mm. Wt. 45.3 g.

End-looped mortar, with a smooth green-grey patina, a little pitted and chipped in places. A large, heavy, ornate example, markedly imbalanced, with a very large, deep zoomorphic terminal and a small, narrow loop. The lightly-curved, strongly tapered bow is slender, with an angular keel and steep, lightly convex walls, which are decorated with an incuse zig-zag design supplemented by lines of punched dots and by a punched dot-in-ring motif, the latter arranged, generally, as one per triangular compartment of the zig-zag. All elements of the incuse decoration are rather imprecisely applied and occasionally bungled. The narrow groove, which runs over the terminal, has an asymmetric V-shaped cross-section with basal facet, probably a product of wear. The bovid-head terminal is broad and well-modelled, with a marked brow ridge, everted horns (both ends broken), ears, small dimpled eyes and nostrils and a slit mouth in the tapered muzzle. The extreme depth of the adjacent keel was probably intended as the beast's dewlap. The understated loop is a small circular eye in a slight expansion of the tapered end.

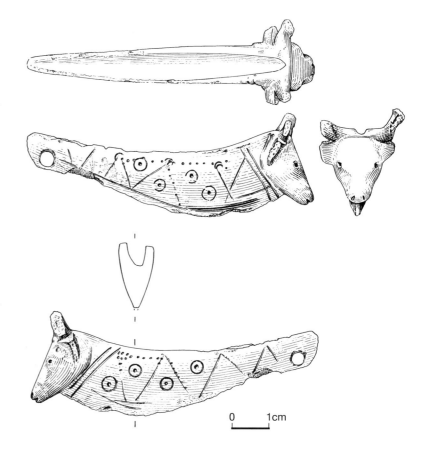

Metal detector find. In private hands.

394. North Creake, Norfolk
L. *c.* 28 mm.

End-looped mortar, Type A, lacking the loop and part of the bow. The steeply-sloped walls are decorated with an incuse triple zig-zag; the keel is angular; and the groove has a U-shaped cross-section. The zoomorphic terminal is highly stylized and rudimentarily formed, with upright horns and a heavy ridged muzzle with down-pointed end. It resembles very closely the terminal of no. 318.

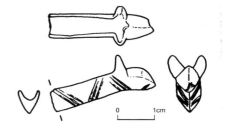

Metal detector find. In private hands.

395. North Ferriby, Humberside

L. 48 mm.

End-looped mortar. A small slender example with only lightly-elliptical bow, low, apparently plain, convex walls, a rounded keel, a U-sectioned groove and a rather square-ended plain terminal. The loop is broken.

Metal detector find from a site on the north foreshore of the Humber. In private hands.

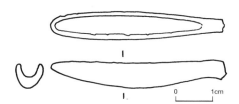

396. Norton Subcourse, Norfolk

L. 42 mm. Wt. 13.19 g.

Centre-looped mortar. The short bow has deep plain walls, with a virtually straight rim, plain blunt-pointed terminals, a broad shallow groove, and a prominent loop with a circular eye.

Metal detector find. In private hands.

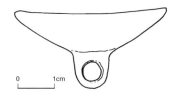

397. Norton Subcourse, Norfolk

L. 57 mm. Wt. 22.4 g.

Centre-looped pestle, with slightly pitted mid-grey-green metallic (tin-enriched) patina, retaining pale brown soil in crevices. A large, heavy example with stout, slightly asymmetric, strongly-curved rod and large plump D-shaped loop. The rod has wear facets on the centre keel and near one tip. Both rod and loop display file-finished facetting.

Metal detector find. In private hands.

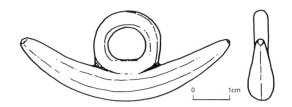

398. Nottinghamshire, unprovenanced

L. 58.6 mm. Wt. 19.8 g.

End-looped mortar, with occasional large and deep corrosion pitting in a dark brown shiny patina, a product of heavy-handed recent cleaning. The strongly-curved bow has a lightly squared keel, steep, plain, convex walls, and a rounded V-sectioned groove which retains the original mid-brown ferrous patina. The terminal is a small simple bovid head with thick muzzle (the tip damaged), horns, and ears (also lacking their tips). The loop is simply-wrought, with a tiny circular eye.

Metal detector find. In private hands, via the antiquity market.

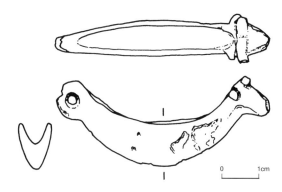

399. Oakley, Suffolk

L. 61 mm. Wt. 24.5 g.

Centre-looped mortar, with a smooth metallic grey (tin-enriched) patina, a little pitted on the smaller terminal. The bow is smoothly curved and the walls have a rounded carination. They are plain except for an incuse (probably punched) crescent, one per wall, to the right of the junction with the loop. The groove has a broad U-shaped cross-section. The terminals are knobbed, with a moulded base, quite worn in places. The better preserved, larger, terminal has an acorn/glans-like appearance. The large D-shaped ring-like loop has a circular eye with some wear polish. The vestigial asymmetric wall markings are intriguing and are certainly the full extent of the wall decoration – nothing else has worn away. Notwithstanding the relative simplicity of the form, this mortar is so similar in dimensions and detail to no. 584 that both are likely to have derived from the same archetype, if not the same mould.

For metal composition see Scientific Analyses.

From excavation, by Suffolk Archaeological Unit, at Oakley, in advance of construction work for the Scole by-pass.

T. Ashwin and A. Tester (eds) (forthcoming) *A Roman settlement in the Waveney Valley: Excavations at Scole, 1993–4*, East Anglian Archaeology.

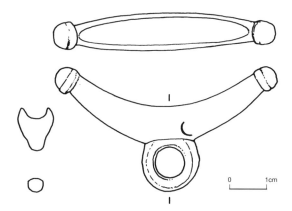

400. Ogof-yr-Esgyrn, ('The Bone Cave'), Dan-yr-Ogof, Powys

L. 73 mm.

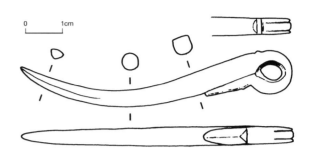

End-looped pestle, with smooth green-brown patina, revealing the golden-coloured metal surface in places. A large, decorative, finely-made example. The long, strongly-curved rod changes from a sub-rectangular cross-section near the loop, through a circular section to a D-shaped section at the upturned tip, which has a wear facet on the convex face. The loop is in the form of a stylized aquatic bird's head with carefully faceted elongated bill. A pair of incuse lines flank a low ridge on the perimeter of the loop and terminate in a slightly worn cross-moulding on the upper edge of the rod. Wear is visible in the slightly elongated eye.

From excavations, 1938–50, of cave deposit; from square N/p = adjacent to 'grave' area of inhumations, probably associated with 2nd century AD occupation debris.

G.C. Boon, 'The Roman material', in E.J. Mason, 1968, 'Ogof-yr-Esgyrn, Dan-yr-Ogof Caves, Brecknock, Excavations 1938–50', *Archaeologia Cambrensis* 117, 18–71, esp. 48, fig. 10, no. 7; Jackson 1985, no. 40. For the cave, see also K. Branigan and M.J. Dearne, 1991, *A Gazetteer of Romano-British Cave Sites and Their Finds* (Sheffield), 176–7.

Cardiff, National Museum of Wales.

401. Old Hunstanton, Norfolk

L. 55.7 mm. Wt. 12.0 g.

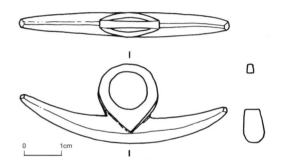

Centre-looped pestle, with fine stable lacquered grey-green patina. The twin-tapered rod has a lozenge-shaped cross-section worn on the keel; the slightly asymmetric and unequal arms have blunt tips; and the large, carefully-wrought loop has a tapered profile, circular eye and sharply-moulded base.

Metal detector find. In private hands.

402. Old Hunstanton, Norfolk (Unillustrated)

L. *c.* 45 mm. Wt. 7.9 g.

End-looped pestle, with short stout rod, markedly swollen towards the asymmetrically-worn, up-turned, pointed tip. The broken loop appears to have been large and, perhaps, ornate.

Metal detector find. In private hands.

403. Otford, Kent

L. 59 mm. Wt. 22.3 g.

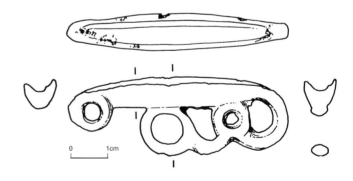

Multiple-looped mortar, with pitted, light green-grey (tin-enriched) patina. A very idiosyncratic example, with fancy scrolled strutting, atypical lightly-convex bow, low, plain, steeply-sloping walls, a squared keel and a shallow U-sectioned groove with very marked basal wear facet, which has resulted in the formation of a 'ledge' on one side. One wall is markedly lower than the other, probably through wear and damage (the rim is extensively chipped), but it may always have been slightly asymmetric as the scrolled strutting is also slightly out of alignment with the bow. Wear in the D-shaped eye of the loop at the end of the scrollwork demonstrates that it was suspended as an end-looped mortar.

For metal composition see Scientific Analyses.

Metal detector find, formerly in private hands.

British Museum, 1993,0703.1.

404. Owmby Cliff, Lincs
L. 56.2 mm. (orig. *c*. 60 mm.) Wt. 13.7 g.

End-looped mortar, with very smooth metallic grey-green (tin-enriched) patina, lightly pocked and accreted at the bow/loop junction and at the terminal. The bow is short, broad and only lightly curved, with plain, convex walls, a rounded, slightly asymmetric keel, and a capacious, broad U-sectioned groove. The lightly down-turned terminal, now chipped, was always plain, and, apparently, open-ended, so that it may have functioned as a spout. The eye of the large circular loop, now broken, was filled with a simple spurred or scrolled openwork design.

Metal detector find. In private hands, via the antiquity market.

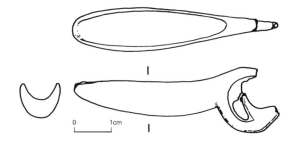

405. Oxborough, Norfolk
L. 34.3 mm. Wt. 6.2 g.

Centre-looped mortar, Type K, with fine pale green patina (sparsely encrusted with a creamy deposit), which preserves the original smooth surface. Both ends of the bow are lacking. The remaining part of the elliptical bow has an angular keel, thin, plain, sloping walls, and a capacious groove of broad V-shaped cross-section with basal facet. The loop is a rather irregularly-shaped ring with an unworn circular eye. In view of the close correspondence to nos 309 and 579 this mortar probably originally had bovid terminals.

Metal detector find. In private hands.

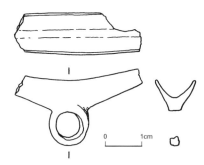

406. Pembridge, Herefordshire
L. *c*. 98 mm.

End-looped mortar, with elliptical bow, apparently plain sloping walls, a relatively broad groove, and a small, simple, knobbed terminal. The loop, worn through in antiquity, is in the form of a stylized bird's head, with marked brow and pronounced everted bill.

Metal detector find. In private hands.

407. Postwick, Norfolk
L. 52 mm. Wt. 23.1 g.

Centre-looped mortar, with elliptical bow, plain walls, a broad shallow groove, and large knobbed terminals, one flattened, the other distinctly and overtly phallic. The centre-loop, with small countersunk eye, has a knobbed finial, possibly intended as a profile of testicles/ scrotum, in view of the juxtaposition with the phallic terminal.

Metal detector find. In private hands.

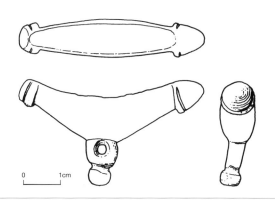

408. Postwick, Norfolk
L. *c*. 31 mm.

Centre-looped pestle. A small, quite crudely-finished example, with a large circular loop on a tall pedestal flanked by a pair of struts, which enclose sub-triangular apertures. Dot-punched decoration on the loop, pedestal and struts encircles the eye and apertures. The twin-tapered rod is short, with slightly blunt tips.

Metal detector find. In private hands.

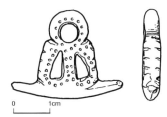

409. Postwick, Norfolk

L. 58.4 mm. Wt. 23.9 g.

End-looped mortar, with heavily-pitted and corroded metallic grey patina. The relatively slender, deep, elliptical bow has a flattened keel, near-vertical plain walls with thick rims, a plain blunt-ended terminal, and a slender groove (partially blocked with soil and corrosion products), which stops short of the terminal but runs onto the top of the loop, where it displays slight wear polish. The sub-circular loop has a tiny circular eye. In several places the surface of this mortar is broken by hollows or perforations, some irregular, some less so. It is impossible to determine whether these are intentional or accidental features, and whether they occurred at manufacture or subsequent to main usage. Whatever the case, the wear at the back of the groove demonstrates that the mortar was finished and used.

Metal detector find. In private hands.

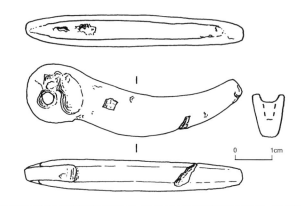

410. Preston St Mary, Suffolk

L. 19.5 mm.

Centre-looped pestle fragment, comprising the large circular centre-loop and the stub of each end of the rod.

Metal detector find. In private hands.

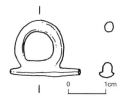

411. Quidenham, Norfolk

L. 55 mm. Wt. 7.7 g.

End-looped mortar, with shiny brown patina. A light example, with slender, parallel-sided, strongly-curved bow, plain, steeply-sloped walls, their thin rims chipped and partially broken, an angular keel, a narrow, deep, capacious V-sectioned groove and a plain, round, up-turned terminal. The simple sub-circular loop has a large eye much elongated through wear.

Metal detector find. In private hands.

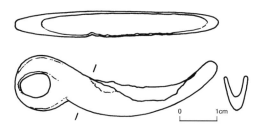

412. Quidenham, Norfolk

L. 55.2 mm. Wt. 8.6 g.

End-looped pestle, with mid-green patina. A simple, elegant example, with circular-sectioned rod, the underside of which is flattened towards the upturned tip. No wear is discernible there, nor in the circular eye of the neatly-formed loop.

Metal detector find. In private hands.

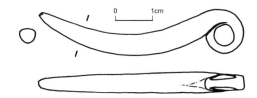

413. Reading area

L. 68 mm. Wt. 8.8 g.

Centre-looped pestle, with grey-green patina. A long slender example with keeled, twin-tapered rod, the two arms of which are markedly asymmetric. The small loop is in the form of a low, slender rectangular plate with circular eye.

Metal detector find. Formerly in private hands, via the antiquity market.

British Museum, 1999,0802.71.

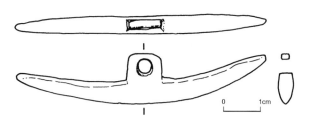

414. Repton, Derbyshire (Unillustrated)

L. 51 mm.

Centre-looped mortar, unavailable for study, with knobbed terminals, a broad V-shaped groove with basal wear slot, a broken loop, and, perhaps, incuse decoration on the bow, though corrosion inhibits inspection.

From excavations, 1985, by Professor Martin Biddle. A residual find in a Saxon or later feature.

N. Wickenden in M. Biddle, publication forthcoming.

415. Richborough, Kent

L. *c.* 40 mm.

Mortar, probably centre-looped. Fragment of a very large example comprising part of the bow with large zoomorphic terminal. The walls are plain and steep, the keel is angular, and the groove is of slender V-shaped cross-section. The head has upright ears (or horns), prominent round bulbous eyes and simple incuse mouth and nostrils on the tapered round-ended muzzle. These features, and the overall shape of the head, give it more the appearance of a horse than a bovid, but certainty is not possible. The size of the head is comparable to the terminals on nos261, 301 and 348, and, as zoomorphic terminals are much less common on end-looped mortars, it is probable that the present example is from a centre-looped mortar and was very likely balanced by a second zoomorphic terminal. A conservative reconstruction gives a length in excess of 100 mm: in reality it was probably much longer.

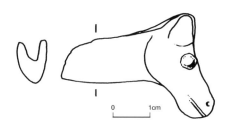

From excavations, 1931–8, diagonal Trench II, 100 ft. along. Effectively unstratified, but apparently from the central row of Claudian granaries, and in the same general area as no. 418, below.

B. Cunliffe, 1968, *Richborough V*, 97, pl. XXXIX, no. 143; Jackson 1985, no. 62.

English Heritage Acc. no. 7351429.

416. Richborough, Kent

L. *c.* 67 mm.

Centre-looped pestle, with robust, crescentic, twin-tapered rod, of lozenge-shaped cross-section, and slender, ring-like, D-shaped loop with heart-shaped eye.

From excavations, 1922–3, Site 1, within the N.W. quadrant of the shore fort.

J.P. Bushe-Fox, 1926, *Richborough I*, 47, pl. XV, no. 32; Jackson 1985, no. 93.

English Heritage Acc. no. 96001769.

417. Richborough, Kent

L. *c.* 46 mm.

Centre-looped pestle, with slender, crescentic, twin-tapered rod, of D-shaped cross-section, and circular ring-like loop.

From excavation, Winter 1924–5, original Finds no. 385.

Context date *c.* AD 280–400+.

English Heritage Acc. no. 7350256.

418. Richborough, Kent

L. *c.* 80 mm.

End-looped mortar, with strongly curved bow, plain, steeply-sloping walls, an angular keel, and a capacious groove of rounded V-shaped cross-section. The terminal knob is very large and elaborate, with neck moulding and incuse, rayed ribbing. The perimeter of the very neatly-wrought loop has a low ridge flanked by a pair of incuse lines, which, with the bill-like projection of the tip of the loop, give the appearance of an aquatic bird's head, very similar in style to pestle no. 400, above.

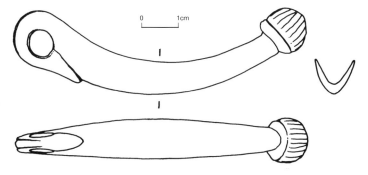

From excavations, 1931–8, Trial Trench IV, Pit 258. Second century AD. This is within Area XVII, inside the stone fort, a little to the south of the west gate. Pit 258 cut one of the foundation trenches of one of the Claudian granaries (H). In the S.W. quadrant of the fort were several burials of later 2nd century date, and it is possible that the mortar originally derived from a disturbed burial.

B. Cunliffe, 1968, *Richborough V,* 97, pl. XXXIX, no. 142; Jackson 1985, no. 7.

English Heritage Acc. no. 96001770.

419. Richborough, Kent
L. *c.* 78 mm.

End-looped mortar, with strongly-curved, tapered bow, apparently plain, thin, steeply-sloping walls, a capacious groove, of deep V-shaped cross-section with basal wear-slot, a cheese-shaped knobbed terminal, and a large circular loop.

From excavation, Winter 1924–5, original Finds no. 378.

Context date *c.* AD 280–400+.

English Heritage Acc. no. 7351530.

420. Richborough, Kent
L. *c.* 53 mm.

End-looped mortar, with short, strongly-curved bow, apparently plain walls, a large bulbous knobbed terminal, and a large circular loop, seemingly worn through.

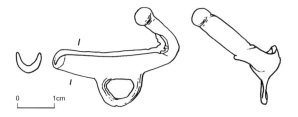

C. Roach Smith, 1850, *The Antiquities of Richborough, Reculver and Lympne, in Kent,* 114, fig. 1; Jackson 1985, no. 14.

Present whereabouts unknown.

421. Ringshall, Suffolk
L. 33.2 mm.

Centre-looped mortar, lacking one end of the bow, the other badly distorted. The bow has an angular keel, apparently plain (though corroded) convex walls, a capacious U-sectioned groove, and a bulbous knobbed terminal. The D-shaped loop is of 'cup-handle' form.

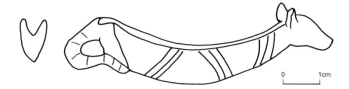

Metal detector find. In private hands.

422. near River Mole, Surrey
L. *c.* 72 mm.

End-looped mortar, Type A, not available for study. The bow has an angular keel, steep, lightly convex walls decorated with an incuse triple zig-zag, and a slender V-sectioned groove, which appears to run over the loop. The zoomorphic terminal, with upright horns/ears and tapered, blunt-ended muzzle, is probably a stylized bovid. The loop, set beneath the other end, was doubtless intended to represent the animal's tail.

This example was illustrated with a small, unscaled, slightly obliquely-drawn sketch, with cross-section, in a reader's letter in *Treasure Hunting* magazine, January 1984, p. 69 (where its dimensions were mistakenly expressed in inches not millimeters). It was said to have been found 'in woodland in Surrey, near the River Mole'.

Present whereabouts unknown, presumably in private hands.

423. Rochester, Kent
L. 53.5 mm. Wt. 7.9 g.

End-looped mortar, with irregular mid-green corrosion-pitted patina. A light, simple example, with a virtually straight bow, plain sloping walls (one rim badly chipped), a rounded keel, and a deep V-sectioned groove with wear polish and an asymmetric basal wear facet. The plain open-ended terminal is more probably an original feature than a product of corrosion/damage. The loop, perhaps a very devolved bird's head, is bent slightly to one side and has a pear-shaped eye.

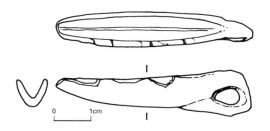

Metal detector find. In private hands via the antiquity market.

424. Rocklands, Norfolk

L. 61 mm. Wt. 8.9 g.

End-looped mortar, with a lacquered pale green patina. A small light example, with slender, lightly curved bow, low, plain, sloping walls, a rounded angular keel and a vestigially-knobbed terminal. The groove, of V-shaped cross-section, has a marked wear-polish and wear-facets on the walls. The narrow basal wear-facet deviates from the longitudinal axis of the groove causing attrition of one rim at the looped end. The slender ring-like loop, with large ovoid eye, is in the form of a stylized aquatic bird's head, with a dished, lightly everted bill. The end of the loop appears to have been worn through in antiquity.

Metal detector find. In private hands.

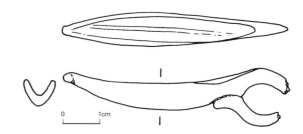

425. nr. Ross-on-Wye/Gloucester

L. 41.1. mm. Wt. 15.1 g.

Centre-looped pestle, with stable, pale olive green and light brown patina. A compact, heavy example, with a short, deep, crescentic, angular-keeled rod and a D-shaped plate-like loop with small circular eye. A smoothed, but nevertheless clear junction line in the rod beneath one end of the loop coincides with the change in colour of the patina from light olive to light brown, and there can be little doubt that the light brown tip was a cast-on repair at the manufacture stage.

'Found at metal detector rally, 27/1/1996, 12 mls. outside Ross towards Gloucester'. In private hands via the antiquity market.

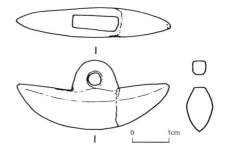

426. Roudham, Norfolk

L. 56.9 mm. Wt. 11.2 g.

Centre-looped pestle, with fine olive-grey patina. The lightly-crescentic twin-tapered rod has a sub-triangular cross-section, marked keel, and blunt tips. Its steeply-sloping sides display wear polish. The ring-like loop has a circular eye.

Metal detector find. Formerly in private hands, via the antiquity market, through which it was falsely attributed the provenance 'Stonea'.

British Museum, 1999,0802.72.

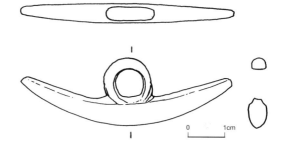

427. Rushall Down, Wilts

L. 74 mm. Wt. 22.4 g.

End-looped mortar, cleaned, with dull golden metal surface and remaining brown-black patina in the groove and on the loop. A relatively heavy example, distinctly axially asymmetric, with an idiosyncratic sinuous bow – the groove is set at one end, and the loop is separated from it by a solid sub-oval-sectioned stem. The walls are low, plain and convex, the keel is rounded, the groove is of shallow U-shaped cross-section, with slight wear polish, and the terminal is a simple low-domed knob. The rather heavy, ungainly loop is tapered, with an ovoid eye, elongated through wear. A thick, collar-like moulding, also worn, separates the loop from the stem.

Rushall Down, west of Casterley Camp, has yielded material of 1st-4th century AD date.

Smith 1918, 58, 59–60, fig. 11; M.E. Cunnington and E.H. Goddard, 1934, *Devizes Museum Catalogue*, Part II, 215–6, pl. lxviii, no. 4; Jackson 1985, no. 12.

Devizes Museum, 361.

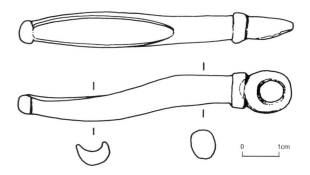

428. Ruskington, Lincs
L. *c.* 84 mm.

Centre-looped mortar, Type H, comprising two joining fragments. The large crescentic bow has low thin walls, simple, small, knobbed terminals, and a broad capacious groove. Adjacent to the loop, exceptionally on one wall only, is a row of three tiny triangular cells, inlaid with blue enamel, their apex pointing towards the loop. Only the stub of the broken loop – D- shaped or lightly heart-shaped – remains.

Metal detector find. In private hands.

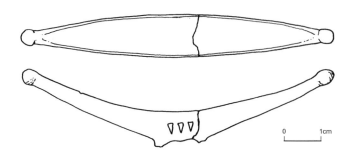

429. Saham Toney, Norfolk
L. 66.8 mm. Wt. 31.4 g.

Centre-looped mortar, Type D, with a fine, smooth, light brown patina overlying pale green corrosion products. In two joining pieces, the breakage appearing recent, probably in-ground plough damage. A well-cast, finely-finished example, with crescentic bow, angular keel, steep, lightly-carinated, plain walls, markedly-flattened, thick rims, and a narrow, V-sectioned groove (partially blocked with a ferrous concretion), with wear polish and narrow basal facet which runs onto the terminals. The low-domed, cushion-like terminal knobs have an elegant neck moulding. A symmetrically-set, diamond-sectioned strut, with neatly-scrolled perforate ends, encloses the very large circular loop (also of diamond cross-section), which has wear polish in the eye.

Metal detector find, from same site as no. 433. In private hands.

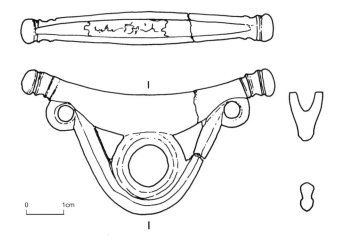

430. Saham Toney, Norfolk
L. *c.* 72 mm.

Centre-looped mortar, Type D, with strongly-curved, slender bow, plain, steeply-sloping walls, a sharply-angular keel, deep V-sectioned groove, and bulbous knobbed terminals. The very large ring-like loop is encircled by a thin strut, which engages with the bow ends.

Metal detector find from the Woodcock Hall site. For the site see R.A. Brown, 1986, 'The Iron Age and Romano-British settlement at Woodcock Hall, Saham Toney, Norfolk', *Britannia* 17, 1–58.

Private hands/antiquity market.

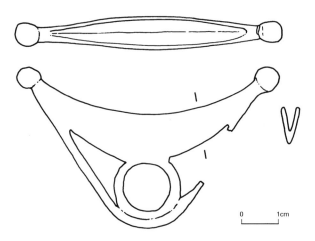

431. Saham Toney, Norfolk
L. 63.4 mm. Wt. 19.3 g.

Centre-looped mortar, with cleaned mid-grey-green patina, lacking most of the original surface. A medium-sized, quite heavy, example, with strongly-curved bow, and plain, convex, thick-rimmed walls, which taper sharply towards the small, simple, round-knobbed terminals. The groove, of shallow V-shaped cross-section, has a basal wear facet and is axially asymmetric, probably through use. The D-shaped ring-like loop has a circular eye.

Circumstances of discovery as no. 430.

Formerly in private hands, via the antiquity market, through which it had acquired the spurious provenance of 'King's Lynn or Norfolk'.

British Museum, 1999,0802.73.

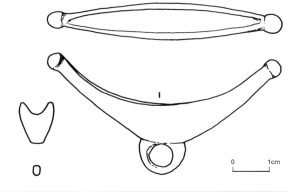

432. Saham Toney, Norfolk

L. 33 mm. Wt. 5.73 g.

Centre-looped mortar, fragment, lacking both terminals, much of the bow, most of the loop and one rim. The elliptical bow has an angular keel, plain sloping walls and a groove of rounded V-shaped cross-section. The fragmentary loop appears to have been of elongated form, perhaps with a heart-shaped eye.

Metal detector find. In private hands.

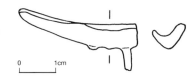

433. Saham Toney, Norfolk

L. 33.1 mm. Wt. 3.1 g.

Centre-looped pestle, with lightly-accreted green-grey patina. A diminutive, light example, of 'rocking-horse' type, with a slender, elliptical, twin-tapered rod of plump, sub-lentoid cross-section. The ring-like loop, broken across its circular eye, is supported on two slender struts, which frame a triangular aperture.

Metal detector find, from same site as no. 429. In private hands.

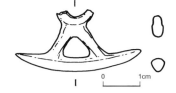

434. Saham Toney, Norfolk

L. 45.2 mm. Wt. 8.3 g.

End-looped mortar, with cleaned mid- to dark-brown patina. A tiny, well-made, example with strongly-curved bow, plain, carinated walls, a chamfered keel, and a neatly-formed, bulbous knobbed terminal. The groove, of V-shaped cross-section with basal facet, is partially blocked with corrosion products. The carefully-profiled sub-circular loop, part of which has broken away, has a tiny round eye.

Circumstances of discovery as no. 430.

Formerly in private hands, via the antiquity market, through which it had acquired the spurious provenance of 'King's Lynn or Norfolk'.

British Museum, 1999,0802.74.

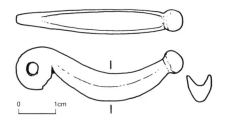

435. Saham Toney, Norfolk

L. 75 mm. Wt. 13.6 g.

End-looped mortar, with smooth dark green-black patina. An elegant, well-made example, with lightly elliptical bow, and plain, convex walls with thin rims. The smooth curvature of the keel gives way to a neat faceting towards the loop. The capacious groove, of rounded V-shaped cross-section, has an axial wear polish. The terminal is a small, neat, button-shaped knob. The loop is elegantly cast in the form of a stylized bird's head with everted bill. Its comma-shaped eye has a wear facet in the normal position.

Metal detector find. In private hands.

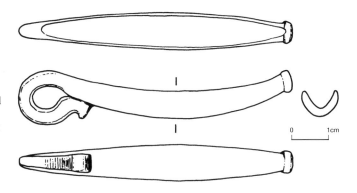

436. St Albans, Herts

L. mortar 83 mm. pestle 62 mm. Wt. mortar 25.7 g. pestle 5.4 g.

Set, comprising an end-looped mortar, and an end-looped pestle, both cleaned, revealing the dull golden-brown metallic surface. Both are finely-finished castings, and their axial asymmetry may have been intentional. The mortar has a broad elliptical bow, quite low, plain, convex walls, a partially flattened keel, a very capacious broad V-sectioned groove with off-centre basal wear slot, and a bulbous knobbed terminal with neatly-wrought neck moulding. Its slender ring-like loop, with large circular eye and simple neck moulding, is out of alignment with the bow as seen from above the groove. The pestle, which fits snugly in the groove of the mortar, has a slender circular-sectioned rod, plumpest towards its upturned tip, which is turned slightly to one side and has a wear facet on the convex face. The circular ring-like loop with its simple neck moulding mirrors that of the mortar.

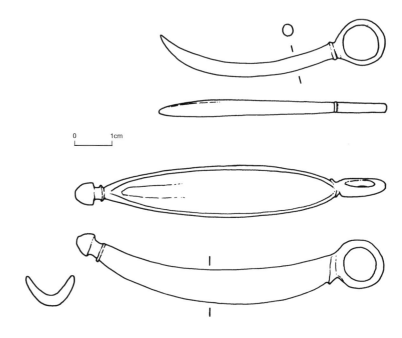

For metal composition see Scientific Analyses.

From excavations, 1966–8, of late Iron Age and Roman cemetery, King Harry Lane, grave no. 203 (SB 40), a cremation in a pottery flagon. Unlike the associated iron toilet set, the cosmetic set had not been burnt. The cremated bone was the remains of an adult, possibly a male.

The grave was assigned to Phase 3, dated AD 40–60.

Jackson 1985, no. 1; I.M. Stead and V. Rigby 1989, *Verulamium: the King Harry Lane site*, English Heritage Archaeological Report 12, 96, 104, 324, fig. 126, 4–5, 326.

British Museum, 1976,0501.505-6.

---

437. St Albans, Herts

L.mortar 67.8 mm. pestle 65.8 mm. Wt. mortar 32 g. pestle 16 g.

Set, comprising a centre-looped mortar and an end-looped pestle, both with a smooth green-grey patina. The mortar is a simple, heavy casting, with lightly-elliptical bow, angular keel, plain, sloping walls, and V-sectioned groove, with marked basal wear facet and polish, which runs over the bulbous, rather phallic, knobbed terminals. The loop is a thick circular disc, with very small cylindrical eye. The pestle is a simple, stout example, with strongly-curved, circular-sectioned rod, which swells towards the upturned tip, on the convex face of which is a marked wear facet and polish. The loop complements that on the mortar -a thick, sub-circular disc, with very small cylindrical eye. It is evident, both from the close stylistic similarity of the loops and from the general appearance of the two components, that they were made together as a set.

From excavations, 1984–6, of the St Stephens (Halsmede) Roman cemetery, by A. Havercroft. Found in a cremation burial (Grave 251 (AKD), together with a glass flask, apparently inside a wooden casket embellished with copper-alloy rings and lion-headed studs.

Context date, late 1st or early 2nd century AD.

The urned cremation, beside the casket, was partially destroyed by early 20th century house footings and proved impossible to sex. However, Ros Niblett has observed (*in litt.*) that where it has been possible to sex the cremated remains found with other lion-headed stud caskets in the cemetery they have all proved to be female. The casket and contents were unburnt, but no traces of pigment were found. A sample taken from inside the base of the glass flask and subjected to Fourier Transform InfraRed spectroscopic analysis (FTIR) in the British Museum Research Laboratory in 1995 (Project 6610) unfortunately yielded no clue as to the former contents. For the site see *Britannia* 16, 1985,293 and *Britannia* 18, 1987,328–30.

St Albans, Verulamium Museum, SABMS 90.985.

---

438. St Albans, Herts
L. 63.5 mm.

Centre-looped mortar, Type C, corroded, with broad, lightly-elliptical bow and steeply-sloping walls, decorated with two series of incuse irregularly-hatched lines centred on a group of three vertical lines at the loop. Two further series of hatched lines embellish the margins of the angular keel. The capacious V-sectioned groove runs onto the terminals. One is a small, stylized bovid head, rather poorly-preserved, with upright (damaged) horns, a marked brow-ridge, and an abraded pointed muzzle. The other, perhaps intended as the beast's tail, is a tiny, simple knob. The D-shaped, plate-like, loop has a circular eye. Closely similar to, and perhaps from the same archetype or workshop as, mortar no. 319. See also no. 357.

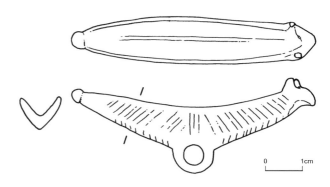

From excavation, 1986, within *Verulamium*, Insula II, by W.H. Manning, R. Niblett and C. Saunders. D86 AL, SF8, in same context as pestle no. 439: Phase 2, early to mid-2nd century AD. Clay levelling under hearth. Although there was no direct association in a closed context it is very probable that the two components had been used together as a set. For the same combination of centre-looped mortar and end-looped pestle see sets nos 319 and 437.

R. Niblett, W. Manning and C. Saunders, 2006, 'Verulamium: excavations within the Roman town 1986–88', *Britannia* 37, 142–4, fig. 42, 15a and b.

St Albans, Verulamium Museum.

439. St Albans, Herts
L. 64.5 mm.

End-looped pestle, with stout, strongly-curved rod, of plump D-shaped cross-section, and simple, circular, discoid loop centrally-set on the end of the rod. Although the eye is rather larger the form and dimensions of this pestle are very close to those of no. 437.

Circumstances of discovery as no. 438.

St Albans, Verulamium Museum.

440. St Albans, Herts
L. 92.5 mm. (orig. *c.* 95 mm.)

Triple-looped mortar. A large, finely-made, ornate example of idiosyncratic form. The long, slender, elliptical bow has an angular keel and steeply-sloping walls with incuse, closely-hatched, triangular and diagonal motifs, symmetrically arranged about the centre loop. A further decorative motif – an incuse zig-zag – occupies the margin of the quite thick, inturned rim. The fairly capacious groove has a rounded V-shaped cross-section. The centre-loop is a large neatly-formed, heart-shaped ring (cf. no. 261), bent slightly to one side, and there is an identical but smaller version (one now broken) beneath the two simple terminals.

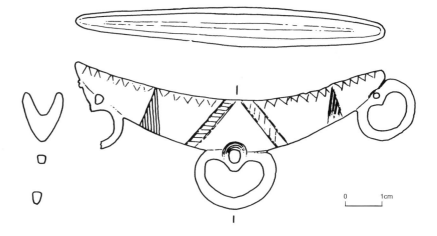

Found, pre-1941, '... in digging out a tree stump west of hypocausted annex. ?Ins. XXIV. Probably a cremation (found associated with a jug).'

St Albans, Verulamium Museum, 79.2156.

441. St Albans, Herts
L. 51 mm. Wt. 17.8 g.

End-looped mortar, with a lightly sand-accreted green patina. A small, well-made, comparatively heavy example, with short, strongly-curved bow, plain convex walls, inturned sharp rim, rounded keel and short, narrow groove of truncated V-shaped cross-section. The terminal is a very precisely-profiled and neatly-moulded knob with a dimpled 'eye' on both sides, and a channelled groove round the circumference. It is mirrored by the knobbed finial of the large loop, which may have been intended as a highly-stylized bird's head.

For metal composition see Scientific Analyses.

Metal detector find. Formerly on the antiquity market.

British Museum, 1986,0402.1.

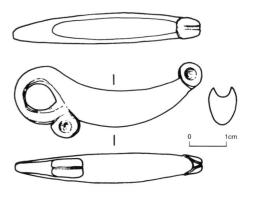

442. St Mary South Elmham, Suffolk
L. 42 mm.

Centre-looped pestle, with large circular loop and crescentic twin-tapered rod with blunt-pointed tips.

Metal detector find. In private hands.

443. St Mary South Elmham, Suffolk
L. 28 mm. Wt. 4.7 g.

Centre-looped pestle, with large circular loop and short elliptical rod with blunt tips.

Metal detector find. In private hands.

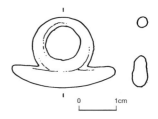

444. Saintes, Charente-Maritime, France
L. *c.* 25 mm.

End-looped pestle?, with green patina. A tiny well-made example, with a short, strongly curved rod. The upturned tip appears complete though perhaps slightly worn. The loop, with small circular eye, may have been intended as a highly-stylized bird's head. The drawing has been sketched from a slide.

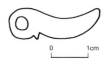

From a rich female inhumation in a stone sarcophagus. The grave goods, including a mirror beneath the head, comprised over 80 objects found inside and outside the coffin. Glass objects at feet; toilet articles next to body. The glass includes a 'stirring rod' and perfume bottles.

Context date *c.* AD 40–50.

Musée Nationale, St Germain-en-Laye.

445. Sall, Norfolk
L. 57.5 mm. Wt. 22.5 g.

Centre-looped mortar, with brown patina, its surface extensively and severely flaked and eroded revealing pitted bright and pale green corrosion products. The elliptical bow has a rounded keel, steeply-sloping plain convex walls with lightly-in-turned rims, now extensively chipped, and a shallow U-sectioned groove, with very marked wear polish, which runs over both terminals. The terminals are in the form of slightly phallic knobs, with incuse radiating grooves, most blocked with a ferrous substance. The form of the broken loop, mounted on a keel plate, cannot be determined, though the opening was evidently not circular and would appear to have been triangular.

Metal detector find, 'from Sall rally site, Sept. '99'. In private hands.

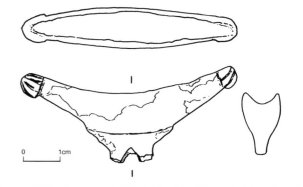

446. Saxlingham Nethergate, Norfolk

L. 36 mm. Wt. 14 g.

Mortar fragment, comprising one terminal and part of the bow, badly pitted by corrosion and with little of the original surface remaining. In consequence the zoomorphic terminal is rather 'fuzzy', but it was evidently a bovid head, with tapered muzzle, horns, ?ears and eyes depicted. In addition, there are remains of what may have been the dewlap and/or strutting along the keel. The bow walls are seemingly plain and convex, the keel lightly rounded, and the groove of asymmetric U-shaped cross-section.

Metal detector find. In private hands.

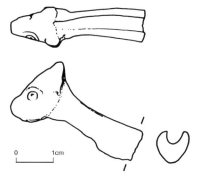

447. Saxlingham Nethergate, Norfolk

L. 38 mm. Wt. 15.5 g.

Centre-looped pestle. A small example with a short, stubby twin-tapered rod and a D-shaped loop with arched eye. On the top of the loop and on the keeled face of the rod there are what appear to be un-cleaned casting flashes, and there is a further blemish on the side of one arm. Such flaws would have precluded use and it is therefore likely that this was a failed casting, jettisoned but never re-melted.

Metal detector find. In private hands.

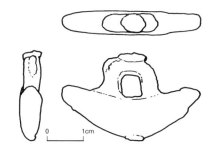

448. Saxtead, Suffolk

L. 49 mm.

End-looped mortar, heavily corroded, except in the groove. A relatively small heavy example, with elliptical bow, angled keel, plain sloping walls with thick rounded rims, and a rounded V-sectioned groove. The apparently simple loop is broken across its eye. The balancing terminal is neatly-moulded, perhaps intended as a very devolved bird's head.

Metal detector find. In private hands.

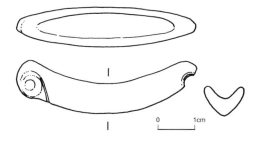

449. Scole, Norfolk

L. 51.4 mm. Wt. 4.3 g.

Centre-looped pestle, with smooth, light grey-green patina. A slender, twin-tapered rod of sub-lozenge-shaped cross-section, with a D-shaped slender ring-like loop. Wear polish is present on the keel, and there are wear facets near both tips, especially so near the shorter tip. It is possible that the distinct asymmetry of the rod is a result of the shortening of that arm through wear.

Metal detector find. In private hands.

450. Scole, Norfolk

L. 40 mm. Wt. 2.6 g.

Centre-looped pestle, with light green patina. A large example (originally well in excess of 50 mm), now lacking both ends of the slender, diamond-sectioned rod, which has a flattened keel beneath the loop. The large ring-like loop has a flattened heart-shaped eye.

From Waterloo, near Scole.

C.H. Gale, 1936, 'Roman Remains in Scole', *Proc. of the Suffolk Institute of Archaeology* XXII, 263 ff., pl. VI, bottom right.

Norwich Castle Museum, 590.962.

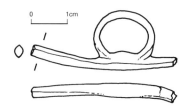

451. Shelford, Cambs
L. 76.8 mm. Wt. 18.2 g.

End-looped mortar, with smooth olive-green patina. An elegant
example with slender gently-curved bow, plain convex walls, an
angular keel, thin rims, a rounded V-sectioned groove, with basal
wear facet, and a small, neatly-formed, domed knob with neck
moulding. The loop, slender with an ovoid eye, is in the form of
a carefully-wrought aquatic bird's head (probably a swan), with
thin curved neck, raised brow-ridge, elongated dished bill with
everted tip, and neatly-rendered circular eye hollows. There is a
pair of incised lines near the tip of the bill, and similar decoration
may once have extended along the now slightly eroded neck from
the brow ridge. A simple incised line beneath the rim at the end of
the groove serves to separate it from the bird's head. The form of
the loop is very similar to that on no. 334, while the knob closely
parallels that on the end-looped mortar of set no. 436.

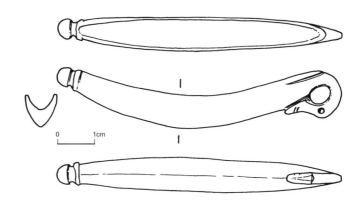

Metal detector find. Formerly in private hands, via the antiquity
market.

British Museum, 1999,0802.75.

452. Shelton, Norfolk
L. 49.5 mm. (orig. *c.* 75 mm.) Wt. 9 g.

Centre-looped mortar, Type J, with a smooth dark olive-brown patina,
preserving most of the original surface. A well-finished example
lacking one terminal and part of the bow. The strongly-curved bow
has an angular keel and thin steeply-sloping walls decorated with an
arc of enamel-inlaid, small, triangular cells, which extend almost to
the terminal. Fourteen survive on each wall, their enamel in good
condition, and they reveal an identical symmetrical arrangement,
originally comprising 19 cells per wall, their apex pointing towards
the keel. Three colours of enamel are used. Starting from the terminal
end the arrangement is three blue, four light green/ turquoise,
five black, two light green/ turquoise. The sequence would have
continued with a further two light green/ turquoise and three blue.
The capacious V-sectioned groove has a basal facet. The small, very
neatly-formed, bovid head terminal has in-turned horns (one broken)
and a ridged, lightly-flared, flat-ended muzzle. The loop is a slender
D-shaped ring with a heart-shaped eye. In form and size virtually
identical to no. 129.

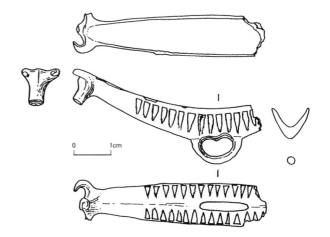

Metal detector find. In private hands.

453. Shenley Church End, Milton Keynes, Bucks
L. *c.* 44 mm.

End-looped mortar, badly corroded and chipped, and lacking the looped end. The bow is
slender, with lightly-angular keel, plain, steeply-sloping walls, a rounded V-sectioned groove,
and a plain, simple, pointed terminal.

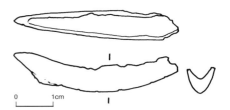

Metal detector find, 'on building site which produced a variety of Roman finds'. In private
hands.

454. Shillington, Beds
L. 53 mm.

Centre-looped mortar, with deep elliptical bow, angular keel, neatly-
moulded thick walls, low-domed terminal knobs and a broad, deep,
V-sectioned groove. The loop, now fractured and distorted, was a
D-shaped ring with large circular eye.

Metal detector find. In private hands.

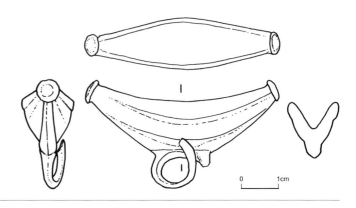

455. Shimpling, Suffolk
L. 38 mm. (orig. *c.* 70 mm.) Wt. 5.1 g.

Centre-looped mortar, Type J, lacking about half of the bow, and with a recent dent near the surviving terminal. The crescentic bow has an angular keel, steeply-sloping thin walls, and a capacious groove of rounded V-shaped cross-section. Adjacent to the loop on both walls is an arc of five slender, elongated, triangular cells (probably originally nine), their apex pointing towards the loop. They are now devoid of any inlay. The surviving small zoomorphic terminal is in the form of a highly-stylized bovid head, with tapered blunt muzzle and vestigial horns. Only the stub of one side of the ring-like loop remains.

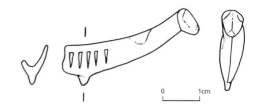

Metal detector find. In private hands.

456. Shipdham, Norfolk
L. 64.1 mm. Wt. 14.4 g.

Centre-looped mortar, with dark brown-black patina. A light casting, with slender crescentic bow, rounded keel, low, plain, convex walls, a relatively capacious groove of rounded V-shaped cross-section, with basal facet, and small pellet-shaped terminal knobs set below each end of the bow. The ring-like loop has a plump D-shaped eye.

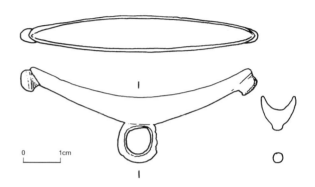

Metal detector find. In private hands.

457. Shipdham, Norfolk
L. 65 mm. Wt. 14.93 g.

End-looped mortar, with elliptical bow, plain walls, broad U-sectioned groove, and simple sub-circular loop. The terminal is a bulbous knob with basal ring-moulding.

Metal detector find. In private hands.

458. Shouldham, Norfolk
L. 62.4 mm. Wt. 26.9 g.

Centre-looped mortar, with lightly-pitted olive-brown patina. A medium-sized, relatively heavy example. The lightly-curved, crisply-facetted bow has a flattened keel, plain carinated walls with quite thick rims, neatly-formed, simple, knobbed terminals, and a V-sectioned groove with basal facet. The circular plate-like loop has a round eye.

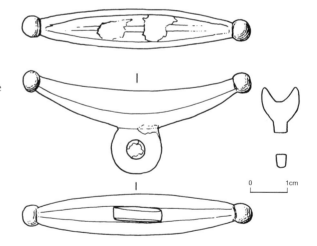

Metal detector find. On the antiquity market, through which its provenance had been reduced to 'from Norfolk'.

459. Shouldham, Norfolk
L. 41.4 mm. Wt. 7.3 g.

Centre-looped pestle, with pale- to mid-green patina. An idiosyncratic, light example, with a strongly re-curved twin-tapered rod, which has the appearance of a pair of bull's horns. The tall trapezoidal loop plate has a circular eye.

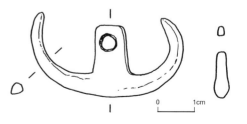

Metal detector find. In private hands.

460. Shouldham/Fincham, Norfolk
L. 55.3 mm.

Centre-looped mortar, with lacquered green patina,
in places denuded to the underlying liver-red coloured
metal. A short, heavy example, of idiosyncratic form, with
broad, lightly-elliptical bow, deep, plain, convex walls, and
slender, U-sectioned groove with basal facet. The large
terminal is a highly-stylized zoomorphic head, perhaps a
boar/pig rather than a bovid, with upright ears, pointed
snout/muzzle and deeply-folded dewlap. The smaller
terminal was clearly intended as the beast's tail. The
D-shaped loop has a small circular eye.

Metal detector find, 1982, near Shouldham/Fincham
parish boundary.

Trett 1983, no. 1; Jackson 1985, no. 68.

Donated to King's Lynn Museum, KL 112.982 (A1685).

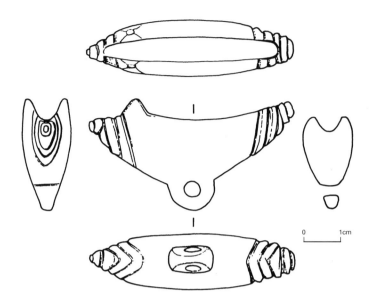

461. Shropham, Norfolk
L. 64.7 mm.

End-looped mortar, with shiny green patina. A heavy example with
lightly-elliptical, very broad bow, plain, sloping walls, angular keel,
wide, shallow, V-sectioned groove, and simple, plain, blunt-pointed
terminal. The slender loop is in the form of a stylized aquatic bird's
head, with circular eye and bill-like extension. Wear polish and basal
facets are visible in the groove.

Found prior to 1974.

Trett 1983, no. 12; Jackson 1985, no. 28.

Donated to King's Lynn Museum, KL 6.974 (A1002).

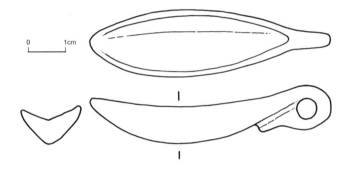

462. Silchester, Hants
L. 72.1 mm.

End-looped mortar, with smooth dark green patina. The elegantly
curved bow has an angular keel, steep, lightly-convex, quite thin,
plain walls, a simple, blunt-pointed terminal, and a capacious
groove, the V-shaped cross-section of which has a deep, axially
asymmetric, basal wear slot. The slender loop, with ornate
inturned scroll, has a wear-elongated heart-shaped eye.

Smith 1918, 56, 58, fig. 4; Jackson 1985, no. 31.

Reading Museum, unregistered, but thought to be almost certainly
from Silchester.

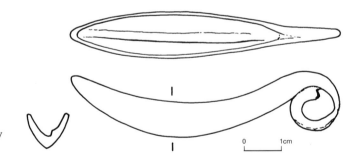

463. Silchester, Hants
L. 62.8 mm.

End-looped mortar, with grey (tin-enriched) patina, encrusted with mid-
green corrosion in many places. A small example with only lightly-elliptical
bow, low, plain, convex walls, a lightly-angular keel, quite thick rim, a plain,
square-ended, lightly-upturned terminal, and a groove of U-shaped cross-
section. The fragmentary loop has a rounded, everted bill-like junction with
the underside of the bow.

Smith 1918, 57–8, fig. 6; Jackson 1985, no. 35.

Reading Museum, unregistered, but thought to be almost certainly from
Silchester.

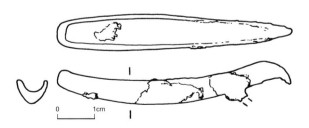

464. Skeffington, Leics

L. *c.* 52 mm.

End-looped mortar, apparently badly corroded and lacking its loop. The crescentic bow has a rounded keel, low, seemingly plain, convex walls, a plain blunt-pointed terminal, and a relatively capacious U-sectioned groove. Only the broken necked junction of the loop remains.

Metal detector find. In private hands.

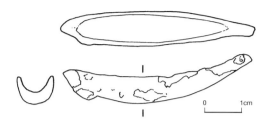

465. Sleaford, Lincs

L. 76 mm. Wt. 18.7 g.

Centre-looped mortar, with olive-brown patina, extensively pitted and eroded (especially at the terminals), revealing the irregular green corroded metal beneath. The elliptical bow has a lightly-facetted keel, low, apparently plain, convex walls, and a V-sectioned groove, with marked wear-scoring and basal wear facet, which runs over the terminals. Both of the small zoomorphic terminals are badly corroded. They have sub-triangular faces, and ears, and may have been intended as stylized bovid heads. The D-shaped loop, with small circular eye, is mounted on a low plinth.

Metal detector find. Formerly in private hands, via the antiquity market.

British Museum, 1999,0802.76.

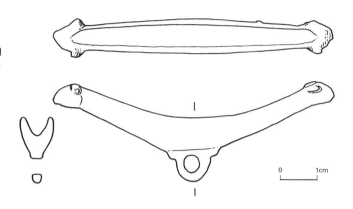

466. Soham, Cambs (Unillustrated)

L. *c.* 85 mm.

Centre-looped mortar, Type L. The elliptical bow is decorated with an incuse triple line motif and has small knobbed terminals and a D-shaped loop plate with small circular eye.

On the antiquity market. Not available for study.

467. Somersham, Suffolk

L. *c.* 60 mm.

End-looped mortar. The bow has a raised axial rib on both walls and another along the keel. They are linked to a transverse neck-moulding at the junction with the large bulbous terminal knob. The deep V-sectioned groove has a distinct wear facet at its base. The thick, neatly-moulded loop has a small, slightly ovoid, eye.

Metal detector find. In private hands.

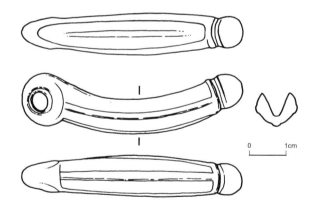

468. South Creake, Norfolk (Unillustrated)

L. 45.5 mm. Wt. 5.3 g.

End-looped pestle, with lightly-curved rod, which swells towards the up-turned pointed tip. The simple sub-circular loop is set below the axis of the rod.

Metal detector find. In private hands.

469. South Ferriby, Humberside

L. 78 mm.

Centre-looped mortar, Type H. The elliptical bow has an angular keel and low, thin, sloping walls with two arcs of six contiguous, small, triangular cells flanking the loop on both faces. The cells retain traces of red enamel, and their apex points towards the loop. The groove is capacious and the terminals are tiny, simple knobs. The large ring-like D-shaped loop has a heart-shaped eye.

Found on a prolific site on the south foreshore of the Humber.

T. Sheppard, 1909, *Notes on a Collection of Roman Antiquities from S. Ferriby, in N. Lincs. Pt. II*, Hull Museum Publications, no. 65, pl. VIII, no. 16, 16a. Smith 1918, 60–61, fig. 13; Jackson 1985, no. 74.

Hull City Museums, KINCM: 883.1942.

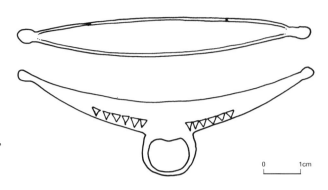

470. South Kyme, Lincs

L. *c.* 39 mm (orig. *c.* 65 mm.)

Centre-looped pestle. A large example lacking one end of the long, crescentic, keeled, tapered rod. The broken end appears to have been smoothed off in antiquity. The large, slender, collar-like loop has an ovoid eye.

Metal detector find. In private hands.

471. Spexhall, Suffolk (Unillustrated)

L. *c.* 30 mm.

Centre-looped pestle, unavailable for study. A small example, with tall-stemmed, small loop, apparently similar in form to no. 544.

Metal detector find. In private hands.

472. Springhead, Kent

L. 80 mm. (orig. *c.* 100 mm.)

Centre-looped mortar, Type H, lacking one terminal and part of the bow and loop. The slender, elliptical bow has an angular keel, and low, thin walls, with an arc of four small hollow-based triangular cells adjacent to the loop on both faces. The cells retain traces of red enamel, and their apex points away from the loop. The capacious V-sectioned groove has a slight basal facet; the remaining knobbed terminal is small and simple; and the fragmentary loop was a D-shaped ring with heart-shaped eye.

From excavations of the religious centre, surface find, SF 2314.

Jackson 1985, no. 77. For the site see S.R. Harker, 1980, 'Springhead – a brief re-appraisal', in W.R. Rodwell (ed.) *Temples, Churches and Religion in Roman Britain*, B.A.R. Brit. Ser. 77(i), 285–288; and B.C. Burnham and J. Wacher, 1990, *The 'Small Towns' of Roman Britain* (London), 192–198.

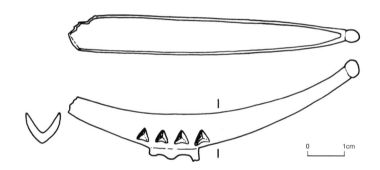

473. Springhead, Kent

L. 62 mm.

End-looped pestle. The curved, sub-circular-sectioned rod is swollen near the upturned, tapered tip. The usual curving facet on the convex face of the tip produces a D-shaped cross-section. Atypically, the simple turned-over loop is set in a different plane to that normally encountered, but see nos 50 and 73.

From excavations of the religious centre, Pit 139, SF 1665.

Context dated mid-late 2nd century AD.

Jackson 1985, no. 56. Site references as no. 472.

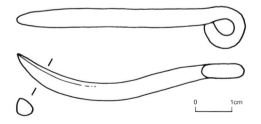

474. Stanway, Essex
L. 38 mm. Wt. 23.8 g.

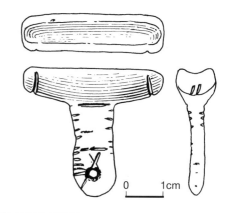

Centre-looped mortar, with a dark grey-green patina. An idiosyncratic example with short bow and long loop plate. The bow is parallel-sided, with virtually no curvature. It has steep, convex, plain walls, a rounded keel, and a shallow groove, of broad U-shaped cross-section, which runs over the terminals. A simple grooved moulding beneath each terminal gives the impression of a vestigial knob, upon the end of which is further incuse decoration, now very eroded. The long, spatulate loop plate has a tiny roughly-cast eye which shows little sign of wear. Instead, suspension may have been by means of the plate itself on which there is very considerable wear, which has erased some of the incuse decoration. The latter comprises notched incisions on the edges, horizontal grooves, and a roughly-cut cross on each face next to the eye.

Metal detector find from Stanway Hall, in general vicinity of Gosbecks temple site and the rich Iron Age burials. No associated objects.

In private hands.

475. Stanwick (Ringstead), Northants
L. 67 mm.

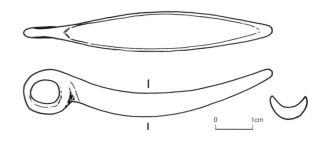

End-looped mortar, with elliptical bow, rounded keel, low, sloping, plain walls, a broad, shallow, U-sectioned groove and a plain, blunt-pointed terminal. The slender ring-like loop has an ovoid eye elongated through wear.

Found during fieldwalking for the Raunds Area Project survey. Publication forthcoming.

476. Stevenage, Herts
L. 75 mm.

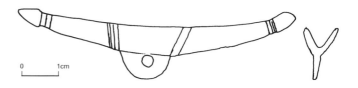

Centre-looped mortar, Type L, with slender, lightly-elliptical bow, rounded angular keel, low, thin, sloping walls, a relatively capacious V-sectioned groove, and neck-moulded, shouldered, terminal knobs, which are distinctly phallic in appearance. The walls are decorated with an incuse diagonal-lined motif flanking the loop, which is a thin, flat, D-shaped plate with small circular eye.

From excavation of a Romano-British farmstead at Lobs Hole, Stevenage, by J. Hunn. LHS – 2'96, 569, SF 4070. Un-dated context.

J. Hunn, T. Doig, D. Hillelson and F. Vardy, 2006, *Lobs Hole, Stevenage: a Romano-British farmstead*, Heritage Network Monograph 1.

477. Stevenage, Herts
L. 33.5 mm.

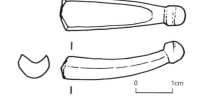

(?) End-looped mortar fragment, lacking the loop and part of the bow. The elliptical bow has a flattened keel, low carinated walls, sharp, inturned rims, and a rounded V-sectioned groove. The terminal is a prominent moulded knob. Probably, but not certainly, an end-looped example.

From excavation of ?Late Iron Age and Roman settlement at Boxfield Farm, Chells Manor, by J. Hunn, for Herts Archaeological Trust. HAT 37 CAA SF 196, an unstratified find from the South Area in the vicinity of a large well, cut in the 1st century AD and backfilled in the 2nd century

A. Wardle, 'Copper-alloy objects' in C.J. Going and J.R. Hunn, 1999, *Excavations at Boxfield Farm, Chells, Stevenage, Hertfordshire*, Hertfordshire Archaeological Trust Report no. 2, 58–9, no. 45, fig. 19.

478. Stoke Holy Cross, Norfolk
L. 42 mm. Wt. 9.12 g.

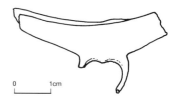

Centre-looped mortar, Type I, with U-sectioned groove, lacking both ends of its elliptical, plain-walled bow. The broken loop was a D-shaped ring with a heart-shaped eye.

Metal detector find. In private hands.

479. Stonea, Cambs
L. 75 mm. Wt. 49 g.

Centre-looped mortar, with extensive brown
iron-staining over a green patina. A heavy,
elaborate casting with a deep, elliptical bow.
The incuse decoration of the steep convex
walls comprises a pair of bellied lines, with
a thin band of zig-zag between the upper
line and the rim. The relatively shallow
groove, of rounded V-shaped cross-section,
runs through the horns of the zoomorphic
terminal. This is a large and detailed bovid
head, with prominent inturned horns, large
everted ears, a short, flat-ended muzzle,
with mouth and nostrils depicted, and deep,
round eye-sockets, which were probably
inset with coloured glass eyeballs, though
neither survives. The other terminal is in
the form of a moulded knob. The relatively
small D-shaped loop has a circular eye.

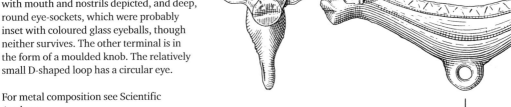

For metal composition see Scientific
Analyses.

Metal detector find, prior to 1980, from the ploughsoil around Stonea Grange Farm.

Jackson 1985, no. 60. R.P.J; Jackson and T.W. Potter, 1996, *Excavations at Stonea, Cambridgeshire 1980–1985*, (London, British Museum Press),
353–4, fig. 114, no. 112.

British Museum, 1982,0602.3.

480. Stonea, Cambs
L. 52.5 mm. Wt. 3.5 g.

Centre-looped pestle, with smooth grey-green metallic patina. The slender crescentic, sub-
circular-sectioned rod has an asymmetric grinding facet on the convex face of one of the upturned
tips. The loop is a simple D-shaped ring.

For metal composition see Scientific Analyses.

From excavation, 1982, of Roman site at Stonea Grange Farm. ST 82 AAG, SF 291. Topsoil/cleaning unit, Blocks 5 and 5a, effectively unstratified.

Jackson 1985, no. 95. R.P.J; Jackson and T.W. Potter, 1996, *Excavations at Stonea, Cambridgeshire 1980–1985*, (London, British Museum Press),
343–5, fig. 109, no. 61.

British Museum, 1985,0201.251.

481. 'Stonea, Cambs'
L. 34 mm. Wt. 4.7 g.

Centre-looped pestle, with a mid-green patina. A small example with short, slender, lightly-curved,
asymmetric arms of D-shaped cross-section, and a comparatively large round loop, its eye blocked with a
ferrous concretion.

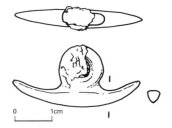

Metal detector find. Formerly in private hands via the antiquity market. In view of the fact that it was
acquired with mortar no. 211, subsequently shown to have been spuriously provenanced Stonea, the
veracity of the provenance of this example cannot be vouchsafed.

British Museum, 1999,0802.79.

482. Stonea, Cambs

L. 67.5 mm. Wt. 27.5 g.

End-looped mortar, with smooth mid-green patina. The virtually straight bow has a flattened keel, and low steeply-curved walls decorated with incuse paired zig-zag lines. The groove, which runs over the plain terminal, has a distinct wear polish and basal wear facet giving it a markedly asymmetric cross-section. The large turned-over loop has a pear-shaped eye.

For metal composition see Scientific Analyses.

Circumstances of discovery as no. 479.

Jackson 1985, no. 19; R.P.J; Jackson and T.W. Potter, 1996, *Excavations at Stonea, Cambridgeshire 1980–1985*, (London), 354–6, fig. 114, no. 113.

British Museum, 1982,0602.4.

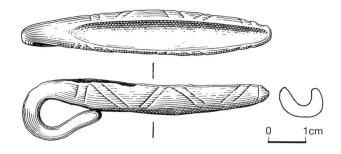

483. Stonea, Cambs

L. 85.2 mm. Wt. 42.3 g.

End-looped mortar, Type B, with metallic grey to brown patina. A heavy casting, the detailed surface treatment of which is difficult to discern because of 1) a thick encrustation of corrosion products everywhere except the groove, and 2) gross over-cleaning of the encrustation in several places on both walls, which has removed both the corrosion products and the original surface. Nevertheless, it is possible to see that the surface of the walls, rim, keel and loop was tin-enriched. The large, strongly-curved bow has flared walls with a sharp carination just below the rim. There is a row of 13 incuse ring-and-dot motifs on each wall, extending from tip to tip of the bow. An area of damage on one wall has been filled (recently) with a hard grey substance. The keel is unusually elaborate, with a herring-bone rib within an axial slot. The terminal is simple and plain. The groove, which runs over both ends, has a U-shaped cross-section and preserves a wear-polish over its full extent. The loop, corroded and over-cleaned, is set beneath the end, in a similar way to that on Type A mortars. It is relatively small, with a circular-eye and a slight extension along the keel.

Metal detector find. Formerly in private hands, via the antiquity market.

British Museum, 1999,0802.77.

484. Stonea, Cambs

L. 50.5 mm. Wt. 14.3 g.

End-looped mortar, heavily corroded, lacking most of the loop, the tip of the terminal, and most of the original surface. The bow is lightly-curved, with a rounded angular keel, apparently plain, sloping walls, extensively chipped rims, and a relatively capacious groove, of rounded V-shaped cross-section, with a deep 'ledged', basal wear slot. The simple terminal has a broken tip. Only the stub of the loop remains.

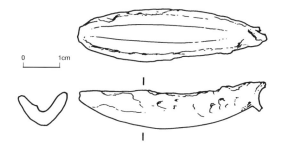

From excavation, 1960, of the Golden Lion Roman settlement site, 2nd–3rd century AD.

T.W. Potter, 1976, 'Excavations at Stonea, Cambs.', *Proceedings of the Cambridge Antiquarian Society* 66 (1975–6), 40, no. 1. Trett 1983, no. 10; Jackson 1985, no. 25.

British Museum, 1985,0503.1911.

485. 'Stonea, Cambs'
L. 77.1 cm. Wt. 22.3 g.

End-looped mortar, with lightly-pitted dark green-grey patina. A finely-made, elegantly-designed example, with slender elliptical bow, lightly-rounded flat keel, carinated plain walls, thin rims, and a relatively capacious, wear-polished, U-sectioned groove, which runs onto the loop and over the terminal. The terminal is a well-formed knob with crisply-cut neck moulding. The loop is in the form of a stylized water-bird's head, with near-circular eye and a prominent, crisply-cut, everted bill.

Metal detector find. Formerly in private hands, via the antiquity market. The given provenance of Stonea is suspect because a pestle acquired from the dealer on the same occasion, and also said by him to come from Stonea, was actually from Roudham (no. 426). Other examples from the same dealer also proved to be falsely provenanced (nos 211, 340, 481).

British Museum, 1999,0802.78.

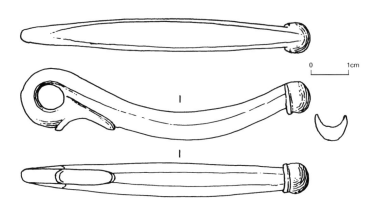

486. Stratton Strawless, Norfolk
L. 52 mm. Wt. 21.8 g.

Centre-looped mortar, with mid-green pitted patina, lacking the original surface everywhere except in the groove. The bow, only lightly curved, has apparently plain convex walls, and a rounded keel, extended at the centre to accommodate the suspension loop. The shallow, narrow, U-sectioned groove is polished through wear; the terminals are plain and very slightly bulbous; and the loop is broken across its small circular eye.

Metal detector find. In private hands.

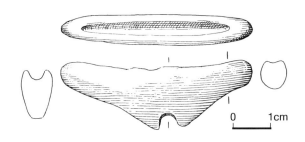

487. Suffolk, unprovenanced
L. 64 mm. Wt. 8.1 g.

Centre-looped mortar, Type H, with olive green patina. A small, light example. The elliptical bow has an angular keel, and low, thin, sloping walls, with a panel of four contiguous, small, triangular cells either side of the loop on both faces, their apex pointing away from the loop. The cells still contain their enamel inlay, which appears to be yellow in every case, but this may be due to degradation. The terminal knobs are tiny; the capacious V-sectioned groove has a basal wear facet; and the loop is a slender D-shaped ring.

Metal detector find. Formerly in private hands, via the antiquity market.

British Museum, 1999,0802.80.

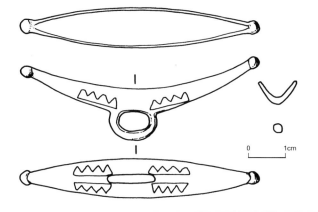

488. Suffolk, unprovenanced
L. 52.7 mm. Wt. 13.3 g.

End-looped mortar, with a mid-green patina, partially accreted with a light coating of pale brown soil. A small, well made example, with plain, finely-carinated walls, rounded keel, and relatively capacious U-sectioned groove, which runs over the terminals. Both terminals are in the form of a simple but elegantly scrolled circular loop, which splays at the junction with the bow.

Metal detector find. Formerly in private hands, via the antiquity market.

British Museum, 1999,0802.83.

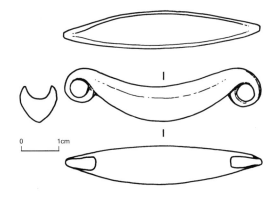

489. Suffolk, unprovenanced
L. 72 mm. (orig. *c*. 77 mm.) Wt. 14.6 g.

End-looped mortar, with a lightly-encrusted green-brown patina. The elliptical bow has a rounded keel, low, plain, convex walls, with a thin rim, a neatly-formed, flat-ended terminal knob, and a deep groove, of rounded V-shaped cross-section. Its asymmetric basal wear facet has encroached on the rim at diagonally opposite ends. The suspension loop, worn through, or broken, in antiquity, is in the form of a stylized bird's head, with marked brow and pronounced everted bill. The latter has a deeply-incised vertical groove when viewed end-on.

Metal detector find. Formerly in private hands, via the antiquity market.

British Museum, 1999,0802.81.

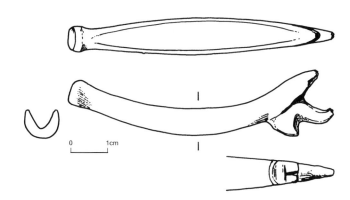

490. (?) Suffolk, unprovenanced
L. 54 mm. (orig. *c*. 58 mm.) Wt. 11.9 g.

End-looped mortar, lacking most of the loop and chipped on rims and keel, with a smooth, lacquered, mid-green patina. The deep, bellied bow is quite short, with only lightly-curved rims, but a strongly-curved angular keel. The steep, lightly-convex walls are plain. The shallow groove, of broad U-shaped cross-section, has wear polish and a slight, off-centre, basal wear facet which runs over the loop. The terminal is a tiny knob. Only the stub of the loop remains, but it appears to have been plain and relatively flat.

Metal detector find. Formerly in private hands, via the antiquity market.

British Museum, 1999,0802.82.

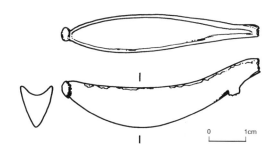

491. (?) Suffolk, unprovenanced
L. *c*. 61 mm.

End-looped pestle. A long example with a large loop in the form of a bird's head with lightly-everted bill. The eye is ovoid, and the upturned tip flattened, both probably worn through use.

Metal detector find. In private hands.

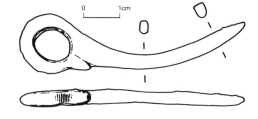

492. Suffolk/Norfolk, unprovenanced
L. 66 mm. Wt. 22.3 g.

End-looped mortar, with a thick, green-brown patina. A heavy, simple example lacking most of the suspension loop. The bow is only slightly elliptical with very thick-rimmed, plain, sloping walls, and a rounded keel, which is markedly asymmetric to the long axis. The V-sectioned groove, with distinct basal wear facet, runs over the plain terminal to form a pouring spout. The broken loop appears to have been a simple circular ring.

For metal composition see Scientific Analyses.

Metal detector find, formerly on the antiquity market.

This mortar was acquired with pestle no. 493. The similarity of their patina, soil coating and corrosion products, together with the form of the groove, make it very probable that the two pieces were used as a set in antiquity, even if not originally made as such.

British Museum, 1993,0901.4.

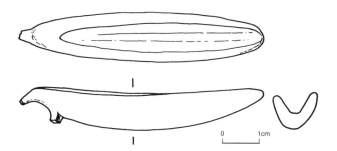

493. Suffolk/Norfolk, unprovenanced

L. 57 mm. Wt. 9.9 g.

Centre-looped pestle, with a thick, green-brown patina. A relatively heavy example, with a collar-like, D-shaped suspension loop and a triangular-sectioned rod. The keeled working face is lightly faceted through use.

For metal composition see Scientific Analyses.

Metal detector find, formerly on the antiquity market.

This pestle fits snugly in the groove of mortar no. 492. In view of the fact that the two share a common patina/soil coating/corrosion products, the vendor's assertion that they were a set is feasible, if incapable of proof. For certain finds of non-matching components used as sets see nos319 and 437.

British Museum, 1993,0901.3.

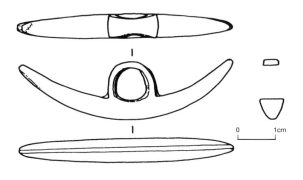

494. Surlingham, Norfolk

L. 63.4 mm. Wt. 15.8 g.

Centre-looped mortar, with mid-green patina lacking the original surface except in the groove and in the angles of the loop assembly. The strongly-curved slender bow has low, plain, convex walls (with abraded rim), a rounded keel, a very shallow U-sectioned groove with wear polish, and sub-spherical terminals, one preserving the last vestiges of a neck moulding. The loop assembly, mounted on a low keel, is broken. It probably comprised a strutted ring surmounting a triangular aperture, as nos 279, 362 and 571. For a near-identical example, but with more capacious groove, see no. 60.

Metal detector find. In private hands.

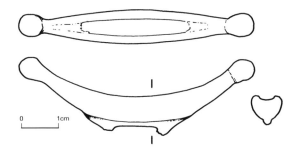

495. Sutton, Suffolk

L. c. 43 mm.

End-looped mortar, Type A, lacking the terminal and part of the bow. The remaining part of the lightly-curved bow is distorted and corroded, with high, steeply-sloping walls, an angular keel, and a narrow groove which runs over the loop. The walls are decorated with incuse lines, in groups of three or four, probably in a zig-zag arrangement. The loop, which lies beneath the end of the bow, is in the form of a stylized bird's head, with prominent brow and elongated bill. If, as is probable, the missing terminal was a bovid head, then the loop may also have been intended to represent the beast's tail. In form and dimensions virtually identical to mortar no. 236.

Metal detector find. In private hands.

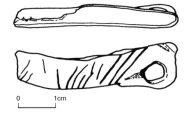

496. Syderstone, Norfolk

L. 69.7 mm. Wt. 38.4 g.

Centre-looped mortar, Type E, with abraded and lightly-pitted grey-green patina. The plump, strongly-curved bow has plain convex walls with a thin upright rim, which is flanked by a line of small punched dots. The slender groove, of rounded V-shaped cross-section, is partially blocked with soil and corrosion products. The heavily stylized zoomorphic terminals, one slightly larger than the other, and perhaps devolved bovids, have a bulbous head, tapered face and flared, lightly-domed muzzle. Each terminal is joined to the centre loop by a sinuous, slender openwork strut (one now broken), which begins as the dewlap beneath the terminal and merges with the lower perimeter arc of the large crescent-shaped loop. The overall form of the mortar compares closely with no. 213 and nos36 and 510, while the form of the strutwork is midway between that of those examples and no. 430, and the treatment of the rim is closely parallelled by no. 65. Like nos 36, 213 and 510, there is a distinct asymmetry of the mortar walls and of the vertical axis of the bow and loop, suggesting, perhaps, a common origin or ancestry for all four examples.

For metal composition see Scientific Analyses.

Metal detector find. Formerly in private hands, via the antiquity market.

British Museum, 1999,0802.84.

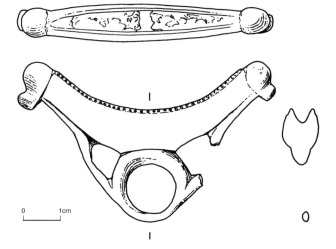

497. Tacolneston, Norfolk

L. 60 mm. (orig. *c.* 80 mm.) Wt. 9.66 g.

Centre-looped mortar, Type H, lacking one terminal and most of the loop.. the crescentic bow has thin sloping walls and a capacious groove of broad, rounded V-shaped cross-section. Adjacent to the loop on both walls is an arc of three thin triangular cells, their apex pointing towards the loop. No trace of their enamel inlay survives. The remaining terminal is in the form of a small knob. The fragmentary loop was a D-shaped ring with a heart-shaped eye.

Metal detector find. In private hands.

498. Tattingstone, Suffolk

L. *c.* 55 mm.

End-looped mortar. An apparently plain, simple example, with low, thick-rimmed walls, a square keel, and a blunt-pointed terminal. The asymmetric U-shaped cross-section of the groove may be a product of wear. The loop has a circular eye and runs some distance along the keel.

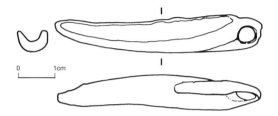

Metal detector find. In private hands.

499. Tattingstone, Suffolk

L. 71 mm.

End-looped mortar, corroded, with a lightly-elliptical bow, a flattened keel, and plain, low, convex walls. The relatively capacious broad groove has been deepened by considerable wear, resulting in a distinct 'ledging' of the inner wall faces and a very thin base. The groove runs over the plain terminal, which is in the form of a simple spout. The original form of the broken loop is indeterminate.

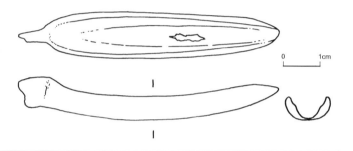

Metal detector find. In private hands.

500. Thelnetham, Suffolk

L. 37.4 mm. Wt. 9.9 g.

A tiny ornate combined brooch and end-looped mortar, with an olive-green patina. The original surface is extensively preserved, but is eroded on the muzzle of the bovid head (giving the false impression that the muzzle is a face, with the nostrils appearing to be eyes), on its horn tips, on the crown of the bird, and on the central convex 'belly', with the scrolled decoration. The solid terminal depicts a highly-stylized ox-head, with prominent drooped muzzle, drilled nostrils and projecting horns. On top of the head is a pair of pierced lugs which retain the axis bar for the hinged brooch pin. The looped terminal is in the form of a fine stylized bird's head, with slender, strongly-curved neck, drilled eyes, and a very prominent, large, elongated, up-turned bill. At the back of the neck is the cast flanged catch-plate for the brooch pin. Worn as a brooch, both terminals would be viewed to good effect, although the bull's head would be inverted. Most prominent of all would be the incised scrolled decoration on the bellied bow. The interior of the bow forms a small grooved mortar of normal form, with broad U-shaped cross-section. Cleaning by the finder has removed any evidence for wear traces in the groove. However, wear polish is visible in two other places: within the looped eye; and under the muzzle of the bovid. It is conceivable that the bird's eyes and the bovid's nostrils were once filled with inlay. While it is very likely that this object functioned both as a brooch and a cosmetic grinder, it is in any case clear that it was at least intended to be seen as a combination of the two. It parallels closely, therefore, the chatelaine type brooch, which was similarly enigmatic in its precise role/ roles.

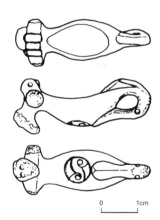

Metal detector find.

British Museum, 2010,8007.1.

501. Thérouanne, Pas-de-Calais, France
L. mortar *c.* 100 mm. pestle *c.* 70 mm.

Set, comprising a centre-looped mortar,
Type J variant, and a centre-looped pestle.
The mortar has an elliptical bow, with a
rounded keel, thin convex walls, and a
capacious U-sectioned groove. Adjacent
to the loop on both walls is a symmetrical
arrangement consisting of an outer arc
of four linked lunate cells enclosing an
inner pair flanking the loop. All retain
their enamel inlay, blue, red, red, blue
in the linked arc, red in the inner pairs.
The terminals are in the form of small
stylized bovid heads, with lightly-flared
blunt muzzles and prominent horns. The
D-shaped ring-like loop has a heart-shaped

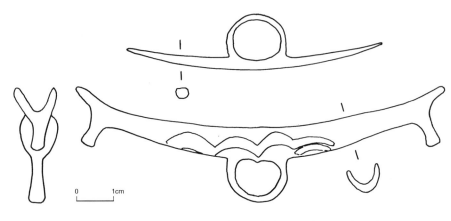

eye. The pestle has a very slender twin-tapered rod, of plump D-shaped cross-section, with pointed tips. The loop is a large D-shaped ring.

From excavation, 1994, of one of the Gallo-Roman cemeteries of *Tarvenna*, the capital of the *Civitas Morinorum*, by Freddy Thuillier, for
Association pour les Fouilles Archéologiques Nationales. Found in grave ST. 17, with an urned cremation, three pottery vessels (two flagons and a
patera), and two glass vessels (a handled cylindrical bottle and a small flagon base stamped with an image of Mercury).
Context date (from vessels), late 2nd century AD.

R.Jackson and F. Thuillier, 1999, 'A British cosmetic set (nécessaire à fard) from Thérouanne (Pas-de-Calais, France)', *Instrumentum* 9, June 1999, 23–4.

Musée Archéologique, Therouanne.

502. Thetford, Norfolk
L. 55 mm.

Centre-looped mortar, lacking both terminals and most of the loop. The strongly-
curved bow has plain, steep, lightly-convex walls, an angular keel, and a capacious,
deep, rounded V-sectioned groove. Only the stub of the heart-shaped loop survives.

Found 1982, near Gallows Hill.

Trett 1983, no. 24; Jackson 1985, no. 91.

Present whereabouts unknown. Presumably in private hands.

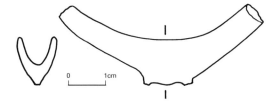

503. Thetford, Norfolk
L. 32.5 mm. Wt. 5.4 g.

Centre-looped pestle, with a shiny mid-green patina and extensive light pitting. A small, light example
of 'rocking-horse' type, quite roughly cast/finished. There is a light facet and wear polish on the base of
the elliptical rod, and a more distinct facet on the side of one of the tips, both of which are chipped. The
A-shaped suspension loop comprises a tiny circular eye in a flat ovoid plate, which is joined to the rod by
two tall struts. There is wear polish in the eye.

For metal composition see Scientific Analyses.

Metal detector find. Formerly on the antiquity market.

British Museum, 1994,0405.6.

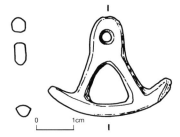

504. Thetford, Norfolk
L. 57 mm. Wt. 21.4 g.

End-looped mortar, with a mid-brown pitted patina. Recent 'cleaning' has
scoured away the original surface from everywhere except the groove. The
bow is short, deep-bellied, and quite strongly curved, with an angular keel,
steep, convex, apparently plain walls, and a shallow U-sectioned groove with
wear-polished surface. The terminal knob is small, simple and flat-ended. The
elegantly decorative loop is in the form of a strongly re-curved head and neck
of a water-bird, its large, ridged, everted bill resting on the keel of the bow. In
consequence, the loop has a comma-shaped eye.

For metal composition see Scientific Analyses.

Metal detector find. Formerly on the antiquity market.

British Museum, 1994,0405.1.

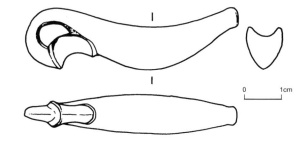

505. Thetford, Norfolk
L. 80 mm.

End-looped pestle. A very large example, with a circular ring-like loop and a long, circular-sectioned rod, lacking the end of its upturned tip.

From Fison Way excavations, 1980–1982, metal-detected topsoil find SF 138.325. Unphased.

T. Gregory, 1992, *Excavations in Thetford 1980–1982, Fison Way. Volume One.* (East Anglian Archaeol. Report no. 53), 129–30, fig. 116,7, where it is mis-identified as the tongue of a Roman military harness buckle

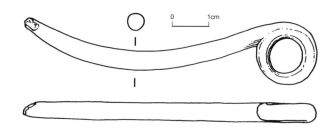

506. Thistleton, Leics
L. 69 mm.

End-looped mortar, with low plain walls, small knobbed terminal, and a narrow loop in the form of a bird's head, with bill-like extension.

From excavation, THV 1960, Site 4, Area XXXIV, Layer 1, i.e. ploughsoil within Building 6, an area of 'ovens' and infant burials. Building 6 lies south of the temple, just outside the precinct. The Building 6 coin list ranges from Trajan to House of Theodosius (AD 104–402).

Jackson 1985, no. 20. For Building 6, see E. Greenfield, *Journ.Rom.Studies* LI, 1961, 175.

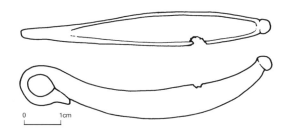

507. Threxton, Norfolk
L. 84 mm. Wt. 33. 8 g.

Centre-looped mortar, with smooth olive-green-brown patina. A large example, with gently-curved bow, angular keel, and steep, lightly-convex walls. The ornate wall decoration comprises interspersed convex and concave angled mouldings, heavily worn at the bow's broadest point adjacent to the loop. The broad, capacious, V-sectioned groove has an axially asymmetric basal wear facet, and the rim of the walls is worn down at diagonally opposite ends. The groove runs over the simple domed terminal knobs. The loop is a large D-shaped ring with wear polish in its heart-shaped eye.

A mid-19th century find, part of the Tom Barton Collection. Trett (1983, 299 no. 9) suggests it is probably from the Saham Toney/ Little Cressingham Roman settlement site.

Jackson 1985, no. 78.

Norwich Castle Museum, 179.950 (6).

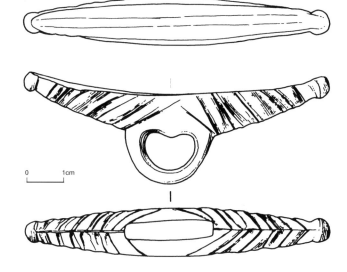

508. Tilbury, Essex
L. 66 mm. Wt. 21 g.

End-looped mortar, with dark green to black patina lightly accreted with cream to green corrosion products. The slender elliptical bow has an angular keel, plain carinated walls with a thin rim, a shallow groove of broad U-shaped cross-section, with a marked basal wear facet, and a small plain ovoid knob, which is little more than a slight swelling of the bow tip. The end loop is remarkable. Of large circular form, it swells to form a bird's head, which can only be properly appreciated when viewed along the keel of the bow with the mortar held upside down. The eyes are formed by two circular cells, which probably originally held glass or enamel inlays, while the beak, formed by the arc of the loop as it meets the underside of the bow, is strongly-ridged. The resulting face is very striking, and in contrast to the normal stylized aquatic bird's head. Considerable wear has elongated the loop's ovoid eye.

For metal composition see Scientific Analyses.

Metal detector find, formerly on the antiquity market.

British Museum, 1992,1201.1.

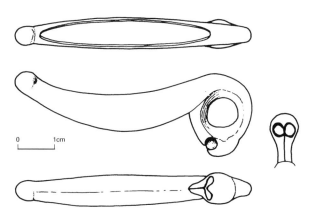

509. Tivetshall St Mary, Norfolk
L. 38 mm. (orig. *c.* 47 mm.) Wt. 8.5 g.

Centre-looped pestle, with a pitted pale and mid-green patina. One end of the crescentic lozenge-sectioned rod is broken. Slight signs of wear are present on the convex face of the surviving end. The tall projecting loop plate has chamfered edges and a small hourglass eye.

Metal detector find. In private hands.

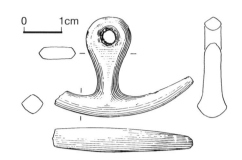

510. Toftrees, Norfolk
L. 49 mm. (orig. *c.* 70 mm.)

Centre-looped mortar, Type E, with lightly-pitted pale green-grey metallic patina. The strongly-curved bow, one end of which is lacking, has plain convex walls, a narrow V-sectioned groove with high wear polish, and a very highly- stylized zoomorphic terminal. At three points on the keel are the remnants of the indented strutwork and the large heavy loop. Although incomplete this mortar was evidently very similar in form to nos36 and 213.

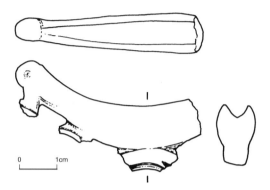

Found 1981/2 and donated to Kings Lynn Museum.

Trett 1983, no. 8; Jackson 1985, no. 89.

Kings Lynn Museum, KL 78.982 (A1678).

511. Tong, Shropshire
L. *c.* 68 mm.

End-looped mortar, with strongly-curved bow, apparently plain convex walls, a plump knobbed terminal, and a circular, ring-like loop, with large circular eye.

Metal detector find. In private hands.

512. Undley, Suffolk
L. 45 mm.

End-looped mortar. A small simple example. The short, lightly-elliptical bow has a rounded keel, plain, sloping walls, a shallow groove of rounded V-shaped cross-section, and a plain blunt-pointed terminal. The neatly-formed ring-like loop displays wear in the large circular eye.

Cambridge, University Museum of Archaeology and Anthropology, 1898.222.

513. Walsoken, Cambs (unillustrated)
L. *c.* 20 mm.

?Centre-looped pestle, if so, of idiosyncratic form, comprising a short plump rod, of olive-stone shape, with twin 'spectacle' type loops surmounting a tall pedestal. For type, see 593.

Metal detector find. In private hands.

514. Walton-le-Dale, Lancs
L. mortar *c.* 53 mm. pestle *c.* 44 mm.

Set, comprising an end-looped mortar and an end-looped pestle. The small mortar has a slender elliptical bow with low plain walls. The thin rims are chipped and the terminal is broken. The ovoid loop, with small circular eye, is slightly constricted at the junction with the bow. The pestle has a plump D-sectioned rod, its upturned tip slightly damaged, and a slender ovoid loop with apparently worn circular eye. Like the mortar loop there is a distinct 'waisting' at the junction of loop and rod. Although not from a sealed context, the form, dimensions and general context of these two pieces leaves little room for doubt that they were made and used as a set.

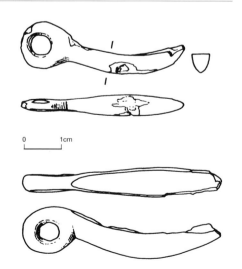

From excavations, 1981–3, of the Roman military depot/industrial site, by A.C.H. Olivier. Found in the backfill of the 1950's excavations, SF 038/252 and SF 038/253. For the site see *Britannia* 13, 1982, 352; 14, 1983, 296–7; 15, 1984, 284–6.

515. Walton-le-Dale, Lancs
L. *c.* 60 mm.

End-looped mortar, lacking the tip of the bow and part of the loop. A finely-made example with slender elliptical bow, thin, plain walls, and a V-sectioned groove. The slight down-curve of the broken terminal suggests it was originally knobbed or spouted. The loop, though damaged, was clearly in the form of a stylized aquatic bird's head, with sharply-cut everted bill and an elegant, neatly-moulded head. The eye is sub-circular.

From excavations, 1981–3, of the Roman military depot/industrial site, by A.C.H. Olivier. SF 041/101, found in an abandonment horizon, assigned to Phase 5/6.

Context date, early to mid-3rd century AD.

For site references see no. 514.

516. Walton-le-Dale, Lancs
L. *c.* 45 mm.

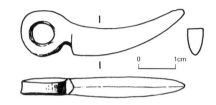

End-looped pestle, with strongly-keeled, blunt knife-like rod and discoidal loop with circular eye. There is a marked step at the junction of rod and loop.

From excavations, 1981–3, of the Roman military depot/industrial site, by A.C.H. Olivier. SF 001/30, unstratified.

For site references see no. 514.

517. Wanborough, Wilts
L. mortar 73 mm. pestle 58 mm.

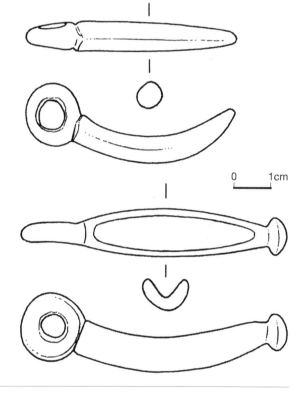

Set, comprising an end-looped mortar and an end-looped pestle, both quite simply made and rudimentarily finished. The mortar has a broad, slightly asymmetric bow, with rounded keel, plain convex walls, a short, broad, V-sectioned groove, and a large, prominent, low-domed terminal knob. The thick, discoidal loop, with sub-circular eye, is, like that of the pestle, inelegant and surprisingly roughly-finished. The pestle has a plump, sub-circular-sectioned rod, with strongly-upturned tip, which fits snugly in the groove of the mortar.

Found, during watching-brief by Swindon Archaeological Society, in an area of disturbed Roman cemetery, of probable later 2nd/early 3rd century AD date. Although unstratified the two pieces are clearly a set, and their survival together is undoubtedly accounted for by their original deposition in a grave.

Jackson 1985, no. 2.

A.S. Anderson, J.S. Wacher and A.P. Fitzpatrick 2001, *The Romano-British 'Small Town' at Wanborough, Wiltshire*, Britannia Monograph Series no. 19 (London), 112, 115, fig. 47, 237.

518. Warlingham, Surrey
L. 43 mm. Wt. 12.7 g.

Centre-looped mortar, with grey (tin-enriched) patina. A small example with severely eroded terminals, badly chipped rims and broken loop. The short bow has steep, lightly-convex walls, beneath the virtually straight rim of which is a low cambered ridge defined by a pair of lightly-incuse lines and a discontinuous row of punched dots. The groove, of broad, very shallow U-shaped cross-section, is wear-polished. The terminals were probably plain, but surface erosion prevents certainty. The broken loop was apparently D-shaped, with a large circular eye.

For metal composition see Scientific Analyses.

Metal detector find, 1983, from Warlingham Court Farm. Donated by finder to British Museum.

British Museum, 1990,0401.1.

519. Warwickshire, unprovenanced (Unillustrated)

L. *c.* 48 mm.

Centre-looped mortar. The elliptical plain-walled bow has a ridged rim, knobbed terminals, and a circular loop.

On the antiquity market. Not available for study.

520. near The Wash, Lincs

L. 48.9 mm. Wt. 7.3 g.

End-looped pestle, with smooth green patina. A well-preserved, neatly-formed example, with a slender, blunt, knife-like rod, worn on the sides and edge. The elongated loop is in the form of a stylized bird's head, with everted bill and large ovoid eye.

Metal detector find. Formerly in private hands, via the antiquity market.

British Museum, 1999,0802.85.

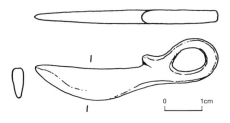

521. Wendover, Bucks

L. 34 mm.

End-looped mortar, fragment, comprising the broken loop and part of the bow. The steeply-sloping convex walls appear plain, as does the remains of the loop, which appears to have had a large tear-shaped eye. At the point of breakage the keel is rounded angular, and the groove is relatively shallow and of asymmetric (?worn) V-shaped cross-section.

Metal detector find. In private hands.

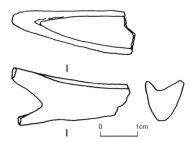

522. Wenhaston, Suffolk

L. *c.* 67 mm.

Centre-looped mortar, of unique form. The lightly-elliptical bow has an angular keel, plain, sloping walls and a comparatively narrow groove which, like the bow, tapers slightly away from the zoomorphic terminal. Only an arc of the broken loop remains. The terminals are remarkable. One is a stylized, bovid head, with horns, brow ridge and a pointed muzzle. The other is, seemingly, anthropomorphic, the only known example to date with a human face. Unfortunately, most of the surface (and, therefore, the detail) has been lost to corrosion, but the remaining fragment appears to preserve parts of the eyes, nose and ?fringe or ?cowl. From the profile it would appear likely that the head was bearded. A further unique feature of this example is that the figured terminals have been inverted, that is to say they have been designed to be seen in an upright position when the mortar was suspended, not when it was in use, as was the norm (Compare, e.g. no. 523).

Metal detector find, from the site of the Roman 'small town'. In private hands.

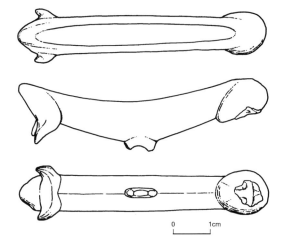

523. Wenhaston, Suffolk

L. *c.* 54 mm.

Centre-looped mortar, Type G, with plain, convex walls, thin inturned rims, and a relatively broad U-sectioned groove which runs onto the terminals. The better preserved terminal is a stylized bovid head, with well-rendered horns, ridged brow and lightly-upturned, ridged muzzle. The second terminal is considerably less well preserved. It, too, appears to have been zoomorphic – small, plump, and slightly heart-shaped, with the hint of ears and muzzle. The large, slender, ring-like loop is distorted.

Metal detector find, 1992, from a low-lying/wet location near to the site of the Roman 'small town'. In private hands.

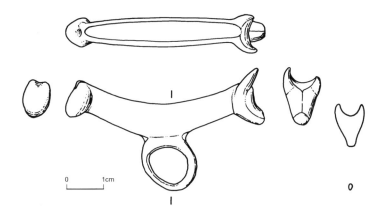

524. Wenhaston, Suffolk

L. 64 mm. Wt. 28.9 g.

Centre-looped mortar, with a smooth, greyish, (tin-enriched) patina, mostly intact, but with a few corrosion patches and a casting blemish near one terminal. A heavy example, with strongly-curved bow, squared-off keel, and plain, steep, lightly convex walls, with an inturned, neatly-formed, thin rim, which continues unbroken around both ends completely encircling the groove. (for a similar feature see mortar no. 65). The groove, of rounded V-shaped cross-section, has a distinct wear polish. The near-identical terminals are in the form of a small bird's head, with a markedly ridged and lightly dished bill. The circular ring-like loop has a round eye with wear in the usual position.

Metal detector find, 1993. In private hands.

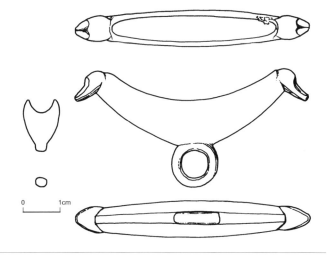

525. Wenhaston, Suffolk

L. *c.* 40 mm.

Centre-looped pestle, with lightly-elliptical, twin-tapered, circular-sectioned, blunt-ended rod. The simple strutted loop, of sub-rectangular cross-section, has a tear-shaped eye and a small triangular piercing.

Metal detector find. In private hands.

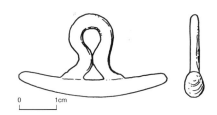

526. Wenhaston, Suffolk

L. 50 mm. Wt. 13.9 g.

Centre-looped pestle, with light-green matt patina. A stout example, with twin-tapered, blunt-tipped, crescentic rod, of sub-trapezoid cross-section, and a tall D-shaped loop with circular eye. There is wear in the eye, as also on the convex face of the rod, where it is most pronounced at the centre and does not extend quite to the tips.

Metal detector find. In private hands.

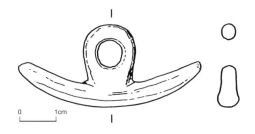

527. Wenhaston, Suffolk

L. *c.* 33 mm.

Centre-looped pestle. A comparatively small example, with short, plump, twin-tapered rod and a circular disc-like loop.

Metal detector find, 1990, from same site as no. 522. In private hands.

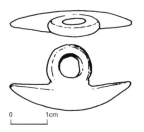

528. Wenhaston, Suffolk
L. 42.5 mm. Wt. 6.1 g.

Centre-looped pestle, with smooth green-grey patina. A neatly-made example with strongly-curved, slightly asymmetric, twin-tapered rod, of plump triangular cross-section. The D-shaped loop is proportionately large.

For metal composition see Scientific Analyses.

Metal detector find, 1989, from same site as no. 522. Subsequently on antiquity market, provenanced only as 'East Anglia'.

British Museum, 1992,1201.3.

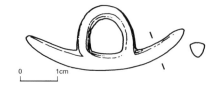

529. Wenhaston, Suffolk
L. *c.* 47 mm.

End-looped pestle, with grey patina, lacking the end of the rod and part of the loop. The strongly-curved rod has a plump oval cross-section which becomes lentoid towards the upturned tip. The loop was evidently a simple ring with circular eye.

Metal detector find, 1991, from same site as no. 522. In private hands.

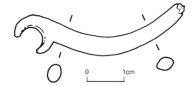

530. Wereham, Norfolk
L. 61 mm. Wt. 10.2 g.

End-looped mortar. A simple example, with low-walled elliptical bow, and a tiny terminal knob, now damaged. The loop has a worn eye.

Metal detector find. In private hands.

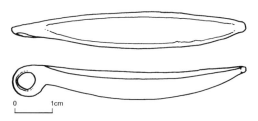

531. West Rudham, Norfolk
L. 55 mm. Wt. 8.91 g.

End-looped mortar, with pitted corrosion, lacking its terminal. The plain bow has a deep, broad, rounded V-sectioned groove. The simple loop has a circular eye with considerable wear.

Metal detector find. In private hands.

532. Wetheringsett-cum-Brockford, Suffolk
L. 33 mm.

Zoomorphic terminal and part of the bow from a large ornate mortar. The surviving part of the bow has an angular keel, steeply-sloping walls, and a V-sectioned groove with basal facet and wear polish. The large terminal is in the form of a bovid head, with prominent in-turned horns (the tips lost to corrosion), marked brow ridge, triangular face, bulbous lentoid eyes, flattened muzzle, drilled nostrils, and part-open mouth. The junction of the back of the beast's head with the groove is marked with a triple incuse moulding, which runs down onto both walls of the bow. It may have been part of a more extensive incuse décor or was perhaps intended to represent the beast's shaggy mane.

Metal detector find. In private hands.

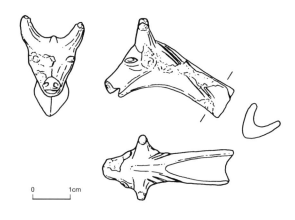

533. Weybourne, Norfolk

L. 58 mm. Wt. 23.6 g.

Centre-looped mortar, with black patina, abraded to underlying green corrosion products in places. 'Oiled' by finder. A relatively heavy example, with short bow, deep, plain, steeply-sloping walls, thick rims, and bulbous, rather phallic, knobbed terminals with ring moulding. The capacious U-sectioned groove, which runs over the terminals, is deep and very heavily worn, asymmetrically, so that one diagonally opposite end of each wall is worn away. The loop is plump, with a small moulded keel plate at the junction with the bow. Its small circular eye is heavily worn.

Metal detector find, 1992. In private hands.

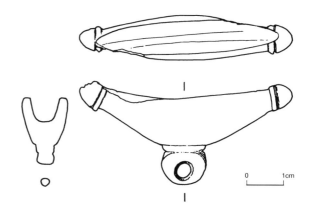

534. Whissonsett, Norfolk

L. c. 57 mm.

Centre-looped mortar, broken at both ends of the bow. The crescentic bow has a bevelled keel, apparently plain carinated walls, and a relatively shallow, rounded V-sectioned groove. Both terminals are lacking. The loop, mounted on a short plinth, has a circular eye.

Metal detector find. In private hands.

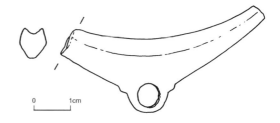

535. nr. Whitchurch, Shropshire

L. c. 52 mm.

End-looped pestle, with pitted and accreted corrosion. The strongly-curved, circular-sectioned rod has an upturned pointed tip. The large loop is in the form of a stylized aquatic bird's head, with long everted bill, marked brow, and tear-shaped eye.

Unstratified find, from excavation, 1972, by Andrew Rogerson, of Romano-British domestic and industrial (ironworking) site, occupied late 1st-3rd century AD.

Shropshire Museums Service.

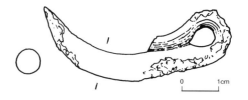

536. Whitton, S. Glamorgan

L. 74 mm.

End-looped mortar. A large, simple example, with long elliptical bow, plain, sloping walls, a chamfered keel, plain, blunt-pointed terminal, and a broad U-sectioned groove. The ring-like loop has a large ovoid eye.

From excavations, 1965–70, of Iron Age and Roman farmstead. Unstratified. The 10 structural phases at Whitton are dated c. AD 30–340.

M.G. Jarrett and S. Wrathmell, 1981, *Whitton: An Iron Age and Roman Farmstead in South Glamorgan* (Cardiff) 179, 180, fig. 72, 40; Jackson 1985, no. 26.

537. Wickford, Essex

L. c. 60 mm.

Centre-looped pestle. A large example, with long, asymmetric, twin-tapered rod, of modified lozenge-shaped cross-section near the upturned tips, and a large D-shaped loop with circular eye.

From excavation, 1971, of Iron Age and Romano-British farmstead, at Beauchamps Farm, by W.J. Rodwell. Found in later Roman subsoil clearance level. N. Wickenden in Rodwell, publication forthcoming.

538. Wickford, Essex

L. 66.7 mm. Wt. 5 g.

End-looped mortar, with corrosion-pitted, dark grey-brown patina, the underlying metal core revealed in places. A very light and simple example, with an extremely slender elliptical bow, rounded keel, very low plain walls, simple pointed terminal, and shallow, broad, V-sectioned groove. The ovoid loop is simply made, with a free end, and has a relatively large tear-shaped eye. It is asymmetrical to the bow. The object could have been worked from a slender rod of rounded rectangular cross-section (c. f. no. 275).

Metal detector find. Formerly in private hands, via the antiquity market.

British Museum, 1999,0802.86.

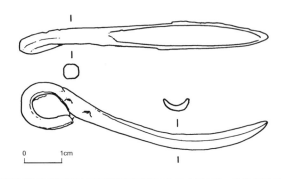

539. Wickham Skeith, Suffolk

L. 18 mm. Wt. 2.93 g.

End-looped mortar, fragment, comprising the end-loop and the stub of the bow, with the beginning of the groove. The loop is in the form of the stylized head of a water-bird, with long curved neck, prominent crown, and elongated dished bill.

Metal detector find. In private hands.

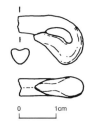

540. Wicklewood, Norfolk

L. 63 mm. Wt. 21.3 g.

Centre-looped mortar, with green patina rather encrusted with a creamy brown deposit. A very finely-made example, with plump, strongly-curved bow, plain, convex walls with inturned rim, and a shallow V-sectioned groove with light basal facet. The prominent knobbed terminals are well-formed spheres with slightly flattened ends. Each has three incuse lines around the girth. The missing loop was connected to a neatly-tapered keel ridge which increases the phallic appearance of the terminal knobs.

Metal detector find from the Crownthorpe Romano-Celtic temple site. Formerly in private hands.

Norwich Castle Museum, 380.985.

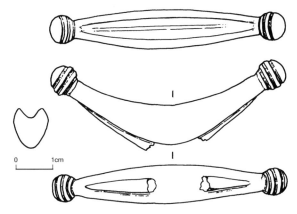

541. Wicklewood, Norfolk

L. c. 60 mm.

Centre-looped mortar, Type D, with elliptical plain-walled bow and knobbed terminals. The prominent loop and scrolled strut assembly is mounted on a low plinth.

On the antiquity market. Not available for study. Veracity of provenance uncertain.

Benet's artefacts of England and the United Kingdom, current values (Cambridge, 2000), 47, no. I14–0103, where it is wrongly sized, spuriously juxtaposed with a non-belonging pestle, and erroneously termed 'woad grinding set'.

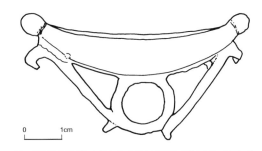

542. Wicklewood, Norfolk

L. 55 mm. Wt. 13.7 g.

Centre-looped mortar, Type D variant, with dusty pale green patina over brownish metallic surface. A light example, with slender, only very gently curved, bow, plain sloping walls, an angular keel, plain, blunt-pointed terminals and a relatively deep groove, of narrow V-shaped cross-section, with an axially asymmetric basal wear facet. The fragmentary, thin circular loop was encircled by a slender strut running onto its lower edge from each terminal.

Metal detector find from the Crownthorpe Romano-Celtic temple site. Formerly in private hands.

Trett 1983, no. 7; Jackson 1985, no. 88.

Norwich Castle Museum, 43.982.

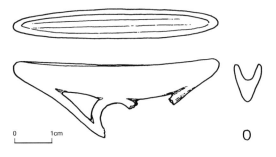

543. Wicklewood, Norfolk

L. 34 mm. (orig. *c.* 39 mm.)

Centre-looped pestle, Type N. The loop plate, in the form of a sitting or swimming duck above a tiny circular eye, is placed centrally on the concave edge of a crescentic, twin-tapered rod, one end of which is broken.

From the Crownthorpe Romano-Celtic temple site.

Trett 1983, no. 23; Jackson 1985, no. 97.

Norwich Castle Museum, 43.983.

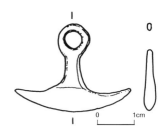

544. Wicklewood, Norfolk

L. 34 mm.

Centre-looped pestle, with a short, crescentic, twin-tapered rod and a small, circular loop mounted on a slender pedestal.

From the Crownthorpe Romano-Celtic temple site.

Trett 1983, no. 22; Jackson 1985, no. 96.

Norwich Castle Museum, 43.983.

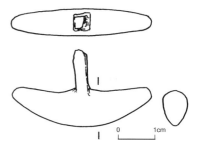

545. Wicklewood, Norfolk

L. 38 mm. Wt. 12.3 g.

Centre-looped pestle, with mid-grey-green patina, recently abraded on the keel, very probably from an ill-considered demonstration of its function. The blunt-tipped, twin-tapered rod is a short, stout, relatively heavy crescent, quite rudimentarily made and finished. The loop, now lacking, was set on a tall slender plinth of sub-rectangular cross-section.

Metal detector find. In private hands.

546. Wicklewood, Norfolk

L. 37 mm. Wt. 7.1 g.

Centre-looped pestle, with a brown, partially accreted, patina. A small, stout, example, with a crescentic, twin-tapered rod, and a large circular loop mounted on a faceted pedestal. A wear facet is present on the convex face of both ends of the rod.

Metal detector find from the Crownthorpe Romano-Celtic temple site. Formerly in private hands.

Norwich Castle Museum, 45.989.

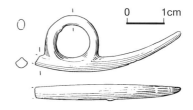

547. Wicklewood, Norfolk

L. 41 mm. (orig. *c.* 58 mm.)

Centre-looped pestle, with light green-brown patina. A large example lacking one end of the long, crescentic, twin-tapered, modified lozenge-sectioned rod. The large D-shaped loop has a circular eye.

Metal detector find from the Crownthorpe Romano-Celtic temple site. Formerly in private hands.

Norwich Castle Museum, 45.989.

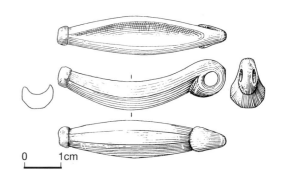

548. Wicklewood, Norfolk

L. 46 mm. Wt. 11.4 g.

End-looped mortar, with a partially pitted dark brown to black patina. A small, finely-made example with a short, plump, strongly-curved bow, a flattened keel, crisply-carinated walls, with a thin rim, a neat, flat-ended, 'button' type knobbed terminal, and a short, broad U-sectioned groove with a high wear polish. The loop is elegantly curled and profiled, and splayed onto the underside of the bow, giving the appearance of a highly-stylized bird's head. There are signs of wear in the small eye.

Metal detector find from the Crownthorpe Romano-Celtic temple site. Formerly in private hands.

Norwich Castle Museum, 45.989.

549. Wicklewood, Norfolk

L. 30 mm. Wt. 7.2 g.

(?) End-looped mortar fragment, comprising one terminal and part of the bow. The surface of the mid-green patina, is rather denuded except in the groove. The walls are sloping and plain, the keel rounded, and the terminal knob a small, flat-ended 'button'. The surviving end of the groove is shallow and U-sectioned, and it has a marked wear polish.

Metal detector find from the Crownthorpe Romano-Celtic temple site. Formerly in private hands.

Norwich Castle Museum, 380.985.

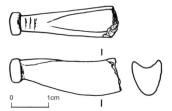

550. Wilderspool, Cheshire

L. *c.* 76 mm.

End-looped mortar, with lightly curved bow, plain convex walls, an angular keel, a shallow groove of rounded V-shaped cross-section, and a moulded, flat-ended terminal knob. The loop, with its bill-like extension, has the appearance of a stylized aquatic bird's head.

From excavations, 1901–4, on the Romano-British 'industrial' site. Found beneath a hearth, 'in the vicinity of the bronze-founder's and enameller's workshop'.

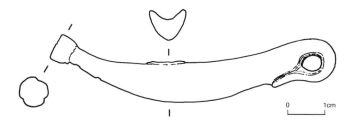

T. May, 1906, 'The excavations on the Romano-British site at Wilderspool', *Trans. Hist. Soc. Lancashire Cheshire* (1906), pl. 1 fig. 1; Smith 1918, 59; F.H. Thompson, 1965, *Roman Cheshire* (Chester) fig. 20,12; Jackson 1985, no. 10.

Warrington Museum.

551. Willersey, Glos

L. 78 mm. Wt. 37.9 g.

End-looped mortar, with a smooth, light green-grey metallic (tin-enriched) patina. A heavy but elegant example, with lightly-curved bow, plain vertical walls, neatly-faceted at their junction with the flattened keel, thick rims, and a narrow, exceptionally shallow, U-sectioned groove, with distinct wear polish, which runs over the loop. The small, low-domed, knob terminal is very regular, with a neat ring-moulding. The loop is large and finely-wrought into the form of an aquatic bird's head, with prominent everted and ridged bill. There is wear-polish at the back of the tear-shaped eye. A further zone of wear polish, on one face of the loop and the adjacent wall of the bow, was probably caused by chafing when the mortar was suspended.

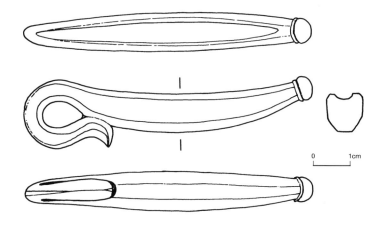

Metal detector find. In private hands.

552. Winchester, nr. Claverley, Shropshire

L. 46 mm. Wt. 11.7 g.

(?) Centre-looped mortar, with brittle, light to olive green patina, extensively destroyed at the terminals and partially flaked away on the walls. The small, crescentic bow has plain carinated walls and an angular keel, which still retains a casting seam. The slender groove, of U-shaped cross-section, has a very marked basal wear facet and correspondingly high wear polish. At the base of the groove, just off-centre, is a negative casting flaw, which evidently did not hinder use. The blunt-pointed terminals were probably always plain. The remains of the struts beneath the bow indicate a central triangular piercing flanked by a pair of rings. It seems probable, in view of this symmetry, that the struts culminated in a central circular suspension loop. The surviving surface remains suggest that the object was finished quite rudimentarily.

Metal detector find. In private hands.

553. Wingham, Kent

L. 43 mm. Wt. 9.65 g.

Centre-looped mortar, deeply-pitted by corrosion. A small example, with apparently plain bow, virtually straight rims, and plain blunt-pointed terminals. The loop, formed by a downward extension of the keeled bow, has a circular eye.

Metal detector find. In private hands.

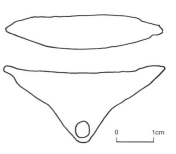

554. Wingham, Kent

L. *c.* 66 mm.

End-looped mortar, with slender, crescentic bow, low, plain walls, a small knobbed terminal with ring-moulding, and a slightly 'coiled' , sub-circular loop with ovoid eye.

Metal detector find, from Crockshard Farm. The finder showed the object to Mrs. Pan Garrard (Canterbury Archaeological Trust), to whom I am most grateful for the pencil sketch from which my drawing was made. By January 1992 the object was no longer in the finder's possession, and it is virtually certain that no. 601, an unprovenanced example which was on the antiquity market in 1993, is one and the same mortar. Its form and dimensions are identical in every respect.

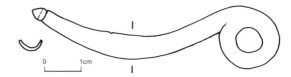

555. Wisbech, Cambs (Unillustrated)

L. *c.* 75 mm.

Centre-looped mortar, Type F, of heavy ornate form with zoomorphic terminals. The walls are decorated with three ridged mouldings which run from rim to keel. The larger terminal is in the form of a bovid head, with blunt muzzle, mouth, eyes, horns and ears rendered. The opposing, smaller, terminal is a highly-stylized animal head, perhaps a cow to complement the horned bull. The stub of the broken loop is present at the base of the central ridged moulding.

On the antiquity market. Not available for study – sketch and photos seen. Veracity of provenance uncertain. In a subsequent re-appearance on the antiquity market the provenance was given as 'probably Norfolk'.

556. Withersfield, Suffolk

L. 59.4 mm. Wt. 16.5 g.

End-looped mortar, with olive patina, half of which has flaked away revealing light green corrosion products beneath. There is slight damage (or a casting flaw) to one rim. The lightly-elliptical bow has a rounded angular keel, plain sloping walls, one preserving a neatly-formed channelled moulding beneath the rim, a bulbous knobbed terminal, and a capacious groove of rounded V-shaped cross-section. The small loop is in the form of a stylized aquatic bird's head, with tiny eye and prominent everted bill.

Metal detector find. In private hands.

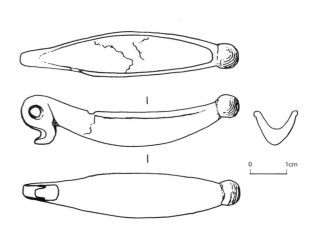

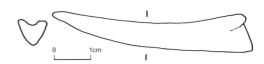

557. Witnesham, Suffolk

L. *c.* 55 mm.

(?) End-looped mortar, very corroded, lacking the loop and part of the bow. The surviving part of the bow is lightly-curved, with an angular keel, low, plain, sloping walls, a simple pointed terminal, and a shallow groove. The expanded end may be the beginning of the loop.

Metal detector find, 1991. In private hands.

558. Wixoe, Suffolk

L. *c.* 63 mm.

End-looped mortar, Type A. The slender, crescentic bow has a sharp-angled keel, and steeply-sloping thin walls, which preserve a pair of incuse angled lines near the loop, probably the last vestige of a more extensive zig-zag motif, as on nos236, 495 etc. The groove is capacious, of narrow and deep V-shaped cross-section. The zoomorphic terminal is probably a very devolved bovid head, with prominent horns (or ears), a marked brow ridge, cursorily-rendered eyes, and a long, tapered, ridged and dished muzzle. The loop, set beneath the opposite, plain, terminal is in the form of a stylized bird's head and was probably also intended to represent the tail of the bovid.

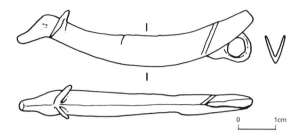

Metal detector find, from the site of a large Roman 'small town'. In private hands.

559. Woodbridge, Suffolk

L. 76 mm.

Centre-looped mortar, Type K, with mid-green patina. A slender, light example with crescentic bow, angular keel and low, lightly-convex walls, which are decorated with an incuse paired inverted V motif adjacent to the loop. The capacious groove, of broad U-shaped cross-section, has a marked basal wear facet, which runs a little obliquely to the longitudinal axis, resulting in wear loss to the rim of diagonally opposing ends of the bow. The groove runs over the terminals, which are in the form of tiny, stylized bovid heads, with only horns and tapered muzzle depicted. The D-shaped, disc-like loop has a large circular eye.

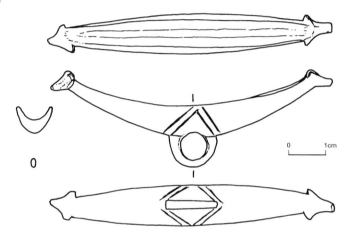

Found, 1977, with coins of 1st–4th century AD date. Other finds included a bronze figurine of Mercury/Cupid.

Trett 1983, no. 13; Jackson 1985, no. 70.

Ipswich Museum, 1977-48.2.

560. Woodeaton, Oxon

L. 71 mm.

End-looped mortar, with smooth grey-brown patina. The gently-curved, parallel-sided bow has low, plain, sloping walls, a chamfered keel, a simple, atypically square-ended, plain terminal, with faceted underside, and a groove, of rounded V-shaped cross-section, with wear-polish in the central zone. The loop is finely-wrought in the form of an aquatic bird's head with a carefully-profiled, elongated bill. There is some wear at the back of the ovoid eye.

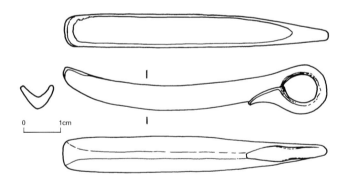

Found before 1900. In addition to the Romano-Celtic temple, of 1st to early 5th century AD date, the site yielded evidence of relatively intense Iron Age activity.

Smith 1918, 57, fig. 5; R. Goodchild and J.R. Kirk, 1955, 'The Romano-Celtic temple at Woodeaton', *Oxoniensia* XIX, 15–37; Jackson 1985, no. 34.

Oxford, Ashmolean Museum, Gordon Coll. 1900 R.131.

561. Wormegay, Norfolk
L. 69.2 mm. Wt. 25.9 g.

End-looped mortar, with heavily-pitted, smooth, mid-green patina.
The plump elliptical bow has an angular keel, plain convex walls,
a small button terminal, and a relatively capacious groove of
rounded V-shaped cross-section with marked wear polish. The loop
is large and ornate, with an openwork trumpet scroll, the thinnest
part of which is distorted and broken. The surviving part is wear-
polished on its inner face.

Metal detector find. In private hands.

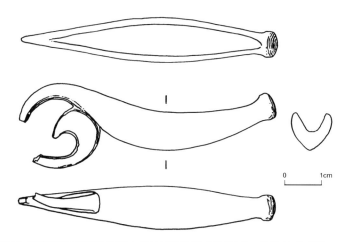

562. Wroxeter, Shropshire
L. 44 mm. Wt. 19.7 g.

End-looped mortar, with a mid green patina. The terminal and part of the bow are
lacking, and the surface, including the point of breakage, is extremely worn and eroded.
The lightly-curved bow has a rounded keel, apparently plain, convex walls, and a
U-sectioned groove with marked basal wear-slot. The heavy loop, although very worn,
was evidently in the form of an aquatic bird's head, with everted bill. The circular eye is
slightly elongated through wear. There are two deep, deliberately-made, notches on one
rim, one on the other rim, another at the broken end, and two more on one wall near the
broken end. Their function is not clear, but they were evidently secondary and may have
been applied when the broken object was re-used, as an amulet?

Shrewsbury, Rowley's House Museum, Wroxeter Coll., no Acc. no.

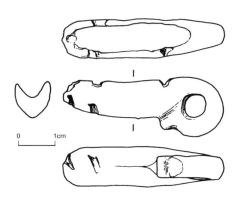

563. Wroxeter, Shropshire
L. 51 mm. Wt. 15.2 g.

End-looped mortar, in poor condition, with heavy emerald green and light blue
corrosion, mineralized, brittle, splitting, laminating and flaking. The terminal and
part of the bow are lacking. The near-straight bow has a rounded keel, steep, lightly-
convex, apparently plain walls, and a rounded V-sectioned groove. The circular loop is
apparently plain, with a circular eye.

Found 23/9/1926.

Shrewsbury, Rowley's House Museum, Wroxeter Coll., B 438.

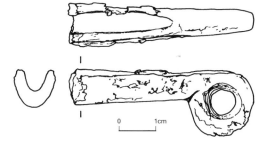

564. Wroxeter, Shropshire
L. 63 mm. Wt. 23.2 g.

End-looped pestle, with smooth, dark-green patina. A large, heavy example.
The thick, blunt, knife-like rod has a deep, upturned tip, with asymmetric
wear-faceting on the convex edge. The large 'coiled' loop has a circular eye.

Shrewsbury, Rowley's House Museum, Wroxeter Coll., A121.

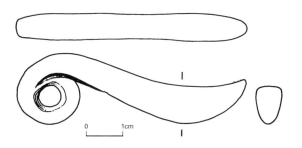

565. Wylye Camp, Wilts
L. *c.* 79 mm.

End-looped mortar, with a deep-bellied bow, plain, steeply-sloping walls, an angular keel, a rounded V-sectioned groove, a large, low-domed terminal knob, and a simple, thick, ring-like loop with ovoid eye.

Smith 1918, 59, fig. 9; Jackson 1985, no. 13.

Salisbury Museum.

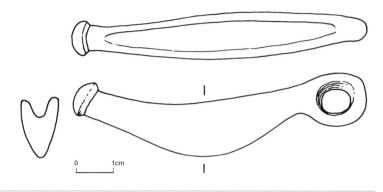

566. Wymondham, Norfolk
L. 33.7 mm. Wt. 4.8 g.

Centre-looped pestle, with brown patina. A diminutive boat-shaped example, with crescentic, smooth-keeled rod. The ornate loop-plate has neatly-made mouldings and a small circular eye, elongated through wear.

For metal composition see Scientific Analyses.

Metal detector find. Subsequently on the antiquity market, when its provenance was given only as 'East Anglia'.

British Museum, 1992,1201.4.

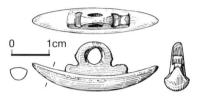

567. Wymondham, Norfolk
L. 52.8 mm. (orig. *c.* 63 mm.) Wt. 8 g.

Centre-looped pestle, with slightly eroded, dusty, light-green patina. A large example, with strongly-curved twin-tapered rod, one tip missing, and a D-shaped collar-like loop with a large circular eye.

Metal detector find. In private hands.

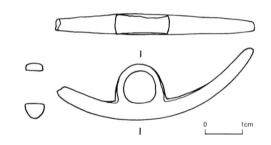

568. Wymondham, Norfolk
L. 23.8 mm. Wt. 2.2 g.

End-looped pestle, lacking most of the rod, with grey-green patina, extensively eroded round the loop. What remains is a short length of the slender, sub-circular-sectioned rod, which terminates in a ring-like loop with large circular eye. Atypically, the loop is set above the line of the rod.

Metal detector find. In private hands.

569. York, N. Yorkshire
L. 63.3 mm. Wt. 19 g.

End-looped mortar, with mid-green patina. The elliptical bow has a ribbed rim and a curving rib flanking the keel. Traces of incuse cabled patterning are preserved in places on the lower rib, with punching in the grooves that flank the rib. No incised decoration is visible on the rim rib. The terminal is a simple blunt point. The groove is of rounded V-shaped cross-section and is separated from the loop. The loop, with small ovoid eye, is in the form of a finely-modelled stylized bird's head, with marked crest and forehead and a strongly-dished bill.

Metal detector find. In private hands, via the antiquity market.

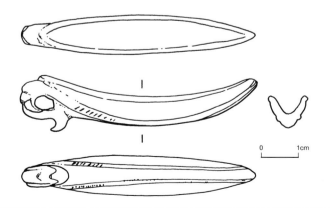

570. York, N. Yorkshire

L. 60 mm.

End-looped pestle, with a stout, lightly-elliptical rod and a finely-wrought loop, in the form of an aquatic bird's head, with a moulded crest and brow, an elongated tapered bill, and a circular eye.

From excavations, 1989–90, of Roman extra-mural site, at 35–41 Blossom Street, south-east of the approach road from Tadcaster. The site revealed ditched enclosures, a sequence of burials and mausolea and a phase of rubbish dumping. Found in ditch fill (part of a site levelling phase).

Context date (pottery), mid-2nd century AD.

York Archaeological Trust 19th Annual Report 1990–91 (1991), 16–17 (where the date is wrongly given as 1st century AD).

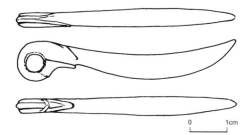

571. York area, N. Yorkshire

L. 38 mm. Wt. 12 g.

Centre-looped mortar, with a smooth, dark-green patina in the groove and flanking the keel, but elsewhere corroded/cleaned away, revealing the uneven metallic surface. A small example with short, elliptical bow, apparently plain, convex walls, a shallow, U-sectioned groove with wear-polish, and plain, blunt-pointed terminals. The small round loop with circular eye surmounts a Y-shaped strut set on a low keel plate. Corrosion has given the loop a deceptively emaciated appearance.

Metal detector find. In private hands, via the antiquity market.

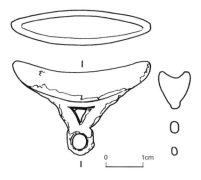

572. York area, N. Yorkshire

L. 53.7 mm. Wt. 14.9 g.

End-looped mortar, with rather pocked, heavy, mid-green patina. The slender, elliptical bow has a rounded keel, plain, steeply-sloping walls, a narrow, shallow, U-sectioned groove, with wear-polish, and a plain, blunt-pointed terminal, now slightly chipped. The broken loop was large and probably ring-like.

Metal detector find. In private hands, via the antiquity market.

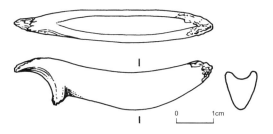

573. ?Yorkshire, unprovenanced

L. 65.3 mm. Wt. 25.3 g.

End-looped mortar, with pale olive-green patina, preserving most of the original surface. An unparalleled, idiosyncratic, example, with deep, slender elliptical bow, bevelled keel, and plain, near-vertical walls, with a central, vertical, low, moulded rib. The very narrow groove, of slender U-shaped cross-section, with wear-polish and marked basal facet, runs over the terminals. Both terminals are in the form of a devolved duck's head, with a tall crown, marked forehead, and deeply-hollowed bill with elongated, everted, trumpet-like tip. The larger terminal has a pierced, small, circular eye for suspension, while the eye of the other terminal is rendered, on one face only, by a shallow punched hollow. Both heads are ornamented with delicately-incised cross-hatching on the crown and incised and dot-punched motifs on the marginal zone.

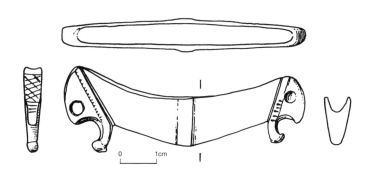

Part of a collection of nine cosmetic mortars sold at auction: Bonhams, December 12th 1996, Lot 19. The provenance is uncertain, according to the vendor.

British Museum, 1997,0101.5.

574. ?Yorkshire, unprovenanced

L. 64.2 mm. Wt. 17.6 g.

End-looped mortar, with fine, very smooth (wear-polished), light- to mid-green patina, preserving most of the original surface. A finely-cast and –finished, unparalleled, elegant example, with smooth elliptical bow, axially-asymmetric neatly-ribbed keel, convex plain walls (one higher than the other), a U-sectioned groove with wear polish and basal facet, and a simple knobbed terminal. The elaborate loop is based on a tendril-and-volute motif, with a heavily-worn incised line running around the margin. This arrangement gives the impression of a highly-stylized bird's head, with the tip of the dished everted bill scrolled back onto the prominent crown, on the perimeter of which is a neatly-recessed grooved moulding. There is wear in the eye.

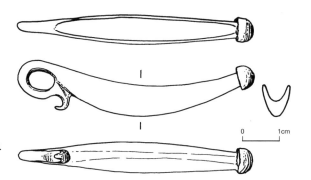

Part of a collection of nine cosmetic mortars sold at auction: Bonhams, 12 December 1996, Lot 19. The provenance is uncertain, according to the vendor.

British Museum, 1997,0101.6.

575. ?Yorkshire, unprovenanced

L. 63.1 mm. Wt. 13.4 g.

End-looped mortar, with a smooth silver-grey patina. A fine casting, well-finished, and of elegant form. The crescentic bow has a rounded keel, plain, steeply-convex walls with narrow rim, a U-sectioned groove with wear polish and basal facet, and a domed-knob terminal. The neatly-made loop is in the form of a stylized bird's head, with large, worn, ovoid eye, prominent crown, and dished, strongly-everted bill.

Part of a collection of nine cosmetic mortars sold at auction: Bonhams, 12 December 1996, Lot 19. The provenance is uncertain, according to the vendor.

British Museum, 1997,0101.7.

576. Unprovenanced (Unillustrated)

L. c. 75 mm.

Multiple-looped mortar, apparently in fine condition, with a long, only lightly-elliptical bow. The walls appear plain, except for a moulding above the triple-perforated central loop plate. There is a further circular ring-like loop at each end of the bow. One is set below the bow in order not to impede the pouring of the contents from the open spout-like end of the groove. The ring at the opposite end was probably the suspension loop.

Metal detector find, provenance not divulged. See *Treasure Hunting*, April 1996, 10–16, esp.11 (photo and text), where the length is given as 7.5 cm.

577. Unprovenanced

L. 93.4 mm. Wt. 26.3 g.

Centre-looped mortar, lacking its loop, with dark olive-green patina. An unusually long, slender, ornate example, which evidently saw long use: the centre-loop, broken in antiquity, had its base ground away (file marks still visible); the groove is very worn; and the incuse decoration on the walls is also heavily worn. The long elliptical bow has very slender ends, a deep centre, and a capacious, deep U-sectioned groove, with heavy wear polish and marked basal facet, which runs over both terminals. One terminal is in the form of a bovid head, with short moulded horns, circular hollow-pitted eyes, an angular-profiled face, and a tapered muzzle. The other terminal, a moulded knob, was evidently intended to represent the beast's tail. The carefully-profiled carinated walls have an angular keel to the head side of the loop and a flat-facetted keel to the tail side. Their upper zone – from rim to carination – is ornamented with a dot-punched zig-zag motif.

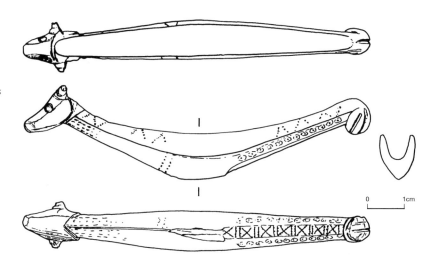

The lower zone at the head end (the beast's neck) is textured with three parallel lines of punched dashes, terminated at the loop by a pair of dot-punched lines at right angles. The lower zone at the tail end is embellished with a line of dot-and-ring punched motifs, while the basal facet has a row of dot-punched cross-in-panel motifs. All of these zones display considerable wear. At the head end the wall rims are very thin.

Part of a collection of nine cosmetic mortars sold at auction: Bonhams, 12 December 1996, Lot 19. This example from a private collection in Sussex, according to the vendor.

British Museum, 1997,0101.9.

578. Unprovenanced

L. 65 mm. (orig. *c.* 78 mm.)

Centre-looped mortar, Type J, with smooth, dark grey-green patina, lacking one terminal, and with recent abrasion on one wall. The crescentic bow has an angular keel and thin, steep walls, with an arc of tiny, narrow triangular cells, their apex pointed towards the loop, 25 on one wall and 24 on the other. The missing cell may have been a casualty of breakage, though the 25th cell is very small, and absolute regularity of size, shape and number of cells was evidently not considered vital. Though much of the enamel inlay is missing, enough survives to, disclose the original arrangement: eight blue, two red, five turquoise, two red, eight blue. The deep, capacious, rounded U-sectioned groove runs onto the surviving terminal, which is in the form of a small, stylized, bovid head, very neatly-modelled, with inturned horns, ridged brow, and flared, flat-ended muzzle. The ring-like, squat, D-shaped loop has wear in the eye.

For enamel and metal composition see Scientific Analyses.

Metal detector find, formerly on the antiquity market.

British Museum, 1990,0702.7.

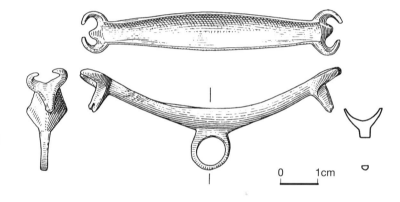

---

579. Unprovenanced

L. 71 mm. Wt. 10.4 g.

Centre-looped mortar, Type K, with light green-brown patina. A light, well-made example, with crescentic bow, low, thin, plain, sloping walls, an angular keel, and a broad, capacious, truncated V-sectioned groove, with clear basal wear facet, which runs over the two terminals. These are small, neatly-modelled, highly-stylized bovid heads. Each has a prominent pair of inturned horns and an elongated, flat triangular head, the better preserved of which retains its grooved mouth. The simple, ring-like loop, slightly asymmetrically cast, has an unworn circular eye. Like the bovid terminals, it retains casting and working marks.

For metal composition see Scientific Analyses.

Metal detector find, formerly on the antiquity market.

British Museum, 1990,0702.6.

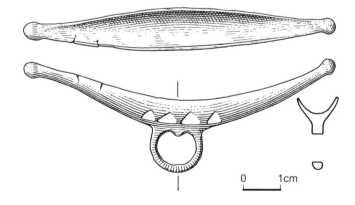

---

580. Unprovenanced

L. 85 mm. Wt. 14.1 g.

Centre-looped mortar, Type H, with pale grey-brown patina. The crescentic bow, slightly distorted and fissured near one terminal, has low, thin, lightly-convex, sloping walls, with an arc of four small, deep triangular cells adjacent to the loop on both faces. The cells, whose apex points away from the loop, are now devoid of inlay. The capacious groove, of broad, rounded V-shaped cross-section, with basal wear facet, stops short of the small, simple knobbed terminals. The large, ring-like, D-shaped loop has a heart-shaped eye.

For enamel and metal composition see Scientific Analyses.

Metal detector find, formerly on the antiquity market. No credence need be given to the vendor's comment that this mortar was said to have been 'found together' with pestle no. 591.

British Museum, 1990,0702.8.

581. Unprovenanced
L. 84 mm. Wt. 68.8 g.

Centre-looped mortar, Type D variant, with smooth grey patina. A large, very heavy, and idiosyncratic example, with an atypical off-set bow of plano-convex cross-section, and a large rectangular loop plate linked to the ends of the bow by a pair of sturdy, rectangular-sectioned struts. The rim of the bow walls is emphasised by a groove below its lip, while its upper edge is decorated with incuse hatching. All other main surfaces, except the curved zone of the convex wall, are decorated with a free, and rather irregular arrangement utilising a much-repeated small stamped S or Z motif, evidently applied with a single punch. The groove is relatively shallow, with a broad U-shaped cross-section. The terminal knobs are large, simple and globular. One has a flat, slightly roughened end, probably a casting flaw. There are two small circular perforations in the loop plate, the outer, slightly larger one of which was probably used for suspension. Small casting blemishes and file-finishing marks are particularly visible on the surfaces within the triangular apertures enclosed by the bow, loop plate and struts; while wear can be discerned especially on the punched decoration near the centre of both walls of the bow.

For metal composition see Scientific Analyses.

Metal detector find, formerly on the antiquity market.

British Museum, 1990,0702.4.

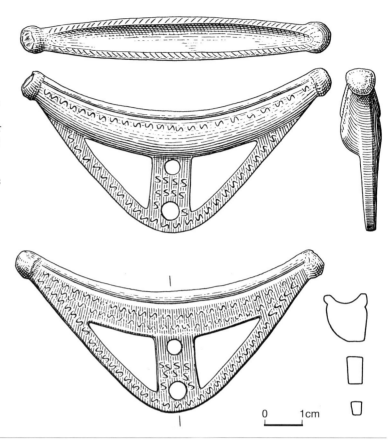

582. Unprovenanced
L. 67 mm. Wt. 44.2 g.

Centre-looped mortar, Type D, with a shiny grey-black patina. A rather ill-proportioned, poorly-cast and rudimentarily-finished example, with a casting flaw above one terminal and on one strut (scroll eye blocked), and an asymmetric and poorly-formed loop and strut assembly. The elliptical bow has plain, steep, convex walls with flattened rims of unequal width, and a deep, narrow, V-sectioned groove, with marked basal wear-facet, which runs over one of the plain, flat-ended terminal knobs. The sub-circular suspension loop, framed by scrolled struts, is disproportionately large.

For metal composition see Scientific Analyses.

Metal detector find, formerly on the antiquity market.

British Museum, 1990,0702.5.

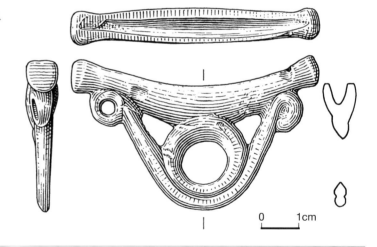

583. Unprovenanced
L. 75 mm.

Centre-looped mortar. A well-made example, with elliptical bow, plain, convex, quite thin walls, a deep, capacious groove, of rounded V-shaped cross-section, with a marked basal wear slot, and worn, triple ring-moulded terminal knobs. The bow dips deeply down to the broken loop, which was probably a D-shaped ring.

Metal detector find. In private hands, via the antiquity market.

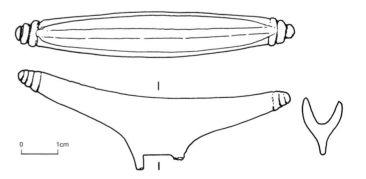

584. Unprovenanced

L. 60 mm. Wt. 22.4 g.

Centre-looped mortar, with a lightly-pitted olive-green patina, which retains a light covering of soil in many places, particularly in the groove. The smoothly-curved, plump crescentic bow has plain, convex walls, a broad, U-sectioned groove, and distinctly phallic knobbed terminals with lightly-incuse base moulding. The loop is an engaged D-shaped ring with large circular eye. Virtually identical to mortar no. 399, and probably from the same mould.

Metal detector find. Formerly in private hands, via the antiquity market. The purchaser was informed by the dealer that this mortar and pestles nos 590, 603 and 605 had been acquired as a collection from someone in the Cambridge area. While that provenance might relate to the collector it does not necessarily apply to the cosmetic grinders.

British Museum, 1999,0802.87.

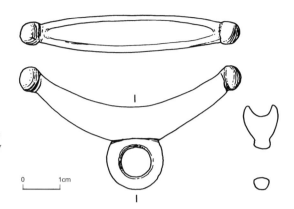

585. Unprovenanced

L. *c*. 74 mm.

Centre-looped mortar, with an apparently plain-walled elliptical bow. Beneath both terminals is a low-domed knob. The large D-shaped loop with circular eye has a moulded bar-like junction with the keel of the bow.

Metal detector find. On the antiquity market.

Unavailable for study, but a single photographed view (with scale) was illustrated in *Treasure Hunting* magazine for Dec. 1992, p. 19. From site referred to only as 'Rubbish Field', no provenance given.

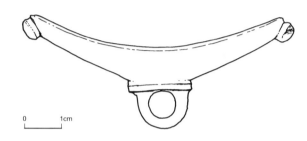

586. Unprovenanced

L. 80.7 mm. Wt. 13.9 g.

Centre-looped pestle, Type O, with smooth mid-green patina. A very large and ornate example, lacking only the tip of one arm. The rod is of rhomboid cross-section with a very light wear facet on the keel. The two non-functional (concave) faces of the rod are decorated with two arcs of three small triangular cells, flanking the junction of loop and rod. The cells, whose apex points away from the loop, contain traces of their degraded enamel inlay, but it is not possible to identify the colour(s) (though one or more appears to have contained green). The large loop is a D-shaped ring with heart-shaped eye. It has been twisted or set slightly obliquely to the rod. So similar to the pestle of set no. 74 as to be probably from the same mould or archetype.

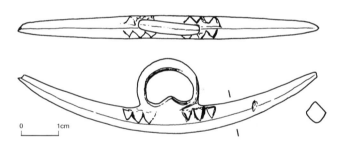

Sold at auction, Bonhams Antiquities, Tues. 25 April 1995, part of Lot 126 (unillustrated). Subsequently application was made for an export licence.

587. Unprovenanced

L. 60 mm.

Centre-looped pestle, with mid-green patina. The crescentic, twin-tapered, rhomboid-sectioned rod has arms of markedly unequal length. There is a little wear on the keel, especially near the centre, but none is visible in the eye of the D-shaped loop.

Metal detector find, donated to Moyses Hall Museum.

Bury St Edmunds, Moyses Hall Museum, 1982. 337.12.

588. Unprovenanced

L. 50.7 mm. Wt. 6.2 g.

Centre-looped pestle, with metallic grey patina. A slender, twin-tapered crescentic rod, slightly asymmetric, of sub-lozenge-shaped cross-section, with a slender D-shaped ring-like loop. Wear polish is visible on the keel and sides of the rod, one tip of which is shorter than the other.

Metal detector find. Formerly in private hands, via the antiquity market. Its provenance was said to be 'Midlands, a local (Birmingham area) find'.

British Museum, 1999,0802.89.

589. Unprovenanced
L. 53.2 mm. Wt. 5.4 g.

Centre-looped pestle, with pale olive to mid-brown patina. The elliptical twin-tapered rod has blunt-pointed tips and a rhomboid cross-section, softened on the lower face through wear. The D-shaped loop has a circular eye, which is also lightly worn on the upper face.

Metal detector find. Formerly in private hands, via the antiquity market.

British Museum, 1999,0802.90.

590. Unprovenanced
L. 37 mm. Wt. 6.2 g.

Centre-looped pestle, with a smooth grey-green patina. A small example of elegant design, though quite roughly-finished. The crescentic, twin-tapered, D-sectioned rod has a little wear on the keel. The prominent strutted loop has a large tear-shaped eye and a small triangular piercing (similar to the loop on mortar no. 362). Wear is visible in the eye, but, more noticeably, around the waist of the strutted loop as though it had been tied and chafed in this region. For a similar wear pattern see mortar no. 474.

Metal detector find. Formerly in private hands, via the antiquity market. See no. 584 for acquisition details.

British Museum, 1999,0802.88.

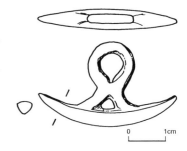

591. Unprovenanced
L. 47 mm. Wt. 12.1 g.

Centre-looped pestle, with a pocked and pitted grey-brown patina. A rather poor, flawed casting, not very carefully finished. The thick, heavy crescentic rod, with plump D-shaped cross-section and blunt-pointed tips, has a lightly-filed facet on the sides. The rather irregularly-finished loop is mounted on a low plinth. There is little sign of wear in its circular eye.

For metal composition see Scientific Analyses.

Metal detector find, formerly on the antiquity market. Said to have been 'found together' with mortar no. 580, but the statement is incapable of proof, and the two objects were evidently not made as a set.

British Museum, 1990,0702.9.

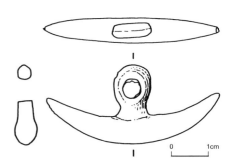

592. Unprovenanced
L. 29 mm.

Centre-looped pestle, Type N, with brown patina. An ornate, atypical example, complete, with a strongly-curved, blunt-ended crescentic rod surmounted by a neatly-modelled sitting or swimming bird. The loop is in the form of a central 'keyhole' perforation.

Metal detector find. On the antiquity market.

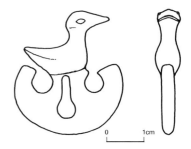

593. Unprovenanced
L. 21.5 mm. Wt. 6.6 g.

?Centre-looped pestle, if so, of idiosyncratic form, with a dark green-black patina. A quite indifferently-finished object, which retains much of the as-cast surface, including small flaws. The short, plump, olive-stone-shaped rod is markedly asymmetric, possibly due to the wear on its keel. The twin 'spectacle' type loops are mounted on a tall slender pedestal. See also 513.

Metal detector find. Formerly in private hands, via the antiquity market. Labelled 'North east England. Lincs./ Yorks.'.

British Museum, 1999,0802.58.

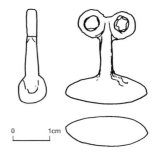

594. Unprovenanced (unillustrated)

L. *c.* 64 mm.

Centre-looped pestle, unavailable for study.

Metal detector find. On the antiquity market. Advertised for sale, unillustrated, in antiquity catalogue, described as 'solid crescent boat shaped. Centre fastening loop missing'.

595. Unprovenanced

L. *c.* 84 mm.

End-looped mortar, corroded, with a long, low-walled bow and large bovid terminal. The loop, beneath the end of the bow, has a circular eye and is in the form of a stylized bird's head, or the bovid's folded tail, or both.

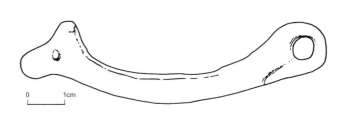

Metal detector find. On the antiquity market.

Unavailable for study, but a single photographed view (with scale) was illustrated in *The Searcher* magazine for April 1995, p. 22, where its provenance was given only as 'from a Roman site'.

596. Unprovenanced

L. 85 mm. Wt. 23.4 g.

End-looped mortar, with a mid-brown to olive patina, retaining traces of light brown soil in many places. The long, crescentic bow has a chamfered keel, and lightly-carinated, thin-rimmed walls. A tiny mushroom-headed stud projects from one wall and a swelling at the same point on the opposite wall signals the former presence of its partner, which evidently broke away and was smoothed down in antiquity. Near the centre of the keel is another tiny stud, and there are the remains of two further studs, one either side of, and equidistant from, it. They also appear to have been broken and smoothed down in antiquity. One wall has a large gash in it, and the smoothed edges suggest that part of this damage may also have occurred in antiquity. The groove, of rounded V-shaped cross-section, is very capacious, with a marked basal wear facet. The terminal is an ornate moulded knob,

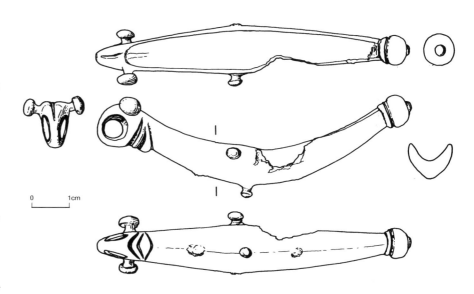

with a nipple-like projection. The loop is highly stylized, but undoubtedly zoomorphic. Viewed end-on, its pair of mushroom-like studs give the appearance more of a ram's head than a bovid. From the side the impression is rather of a duck's head, and it may be that such a combination was intentional. There are slight traces of wear in the countersunk circular eye.

Metal detector find. Formerly in private hands, via the antiquity market.

British Museum, 1999,0802.91.

597. Unprovenanced
L. 84.4 mm. Wt. 49.5 g.

End-looped mortar, Type B, with a fine pale green-grey
patina preserving all of the original surface. A finely-
wrought and –finished heavy casting, with strongly-curved
bow, and sharply-carinated walls, each decorated with an
arc of eight incuse ring-and-dot motifs which extend from
tip to tip of the bow. Adjacent to the loop on one wall the
ring-and-dot has been double struck, the first impression
being poorly-placed. Both decorated faces display a
considerable wear polish. The elaborate keel comprises a
herring-bone rib recessed in an axial slot. The groove, which
runs onto both terminals, has a broad, rounded V-shaped
cross-section with basal facet and a marked wear polish.
Both terminals are simple and plain. Beneath one is the
relatively small loop, with a circular eye and neatly-formed
dished moulding, giving the impression of a highly-stylized
bird's head.

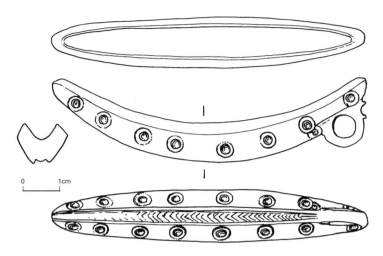

Part of a collection of nine cosmetic mortars sold at
auction: Bonhams, 12 December 1996, Lot 19. From an 'Old
collection', according to the vendor.

British Museum, 1997,0101.8.

598. Unprovenanced
L. 61.3 mm. Wt. 11.1 g.

End-looped mortar, with a lightly-pitted brown patina, incautiously cleaned.
A smallish but quite heavy example, comprising a slender, low-walled,
elliptical bow, with rounded keel, plain steeply-sloping walls, a slender groove
of shallow, rounded V-shaped cross-section, and a small, simple, knobbed
terminal. The loop is in the form of a highly-stylized bird's head, with small
circular eye and simply-moulded dished bill.

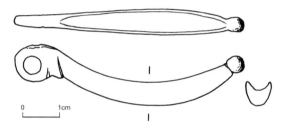

Metal detector find. Formerly in private hands, via the antiquity market.

British Museum, 1999,0802.92.

599. Unprovenanced
L. 59.7 mm. Wt. 15.5 g.

End-looped mortar, with mid-grey-green patina, extensively pitted and
flaked, especially at the rims. The bow, only lightly elliptical, has a rounded
angular keel, plain, steeply-sloping walls, and a U-sectioned groove with
highly wear-polished surface. The terminal has broken away – not recent
damage. The loop is in the form of a highly-stylized bird's head, with a wear-
polished circular eye and a dished bill.

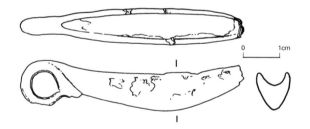

Metal detector find. Formerly in private hands, via the antiquity market.

British Museum, 1999,0802.93.

600. Unprovenanced
L. 68 mm. Wt. 12.5 g.

End-looped mortar, with lightly pitted cleaned metallic surface. The
slender, lightly-elliptical bow has a broad, gently-curved keel, low,
plain, near-vertical walls, a U-sectioned groove, and a tiny, vestigial,
terminal knob. The carefully-profiled, ring-like, circular loop has
neatly-applied incuse linear ornament around the circumference
and at the junction with the groove.

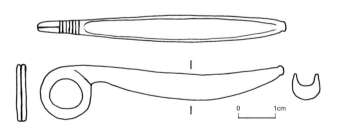

For metal composition see Scientific Analyses.

From the Ransom Collection; no provenance is given for the object,
but much of the collection was formed in and around Hitchin, in
Bedfordshire, and in London.

Smith 1918, 55, fig. 2; Jackson 1985, no. 21, where the provenance 'Hitchin' was incautiously given.

British Museum, 1915,1208.128.

601. Unprovenanced (but see no. 554)
L. 67 mm. Wt. 17 g.

End-looped mortar, with lightly pitted dark-green to black patina. The crescentic bow is slender, with low, plain, convex walls, one of which has recent damage to the rim, though it was evidently lower than its partner even before the damage occurred. The groove, also, is slightly asymmetric, probably as a result of wear. It is of rounded V-shaped cross-section and runs onto the loop. The small knobbed terminal has a ring moulding. The neatly-formed, slightly 'coiled' loop is sub-circular and tapers from top to bottom. It has an ovoid eye elongated through wear.

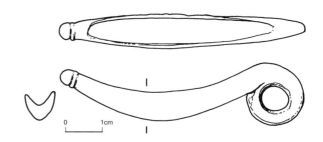

For metal composition see Scientific Analyses.

Metal detector find. On the antiquity market in 1993. While it is impossible to prove, it seems virtually certain that this is the mortar found at Wingham (no. 554 above), which subsequently 'lost' its provenance on the antiquity market.

British Museum, 1994,0405.2.

602. Unprovenanced
L. 57.8 mm. Wt. 14.8 g.

End-looped mortar, with a dark green-black patina. The bow is only lightly elliptical, with a rounded angular keel, plain, steeply-sloping walls, a capacious U-sectioned groove, and a simple open-ended spout. The simple loop has an ovoid eye elongated through wear.

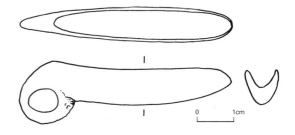

Metal detector find. Formerly in private hands, via the antiquity market.

British Museum, 1999,0802.94.

603. Unprovenanced
L. 66 mm. Wt. 10.6 g.

End-looped pestle, with a smooth green patina. A large, elegant, strongly-curved example. A collar-like expansion with lightly-incuse mouldings divides the rod into a handle and a functional end. The latter has a marked wear facet on the underside of its upturned tip, which is of lentoid cross-section. The handle, of ovoid cross-section, terminates in a large coiled loop with a sub-circular eye, in which are traces of wear-polish. The very worn sides of the moulded collar attest, in any case, considerable wear from suspension.

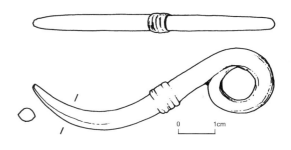

Metal detector find. Formerly in private hands, via the antiquity market. See no. 584 for acquisition details.

British Museum, 1999,0802.95.

604. Unprovenanced
L. 57.5 mm. Wt. 9.1 g.

End-looped pestle, with a rather uneven mid-green patina and light brown soil accretion in places. The elliptical rod has a plump oval cross-section and swells just before the blunt-pointed tip. The loop is round, with a small circular eye.

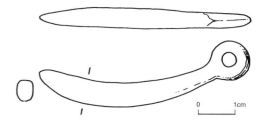

For metal composition see Scientific Analyses.

Metal detector find. Formerly on the antiquity market.

British Museum, 1994,0405.5.

605. Unprovenanced

L. 52 mm. Wt. 11.5 g.

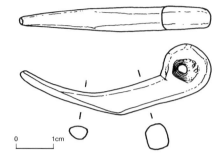

End-looped pestle, with a dark brown (iron-stained) patina over mid-green corrosion products. The rod, of rounded rectangular cross-section at its looped end, is strongly curved towards the tip, which is complete. The concave face is as-cast, but the angular convex face is a product of extremely heavy and/or prolonged usage, which has virtually worn through the rod. Several angle facets are visible. The loop, of crude, heavy form, is set, atypically, above the concave curve. Its eye appears never to have been worked after casting, shows absolutely no wear (in stark contrast to the rod), and cannot ever have been used for suspension.

Metal detector find. Formerly in private hands, via the antiquity market. See no. 584 for acquisition details.

British Museum, 1999,0802.96.

606. Unprovenanced (unillustrated)

L. *c.* 57 mm.

End-looped pestle, unavailable for study.

Metal detector find. On the antiquity market. Advertised for sale, unillustrated, in antiquity catalogue, described as 'solid boat shaped with large end suspension loop. Complete.'

Uncertain examples

607. Amersham, Bucks

L. 35 mm.

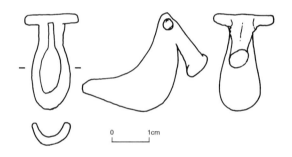

?End-looped mortar. The excessively short, deep crescentic bow has plain walls, a U-sectioned groove, and a large bovid terminal with straight horns, long tapered face, and a bulbous, flat-ended muzzle. It seems that a loop may have broken away from the other end of the bow. If this is a cosmetic grinder it is a most atypical example.

From archaeological investigation, 1983–9, of Roman site at Mantles Green.

Aylesbury, Bucks. County Museum, 1988.98.2.

608. Ashtead, Surrey

L. *c.* 63 mm.

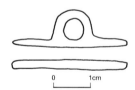

?Centre-looped pestle, with barely discernible curvature of the rod, and a large D-shaped loop with circular eye.

From excavations, 1924–7, of Roman villa and bath house.

A.W.G. Lowther, 1927, 'Excavations at Ashtead, Surrey', *Surrey Archaeological Collections* 37, 144ff, fig. 2, no. 12.

609. The Caburn, E. Sussex

L. *c.* 28 mm.

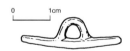

?Centre-looped pestle. A diminutive example, with blunt-ended, lightly curved rod, and an arched loop.

From excavation, 1925, of the Iron Age hillfort. Found in Pit 95 at 15 inches.

E. and E.C. Curwen, 1927, 'Excavations in the Caburn, near Lewes', *Sussex Archaeological Collections* 68, 1–59, esp. 15, and pl. V no. 34.

610. Little Waldingfield, Suffolk

L. 44 mm.

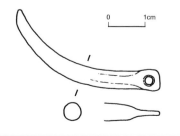

?End-looped pestle. The crescentic, circular-sectioned rod has the normal tapered, upturned tip, but the loop, a simple flattening of the opposite end of the rod, with tiny circular eye, is atypically understated.

Metal detector find. In private hands.

9. Bibliography

N.B. Published references for individual catalogued finds are incorporated in the relevant catalogue entries and are not repeated here.

Abdy, R., Leins, I. and Williams, J. (eds) 2002, *Coin Hoards from Roman Britain, Volume XI* (Royal Numismatic Society, Special Publication no. 36, London).

Ager, B. 2006, 'A lead model for a late 5th- or early 6th-century sword-pommel', *Medieval Archaeology* 50, 2006, 243–9.

Allason-Jones, L. 2002, 'Enamelled flask from Catterick Bypass (Site 433)', in Wilson 2002, 78–80.

Atkinson, M. and Preston, S.J. forthcoming, *Excavations at the Iron Age and Roman Settlement at Elms Farm, Heybridge, Essex 1993–5* (East Anglian Archaeology monograph, forthcoming).

Bagnall Smith, J. 1999, 'Votive objects and objects of votive significance from Great Walsingham', *Britannia* 30, 1999, 21–56.

Bayley, J. and Budd, P. 1998, 'The clay moulds', in Cool and Philo (eds) 1998, 195–222.

Bayley, J. and Butcher, S. 2004, *Roman Brooches in Britain. A technological and typological study based on the Richborough collection* (Society of Antiquaries of London, London).

Bierbrier, M. 1997, 'New light on ancient faces', *British Museum Magazine* 27, 36–9.

Bird, J. 1997, 'A Romano-British linch-pin head from Chelsham', *Surrey Archaeological Collections* 84, 187–9.

Bird, J. 2007, 'Catalogue of Iron Age and Roman artefacts discovered before 1995', 34–69, in R. Poulton 'Farley Heath Roman temple', *Surrey Archaeological Collections* 92, 1–147.

Bishop, M.C. 1988, 'Cavalry equipment of the Roman army in the first century AD', in J.C Coulston (ed.) *Military Equipment and the Identity of Roman Soldiers. Proceedings of the Fourth Roman Military Equipment Conference* (BAR International Series 394, Oxford), 67–195.

Brailsford, J.W. 1962, *Hod Hill Vol. One: Antiquities from Hod Hill in the Durden Collection* (London).

Branigan, K. and Bayley, J. 1989, 'The Romano-British metalwork from Poole's Cavern, Buxton', *Derbyshire Archaeological Journal* 109: 34–50.

Brown, A.E. (ed.) 1995, *Roman Small Towns in Eastern England and Beyond* (Oxbow Monograph 52, Oxford).

Burnham, B.C. 1995, 'Small towns: the British perspective', in Brown 1995, 7–17.

Carr, G. 2005, 'Woad, tattooing and identity in later Iron Age and early Roman Britain', *Oxford Journal of Archaeology* 24(3), 273–92.

Cool, H.E.M. and Philo, C. (eds.) 1998, *Roman Castleford. Excavations 1974–85, Volume I: The small finds* (Yorkshire Archaeology 4, West Yorkshire Archaeology Service, Wakefield).

Cool, H.E.M., Lloyd-Morgan, G. and Hooley, A.D. 1995, *Finds from the Fortress* (CBA/ York Archaeological Trust, York).

Cooney, G., Becker, K., Coles, J., Ryan, M. and Sievers S. (eds) 2009, *Relics of Old Decency: archaeological studies in later prehistory. Festschrift for Barry Raftery* (Dublin).

Cowell, M. 1998, 'Coin analysis by energy dispersive x-ray fluorescence spectrometry', in A. Oddy and M. Cowell (eds) *Metallurgy in Numismatics 4* (RNS, London), 448–60.

Craddock. P.T. 1978, The origins and early use of brass', *Journal of Archaeological Science* 5(1), 1–16.

Crummy, N. 1983, *The Roman Small Finds from Excavations in Colchester 1971–9* (Colchester Archaeological Report 2, Colchester).

Crummy, N and Eckardt, H. 2003, 'Regional identities and technologies of the self: nail-cleaners in Roman Britain', *Archaeological Journal* 160, 44–69.

Crummy, P., Benfield, S., Crummy, N., Rigby, V. and Shimmin, D. 2007, *Stanway: An élite burial site at Camulodunum* (Britannia Monograph Series no. 24, London).

Cuddeford, M. 2008, 'Woad grinders they are not!', *Treasure Hunting* October 2008, 70–1.

Davey, N. and Ling, R. 1982, *Wall-painting in Roman Britain* (Britannia Monograph Series no. 3, London).

Davies, J.A. 2009, *The Land of Boudica. Prehistoric and Roman Norfolk* (Oxford).

Davies, J.A. and Gregory, T. 1991, 'Coinage from a *Civitas*: a survey of the Roman coins found in Norfolk and their contribution to the archaeology of the *Civitas Icenorum*', *Britannia* 22, 65–101.

Down, A. and Rule, M. 1971, *Chichester Excavations I* (Chichester Civic Society Excavations Committee, Chichester).

Eckardt, H. 2005, 'The social distribution of Roman artefacts: the case of nail-cleaners and brooches in Britain', *Journal of Roman Archaeology* 18, 139–60.

Eckardt, H. 2008, 'Technologies of the body: Iron Age and Roman grooming and display', in Garrow, Gosden and Hill 2008, 113–28.

Eckardt, H. and Crummy, N. 2006, "Roman' or 'native' bodies in Britain: the evidence of Late Roman nail-cleaner strap-ends', *Oxford Journal of Archaeology* 25(1), 83–103.

Eckardt, H. and Crummy, N. 2008, *Styling the Body in Late Iron Age and Roman Britain: a contextual approach to toilet instruments* (Monographies *instrumentum* 36,Montagnac).

Fell, C. 1936, 'The Hunsbury Hillfort, Northants', *Archaeological Journal* 93, 57–100.

Forbes, R.J. 1955, 'Cosmetics and perfumes in antiquity' and 'Paints, pigments, inks and varnishes', in *Studies in ancient technology III* (Leiden), 1–49 and 202–55.

Garrow, D., Gosden, C. and Hill, J.D. (eds.), 2008, *Rethinking Celtic Art* (Oxford).

Green, M. 1989, *Symbol and Image in Celtic Religious Art* (London).

Green, M.J. (ed.) 1995, *The Celtic World* (London/ New York).

Guillaumet, J.-P. and Eugène, A. 2009, 'Á propos de trios objets métalliques, témoins des relations entre le pays éduen et les Îles Britanniques', in Cooney *et al.* (eds) 2009, 241–8.

Gurney, D. 1986, *Settlement, Religion and Industry on the Fen-Edge: three Romano-British sites in Norfolk* (East Anglian Archaeology 31).

Gurney, D. 1995, 'Small towns and villages of Roman Norfolk. The evidence of surface and metal-detector finds', in Brown 1995, 53–67.

Hawkes C.F.C. and Hull, M.R. 1947, *Camulodunum* (Society of Antiquaries of London Research Report 14, London).

Henig, M. 1995, *The Art of Roman Britain* (London).

Henry, F. 1933, 'Émailleurs d'occident', *Préhistoire* II, 1, 65–146.

Hill, J.D. 1997, "The end of one kind of body and the beginning of another kind of body'? Toilet instruments and 'Romanization' in southern England during the first century AD', in A. Gwilt and C. Haselgrove (eds) 1997, *Reconstructing Iron Age societies. New approaches to the British Iron Age* (Oxbow Monograph 71, Oxford), 96–107.

Holder, P.A. 1982, *The Roman Army in Britain* (London).

Hook, D. and Craddock, P.T. 1996, 'The scientific analysis of the copper-alloy lamps: aspects of classical alloying practices' , in D.M. Bailey, *A Catalogue of the Lamps in the British Museum. IV Lamps of Metal and Stone, and Lampstands* (London), 144–64.

Hunter, F. 2008a, 'Celtic art in Roman Britain', in Garrow, Gosden and Hill 2008, 129–45.

Hunter, F. 2008b, 'Two unusual Romano-British dragonesque brooches from Well, North Yorkshire', *Yorkshire Archaeological Journal* 80, 15–20.

Hunter, F. 2009, 'Miniature masterpieces: unusual Iron Age brooches from Scotland', in Cooney *et al.* (eds) 2009, 143–55.

Jackson, R. 1985, 'Cosmetic sets from Late Iron Age and Roman Britain', *Britannia* 16, 165–92.

Jackson, R. 1993, 'The function and manufacture of Romano-British cosmetic grinders: two important new finds from London', *Antiquaries Journal* 73, 165–9.

Jackson, R. 2006, 'Colchester, cosmetic sets and context', in P. Ottaway (ed.) *A Victory Celebration: papers on the archaeology of Colchester and Late Iron Age – Roman Britain presented to Philip Crummy* (Colchester Archaeological Trust, Colchester), 105–12.

Jackson, R. forthcoming a, 'Cosmetic set', in I.P Garrard 'Other Roman objects of copper alloy', in P. Bennett *Excavations in the Castle Street and Stour Street areas* (The Archaeology of Canterbury, Vol. VI, forthcoming).

Jackson, R. forthcoming b, 'The cosmetic grinders', in Atkinson and Preston forthcoming.

Jackson, R.P.J. and Potter, T.W. 1996, *Excavations at Stonea, Cambridgeshire, 1980–85* (London).

Jackson, R. and Thuillier, F. 1999, 'A British cosmetic set (nécessaire à fard) from Thérouanne (Pas-de-Calais, France)', *Instrumentum* 9, 23–4.

Jacques, A. and Prilaux, G. (eds) 2003, *Dans le sillage de César: traces de Romanisation d'un territoire, les fouilles d'Actiparc à Arras.* Exposition au Musée des Beaux-Arts d'Arras, du 27 septembre 2003 au janvier 2004 (Arras, Musée des Beaux-Arts).

James, S. and Rigby, V. 1997, *Britain and the Celtic Iron Age* (London).

Jarrett, M.G. 1994, 'Non-legionary troops in Roman Britain: part one, the units', *Britannia* 25, 35–77.

Johns, C.M. 1982, *Sex or Symbol: Erotic Images of Greece and Rome* (London).

Jundi, S. and Hill, J.D. 1998, 'Brooches and identities in first century AD Britain: more than meets the eye?', in C. Forcey, J. Hawthorne, R. Witcher (eds) *TRAC 97. Proceedings of the seventh annual theoretical Roman archaeology conference, Nottingham 1997* (Oxford), 125–37.

Kaufmann-Heinimann, A. 1998, *Götter und Lararien aus Augusta Raurica. Herstellung, Fundzusammenhänge und sakrale Funktion figürlicher Bronzen in einer römischen Stadt* (Forschungen in Augst 26, Augst).

Künzl, E. 2005, 'Grossformartige Emailobjekte der römischen Kaiserzeit', in S.T.A.M. Mols *et al.* (eds) *Acta of the 12th International Congress on Ancient Bronzes, Nijmegen 1992* (Nederlandse Archeologische Rapporten 18, Amersfoort), 39–49.

Künzl, E. 2008, 'Enamelled bronzes from Roman Britain: Celtic art and tourist knick-knacks', *Current Archaeology* 222 (Vol. XIX, no. 6), 22–7.

Leins, I. 2002, 'Itteringham, Norfolk', in Abdy *et al.* (eds) 2002, 77–83.

Mackreth, D. 1994, 'Late La Tène brooch', in Thorpe *et al.* 1994, 49–50.

Mackreth, D. 2009a, 'Brooches', in S. Trow, S. James and T. Moore, *Becoming Roman, Being Gallic, Staying British: Research and excavations at Ditches hillfort and villa 1984–2006*, (Oxford), 132–43.

Mackreth, D. 2009b, 'An unusual Romano-British brooch from Norfolk, with a note upon its probable affinities', *Britannia* 40, 137–49.

Martin, E., Pendleton, C. and Plouviez, J. 2008, 'Archaeology in Suffolk 2007', *Proceedings of the Suffolk Institute of Archaeology and History* 41(4): 505–42.

Mattingly, D. 2006, *An Imperial Possession: Britain in the Roman Empire, 54 BC–AD 409* (London).

May, J. 1971, 'An Iron Age spout from Kirmington, Lincolnshire', *Antiquaries Journal* 51, 253–9.

Megaw, R. and Megaw, V. 1989, *Celtic Art* (London/New York).

Menzel, H. 1966, *Die römischen Bronzen aus Deutschland II: Trier* (Mainz).

Menzel, H. 1986, *Die römischen Bronzen aus Deutschland III: Bonn* (Mainz).

Middleton, A. and Humphrey, S. 2001, 'Pigments on some Middle Kingdom coffins', in W.V. Davies (ed.) *Colour and Painting in Ancient Egypt* (London), 10–16.

Millett, M. 1995, 'Strategies for Roman "small towns"', in Brown 1995, 29–37.

Miron, A. 1989, 'Toilettbestecke mit Scharnierkonstruktion', *Archaeologia Mosellana* 1, 41–65.

Murawski, P.G. 2003, *Benet's Artefacts of England & the United Kingdom. Current values* (Ely).

Niblett, R. 2000, 'Funerary rites in Verulamium during the early Roman period', in J. Pearce, M. Millett and M. Struck (eds) *Burial, Society and Context in the Roman World* (Oxford), 97–104.

Niblett, R., Manning, W.H. and Saunders, C. 2006, 'Verulamium: excavations within the Roman town 1986–88', *Britannia* 37, 53–188.

Nicolay, J. 2008, *Armed Batavians: use and significance of weaponry and horse gear from non-military contexts in the Rhine delta (50 BC to AD 450)* (Amsterdam).

Oldenstein, J. 1976, 'Zur Ausrüstung römischer Auxiliareinheiten', *Bericht der Römisch-Germanischen Kommission* 57, 49–284.

Perez-Arantegui, J. 1996, 'Analysis of the products contained in two Roman glass unguentaria from the colony of Celsa, Spain', *Journal of Archaeological Science* 23, 649–55.

Philpott, R. 1991, *Burial Practices in Roman Britain. A survey of grave treatment and furnishing AD 43–410* (BAR British Series 219, Oxford).

Piggott, S. 1953, 'Three metal-work hoards of the Roman period from southern Scotland', *Proceedings of the Society of Antiquaries of Scotland* 87, 1–50.

Plouviez, J. 1995, 'A hole in the distribution map: the characteristics of small towns in Suffolk', in Brown 1995, 69–80.

Read, B. 2010, *Metal Buttons c. 900 BC – c. AD 1700* (Langport).

Richmond, I. 1968, *Hod Hill. Vol. Two: excavations carried out between 1951 and 1958 for the Trustees of the British Museum* (London).

Rigold, S. E. 1970, 'Six copper-alloy objects from St Augustine's, Canterbury', *Antiquaries Journal* 50, 345–7.

Riha, E. 1986, *Römisches Toilettgerät und medizinische Instrumente aus Augst und Kaiseraugst* (Forschungen in Augst 6, Augst).

Singer, P.N. 1997, *Galen. Selected Works* (Oxford).

Smith, R.A. 1918, 'On a peculiar type of Roman bronze pendant', *Proceedings of the Society of Antiquaries of London* 2nd series, vol. 30, 54–63.

Smith, R.A. 1922, *A Guide to the Antiquities of Roman Britain in the Department of British and Mediaeval Antiquities, British Museum* (Printed by order of the Trustees, London).

Stead, I.M. and Rigby, V. 1989, *Verulamium: the King Harry Lane site* (English Heritage Archaeological Report 12, London).

Stirland, A. 1989, 'The cremations from the Iron Age cemetery', in Stead and Rigby 1989, 240–4.

Thorpe, R. Sharman, J. and Clay, P. 1994, 'An Iron Age and Romano-British enclosure system at Normanton-le-Heath, Leicestershire', *Trans. Leicestershire Archaeol. and Hist. Soc.* 68, 1–63.

Tite, M., Pradell, T. and Shortland, A. 2008, 'Discovery, production and use of tin-based opacifiers in glasses, enamels and glazes from the Late Iron Age onwards: a re-assessment', *Archaeometry* 50 (1), 67–84.

Toynbee, J.M.C. 1964, *Art in Britain under the Romans* (Oxford).

Trett, R. 1983, 'Roman bronze "grooved pendants" from East Anglia', *Norfolk Archaeology* 38 (3), 219–34.

Wainwright, G.J. 1979, *Gussage All Saints: an Iron Age settlement in Dorset* (DoE Archaeological Report 10, London).

Williams, J. 2007, 'New light on Latin in pre-conquest Britain', *Britannia* 38, 1–12.

Wills, J. and Dinn, J.L. (eds) forthcoming, *Excavations at Beckford, Worcester, 1972–9* (CBA Research Report).

Wilson, P. 2002, *Cataractonium: Roman Catterick and its hinterland. Excavations and research, 1958–1997. Part II* (CBA Research Report 129, York).

Worrell, S. 2005, 'Roman Britain in 2004. II. Finds reported under the Portable Antiquities Scheme', *Britannia* 36, 2005, 447–72.

Worrell, S. 2006, 'Roman Britain in 2005. II. Finds reported under the Portable Antiquities Scheme', *Britannia* 37, 2006, 429–66.

Worrell, S. 2008, 'cosmetic sets', in 'Roman Britain in 2007. II. Finds reported under the Portable Antiquities Scheme', *Britannia* 39, 2008, 347–51.

10. Concordances

Concordance, by county, place and catalogue number

Bedfordshire
Shillington — 454

Berkshire
Aldworth — 4
Reading area — 413

Buckinghamshire
Amersham — 5, 607
Lillingstone Dayrell — 307
Magiovinium, Bletchley — 334–6
Shenley Church End — 453
Wendover — 521

Cambridgeshire
Cambridge — 66
Cambridge area — 67
Elm — 174
Ely — 176
Fengate — 187
Grandford — 204–7
Huntingdon area — 277
Linton — 314
March area — 338
Shelford — 451
Soham — 466
Stonea — 479–84
Stonea? — 485
Walsoken — 513
Wisbech — 555
unprovenanced — 68–71

Cheshire
Chester — 90–1
Meols — 341
Wilderspool — 550

Cumbria
Carlisle — 79
Kirkby Thore — 300

Derbyshire
Elmton — 175
Repton — 414

Dorset
Gussage All Saints — 226
Hod Hill — 268
unprovenanced — 149–53

Durham County
Unprovenanced — 157

East Anglia
unprovenanced — 158–68

East Anglia/Cambs.
unprovenanced — 169–70

Essex
Church End — 99
Colchester — 109–28
Colchester area — 129–30
Gosbecks — 203
Great Chesterford — 208–9
Great Chesterford area — 210
Great Yeldham — 223
Harlow — 233–4
Hatfield Broad Oak — 237
Henham — 239
Heybridge — 246–52
Maldon — 337
Stanway — 474
Tilbury — 508
Wickford — 537–8
unprovenanced — 178–82

Glamorgan, South
Whitton — 536

Gloucestershire
Cirencester — 100–3
Kingsholm — 295
Lydney Park — 332
Ross-on-Wye area — 425
Willersey — 551
unprovenanced — 200–1

Gwent
Caerleon — 62–3
Newport — 354

Hampshire
Breamore area — 47
Silchester — 462–3

Hereford and Worcester
Beckford — 22

Hertfordshire
Ashwell — 9–11
Baldock — 16
Harpenden — 235
Pembridge — 406
St Albans — 436–41
Stevenage — 476–7
unprovenanced — 243

Humberside
Brigg — 52
Dragonby — 154–5
Grimsby — 224
North Ferriby — 395
South Ferriby — 469
unprovenanced — 274

Isle of Wight
Chessell Down — 89

Kent
Boughton Monchelsea — 30
Brenley Corner — 50
Canterbury — 73–6
Darenth — 140
Deal/Canterbury — 141
Faversham — 184
Horton Kirby — 273
Keston — 292
Minster-in-Sheppey — 348
Otford — 403
Richborough — 415–20
Rochester — 423
Springhead — 472–3
Wingham — 553–4
unprovenanced — 290–1

Lancashire
Walton-le-Dale — 514–6

Leicestershire
Ashby Folville — 6
Cossington — 136
Enderby — 177
Leicester — 305
Melton Mowbray — 340
Normanton-le-Heath — 391
Skeffington — 464
Thistleton — 506

Lincolnshire
Bourne — 31
Fishtoft — 192
Gate Burton — 198
Great Sturton — 212
Laughterton — 304
Lincoln — 308
Long Bennington — 329
Morton — 350–1
Owmby Cliff — 404
Ruskington — 428
Sleaford — 465
South Kyme — 470
The Wash area — 520
unprovenanced — 309–11

Lincs./E. Yorkshire
unprovenanced — 312

Lincs./Leics.
unprovenanced — 313

London
318–28

Norfolk
Alderford — 1–2
Ashill — 7–8
Ashwicken — 12
Attlebridge — 13
Bawburgh — 20
Beeston — 25
Besthorpe — 26
Billingford — 27
Blakeney — 28
Brampton — 34–8
Brettenham — 51
Brisley/Stanfield — 54
Broome — 56
Burlingham — 60
Caister-on-Sea — 64
Caistor St Edmund — 65
Carleton Rode — 77–8
Colkirk — 133
Congham — 134
Corpusty — 135
Costessey — 137
Cranwich — 138
Cranworth — 139
Denton — 143
Diss — 144–5
Ditchingham — 146
Ditchingham area — 147
East Bilney/Stanfield — 171
Felthorpe — 186
Fincham — 188–90
Forncett — 193
Foulden — 194
Fring — 196
Garboldisham — 197
Great Walsingham — 213–20
Great Yarmouth — 221
Great Yarmouth area — 222
Haddiscoe — 230
Harleston — 232
Hevingham — 244–5
Hillington — 253
Hindringham — 255
Hockwold — 260–7
Holme Hale — 269
Holt — 270
Hopton-on-Sea — 271
Horsham St Faith — 272
Ingoldisthorpe — 282–5
Itteringham — 286–7
Kelling — 288
Kenninghall — 289
Keswick — 293–4
Kings Lynn — 296–7
Kings Lynn area — 298
Lynford — 333
Marsham — 339
Middleton — 344
Mileham — 345–7
Morningthorpe — 349
Mundham — 352
North Creake — 393–4
Norton Subcourse — 396–7
Old Hunstanton — 401–2
Oxborough — 405
Postwick — 407–9
Quidenham — 411–2
Rocklands — 424
Roudham — 426
Saham Toney — 429–35
Sall — 445
Saxlingham Nethergate — 446–7
Scole — 449–50
Shelton — 452
Shipdham — 457
Shouldham — 458–9
Shouldham/Fincham — 460
Shropham — 461
South Creake — 468
Stoke Holy Cross — 478
Stratton Strawless — 486

Cosmetic Grinders in the British Museum Collections

Complete sets in bold type

Cat. no.	BM Reg. no.	Provenance	Cat. no.	BM Reg. no.	Provenance
4	1999,0802.1	Aldworth	309	1990,0502.1	Lincs.
36	1999,0802.2	Brampton	310	1990,0502.2	Lincs.
39	1999,0802.3	Brandon	313	1999,0802.42	Lincs./ Leics.?
40	1999,0802.4	Brandon	324	1851,0228.7	London, Thames
41	1999,0802.6	Brandon	340	1999,0802.43	Melton Mowbray
42	1999,0802.7	Brandon	345	1999,0802.44	Mileham
45	1999,0802.8	Brandon	348	1987,1004.1	Minster-in-Sheppey
46	1999,0802.5	Brandon?	351	1996,1001.1	Morton
59	1999,0802.9	Burgh Castle	353	1999,0802.45	Newark-on-Trent area
67	1999,0802.10	Cambridge area	356	1997,0101.3	Norfolk
68	1999,0802.14	Cambs., south	357	1999,0802.46	Norfolk
69	1999,0802.12	Cambs.	358	1997,0101.4	Norfolk
70	1999,0802.11	Cambs.	359	1999,0802.47	Norfolk
71	1999,0802.13	Cambs.	361	1999,0802.51	Norfolk
81	1999,0802.15	Catterick area	362	1986,0801.1	Norfolk
82	1999,0802.16	Catterick area	363	1999,0802.48	Norfolk
89	1867,0729.125	Chessell Down	364	1999,0802.49	Norfolk
96	1994,0701.1	Chichester area	365	1999,0802.50	Norfolk
97	1995,0502.1	Chichester area	366	1999,0802.52	Norfolk
127	1870,0402.250	Colchester	367	1999,0802.55	Norfolk
140	1999,0802.17	Darenth	368	1999,0802.56	Norfolk
144	1999,0802.18	Diss	369	1999,0802.53	Norfolk
147	1993,0901.1	Ditchingham area	370	1999,0802.54	Norfolk
149	1999,0802.19	Dorset	371	1999,0802.57	Norfolk
151	1994,0405.4	Dorset	372	1986,0801.2	Norfolk
152	1994,0405.3	Dorset	373	1997,0101.1	Norfolk
153	1999,0802.20	Dorset	374	1999,0802.60	Norfolk
162	1999,0802.22	East Anglia	375	1999,0802.59	Norfolk
163	1992,1201.2	East Anglia	376	1999,0802.69	Norfolk
164	1999,0802.21	East Anglia	377	1999,0802.61	Norfolk
167	1999,0802.23	East Anglia	378	1997,0101.2	Norfolk
168	1999,0802.24	East Anglia	381	1999,0802.62	Norfolk
169	1999,0802.25	East Anglia/ Cambs.	382	1999,0802.65	Norfolk
170	1999,0802.26	East Anglia/ Cambs.	383	1999,0802.64	Norfolk
176	1999,0802.27	Ely	384	1999,0802.66	Norfolk
178	1999,0802.28	Essex	386	1999,0802.63	Norfolk
179	1986,0802.2	Essex	388	1999,0802.67	Norfolk
180	1986,0403.1	Essex	389	1986,0301.1	Norfolk
181	1986,0802.1	Essex	390	1999,0802.68	Norfolk
182	1999,0802.29	Essex	392	1999,0802.70	Northampton area?
183	1999,0802.30	Eyke	403	1993,0703.1	Otford
184	1260.70 (Gibbs Bequest)	Faversham	413	1999,0802.71	Reading area
200	1999,0802.31	Gloucestershire area	426	1999,0802.72	Roudham
201	1999,0802.32	Gloucestershire area	431	1999,0802.73	Saham Toney
211	1999,0802.33	Gt Cornard	434	1999,0802.74	Saham Toney
212	1991,1101.1	Gt Sturton	**436**	**1976,0501.505-6**	**St Albans**
221	1999,0802.34	Gt Yarmouth	441	1986,0402.1	St Albans
224	1990,0702.3	Grimsby	451	1999,0802.75	Shelford
230	1993,0901.2	Haddiscoe	465	1999,0802.76	Sleaford
232	1999,0802.35	Harleston	479	1982,0602.3	Stonea
237	1999,0802.36	Hatfield Broad Oak	480	1985,0201.251	Stonea
260	**1990,0702.1-2**	**Hockwold**	481	1999,0802.79	'Stonea'
261	1977,0403.1	Hockwold	482	1982,0602.4	Stonea
268	1960,0405.466	Hod Hill	483	1999,0802.77	Stonea
274	1999,0802.37	Humberside	484	1985,0503.1911	Stonea
277	1999,0802.38	Huntingdon area	485	1999,0802.78	'Stonea'
278	1957,1003.6	Icklingham	487	1999,0802.80	Suffolk
286	**2001,0801.1-2**	**Itteringham**	488	1999,0802.83	Suffolk
287	**2001,0801.3-4**	**Itteringham**	489	1999,0802.81	Suffolk
289	2010,8005.1	Kenninghall	490	1999,0802.82	Suffolk?
290	1999,0802.39	Kent	492	1993,0901.4	Suffolk/ Norfolk
292	1927,1011.1	Keston	493	1993,0901.3	Suffolk/ Norfolk
296	1999,0802.41	Kings Lynn	496	1999,0802.84	Syderstone
298	1999,0802.40	Kings Lynn area	500*	2010,8007.1	Thelnetham

Cat. no.	BM Reg. no.	Provenance
503	1994,0405.6	Thetford
504	1994,0405.1	Thetford
508	1992,1201.1	Tilbury
518	1990,0401.1	Warlingham
520	1999,0802.85	Wash area
528	1992,1201.3	Wenhaston
538	1999,0802.86	Wickford
566	1992,1201.4	Wymondham
573	1997,0101.5	Yorkshire?
574	1997,0101.6	Yorkshire?
575	1997,0101.7	Yorkshire?
577	1997,0101.9	Unprovenanced
578	1990,0702.7	Unprovenanced
579	1990,0702.6	Unprovenanced
580	1990,0702.8	Unprovenanced
581	1990,0702.4	Unprovenanced
582	1990,0702.5	Unprovenanced
584	1999,0802.87	Unprovenanced
588	1999,0802.89	Unprovenanced
589	1999,0802.90	Unprovenanced
590	1999,0802.88	Unprovenanced
591	1990,0702.9	Unprovenanced
593	1999,0802.58	Unprovenanced
596	1999,0802.91	Unprovenanced
597	1997,0101.8	Unprovenanced
598	1999,0802.92	Unprovenanced
599	1999,0802.93	Unprovenanced
600	1915,1208.128	Unprovenanced
601	1994,0405.2	Unprovenanced
602	1999,0802.94	Unprovenanced
603	1999,0802.95	Unprovenanced
604	1994,0405.5	Unprovenanced
605	1999,0802.96	Unprovenanced

* brooch/ cosmetic mortar

Cosmetic Grinders Analysed in the British Museum Department of Conservation and Scientific Research

All surface-analysed by XRF
D = additional drilled analysis
Bold type = results discussed in text

Cat. no.		Cat. no.	
96		399	
147		403	D
151		436	
152	D	441	
163		**479**	D
179	D	480	
180		482	
181	D	492	D
184		493	
212		496	
224		503	
230		504	D
260		508	
261		518	
268		528	
278		566	
292	D	**578**	D
301		579	
309		580	
310	D	581	D
318		582	D
324		591	
348	D	600	
362		601	
372	D	604	
389	D		